SPIN Z

CW01081165

سپین بیری

Old Man in Helmand

A true story by
CHRIS GREEN

Spin Zhira:
Old Man in Helmand
Third UK Edition 2017
www.spinzhira.com

This Third Edition
published in 2017 by OMiH Ltd

First published in Great Britain
in 2016 by OMiH Ltd

Copyright © OMiH Ltd 2017
The right of Chris Green to be identified
as the author of this work has been asserted
in accordance with the Copyright,
Designs and Patents Act 1988.

ISBN 978-0-9934287-4-6

Edited by Kate Hudis
katehudis@wordscandance.com
www.wordscandance.com

Design by Them®
www.them.co.uk

For
Harry and Alfie

HOPE FOR THE BEST.
1. Hope for the best.
2. Plan for the worst.
3. Prepare to be surprised.

Destroying a home or property jeopardises the
livelihood of an entire family - and creates
more insurgents

- General Stanley McChrystal, August 2009

Among the calamities of war may be justly
numbered the diminution of the love of truth,
by the falsehoods which interest dictates and
credulity encourages.

- Samuel Johnson, November 1758

Get a fucking pistol as soon as you get out
there mate and keep one in the chamber at
all times.

- Major Dave Groom, January 2012

DISCLAIMER

This is a true story based on personal recollections.

It is not an officially sanctioned memoir.

It has not been endorsed by the Ministry of Defence.

It may differ from authorised accounts.

The views and opinions expressed are entirely my own.

CONTENTS

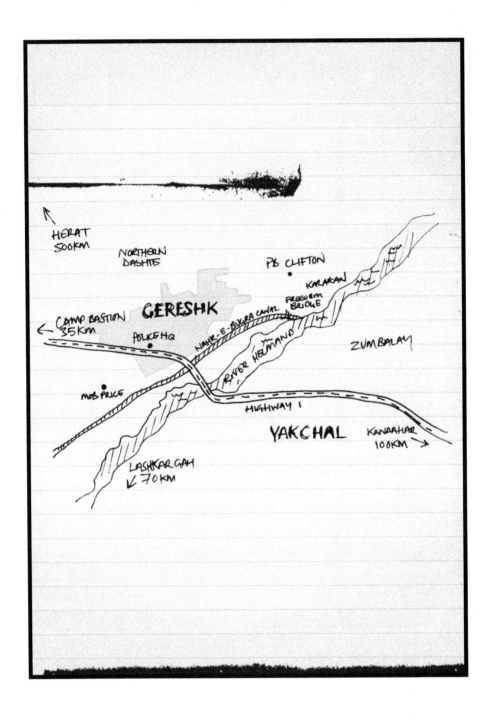

AFGHANISTAN FATALITY AND CASUALTY TABLES
UK Military Fatalities and Casualties[1]
01 January 2012 – 30 September 2012

2012	Fatalities[2]				Casualties[34]			Field Hospital Admissions[5]			Aeromed Evacuations
Month	Total	KIA[6]	DOW[7]	Other[8]	Total	VSI[9]	SI[10]	Total	WIA[11]	DNBI[12]	
Jan	3	1	1	1	3	3	0	79	17	62	94
Feb	1	1	0	0	2	1	1	63	4	59	123
Mar	9	9	0	0	4	4	0	53	10	43	95
Apr	3	1	2	0	3	1	2	91	10	81	86
May	5	5	0	0	9	4	5	89	33	56	114
Jun	4	4	0	0	4	1	3	78	21	57	108
Jul	3	3	0	0	6	3	3	98	33	65	126
Aug	3	2	1	0	3	0	3	71	23	48	97
Sep	8	4	1	3	1	0	1	88	35	53	85
Total	39	30	5	4	35	17	18	710	186	524	928

Source: Initial NOTICAS[13]   Source: UK and Coalition Medical Facilities   Source: AECC[14]

1. Source: Ministry of Defence. First published 14 November 2012.
2. Some deaths may not have clearly defined cause information and could be subject to change.
3. The VSI and SI data includes personnel with an initial NOTICAS listing of VSI or SI who were alive at the time of discharge from their first hospital episode in the UK.
4. The personnel listed as VSI or SI may also appear in the UK field hospital admissions and aeromed evacuations data.
5. The admissions data contain UK personnel admitted to any field hospital, whether operated by UK or Coalition Medical Facilities.
6. Killed in Action
7. Died of Wounds
8. These data include all deaths occurring as a result of accidental or violent causes while deployed and deaths due to disease related causes during the deployment.
9. Very Seriously Injured
10. Seriously Injured
11. Wounded in Action
12. Disease or Non Battle Injury
13. Only the most serious casualties are subject to a NOTICAS notification.
14. Aeromedical Evacuation Control Centre

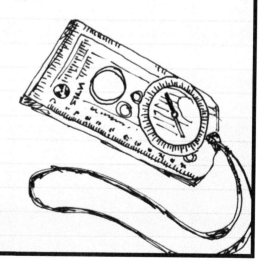

Latitude:	52.07
Longitude:	0.58
Elevation:	46m
Met:	Overcast, visibility poor, H:9°L:6°
DTG[1]:	071000ZJUN14

IN DECEMBER 2012, in a Christmas missive to friends and family, my late father wrote

...so last month he returned home and we all breathed again. It was a considerable experience. In so many of the photographs there is this grey haired man among all the young 19/21 year old squaddies.

The grey haired man is me and his comment inspired the title of this book which is first and foremost the true story of my considerable experiences as a *Spin Zhira*, literally 'White Beard' in Pashtu, or 'Old Man' in Helmand province, Afghanistan.

According to the Department for International Development, life expectancy in Helmand is 44 years. Another study identifies that, in 2012, the average age of the British squaddie was 20. By either measure I was, indeed, an old man in Helmand and I have the white beard to prove it. In this capacity I was privileged to witness the incredible bravery and devotion to duty of the young men and women of the British and Danish Armed Forces as they fought a counter-insurgency campaign for which there was little popular mandate in their home countries. It is a war which, for all their extraordinary efforts, I have no doubt history will judge them to have lost by almost any measure other than body count.

****

---

[1] **DTG**: Date Time Group.

Using the DTG, 10.30 GMT on 11th April 2012 is written as 111030ZAPR12.

The Armed Forces use the 24-hour clock. This means that 20.15 hours, pronounced twenty fifteen hours, is 8.15pm.
Soldiers usually avoid midnight and refer to 23.59 or 00.01 hours.

Time zones: The suffix Z (Zulu) denotes Greenwich meantime (GMT). A (Alpha) denotes GMT + 1 hour. B (Bravo) denotes GMT + 2 hours and so on. Afghanistan is 4 ½ hours ahead of GMT but uses the suffix D (Delta).

Literacy levels in rural Helmand Province are almost non-existent. Some of those few who claim to be able to read have, in reality, merely learned tracts from the Qur'an[1] or other texts by rote and cannot read at all.

In the absence of written histories much of Helmand's past is therefore preserved and chronicled through oral tradition and the story-telling of the village elders or *spin zhiras*. This has proved to be a highly effective method of capturing and recording history, even if it is subject to greater inaccuracy with each successive telling.

Muslim societies, especially illiterate societies like those in rural Helmand, are keenly aware of their past. The decisions they make today are routinely shaped by events of many centuries before.

By contrast, Western societies have invested heavily in the writing and teaching of history but tend to have very low levels of historical knowledge and dismiss its relevance in shaping their lives. The phrase *that's ancient history* is commonly used to reject something as unimportant or of little value.

Since I did not keep a diary or take extensive notes at the time, the events described in this book are my oral history.

My version of the truth.

---

[1] **Qur'an** (also **Quran, Koran, Kuran**): The central religious text of Islam, which Muslims believe to be a revelation from Allah. Respect for the written text of the Qur'an is an important element of religious faith for most Muslims, and the Qur'an is treated with reverence. Based on tradition and a literal interpretation of Qur'an 56:79 *(none shall touch but those who are clean)*, many Muslims believe that they must perform a ritual cleansing with water before touching a copy of the Qur'an, although this view is not universal. Worn-out copies of the Qur'an are wrapped in a cloth and stored indefinitely in a safe place, buried in a mosque or a Muslim cemetery, or burned and the ashes buried or scattered over water.

```
Latitude    51.87
Longitude   -0.42
Elevation   125m
Met         Overcast, occasional rain, H:8°L:5°
DTG         072100ZMAR10
```

I was prepared to overlook
the fact he'd just called me a
fucking cunt, sir. Sir.

SUV: Suburban Utility Vehicle
SUSAT: Sight Utility Small Arms Trilux
SA80 A2 L85: British Army standard issue assault rifle
TA: Territorial Army
G4: Logistics
IED: Improvised Explosive Device
PJHQ: Permanent Joint Headquarters

Latitude:	51.87
Longitude:	-0.42
Elevation:	125m
Met:	Overcast, occasional rain, H:8°L:5°
DTG:	072100ZMAR10

ON 7th MARCH 2010 at approximately 9 pm, somewhere between Coventry and Luton, I made a decision to give up my secure but largely unremarkable existence and go in search of adventure in the service of my country.

In the comfort of the air-conditioned cabin of my powerful SUV, it did not seem to be a particularly difficult decision to make.

This is the story of what happened next:

Latitude:	31.79
Longitude:	64.67
Elevation:	852m
Met:	Sunny H:37°L:10°
DTG:	091117DSEP12

MIRAJDIN LAY IN wait less than 250 metres from the huge explosive device he'd buried on the track junction. Inshallah, his patience and daring would soon be rewarded. He would avenge the deaths of his revered commander Mohammed Momin, assassinated on the banks of the river Helmand and those of his brothers-in-arms who had perished resisting the infidels' incursion into their homelands just eight days earlier.

Assembling and positioning the bomb had been dangerous and audacious, his intelligence unreliable. Working under cover of darkness, Mirajdin had assembled the deadly components in his father's compound before digging a huge pit to accommodate the 20 yellow palm oil containers that housed the main charge of fertiliser based explosive.

As he'd been acutely aware, this had been the riskiest part of the operation. Not only was the home-made explosive mixture highly unstable but he had to avoid detection by the infidels' invisible eyes in the sky. Many brave emplacers had died positioning their devices, vaporised by their own explosives, or by the infidels' Hellfire missiles. He had required good fortune, as well as a cool head and a steady hand, and Allah had smiled upon him.

Next, he had buried the command wire with which to detonate the device in a 250 metre long trench that ran from the bomb to his current hiding place. Finally, just as his mentor Haji Jalander had instructed, he had painstakingly concealed all evidence of his handiwork ensuring that none of the telltale ground signs, such as discoloration, disturbance or subsidence, remained to betray him.

Mirajdin had worked diligently and risked much for this moment and his labour had already been rewarded. An hour earlier the infidels had driven mine detection vehicles down the track but had failed to locate his device. He'd resisted the temptation to detonate the bomb under the American mine plough. A greater prize would follow.

All that was now required was patience.

Clouds of dust to the south indicated the imminent arrival of the kafir invaders as their lumbering armoured vehicles left the relative safety of the blacktopped highway and headed north on the unmetalled road into Zumbalay. The infidels, cowering inside their vehicles, were coming to meet their fate.

Mirajdin had been trained in bomb making while studying at a religious seminary in the Pakistani province of Baluchistan. His device was the product of more than one country. The detonator was a blasting cap made in China, the firing cable from Iran. The main charge had been produced in a chemicals factory owned by a company traded on the derivatives markets in the United States of America.

Mirajdin's pulse raced and he prayed his nerves would not fail him. As he had done a thousand times already that morning, he committed himself to Allah's will.

Latitude:	56.26
Longitude:	6.84
Elevation:	2,346m
Met:	Plenty of sunshine H:5°L:-3°
DTG:	071530AFEB13

LIAM STARED INTO the abyss, took a long toke[1] on the doobie[2], passed it to Ritchie with fingers made clumsy by thickly insulated gloves, and giggled. I followed his gaze and, without the benefit of mind altering drugs, found no humour in our situation.

A huge cornice loomed above us. The overhanging edge had turned to ice and in the weak rays of the afternoon sun it gleamed with yellowed and ugly menace. As surely as night turns to day, but with far less predictability, the forces of nature demanded that it must tumble into the valley below. Two stoned snow boarders and a grey-bearded man well beyond his middle years would do little to arrest its downward trajectory.

Directly beneath our precarious perch a narrow couloir dropped steeply to an immense snow field which descended without a single blemish of human intervention into the valley below. Our desire to be the first to tag this example of nature's perfection had got us this far, but Mother Nature was not quite ready to give up the prize that waited below.

First we would have to prove ourselves worthy.

The couloir was little more than an interruption between two cliff faces. In no place more than 30 metres wide, it descended for about 300 metres. On the right the cliff rose jagged and imposing to the mountain's summit; on the left it dropped almost vertically to the valley floor below. In order to descend this narrow traverse it would be necessary to put in four, perhaps five, turns. Every one of these turns would be above the No Fall line.

In the lexicon of off-piste skiing this is an imaginary line drawn on any descent above which a fall may lead to serious injury, but will more

---

[1] **Toke**: inhale from a cigarette, typically one containing cannabis.

[2] **Doobie**: Marijuana cigarette

probably result in death. The term was coined by the legendary French extreme skier, Patrick Vallençant, who lived by the motto *si tu tombes, tu meurs*. If you fall, you die. On 28 March 1989, aged 43, he tragically succumbed to his own axiom. In fifteen years of skiing I had never made more than two consecutive turns above the No Fall line.

The preceding night had seen heavy snowfalls across the Alps and the morning had dawned bright and blue. Like all dedicated off-piste skiers, I subscribed to several meteorological reports which I scanned daily with religious zeal. Consequently, anticipating these conditions, I had risen before dawn. The sky was clear, the air was still. More importantly, on my balcony rail was a six centimetre deep layer of perfectly formed ice crystals. I gently blew on them and they dispersed. Even more snow was likely further up the mountain. Conditions were perfect.

Although the ski industry would have you believe that every day in the mountains is a perfect powder day, in truth this combination of conditions occurs perhaps half a dozen times each season. My body tingled with excitement as I made my usual breakfast of porridge and coffee.

As the sun broke cover over the mountains, I loaded up my battered old 4x4 which had superseded the shiny SUV of my previous life. Snow covered peaks turned pink with early morning light as I drove down the narrow, rutted track to the lift station. Despite the early hour, a steady stream of headlights bobbed and weaved in my rear view mirror and even though the lifts would not open for another half hour, four or five cars had arrived ahead of me.

There was a palpable hum of excitement and anticipation. Everyone busied themselves making preparations for the day ahead as we waited for the lifts to open. True to their stereotypes, skiers wore performance mountain clothing of sober hue and sensible cut, boarders wore baggies in a riot of clashing colours.

When I first got into skiing in my early thirties, many skiers were pretty negative about boarders, accusing them of being reckless and out of control. These days, despite the difference in fashion tastes, there's little animosity between us. We've learned to respect each other and jog along together, united by our shared love for snow covered mountains.

There was no hostility between the different groups but there was little conversation either. There are no friends on a powder day and we were all in open competition to be the first to tag the mountain. No one was about to reveal their game plan lest this give one of the other groups an advantage.

As a solo skier, I was completely ignored.

Skiing alone in the backcountry is not recommended. In fact it's actively discouraged. Such recklessness negates any duty of care the lift operator may have, and automatically voids insurance cover. This is because it significantly increases risk. Even the most experienced skier can have a bad day. Without colleagues to assist or to raise the alarm, an otherwise trivial incident can quickly escalate into a matter of life or death.

Danny Boyle's excellent film *127 Hours* tells the true story of Aron Ralston, who is forced to commit one of the most extreme and desperate acts imaginable to save his life. It vividly illustrates how nature's unpredictability can quickly lead to disaster, even for the most experienced outdoorsman.

I'm aware of the danger. I've watched Danny's film and read Aron's book. I've heard or read countless other tales of solo misadventure. But I'm still driven to ski the backcountry alone. I'm alive to the risks just as the heroin junkie, the smoker, or the sugar addict is alive to the health implications of their habit, but I don't ski solo entirely by choice. The pleasure of backcountry skiing is heightened rather than diminished when the experience is shared. The truth is that few of my contemporaries have either the time or the inclination to ski at this level or intensity. Those who are tempted are quickly reminded by partners, children or employers of their other responsibilities.

This, perhaps, is the true nature of my addiction; that I do not hear or choose to ignore these other voices.

Generally I try to mitigate the risks of solo skiing by avoiding north-facing slopes (where 70% of all avalanches occur), by skiing as close as possible to the piste, or by skiing in terrain that is overlooked by chair lifts or other ski industry infrastructure. Today none of these precautions will be possible. In order to feed my addiction to white powder I must go deep into the backcountry and forests of the Porte du Soleil. I cannot tell others where I'm going, or even leave a note in my car, as I do not know myself. My outline plan must remain flexible depending on conditions, and on whether or not others have beaten me to the powder fields that I seek.

The morning goes well for me. Conditions are perfect and I'm skiing well too. I'm feeling pretty pleased with myself as I leave linked S-shaped tags all over the mountain. I have chosen terrain that most would consider too demanding or risky but this simply heightens the pleasure of each successful descent. I know others will see my tracks and choose not to follow.

By mid-afternoon I've skied without a break for hours. I'm exhausted. It's getting harder and harder to find areas which are not already tracked out. I'm considering calling it a day when I meet Liam and Ritchie. It's a chance encounter. I make an idiot of myself getting on a chair lift and end up a tangle of poles and skis. Liam and Ritchie help me out while simultaneously subjecting me to some banter, which I appreciate. I've always enjoyed a bit of banter, even when on the receiving end.

They correctly assume I'm not a member of the local Gendarmerie and skin up[1] an enormous reefer[2]. Despite a temperature differential of about 60 degrees, the pungent aroma instantly transports me back to Afghanistan. Just a few months ago I'd been fighting for my life in the ganja fields of Zumbalay. Could these boys be smoking the harvest of those very same fields that we'd used for cover to break contact with the Taliban?

Ritchie proffers the marijuana cigarette. I've worked with stoners, smokers, caine-heads and alkies of varying levels of addiction, all of my adult life. For the most part they seem to function pretty well, so I'm personally content to live and let live. However, as a reserve officer in the British Army, I'm duty bound to decline his offer.

As the boys chill out we share our love of the mountains and agree it's been a very special day. They're both habitual seasonaires who know the area well. They invite me to join them on a run just a short distance from the top of the chairlift, a run that they think will still be untouched.

It's an offer I can't refuse.

---

[1] **Skin up**: to roll a marijuana cigarette

[2] **Reefer**: Marijuana cigarette

By the time we get to the top of the chair there is already a small group of German skiers gingerly peering over the safety barrier. They clearly like what they see but are not so sure about the route. There is animated debate, interspersed with lots of pointing. We have competition at the drop-in and there's no time for a briefing. The boys tell me to follow, climb over the barrier, and then they're gone.

I look at the Germans.

The Germans look at me.

Now they know the route I have only a moment before they will push past and claim the prize.

I could wave them on with a cheery *guten tag* which, together with *zvei bier, bitte,* is the extent of my German language skills. It's the right thing to do. I've had a glorious day. I've only just met Liam and Ritchie. I wouldn't even recognise them again but for their outlandish apparel. Throughout our short acquaintance their faces have been hidden behind beanies, mirrored goggles and ice-encrusted, wispy beards. My legs are tired, I'm too old to be doing this stuff, there's cold beer on the balcony back at the chalet ... and I need to wash the 4x4.

There are numerous good reasons not to follow my new stoner friends over the safety barrier, not least because that barrier was put there for a reason.

Sensing my hesitation, the Germans begin to crowd towards me. I duck under the barrier, simultaneously absolving the lift company of any responsibility for my well-being and voiding my accident insurance policy. Liam and Ritchie are way down the valley looking back up in my direction. I see them, and launch.

Immediately my skis and most of my legs disappear into thigh-deep powder. I have to raise my poles high to stop them dragging and putting me off balance. Tom Goldney, one of my former instructors and a skiing inspiration, once described off-piste skiing to me as a *series of linked corrections*. It made a lot of sense to me at the time and still does today. Good skiers may appear to be gliding down the slopes with ease, but in reality it's a constant battle to maintain optimum position and balance.

Gravity takes over and I start to accelerate. My skis begin to float in the powder beneath and with each turn they briefly pop to the surface before disappearing once more. After two or three turns I'm into a natural rhythm, and now comes the rush I've been seeking. But even this intoxicating moment is tinged with regret. No matter how many times I do this, it will never be enough. I will always need more powder, more lines, more slopes, more linked turns. I've already surrendered my marriage, my job and my life savings to feed my addiction. How much more am I prepared to sacrifice?

I don't know the answer to the question.

I push these concerns to the back of my mind and submit myself to the moment.

I join Liam and Ritchie and we high five each other. They spark up the reefer once more and we look back up the way we've come at the lines we've carved across the mountain. We discuss our route selection, the snow condition, the thrill of the ride. There is no longer any sign of the Germans at the drop-in, presumably they've moved on in search of fresh tracks of their own.

For the next couple of hours we ski together, tackling progressively steeper and more demanding pitches. These two young boarders are pushing me to my limits and beyond. There's no peer pressure, I know I can pull out at any point and retire with grace and dignity. I'm here because I want to be here. Then they ask me if I know of a run they call *The Cornice*? Would I like to try it? They say it's *a bit of a trek*, which means it's even further off the beaten track. They say the drop-in is *a bit gnarly,* in much the same way that soldiers will describe a firefight as *a bit crunchy*.

I recognise these signs.

I should know better.

I agree we should give it a go.

Latitude:	51.95
Longitude:	-3.56
Elevation:	196m
Met:	Overcast, periods of rain H:9°L:5°
DTG:	101100ZJUN11

CONTACT FRONT!

The cry went up simultaneously from at least three of the lads in the section. Most of them were behind me so it was impossible to tell who had initiated the contact.

I knew this moment was coming but my heart still leapt into my mouth. In the minutes ahead I would be stretched to my physical limits. Adrenaline was already coursing through my veins in anticipation.

I squeezed off a couple of rounds in the general direction of the enemy. These were not accurate shots; I didn't even attempt to use the SUSAT[1] optical scope on my SA80 A2 L85[2], British Army standard issue assault rifle. I wanted to maintain some situational awareness and in particular preserve my peripheral vision in case one of my own blokes ran between me and the target.

Releasing the trigger, I placed my right index finger across the trigger guard. In the same movement, I slid my left hand down the fore grip, punched the safety catch on with my thumb and started running forward. I already knew where I was headed. Even before the contact was initiated I had identified a small berm[3], about 25 metres ahead, as my next point of cover.

But I wasn't going to make it.

---

[1] **SUSAT**: Sight Unit Small Arms Trilux. A x4 optical gunsight with tritium-powered illumination for use in low light conditions fitted to the SA80 but now largely replaced by the ACOG (Advanced Combat Optical Gunsight) or the ELCAN Specter OS x4 Lightweight Day Sight (LDS).

[2] **SA80 A2 L85**: The SA80 A2 L85 is a 5.56mm gas-operated assault rifle manufactured by Heckler & Koch. It is a member of the SA80 family of assault weapons and serves the British Armed Forces as Individual Weapon (IW) and Light Support Weapon (LSW).

The SA80 series of rifles entered service with the British Army in 1985 and underwent a major mid-life update in 2002, during which the SA80 A1 rifles were upgraded to the SA80 A2 standard.

[3] **Berm**: A low earth wall, usually adjacent to a ditch. The digging of the ditch often providing the soil from which the berm is constructed.

The combined weight of combat body armour and ceramic plates, mark 6 ballistic nylon fibre helmet, over 300 rounds of 5.56mm ammunition, two litres of water and enough food and essentials to sustain me for 24 hours was slowing me down and I was making myself an easy target.

I was going to have to crawl on my belt buckle the rest of the way. I crashed to the ground and moved as fast as I could while keeping my backside as close to the ground as possible – no-one wants to suffer the indignity of getting shot in the arse.

Where were the others? 'Joe Ninety' was now behind me to my left, I'd seen him as I hit the deck. 'PB' must be to my right and beyond him 'Double A', but I hadn't seen them. They were out there somewhere but no one was returning fire and I was worried we were losing momentum. I guessed that they, like me, were busy crawling forward into cover. Knowing that I must be closest to the berm I redoubled my efforts to get there to give them covering fire and allow them to move up level with me to form a baseline.

The berm was no more than 15 or 20 metres away, but I reached it soaked in sweat and covered in sheep shit. At least, I hoped it was sheep shit. Being the most efficient processor of grass on the planet I knew from experience that the sheep's shit neither sticks, nor stinks, too much.

Encased as it was in ballistic nylon fibre, my head was cooking up nicely and sweat was pouring down my forehead and into my eyes. Before I could return fire I had first to wipe my eyes with my shit covered hands. Please let it be sheep shit.

Now I could see and this time I used the optical scope. Lining the tip of the sight post up on the centre mass of the target I double tapped the trigger. The shot fell high and to the right. I was breathing too hard. I tried to control my breathing by exhaling as slowly as I could, simultaneously taking up the first pressure on the trigger. At the bottom of this breath I gently squeezed through the second pressure. Although I could still feel my heart pounding against the ceramic plate in my body armour the shot was good and I followed it up with two more in rapid succession.

On my left I heard Joe Ninety open up with a series of single shots. Shortly afterwards on my right PB and Double A started to get involved too. We were back in the fight. Now I could take stock of our situation. I lowered my weapon, applied the safety catch, and allowed myself to slide backwards down the crest of the berm and out of sight of the enemy.

We were an eight man patrol, most of us new to one another. We'd met a few days ago but this was our first outing together. Fifteen minutes earlier we'd loaded and made ready our assault rifles, and immediately stepped off into a small river. The shallow water quickly penetrated my gortex gaiters and began to fill my boots, a familiar but unwelcome sensation. Trying to set an example, I deliberately pushed into deeper water. If I minced about trying to keep my feet dry the others would surely follow suit. Of course there was no guarantee that the opposite was also true, but I hoped they would get the message.

The section was made up of two fire teams, each of four men. As the section commander I took charge of the 'Charlie' team while my second-in-command, Lance Corporal 'Ron' McCabe, took charge of 'Delta'. I'd been briefed that he was a trouble maker with a history of discipline issues. He certainly looked the part with a distinctive rose tattoo on his neck. But despite the warning and the tattoo, I instinctively liked him. I guessed that trouble probably paid him a visit after a few drinks, but from the little I'd seen of him he struck me as a capable and competent soldier. I hoped I was right. I would be relying on him to keep me alive.

My own team consisted of Ranger Heyward, otherwise known as Joe Ninety due to his striking resemblance to the 1960s puppet, Private Price Brown, known as PB, and Ranger Aneyanwu or Double A for short. British military standards required that, as an officer, I should not refer to other ranks by Christian name. So I called Ranger Heyward Ninety, and PB and Double A by their nicknames which were abbreviations of their surnames. They all called me Sir, not out of respect but because I was just another *Rupert* to them and they hadn't bothered to learn my name. Ron McCabe, being a bit neckier than the other lads, even avoided calling me Sir by referring to me as Boss. I hadn't challenged him on this, and according to the Royal Military Academy, Sandhurst manual I'd failed the first test of moral courage by not doing so. I'd last visited the Academy back in 1988, long before Ron McCabe was born and I wasn't about to lose any sleep over it.

From my new position I could see PB and Double A were about ten metres to my right in good cover, returning fire at a steady rate of roughly one round every six seconds.

Happy days, nothing wrong there.

On my left I could see Ninety had also found good cover and was getting rounds on target. Beyond him Ron McCabe and Delta were now 75–100 metres away. But although they had good cover, I judged that they were not in a position to return fire effectively. I signalled to Ron to bring his team up closer to my own. This would involve more crawling and more sheep shit, but he didn't hesitate. To cover this move I yelled across to PB and Ninety to increase their rate of fire and crawled back into a position where I could get some more rounds on target myself.

Waiting for Ron to join me I ran through my plan one more time in my head. I was confident the plan itself was sound, but I wanted to mentally rehearse how to communicate it to him. I had to be absolutely certain he would understand what I was trying to achieve and what his role would be.

The berm behind which we were currently sheltering ran left to right across our axis of advance. On the right it petered out just short of some stunted trees; on the left it ran back down to the river along which we had originally advanced. I reckoned we could use this to get to within 25 metres of the enemy positions without being seen.

I would leave Delta behind on the berm to provide fire support and take Charlie down to the river. We could then advance up the river bed. I would leave PB and Double A somewhere on the bank where they could provide an additional point of fire[1], before assaulting onto the enemy position with Joe Ninety.

It wasn't a complicated plan but when you're crawling around in front of your own guns it's just as easy to be hit by friendly fire as it is by the enemy. *Blue on blue,* as it's known, is everyone's worst nightmare. I didn't want it happening to me.

As soon as Ron and his team arrived I briefed him on the plan and set off back down the bund line[2] towards the river with Ninety, PB and

---

[1] **Point of Fire**: A location from which an enemy can be engaged with suppressive fire threatening casualties to those who expose themselves to it and which, when coordinated with the manoeuvre of forces achieves the destruction, neutralisation or suppression of the enemy.

[2] **Bund line**: Built-up natural defence line, such as a low hedgerow or berm.

Double A in hot pursuit. I hadn't had a chance to brief them yet, but they all knew that wherever I was going they were going too. I could hear Delta blazing away behind us while Ron bellowed at them to conserve ammunition and slow their rate of fire.

The berm afforded limited cover which meant we could only run bent double but, despite this, we made quick progress until the bund petered out about ten metres short of the river bank. We would need to break cover and dash these last few metres. Stopping just short of the open ground, I quickly explained to the lads my plan and their individual roles. I could see that Ninety was made up to be joining me for the final assault. Then I explained we should individually make the dash across to the cover of the river bank. PB set off first. As soon as he disappeared Double A followed, then Ninety and I in rapid succession.

The river bank was about six feet above the level of the water and, in my haste to reach cover, I simply launched myself over the edge into thin air. The lads had all done pretty much the same thing and I landed on top of a heap of bodies in the river. Being the first one to cross the open ground, PB was now at the bottom of this pile and from the look on his face he wasn't particularly enjoying the experience. At 43, PB was probably one of the oldest, if not the oldest, private soldier in the British Army. His paper round as a child must have been a hard one and he wore every single one of those 43 years in the lines on his face. Beneath this craggy exterior was a man of steel; PB was easily fitter than most lads half his age and was basically unbreakable. Providing a soft landing for three fully laden soldiers might not have been at the top of his 'to do' list that morning but it still wasn't a big drama for him.

Given that I'd fallen on him from a great height, I was prepared to overlook the fact that he'd just called me a *fucking cunt, Sir*. As far as I was concerned, PB was gleaming.

It took us a few moments to sort ourselves out and then we were off again. By now we were all blowing hard and the exertion of running in knee-deep water was exhausting us still further. To make matters worse the river bed was strewn with extremely slippery boulders, making it hard going under foot. I heard Ninety cry out directly behind me, followed by a loud splash. He must have lost his footing and fallen forward into the river but I didn't stop, I didn't even look round to check he was OK. He'd have to sort himself out; I needed to get back to a point where I had line of sight of the enemy to reassess the situation and see if my plan was still valid.

After about 100 metres I came to a slight bend in the river that afforded me a good view of the enemy position. I stayed in cover, greedily sucking air into my aching lungs, while I waited for the others to join me. At 46, I was really getting too old for this. With the exception of Ninety, who looked to me like he couldn't possibly be a day over 14, we were all on the old and grey side. There was a good reason for this. We were all reservists, the modern-day equivalent of 'Dads Army', all doing our bit for our country in our spare time. In my case I had spent ten years in the regular army, serving in Iraq, South Armagh and Bosnia before giving it up to settle down, get married and become a father. Fifteen years later, with my marriage on the rocks, here I was, back in green again, soaked to the skin, covered in sheep shit and about to take the fight to the enemy.

I could see that Ninety was in pain but he dismissed my enquiry with a wave of his hand. I indicated to PB and Double A to stay here and provide an additional point of fire onto the enemy position while Ninety and I went forward. This would be the most dangerous part of the patrol. Not only were we about to engage the enemy at close range, but also we would be crawling forward under a considerable rate of covering fire from our own guns.

With rounds cracking over our heads, Ninety and I inched forwards, keeping our bodies as close to the ground as possible. Every few metres I had to stop to readjust my helmet which kept falling forward over my eyes. By now I was exhausted. Only adrenaline was keeping me going as I zoned out and focussed solely on the task in hand.

After what seemed an age we got to within just a few metres of the enemy position. Lying on my back I motioned to Ninety that we would assault from this point and pulled a fresh magazine of 30 rounds from my webbing. I wanted to go over the top with a full mag[1]. Ninety changed mags too, clearly thinking along the same lines. I could hear lots of crack and thump as Ron and Delta team back at the berm, and PB and Double A on the river bank, continued to pour fire into the enemy position. I prayed that they could see me. In the next few moments I was going to stand up and charge the position. If they didn't instantly switch fire I was going to be mown down by my own blokes.

---

[1] **Mag**: slang for magazine. A container or detachable receptacle for holding a supply of ammunition cartridges to be fed automatically into the breech of a weapon.

Glancing back at Ninety a second time I saw to my horror that he was about to launch himself onto the enemy position without me. I grabbed his arm and pulled him back into the tiny depression we were using for cover. Despite his boyish good looks I could see the murderous intent in his eyes and feel the tension in his body. I couldn't hold him back for much longer but protocol must be observed.

As the senior rank present it was my job to go in first.

I took a couple of deep breaths, composed myself as best I could and leapt to my feet while simultaneously firing into the enemy position. I could see my rounds striking the ground and could hear and feel Ninety's rounds passing me just a few metres away. We were so close that the hot, empty cases from his weapon were striking my helmet and face as they ejected from the firing chamber. I kept on running and firing until I was about 15 metres beyond the position and then threw myself down, gasping for breath and grateful to be alive.

But there was no time to celebrate. Having successfully cleared the position we needed to regroup and resume the patrol. Ninety was on my left, scanning his arcs, clearly still full of fight and looking forward to another scrap. I, on the other hand, was completely exhausted and looking forward to a bath.

I looked back to PB and Double A's position on the riverbank and signalled for them to come forward and join us. Ron and his team were nowhere to be seen on the berm. I guessed they were somewhere in the river, making their way to us, using the same route we'd just proved clear of mines, booby traps or explosive devices.

PB and Double A reached us and immediately took up fire positions on Ninety's left. With the section reassembling I was able to take stock of the situation. To our front the ground rose in a gentle convex slope to the top of a small hill. The words *frying pan* and *fire* sprang to mind.

Army gobbledegook would define this geographical feature as *key terrain*. This describes *any locality, or area, the seizure or retention of which affords a marked advantage to either combatant.* In layman's terms this meant it would be much better for us if we were up there rather than the enemy. I decided we should relocate to this position as soon as the other team arrived.

Ron was not the name Lance Corporal McCabe's mother had given him when he was born. Like all TA soldiers the army was not his main source of income. When he wasn't running around in green kit – or getting into fights in bars – Ron worked in the adult entertainment industry. Naturally, he was the envy of all his peers with more conventional jobs and it was not long before he earned the nickname Ron in reference to the famous American porn star Ron Jeremy. The lads continually pestered him for work placement opportunities and he was always put in the line-up to meet visiting dignitaries. It's a pretty safe bet that, by way of small talk, a VIP will ask a TA soldier what they do in Civvy street. Ron was unapologetic about his career choice and it was always a pleasure to see how they tackled his response to this question.

One of the key tasks of any second-in-command is to take care of the section's administrative needs, or *G4,* as it is referred to in the army. Currently our immediate needs were limited to bodies, bullets and water.

Was everyone accounted for?

Was anyone injured?

How much ammunition and drinking water did we have left?

As Delta had been providing fire support throughout the contact they'd fired more rounds than anyone else. As soon as Ron arrived he set about redistributing ammunition across the section. As he did so he was also quietly checking that everyone was OK and establishing how much water they had left. This reminded me that I was now dehydrated myself.

I greedily sucked down about a quarter of my own allowance. I didn't offer it to anyone else. Everyone knows the rules. While it's good practice to share and redistribute ammunition, this does not extend to water. Each man must look after his own needs and water is shared only in extremis if someone is obviously going down with heat exhaustion or dehydration.

Ron completed his rounds and gave me a quick G4 update. Everyone was OK and had at least one full water bottle. We all had about three mags or 90 rounds each after redistribution, which meant that we'd expended about two thirds of our ammunition in the contact. We'd need a resupply soon but not before we got onto the high ground. I outlined my concerns to Ron and we agreed that he would go firm while Charlie patrolled onto the feature in a single bound. As soon as we were static he would follow on and join us in an overwatch position.

As we stepped off with Ninety once more taking up point I heard a shout from behind us and looked back to see a man in a yellow high-visibility jacket. It was Major Guy Lock, our Training Major, and he was signalling for us to stop. Up until this moment I had been totally absorbed in the task at hand and not really aware of his presence, or that of the other range safety staff who had been shadowing us throughout the patrol, but now the bubble was burst.

As he approached he gave me an almost imperceptible nod and a half smile, *Not bad for an old fucker, Chris*, he said. Without the need for further prompting the lads formed a straight line with their weapons facing down the range. One of the range safety staff then bellowed the order, *Unload! For inspection, Port Arms!*

Working almost entirely on instinct and muscle memory I checked the safety catch was on, depressed the magazine release catch, removed the magazine from the weapon and placed it back in my webbing pouch. I then pulled the working parts to the rear and engaged the holding open device before visually and manually checking there were no rounds in the chamber or the magazine housing. I allowed the working parts to go forward before taking an aimed shot, firing off the action. There was an audible click as the firing pin was engaged. I checked safety again before pulling the working parts to the rear once more. This time I waited for the weapon to be visually inspected by a member of the range staff who then gave the command, *Ease springs.*

The patrol was over and with it the culmination of five days *Live Firing Tactical Training* in Sennybridge, Brecon. This was my first step in a 12-month journey that would lead to deployment to Helmand Province, Afghanistan. On this occasion, although the bullets we had expended had been real and deadly enough, the enemy had been wooden targets and there had been no return fire to worry about. But the exercise was not without risk. One soldier would be killed and several others seriously wounded on live firing ranges over the coming months as we prepared for deployment.

Although we didn't know it yet we were bound for the two-way range known as the Upper Gereshk Valley, or UGV. Often referred to as *The University of Close Quarter Combat*, the UGV is a largely rural area of Helmand Province where poppy cultivation is the main source of income and where Taliban shadow governance predominates.

I was to learn more about the area months later in a briefing given by our Intelligence Officer, Captain Alex Bayliss. He summed up by describing it as the 'Heart of Darkness'. To get a feel for the place he further suggested that I watch a movie called *Armadillo* by Danish film maker Janus Metz. At the time, and after watching the film, I assumed that Alex was bigging up the threat in a display of casual bravado that is typical of the young British Army officer, but his assessment would prove to be chillingly accurate.

In the nine months from January to September 2012 the combined Afghan, Danish and British force with whom we would work was engaged in over 400 small arms contacts, suffered 117 improvised explosive device (IED) strikes and discovered a further 241 IEDs. We also tragically lost 28 of our number killed in action, with a further 149 wounded in action. All in an area roughly the size of the Isle of Wight.

This exercise was not only my first step towards Afghanistan. It was also further definitive proof that I was experiencing a mid-life crisis. Some months earlier, while surfing the internet, I'd stumbled across an article on the subject. Although I hadn't cheated on my wife, bought a sports car, run off with the baby-sitter or purchased a hair-piece, I reckoned I was already hitting most of the bases.

On leaving the army in 1996, I'd worked hard to climb the corporate ladder, achieving a degree of success which had brought wealth but not happiness. I felt trapped on a treadmill. My employers kept paying me ever larger salaries but demanded more and more of my time in return. My beautiful wife, Jane[1], also enjoyed the trappings of success and required a seemingly inexhaustible supply of designer clothes, beauty treatments and visits to the hair salon, all of which required funding. Not to mention the trophy house with its prestigious SE21 postcode in Dulwich Village. This we filled with expensive designer furnishings so that we might employ a housekeeper to keep it all clean. Then there were the exotic but tediously sanitised holidays which we bragged about to our friends and neighbours.

I yearned for something more meaningful than this life of comfortable consumerism. Ironically, as a marketing specialist it was my job to encourage others to buy more and more goods and services for which

---

[1] **Jane**: Not her real name.

I personally cared less and less. Skiing had become my escape valve. But it was also a source of constant friction between Jane and me as I sought to spend more and more time in the mountains.

When we finally divorced in 2013 she cited my excessive skiing as 'a cause of upset and unreasonable behaviour'. Her advocate, whom it would have given me great pleasure to meet in a dark alley, sneered in court sessions at my ambition to become a ski instructor, as if this was somehow a pathetic and worthless aspiration.

The internet article I'd stumbled across identified that the man in mid-life crisis would *revive old interests from years past* and *make sudden life-changing decisions, usually without consulting his wife or partner*. By attending the live firing training I had effectively signalled to the army my commitment to deploy to Afghanistan, a secret ambition I'd harboured for over a year but not yet declared to my wife. I would not do so for some months to come.

But what had specifically revived my interest in the military after a 15-year absence, what had started me on the path that would lead ultimately to Afghanistan, was the death a year before of a friend and former army colleague.

Latitude:	46.26
Longitude:	6.84
Elevation:	2,346m
Met:	Plenty of sunshine H:5°L:-3°
DTG:	071600AFEB13

RITCHIE, LIAM AND I had quickly established a pecking order. As the more experienced boarder, Ritchie was our Alpha. As such he was entitled to the richest pickings the mountain had to offer but, to maintain his leadership role, he must also take the greatest risks in proving the route. As the newcomer I gratefully accepted last place. It meant that I didn't get to ski quite the best lines but even after Ritchie and Liam had had their fill of the mountain there was still plenty left for me. Consequently, there was no need to discuss how we would tackle the couloir. Ritchie tamped the reefer between forefinger and thumb of his gloved hand and thrust it into one of the many pockets in his voluminous mock-camouflage jacket. He made some tiny adjustments on his board, punched Liam's outstretched fist, winked at me and said simply *See you at the bottom.*

He dropped into the couloir making no attempt to control his downward trajectory and surfed an almost perfectly straight line down the middle of the narrow ledge. He was taking an enormous risk. As he continued to accelerate, he was reducing his options and simultaneously increasing his margin for error. Within seconds he was travelling too fast to turn in the narrow confines of the couloir and I watched with a mixture of horror and admiration as he hurtled ever faster down to the powder fields below. About 30 metres from the bottom of the couloir he hit some unseen obstacle beneath the snow which acted as a ramp and launched him into thin air. Incredibly, he managed to hold his position on the board as he shot out of the couloir before disappearing in an explosion of powder as he landed in the snow field below.

One down, two to go.

I could see from the look in Liam's eyes that he was nervous. It was the same look I'd seen many times before in the eyes of young soldiers in Afghanistan as they prepared to leave the relative security of the patrol base and face the uncertain dangers of the Green Zone[1].

---

[1] **Green Zone (GZ):** Fertile, cultivated land irrigated by the Helmand River.

..e stared at the slope for several moments, mentally composing himself before side-slipping down to the mouth of the couloir and the point of no return.

He was solely focussed on staying alive. I gave him no words of encouragement for fear of breaking his concentration as he continued to side-slip down to the narrowest section. At this point he stopped again for several long seconds. Although I hardly knew Liam I knew exactly what he was thinking. The side-slip is the safest and most stable method of negotiating steeps, I'd used it myself a thousand times before to get out of tricky situations, but it wins no points for style or glamour. Having successfully negotiated the more dangerous top section of the couloir, he was now considering whether or not to up the stakes and surf the bottom section. He began to make a tiny back and forth rocking motion on his board which I recognised from prior observation as the indication that he had made his decision and was about to launch.

Unlike Ritchie, Liam controlled his rate of descent by bringing the edges of his board across the fall line to act as a brake, in a succession of S-shaped turns. However, on such a steep and confined slope he could hold each turn only momentarily and he was still travelling at speed when he hit the same unseen obstacle that had launched Ritchie and was similarly propelled into thin air. He too landed in an explosion of powder, tumbling head over board a couple of times before coming to a stop. From this prone position I saw him punch the air several times and I knew it would not be long before he was firing up the spliff once again in celebration.

Two down, one to go. Now it was my turn.

Latitude:	51.64
Longitude:	-0.19
Elevation:	81m
Met:	Partly cloudy, some sun H:10°L:7°
DTG:	070645ZMAR10

DAWN BROKE AS we were speeding north along the motorway. I'd picked Mark up from his military home in north London before first light to avoid the morning rush hour. Although we hadn't seen each other in over 12 months we sat in companionable silence as my expensive 4x4, another potent symbol of my commercial success, ate up the miles to our destination.

Mark and I had served together in the Balkans in 1995, running convoys into towns now long forgotten by the media; Gorni Vacuf, Vitez, Sarajevo, Gorazde. Although I left the regular army shortly afterwards, we had remained great friends and I had subsequently been best man at his wedding and was god-father to his eldest daughter.

Over a brew in a Happy Eater, Mark brought me up to speed with his career and his family. Things were going well for him. He was currently doing a demanding job based out of the Permanent Joint Headquarters[1] (PJHQ) in London, travelling to some interesting places that don't appear on most commercial airlines' list of destinations.

He was also close to being 'pink listed', an internal army document listing those eligible for promotion to Lieutenant Colonel. At his age, this was an indicator that Mark had been singled out for future stardom and from now on he could enjoy a bigger office, a better salary and the grudging respect of his peers who would now be behind him on the career ladder. Despite this success, Mark was clearly troubled by the strain of service life on his marriage and family, especially the effect of his extended periods away from home.

Continuing on our journey, we once more settled into silence. I guess we were both reflecting on the life of the man whose funeral we were travelling to attend. Major John Wallace-Dutton had served with us in Bosnia. Like Mark he had continued in the army after I had left.

---

[1] **PJHQ**: Permanent Joint Headquarters. Situated in Northwood, London PJHQ is the UK's tri-service headquarters from where all overseas military operations are planned and controlled.

Determined to strike out on my own, to break the umbilical with service life and make a success of myself in civvy street, I had avoided the reunions, dinners and parades that are a regular feature on every regiment's social calendar and to which members past and present are invited. My refusal to look back had not been without cost and as the years passed I received fewer of these invites and lost touch with many friends and colleagues with whom I had once been close. John had been one such friend.

In the summer of 2009 I unexpectedly received an invite to attend the centenary celebrations of the unit I had served with in Gulf War 1 in 1991 and again in Bosnia in 1995. My two boys Harry and Alfie, then aged six and three, knew nothing of my former army life and, on a whim, I decided we should attend. Jane was less keen but agreed to go along.

The outing was not a great success.

Alfie, as every three year old is perfectly entitled to do from time to time, was being a handful. Harry was bored by the parade, and Jane wanted to leave even before we arrived. After a thirteen year absence, almost no one knew who I was and we were largely ignored. John was one of the few people who recognised me and bounded over to stay hello, shaking my hand in a crushing embrace with his enormous boxer's fist.

John was a huge bear of a man. His presence was hard to miss even if he hadn't been such a snappy dresser. He was, as usual, immaculately turned out. His vast barrel chest strained against his double-breasted blazer with regimental buttons. His crisp white shirt the perfect setting for a tie emblazoned with the crossed *kukri*'s of the Brigade of Gurkhas, the legendary fighting force to which he proudly belonged. To complete the ensemble he had chosen a pair of burgundy red cords that a lesser man would have found hard to carry off but which John wore with casual aplomb.

Both through physical presence and force of character John was not a man you could ignore but he also possessed a gentle good humour that made him fun to be around. Although he could be tough and ruthlessly professional when required, he had always been much loved and admired by those under his command. Clearly he had not lost his touch in the intervening years and we were constantly interrupted by soldiers approaching him to say hello. It was a pleasure to be reacquainted with him after such a long time and I would have happily stayed and chatted with him for longer, but I could feel Jane's impatient presence on my shoulder, so we said our goodbyes and promised to stay in touch in the way that all soldiers do but seldom deliver on.

A few months later I was to learn from Mark that John had terminal cancer. Like Mark, he was married with three young children who would soon be growing up without their father.

Latitude:	46.26
Longitude:	6.84
Elevation:	2,346m
Met:	Plenty of sunshine H:5°L:-3°
DTG:	071615AFEB13

AS LIAM HAD done before me, I side-slipped down into the couloir and the point of no return. The walk to the drop-in through deep snow in my inflexible ski boots had been arduous, aggravating an old blister on the inside of my left heel. I'd been stationary for about ten minutes while first Ritchie and then Liam had negotiated the descent. Waiting, I had felt the blood congealing in my boot around the wound. Now I was moving again my woollen sock detached itself from the blister. I dismissed the excruciating pain.

Snow conditions are many and varied. Experienced skiers and boarders continually adjust their technique in response to the signals that are transmitted through the base of their skis or board. I had just a few metres in which to plan how to tackle this descent, and I needed to process these signals before committing myself. I simply could not allow the pain in my heel to distract me from this task.

I was now at the top of the couloir with the cornice to my back. I could feel its malevolent presence behind me and briefly wondered if Ritchie and Liams' descent had in some way altered the delicate balances that maintained its gravity defying position. Nine months in Afghanistan had taught me not to worry about things over which I had no control. Nonetheless I did not want to hang around for too long in this exposed and vulnerable position.

Looking down the length of the couloir I judged where to make each turn in order to control my descent. The No Fall line looked to be just below the point at which Liam had stopped side-slipping. I reckoned on four turns from my current position to that point. I would need to turn my skis in order to control my rate of descent, but each turn would also increase the risk of error which, above the No Fall line, was likely to prove fatal. The stakes could not have been higher. I made some minor adjustments to my body position and committed myself to the slope.

Almost immediately I was in trouble. Warren Smith, of the eponymous Ski Academy in Verbier, urges his students to attack the slope from the very first turn. I had been too hesitant in my approach and my left ski was now pulling away from me under the snow. In order to bring my skis back together under my body I would have to execute a quick turn.

I didn't make this decision consciously, it was an instinctive and automatic reaction to regain control of my skis, but my plan was already in disarray. Now I would be making things up as I went along, and I was not yet out of trouble.

The manoeuvre had put me dangerously close to the edge of the couloir and the long drop into the valley below. My next turn was equally rapid but much more deliberate. In my peripheral vision I saw snow disturbed by my presence so close to the cliff edge tumbling into the void. No time to consider my lucky escape. I was heading towards the cliff wall on the other side of the couloir just above the narrowest point, where only the most confident skier would risk a turn. I would have to turn again in order to slow my descent above this most dangerous section.

Three turns in. This was uncharted territory. I'd never before made more than two turns above the No Fall line. I shot through the narrow section trying to maintain my body position over the tips of my skis and punched my left arm forward and down as I threw my hips over my skis into turn four. Now I was through the most dangerous point and my confidence soared.

I could do this.

I was going to make it.

With my self-belief at an all time high the next two turns were easy, almost lazy, and I knew I was putting on a good display for Liam and Ritchie who would be watching from their vantage point below. All that was left for me to negotiate was the unseen obstacle that had launched them both skywards.

I enjoy catching some air with the best of them, but my ambition in this regard is modest. I reckon my bones are too old and brittle to tackle serious jumps. As a general rule I leave the half pipe, the fun park and the big cliff drops to the youngsters who are not only braver and more reckless, but who also heal from their injuries more quickly. But now, awash with adrenaline, I threw caution to the wind, allowed my skis to point directly down the slope and let gravity take over.

I could clearly see from their tracks in the snow where both of the lads had lost contact with the ground. Approaching this point I let my knees flex to soak up some of the energy transmitted through the base of my skis by the unseen object below the snow. With my thighs almost in my chest I straightened my legs as explosively as I could and was airborne. Instantly I tucked my legs up again to stay over my skis and held this position for what seemed like an age. In the split second before regaining contact with the snow I straightened my legs, keeping my knees soft in an attempt to land the jump. I knew the theory well enough but in truth this was so far beyond any jump I'd ever tackled before that I really didn't know what to expect. I was completely unprepared for what happened next.

Although I had tried to stay over the tops of my skis, human instinct, evolved over millennia, tells us that the best way to break a fall is to sit down. All skiers, if they are going to progress to any reasonable standard, have to unlearn this in-built reflex.

In Warren Smith Ski Academy classes I'd been taught the mantra that falling forwards was OK – at least you were trying – but falling backwards was not. This was so ingrained in my psyche that I'd even passed it on to my own children. But now, in unfamiliar territory, attempting something well beyond my level of experience, the instinct of evolution took over. As my skis made contact with the snow, detonating an explosion of powder that completely engulfed me, I was thrown backwards with such force that I was powerless to prevent it. I'd failed to correctly anticipate the landing, my body position had been completely wrong.

As I was thrown on my back and had the wind knocked out of me I had a brief vision of my eldest son, Harry, telling me *you weren't trying hard enough, Daddy*. But then, just as suddenly, I was propelled forward once again by forces unknown. Incredibly, I was up and over my skis again, out of breath, but back in control. It was a complete fluke but I'd landed the jump!

As I'd been obscured in powder at the time I was pretty sure Ritchie and Liam had not seen me fall. In any case, I was back on my feet and they were both far too generously spirited to deny me the jump. Decelerating through a couple of looping turns into the powder field I allowed the euphoria of the descent and the jump to wash over me. I could feel the endorphins, my own private narcotic, surging through my nervous system and brain, far more powerful and more rewarding than any opiate harvested in Afghanistan.

Latitude:	52.13
Longitude:	-3.78
Elevation:	391m
Met:	Partly cloudy, some sun H:10°L:7°
DTG:	071000ZMAR10

JOHN'S FUNERAL, LIKE the rest of his life, was outstanding. He couldn't have organised it better himself, which knowing John he probably had done.

By the time Mark and I arrived at the picture postcard village in North Wales, dawn had given way to a perfect spring morning. Frost feathered the slate tiles of the Norman church at its centre. Larks could be heard singing high above the hedgerows.

The village was not prepared for the influx of people who had come to pay their respects and the little streets were packed with cars parked nose to tail well beyond the village boundary. We abandoned the SUV on the end of one such line and started walking.

On the wind we could hear the lament of a lone piper calling us to prayer. Resplendent in a tailored charcoal pinstriped suit, Mark had received some admiring glances from the girls behind the hotplate when we'd broken our journey at the Happy Eater. I wasn't about to tell him, but dressed as he was, with his shock of dark hair, olive skin and rugged good looks, it was easy to see why his beautiful and talented wife had fallen for him. As we approached the church the cast iron heel protectors on his highly polished shoes seemed to mark time with the regimental piper.

I'd briefly met with John and Mark about three months prior to John's death, by which time he was grievously ill. The cancer and the radiation therapy had reduced him to a pale shadow of his former self, although he retained his perfect gentleman character and self-deprecating humour. As we said goodbye on that occasion I'd struggled to hold his gaze as he'd looked deep into my eyes. We both knew it was for the last time.

John's funeral did not mourn his death but celebrated his life to a sell-out crowd.

The Health and Safety Executive would have had a big drama. The church's capacity was exceeded two- or three-fold and its Norman designers had not thought to include emergency exits or adequately signed escape routes. Although John had opted not to have a military funeral, the aisles were full of men and women in drab green service dress uniforms, decorated with bright splashes of colour from the ribbons of their medals. A plethora of pretty baubles which offered a clue to the tempo of operations the army had endured during the fifteen years in which I'd been getting rich and fat.

To judge from the highly polished belts, straps and shoes on display most of those present must have spent an industrious hour or two the previous night bulling leather with Kiwi parade gloss and Selvyt polishing cloth, just as we'd been taught at the Royal Military Academy. I would learn later that John was so highly regarded by the military community that operations in Afghanistan had been temporarily suspended in order to hold a service of remembrance in his honour at Camp Bastion.

The church was so packed that I could not see John's wife, Jo, and their three children. I guessed that, even in their grief, their hearts must have swelled with pride as they listened to the eulogies to an extraordinary man, husband and father.

Although he had never mentioned it to me, from one of these tributes I learned that John had done a stint in Iraq. In his spare time, using his ingenuity, a few bits of wood and some scrap metal, John had built a gym complete with makeshift boxing ring. He'd then marketed his creation by inviting all comers to try and take a swing at an officer, something that under normal circumstances would most likely result in instant dismissal and court martial. Word got around and naturally there were one or two likely lads who fancied themselves up for the challenge. All of whom had ended up on the canvas at the wrong end of John's massive fists.

I could just imagine him helping some poor tattooed head-banger back to his feet, dusting him down and offering him some quiet words of encouragement to come back and have another go when he was feeling better. It would have been so typical of John's unique sense of humour.

Following the service we all retired to a local hotel where John's life was celebrated in the way he would have wanted, with fond reminiscences over a pint. As the alcohol flowed, I listened to ever more raucous and outlandish tales. I could not help but contrast the life of this wonderful, charming extrovert with my own, which to my mind had become stale and dull.

As we barrelled back down the motorway that night in my expensive gas guzzler, Mark snoring softly beside me in the passenger seat, I realised that somewhere along the way I'd confused the acquisition of possessions with the attainment of happiness.

Inspired by John's remarkable life, and the sheer vitality and energy of his army colleagues, I resolved to return to active duty after a fifteen year absence and deploy to Afghanistan. It was another two years before I climbed aboard the ancient RAF TriStar aircraft that would deliver me, together with 40 colleagues from the 1st Battalion Grenadier Guards, to Camp Bastion and the start of 239 days in Helmand Province.

For most of those two years I kept my ambition a closely guarded secret from friends and family, shamefully concocting a series of ever more elaborate and unlikely excuses for my absences from work and home as I trained for deployment.

But my resolve never once wavered.

Latitude:	46.26
Longitude:	6.84
Elevation:	2,346m
Met:	Plenty of sunshine H:5°L:-3°
DTG:	071700AFEB13

RITCHIE, LIAM AND I had successfully completed the quest that Mother Nature had set. We had willingly risked our lives in her service and now we were ready to claim our prize. Still buzzing from our successful descent through the drop-in we marvelled at the perfection of the powder fields even as they yielded to our embrace. Turn after perfect turn we placed our mark on the mountain, certain in our knowledge that no one would have the courage or determination to follow us through the entry point and despoil our legacy – at least until the next snows came.

It was the perfect end to a perfect day. We celebrated with Vin Chaud on the terrace of a restaurant in the village below the powder field. Looking back up the way we had come it was easy to make out our tracks through the drop-in and into the powder below. With the setting sun once more turning the mountain peaks pink we took photos of our tracks, noisily discussing our descent in less than perfect language as we came down from our adrenaline high.

The restaurant's other patrons kept a respectful distance, perhaps from disapproval at our boisterous presence on the balcony, perhaps from grudging admiration at the tracks we had carved on the mountain. All too soon it was time to leave or risk missing the last chairlift home. As we made our way to the exit a man of about my own age leaned across to his partner and said in a broad Yorkshire accent *bloody idiots must have a death-wish or summat' carrying on like that*. Given our unruly behaviour it was not unreasonable that he might bear some ill will towards us, but he was wrong about one thing. I couldn't speak for Liam and Ritchie, but for my own part it wasn't a death wish that had driven me into the Porte du Soleil backcountry.

I'd been celebrating my life and my limbs after nine months in the killing zone of Helmand's front line.

Latitude   51.47
Longitude   -0.10
Elevation   9m
Met   Cloudy with some showers H:8°L:5°
DTG   061930ZAPR10

I couldn't decide if I was
participating in a spectacular
BBC period drama or a Terry
Gilliam epic fantasy

ATP: Annual Training Package
MOD: Ministry of Defence
PT: Physical Training
LA: Los Angeles

Latitude:	51.47
Longitude:	-0.10
Elevation:	9m
Met:	Cloudy with some showers H:8°L:5°
DTG:	061930ZAPR10

REJOINING THE ARMY after a 15 year absence turned out to be surprisingly easy. One evening in the late spring of 2010, a few weeks after John's funeral, I cycled over to my local Territorial Army[1] Centre in Camberwell – home of D (London Irish Rifles) Company, The London Regiment – and presented myself at the gate for re-enlistment. I was invited inside and joined half a dozen other would-be recruits, all of whom were less than half my age, for a series of presentations on life in the Territorial Army (or TA). The recurring theme of these briefings was the opportunity to join the Regular Army on operations in Iraq and Afghanistan, which suited me perfectly. I'd clearly come to the right place, although I wasn't planning to declare my hand just yet.

Not everyone, it seemed, was quite so enthused by this prospect. There was some shuffling of feet when a huge, shaven-headed soldier helpfully explained that the primary role of the infantry was to place a bayonet in the chest of the Queen's enemies. He was clearly a man who enjoyed his work, and his expletives, and he went on to describe the intricacies of this procedure in some detail, using language that would have made Harry's primary school teacher blush.

A number of the other soldiers who briefed us had recently returned from operations and talked of their experiences. Sticking bayonets in people did not actually seem to be part of the daily routine but it was nonetheless obvious that they had all put themselves in harm's way in the service of their country. One or two were eager to return to the action as soon as possible, others seemed more world-weary, but they were all clearly proud of their service. I was full of admiration for them.

The evening culminated in a briefing from the Company Commander, Major Crispin Swayne, a thoroughly charming and likeable man of about my own age. He thanked us all for our interest in the Territorial Army and expressed his hope that in the not too distant future he would be able to welcome us back to the London Irish Rifles as fully

---

[1] **TA**: Territorial Army now renamed the *Army Reserve*

trained recruits. As the only person present with prior military service I was singled out for a one-to-one interview with Major Swayne and was instructed to wait outside his office.

The London Irish Rifles has a proud history as a volunteer rifle regiment dating back to 1859. It first saw service in the Boer War and went on to distinguish itself in both World Wars. Today it is much reduced in size and forms one of four rifle companies that make up The London Regiment. Much of this rich history is chronicled on the walls of the TA centre and I was literally immersed in the past as I waited in a corridor lined with pictures and paintings. Illustrious senior officers competed for space with impossibly young men, posthumously decorated for their bravery in battle. They all stared gravely down at me. A silent pre-screening panel, assessing my suitability to become one amongst their number.

Given they were all long since dead, this was not part of my plan. But after listening to the young soldiers earlier in the evening, I understood that it was a distinct possibility.

In the months ahead Crispin and I would become firm friends. Although neither of us could have foreseen it at the time, I would eventually replace him as D Company's Commander. As an ex-Regular himself he was able to explain the process of re-enlistment, and it was all good news. I would not be required to complete basic training for a second time. All that was needed was a successful interview with the Commanding Officer of The London Regiment, a medical check-up, and the approval of Army Manning and Records in Glasgow. I was well past the upper age limit for enlistment into the TA but Crispin assured me that this need not be a problem. So long as the Commanding Officer was suitably impressed at interview and put in a good word for me with Manning and Records, all would be well.

And he was right. A few weeks after meeting with the Commanding Officer, and a very perfunctory medical which did little more than confirm I was still breathing and had two knees in reasonably good working order, an unremarkable brown envelope with a Glasgow date stamp on the reverse dropped through our letterbox. It contained a single sheet of recycled paper with the capitalised headline:

APPOINTMENT TO A TERRITORIAL ARMY COMMISSION 30132918 CAPT C D S GREEN – LONDONS (V).

Three lines of text confirmed my appointment to a *TA Group A*

Commission and concluded *The officer is to report for duty on 03 Aug 2010.*

I was in.

Latitude:	50.44
Longitude:	-5.00
Elevation:	85m
Met:	Sun with some clouds H:17°L:15°
DTG:	280600ZAUG10

MY FIRST ASSIGNMENT with my new regiment was to attend the two week annual training package, or ATP as it is known. Every TA unit is expected to undertake two weeks of collective training each year. The London Regiment had elected to conduct its ATP at RAF St Mawgan, near Newquay in Cornwall. It wasn't entirely clear what my duties would be but this didn't seem to matter so long as I turned up with all the kit with which I had recently been issued.

The year prior to my leaving regular service in 1996, the army had introduced new clothing and personal equipment which had been collectively labelled 'Combat '95'. Like the rest of the British public, I was aware of the debate about under-resourcing in the army. Hardly a day went by without talk of the inadequacy of Snatch Land Rovers, or the shortage of helicopters in Afghanistan.

The debate was vividly brought home to me by my kit issue.

In the 15 years I'd been away there appeared to have been no upgrades or improvements to Combat '95, other than there seemed to be less of it. 'Barrack dress' and 'lightweights' had been removed as orders of dress, as had the Jersey, Heavy Wool – which was probably a good thing. Although Nuclear, Biological and Chemical (NBC) protective clothing had been rebranded as Chemical, Biological, Radioactive and Nuclear (CBRN), it was otherwise unchanged and in any event was 'dues out' and not available for issue.

I was later to discover that giving old bits of kit new names was a recurring theme. The ancient FV432 armoured personnel carrier, a relic of the 1960s Cold War, had returned to service as the 'Bulldog'. The Lynx helicopter, somehow forced upon the British Army by Westland in a deal dating back to the 1970s, was now the 'Wildcat'.

The Lynx was originally much loved by pilots for its ability to do a barrel roll. This feature made it tremendous fun to fly, but turned out not to be a battle winning capability and did little to compensate for its failings. It was too small to be an effective troop carrier, and lacked the integrated weapon systems of an attack helicopter. It had first come in to service in the year Showaddywaddy topped the charts with *You got what it takes* but as a military helicopter it could never aspire to the title of that particular hit single.

A Lynx would later get me out of trouble whilst on a fighting patrol in the insurgent stronghold of Zumbalay. Following a pre-dawn infiltration to probe enemy strengths and dispositions our presence had proved unpopular with the local Taliban. A number of small arms engagements ensued before the insurgents succeeded in blocking our exfiltration route. It was time to call for some air support and an Apache attack helicopter, callsign *Ugly*, was requested.

The *Ugly* is an awesome killing machine and the Taliban know better than to try and take it on. Its presence alone would be enough to make them go to ground and secure our safe passage. But we were informed that our request would be met by a different attack helicopter, callsign *Crucial*. This callsign was unknown to me and, when it came on station a few minutes later, I was dismayed to discover that it was nothing more than a Lynx with a 50-calibre machine gun mounted in the door. Calling this an attack helicopter and thus comparing it with an Apache was like comparing the space shuttle with a paper aeroplane.

As I had anticipated, the *Crucial* did not have the desired effect on our adversaries, at least until the door gunner opened up with his 50, killing two of their number and giving us the opportunity to break cover and hot foot it back to the relative safety of our desert leaguer[1]. I was grateful to the Lynx pilot and his crew, they may well have saved our lives, but I still reckoned the Lynx should have retired about the same time Showaddywaddy called it a day.

Even the Land Rover in which I travelled that summer from central London to Cornwall had been renamed the 'Wolf'. It was hard to imagine a more inappropriate name. The gutless beast was nearly as old as I was and incapable of speeds in excess of 45 miles per hour. From where I was sitting on the sweaty vinyl cushion of that ancient vehicle, it didn't feel like the MoD was investing in its strategic reserves.

---

[1] **Leaguer** (from South African Dutch **Laager**): A temporary defensive encampment surrounded by armoured vehicles – a military term originating from the Boer War.

But at the time I wasn't worrying too much about MoD policy. I was just glad to be out of the house.

By now Jane and I were barely communicating.

As a freelance marketing consultant I worked from home a lot and had converted one of the back bedrooms into a study. Jane had taken to sleeping in this room and so we passed each other each morning and evening on the landing as I commuted from bedroom to study and back again.

It wasn't much of a life.

To make matters worse I was running out of work. As contracts expired I wasn't replacing them. I was going through the motions, attending power lunches, making phone calls, working my network, but with precious little to show for it. I told myself it was the economic downturn. This may have been a factor, but the truth is that my heart was just not in it and I suspect that would-be clients could sense my lack of commitment. Instead I explored some new business ventures with friends. While it was fun to imagine myself as the next Richard Branson, I was only fooling myself.

Jane took little if any interest in my work, or lack of it, and continued to live the life to which she had grown accustomed. Perhaps I should have spoken to her about our situation and asked her to rein in her spending, but I resented the fact that we even needed to have this conversation. How could she not see what seemed so obvious to me? Instead I just raided my savings, hoping that something would come along soon, while privately despairing at my wife's insensitivity to our situation. It was a slippery slope from which our marriage would never recover and I was incensed when Jane suggested expensive therapy sessions as a solution to our problems.

By the time September came around it was a relief to get away. Besides the TA were going to pay me, so it was money in the bank. Not quite the salary I was used to, but better than a slap on the belly with a wet fish, as my mother used to say.

I've no doubt Jane was glad to see the back of me too, but it wasn't only Jane I was leaving behind. It would not be the first time in their young lives that I'd been separated from my sons, Harry and Alfie but I was painfully aware that this was the start of something different. If I succeeded in getting to Afghan, I would be away for months at a time. I might not come home at all.

The thought of abandoning my children in this way was both mentally and physically so painful that I put it to the back of my mind and told myself I would not be the first soldier, or the last, who would be leaving loved ones behind to deploy on operations. But I had a nagging doubt that, in this regard, my situation was different.

In March 2009, skiing legend Shane McConkey tragically died while trying to perform a complex stunt for an extreme skiing film. He was a prominent and extrovert athlete who had already appeared in many similar films, and his death shocked the skiing community. It opened up a fierce and very public debate in skiing chat rooms and on-line forums.

McConkey was married with a three year old daughter, the same age as my son, Alfie. There were some who thought that McConkey should have given up his daredevil lifestyle when his daughter was born and that his death, while tragic, was an inevitable consequence of his own recklessness. While some hailed him as a hero, others were of the opinion that he performed these 'pointless' stunts purely for his own personal gratification and enrichment. Calling him a hero and, in so doing, comparing him to soldiers who had sacrificed their lives in the service of their country was, some argued, inappropriate.

I didn't have a dog in this fight and did not contribute to the debate, but it got me thinking. I could never compare myself to McConkey in proficiency as a skier. But perhaps we did have something in common. I too had responsibilities to my young children. Wasn't my own yearning for a life less ordinary just as reckless and 'pointless'? I didn't need to go to Afghanistan for any reason other than that I wanted to. I was voluntarily putting myself in harm's way exactly as McConkey had done.

I didn't like to confront these thoughts too deeply. Anyway at my age I reckoned I'd be sitting behind a desk somewhere in the rear headquarters so far behind the lines that I'd probably have to send my laundry forward. In the months ahead, once I'd declared my intention to deploy, I would use this *rear headquarters* line whenever friends or family members raised their concerns. The sceptical looks I received in response indicated they were unanimously unconvinced by the argument.

Jane would frequently remind me that I was failing in my responsibilities to my children. But by then all forms of communication had collapsed, other than increasingly vitriolic text messages.

My first two weeks in the Territorial Army were a blast. On arrival at RAF St Mawgan, I was assigned the position of Regimental Signals Officer, or RSO for short. I knew almost nothing about signals but this didn't seem to matter because we had almost no radios, no secure communications or 'crypto', and only a handful of soldiers in the signals platoon. I left the much diminished platoon in the capable hands of the Regimental Signals Warrant Officer and went in search of things to do.

My first port of call was the recruit training wing. It had been 15 years or more since I'd last handled an assault rifle and I didn't want the first opportunity to reacquaint myself to be with live ammunition. The SA80 is the standard issue personal weapon of the British Army. It first came into service in 1988, the year I joined the regular army and consequently I'd been trained in its use at the Royal Military Academy, Sandhurst. It had not proved a popular weapon and was considered both fragile and unreliable. I'd had my fair share of problems with it but I knew it had since undergone an expensive Heckler and Koch upgrade. 200,000 units had been recalled and re-manufactured at a cost to the taxpayer of £400 each.

I assumed that the upgrade would necessitate some changes in weapon handling skills and drills, but was surprised to find that this was not the case. In fact, apart from a few minor alterations to the cocking handle and the magazine release catch, it was hard to see where tax payers' money had been invested. The only new drill was the 'forward assist' which ensured that the working parts were fully engaged once the weapon had been cocked. I didn't recall this being a problem with the old weapon and cynically wondered if the upgrade had, in effect, only created new problems.

Although the Ministry of Defence proudly boasted that the upgraded weapon was *the most reliable of its type in the world,* unlike the Russian AK47 or the American M16, there hadn't been a rush in the world's arms market either to purchase or to copy the weapon. In fact the only export orders had come from Bolivia, Jamaica and, following British military intervention in the civil war there, Sierra Leone.

It was hardly a positive endorsement of the MoD's claims.

After a pleasant enough afternoon in the company of a dozen or so recruits-in-training and their instructors, I was ready to take a weapon handling test. As an officer it would be a big embarrassment if I failed this most basic test of my soldiering skills. News would quickly pass through the regiment, undermining my credibility and standing with my colleagues, perhaps irrevocably, but I was feeling pretty confident. I'd been surprised at how quickly I'd remembered the drills. They'd been so thoroughly imprinted in my brain and muscle memory 22 years before that after just a few hours I was fully reacquainted with the weapon.

I easily passed the test but, much to my annoyance, I forgot to perform the new forward assist manoeuvre in one of the drills. This was not deemed a critical error but it did cost me a few points, and the perfect score I desired. Months later, outside an Afghan National Army checkpoint in one of the most heavily contested areas of our district, making ready prior to a patrol, I would call upon the forward assist to correctly chamber a round in my weapon. Had I failed to perform the drill on this occasion it would have resulted in a misfire. I was grateful that I'd learned my lesson in the classroom at RAF St Mawgan.

The following morning was scheduled for Battalion Physical Training, or PT. At our initial all-ranks briefing on arrival in St Mawgan the Training Major, Guy Lock had assured us that this would not be a thrashing. But I was unconvinced. Major Lock's reputation preceded him. A Coldstream Guards officer, he had been wounded in action in Afghanistan while commanding the Guards Parachute Platoon[1], part of the 3rd Battalion, The Parachute Regiment. He had subsequently been posted to The London Regiment as Training Major while recovering from his injuries.

Over the coming months I would get to know Guy well but I was initially wary of him. Airborne Forces operate in the vanguard and are therefore trained to fight in the most demanding of circumstances, often against superior numbers. They attract supremely tough and resilient soldiers to their ranks, and they have a reputation for intolerance and arrogance. Guy appeared to me to conform to this stereotype. He was shaven-headed, a style generally frowned upon in the officer corps, and his combat fatigues had clearly seen better days.

---

[1] **Platoon**: In the British Army, a rifle platoon from an infantry company consists of three sections of eight men, plus a signaller (radio operator), a platoon sergeant and the platoon commander (either a second lieutenant or lieutenant).

His smock was frayed and torn, his trousers were faded several shades lighter than the new pair with which I had just been supplied, and his non-standard issue boots were heavily scored and dulled by use.

He looked every inch the combat veteran that he was.

Like the weapon handling test the previous day, that morning's PT session would be another important milestone for me. Soldiering is a physically demanding business and it's every soldier's responsibility, regardless of rank, to maintain the highest standards of physical fitness at all times. My credibility would be severely compromised if I proved unable to keep up. This preyed on my mind as I made my way to the muster point in the early morning half light.

I stood shivering in thin PT shorts and vest while a roll call was taken. This took several minutes as a number of my new brothers-in-arms were mysteriously unaccounted for. The Regimental Sergeant Major became increasingly enraged as sheepish latecomers were rounded up but eventually we were assembled in three ranks in preparation for a squaded run.

Our PT session that morning was to be led by Sergeant 'D-Day' Dawson. D-Day had seen action in Iraq, where he had sustained serious head injuries when the vehicle he was commanding was struck by an improvised explosive device, or IED. He had returned to duty, but would carry the scars of that encounter with the enemy for the rest of his life. His presence was another reminder to me of the dangerous business I was getting myself into.

Despite my scepticism, Major Lock was true to his word and we set off on a gentle lap of the camp perimeter road. To me the pace seemed undemanding and I was still cold from the long wait at the muster area when, after no more than half a mile, a rather overweight individual dropped out of the ranks and stood at the side of the road, bent double clutching his knees and gasping for breath. A few miles later he had been joined by perhaps half a dozen others in a similar breathless condition. I never did discover who that first hapless individual was, and never saw him again, but it was a surprise to learn that obesity was a problem, even in a battle hardened unit with a record of operational service like that of The London Regiment.

I suppose it is a reflection on our society as a whole that even the army is not immune to the over-eating epidemic. Nor is this problem confined to the Territorial Army. In Afghanistan I was to come across soldiers who were clearly eating too much and not exercising enough, even though they must have been aware this was compromising their operational effectiveness, potentially putting their lives and those of their comrades at risk.

It doesn't help that the MoD continues to feed soldiers with crap. The traditional 'full English breakfast', rich with sodium and saturated fat, remains the daily staple of every cookhouse from Aldershot to Afghanistan. Despite claims to the contrary, it would seem that the MoD has little interest in the health and well-being of its soldiers. How else is it possible to explain the inclusion of hydrogenated vegetable oils in the rations it supplies to its servicemen on operations?

The stupidity of introducing an ingredient medically proven to be linked to heart disease and obesity into the diet of men and women who are required to maintain optimum levels of health and fitness seems obvious to me, but appears lost on civil servants at the MoD.

However, this stupidity pales into insignificance when compared to that of dispensing a drug known to induce hallucinations, aggression and psychotic behaviour to men and women entrusted with instruments of death and destruction.

As improbable as this may seem, and despite years of repeated warnings, the MoD issues Lariam to troops as its anti-malarial prophylactic of choice. It's a drug that, according to the manufacturer, may *induce potentially serious neuropsychiatric disorders* including *hallucinations, psychosis, suicide, suicidal thoughts and self-endangering behaviour*. The MoD, apparently unconcerned by this warning, doggedly refuses to switch to an alternative. Even after the US Army introduced a ban, and UK Service Chiefs queued up to criticise the policy, the MoD insisted on its continued use.

Major General Julian Thompson, who commanded 3 Commando Brigade in the Falklands War, came to the conclusion this was because *the MoD has a large supply of Lariam, and some chairborne jobsworth has decreed that, as a cost-saving measure, the stocks are to be consumed before an alternative is purchased.*

My personal conclusion is slightly at odds with the Major General's. It seems to me that the MoD mandarins continue to risk the mental health of their soldiers because they are themselves as mad as a box of frogs.

All those who served in the Iraq and Afghan wars will have been issued Lariam under the generic name mefloquine. Nearly 1,000 UK service personnel are known to have been admitted to psychiatric hospitals, or treated at mental health clinics, as a result of being prescribed the drug. In 2012, more British veterans of the two conflicts took their own lives than soldiers died fighting the Taliban in Afghanistan over the same period.

It is a terrible coincidence that the side effects of Lariam closely resemble those linked to Post Traumatic Stress Disorder (PTSD). Some experts believe that Lariam amplifies the effects of PTSD and the British Army now faces a mental health catastrophe. The Ministry of Defence, on the other hand, continues to maintain that the incidence of mental health issues in army personnel is broadly in line with the general population, and continues to prescribe mefloquine.

On the night of 11th March 2012, US Army Staff Sergeant Robert Bales murdered 16 Afghan civilians in Kandahar Province in a brutal and apparently motiveless attack. Bales could not explain his actions and admitted *There's not a good reason in this world for why I did the horrible things I did.*

Bales' killing spree was incomprehensible not only to him but also to everyone in Task Force Helmand. Threat levels were raised in anticipation of retaliatory attacks, and we all speculated on the impulse that led him to leave the security of his patrol base before sadistically slaying innocent women and children. While we could find no rational explanation, the makers of Lariam thought they knew the answer.

A month after the mass killings Roche, who manufacture Lariam and claim on their website to be *passionate about transforming patients' lives,* notified the US Food and Drug Administration that Bales had been given the anti-malarial drug (in direct contradiction to US military rules) and *developed homicidal behaviour and led to Homicide killing 17* [sic] *Afghanis.*

Although it never occurred to me that mass murder could be linked to the seemingly innocuous little white tablets with which I'd been issued, I'd already stopped taking them. No one had counselled me on their potential side effects but they'd caused me to feel so unwell that I'd decided I would be better off with malaria.

Latitude:	50.44
Longitude:	-5.00
Elevation:	85m
Met:	Partly cloudy H:21°L:15°
DTG:	111943ZSEP10

RAF ST MAWGAN is situated on one of Britain's most picturesque coastlines, midway between Newquay in the south and Padstow in the north. It's an area of outstanding natural beauty that is also home to a variety of military training areas. Major Guy Lock had ensured we made best use of them all.

For the next ten days we conducted exercises at platoon and company level. For me, there was very little to do other than enjoy some combat camping in idyllic surroundings and spend time getting to know some of the characters who made up the regiment. Getting back to basics was an absolute pleasure and I enjoyed living rough for a few days on the cliffs overlooking Perrin Bay under a makeshift shelter constructed from my camouflage poncho. It was in stark contrast to the four and five star hotels I'd enjoyed in New York, Chicago, LA, Seattle, Cannes, Rome, Venice, Florence, Vienna, and elsewhere to which I'd travelled as a business executive. I couldn't have been happier.

Together with my little band of signallers I'd been tasked to set up an exercise control point, or Excon, and await the arrival of the exercising troops who would be due in a few days time. From our vantage point I watched the waves rolling in from the Atlantic and enjoyed the light-hearted banter of these soldiers who relentlessly joshed and teased one another as they patiently waited for something, for anything, to happen.

A capacity for waiting is an essential soldierly quality. I was more than happy to while away the time in the company of these men. Even when I woke one morning after a particularly heavy rainstorm to find my shelter had become a staging area for dozens of disgustingly slimy slugs my spirits were not dampened.

All too soon, ATP was over and it was time to return home. I'd still not declared my intention to mobilise but reckoned I'd put in a sufficiently good showing that my application, when it came, would be viewed favourably.

On the eve of our departure the Quarter Master, Major 'Dutch'

Elms, laid on a spectacular dinner under canvas for the Officers' and Sergeants' Messes on the cliff tops above Watergate Bay. Somehow he'd managed to transport all the mess furniture from London to a farmer's field right on the cliff edge where he'd established a field kitchen and two huge mess tents.

As cows grazed nearby, nearly 100 men and women, all dressed in regimental mess kit or black tie, watched a spectacular sunset from the comfort of deep leather Chesterfield sofas while being served champagne cocktails from silver salvers.

It was a surreal scene in the finest tradition of Mad Dogs and Englishmen.

When dusk fell Highland bagpipers of the regiment's A (London Scottish) Company sounded the calls for dinner and we sat down in the middle of the field at a huge antique mahogany dining table bedecked with silver candelabra, rose bowls, figurines and tontine[1] boxes, some dating back to 1779 when antecedents of the regiment were first formed.

I couldn't decide if I was participating in a spectacular BBC period drama or a Terry Gilliam epic fantasy, but it was certainly a night to remember. At about 2am, with the party still in full swing, I decided to call it a day. Without any clear idea of how to get back to my billet I set off across the field in what I hoped was the right direction. With the lights from the party to my back I was quickly engulfed in the inky black night but this did not worry me. Providing sufficient quantities of alcohol have been consumed, like most other homo sapiens I know, I have a homing instinct to rival the carrier pigeon.

In any event, as I made my no doubt erratic path across the field, I encountered sufficient clues to give me confidence I was heading in the right direction – the first of these being the Adjutant, Captain Toby Davidson, and the Quarter Master standing toe-to-toe engaged in a furious argument. They were normally great friends and I never did discover why they had fallen out. Certain my presence was

---

[1] **Tontine Box**: Tontine boxes were popular amongst the officer class in the 18th and 19th Centuries. Prior to departing on a military campaign or expedition, each participating officer paid an agreed sum into a fund which was used to purchase a piece of silverware, usually a box, on which their names were engraved. On return from duty the box would then be sold and the proceeds divided amongst the surviving members. In some cases no officers survived and the boxes have remained the property of the Officers' Mess to which they belonged, a poignant reminder to their successors of their sacrifice.

undetected, I briefly considered waiting to see if the two of them would come to blows. But, entertaining as this spectacle might have been, I concluded that it would be more prudent to make a discreet detour.

Shortly afterwards I came to a hedge that marked the perimeter of the field, beyond which I could see a single-track metalled road. Confident this must be my own personal yellow brick road that would magically lead me back to RAF St Mawgan I began to search for a suitable crossing point. As I tramped along the hedgerow I heard the unmistakable sounds of a couple engaged in what might best be described as extra-curricular activities. They were clearly doing their best to keep the noise to a minimum to avoid detection. Not wishing to put them off their stride, I again found myself making a discreet detour.

After some further searching I successfully crossed the hedge by a combination of stumbling and falling, and continued on my journey. I'm not entirely sure how long I walked along the road. At one point my head was spinning so much I had to sit down and take a breather. Eventually I spied lights ahead in the distance and correctly guessed this must be the guard post at the front entrance to the camp. Shortly afterwards I presented myself to the gate guard who seemed completely unfazed by my dishevelled appearance at such an early hour. After checking my military identity card he snapped up a smart salute, wished me a good morning, and allowed me access.

Stumbling over to the accommodation block I came across the supine figure of Guy Lock, the Training Major, fast asleep on a grass verge with a beatific smile on his face. He'd removed his mess wellingtons and placed them neatly to one side but was otherwise fully dressed in his mess kit, his scarlet tunic adorned with an impressive array of campaign medals and much coveted para wings on the shoulder of his right arm.

His journey must have been similar to my own. Not realising just how close he was to his goal, I presumed he had, like me, stopped for a brief sojourn, but then fallen asleep where he lay. He seemed genuinely pleased to see me when roused but, when I pointed out how close he was to his accommodation, declared he was *perfectly comfortable, thank you*, rolled over and promptly went back to sleep. When I persisted he rather grudgingly picked up his boots, tucked them neatly under his arm, and wandered off in his stockinged feet.

We would not see each other again for several weeks. Our next meeting was a rather more formal occasion at which I would volunteer for operational deployment.

Latitude:	51.44
Longitude:	-0.09
Elevation:	32m
Met:	Haze, mostly cloudy H:18°L:15°
DTG:	121800ZSEP10

MY RETURN HOME the following evening, after another long sweaty journey in the ageing Wolf, was not a triumphant one. Within hours of stepping across the threshold of our magnificent Edwardian stained glass front door with its enormous hexagonal brass pull and letter plate my spirits were thoroughly deflated.

Harry and Alfie were pleased to see me. Full of questions about my experiences with the *real soldiers*, wanting to know if they'd given me a shooter, not quite believing me when I told them that I'd slept outside on the ground.

Jane barely acknowledged my presence. After I'd bathed the boys and put them to bed I found myself alone in the front room. I stared at my reflection in the antique gilt-framed mirror above the mantelpiece and knew I was in the shit. But the silent treatment didn't last long. The following morning Jane told me she was moving out and taking the boys with her. When she explained that she'd found a cottage for rent close to the city of York, near to her parents and in the catchment area of an excellent primary school, I didn't object. In truth the news came as a relief. I didn't know how on earth I was going to continue to pay the mortgage on our trophy property in Dulwich.

Since it turned out that Jane was expecting me to continue to foot the bill for her extravagant lifestyle, perhaps I should not have allowed financial considerations to cloud my judgement. I shall forever regret the fact that I did not properly consider the impact of our separation on our children, Harry and Alfie. I reasoned to myself that, given I was bound for Afghanistan, it actually made sense for them to be closer to their much loved grandparents.

Both boys would later make heartbreaking appeals to me to get back together with Mummy. I would do almost anything for my children, including going to fight a war over 3,500 miles away, but I couldn't even begin to reconcile my differences with Jane. As Alfie would explain to me, he loved Mummy and he loved Daddy, so why didn't we love each other?

In the summer of 2011, while I was in Canada training for deployment, Jane and her parents took the boys on holiday to Portugal. In one of their holiday snaps Harry and Alfie are standing together on a golden beach at sunset. Harry has a protective arm draped over his younger brother who is dressed in just vest and underpants. Both boys are waving and smiling directly at the camera.

It's a perfect picture but also a painful one.

In my imagination the boys are waving goodbye to me. The image became not only a visual metaphor for the possibility that I might not return from Afghanistan, but also a touchstone of terrible realisation of the sense of abandonment that I was imposing on my children, the people I loved most in the world.

Three months later, in December 2010, the movers arrived in a pantechnicon into which the entire contents of our family home were slowly and methodically disgorged. By the second day everything had gone. The house that Jane had interior decorated at great expense, and with incredible attention to detail, was empty – a hollow shell of hopes, dreams and aspirations that would never be rekindled.

I'd purchased the property in the hope that it would make Jane happy and that, in turn, I could be happy too. But it hadn't worked out that way. The mortgage burden had been a constant anxiety that I came to resent and so I had never truly enjoyed living there. But rattling around the empty house, alone, was an even gloomier experience.

Ironically perhaps, Jane had taken all the custom-made curtains, and I took to living in the back of the house so as not to frighten the neighbours. With no furniture to speak of, I moved into what had been the rear reception room where Jane had abandoned an old but still functional television. I set myself up with a blow-up mattress, my army issue sleeping bag and a kettle.

It was without doubt a devastating low point in my life, but it wasn't the lack of possessions that bothered me. Later, in Afghanistan, I would enjoy the simplicity of a life where all my personal belongings would fit in a small grip bag that I kept in my bed space. I would routinely deploy out to one of the patrol bases or onto the ground for several days with nothing more than a small day sack.

In common with our neighbours, most of whom had children of similar ages to our own, we'd always maintained an open door policy, and it was not unusual to return home from work to find the house full of kids. Now the house was silent, empty not only of furniture, but also of the voices of our children and their friends. To me it was a silence that screamed of failure.

Of course it was not the first time I'd experienced failure. Failed exam grades, sporting disappointments, romantic disasters, jobs lost. I'd had my fair share but nothing to match the completeness of my current predicament. In the face of my failed marriage, the heartbreaking separation from my children, and financial ruin, Afghanistan seemed like an obvious choice.

During this period I stumbled across the writings of John Stuart Mill who, in 1862, wrote:

When a people are used as mere human instruments for firing cannon or thrusting bayonets, in the service and for the selfish purposes of a master, such war degrades a people. A war to protect other human beings against tyrannical injustice; a war to give victory to their own ideas of right and good, and which is their own war, carried on for an honest purpose by their free choice, – is often the means of their regeneration. A man who has nothing which he is willing to fight for, nothing which he cares more about than he does about his personal safety, is a miserable creature.

I was looking for regeneration and Mill seemed to offer the solution. A war to protect other human beings against tyrannical injustice was just what I now needed to restore my self-esteem.

Latitude:	51.44
Longitude:	-0.09
Elevation:	32m
Met:	Some cloud, bright spells H:10°L:7°
DTG:	231600ZMAR11

IN THE SPRING of 2011 I gave up all pretence of trying to rebuild my consultancy business and devoted myself full-time to training and preparation for mobilisation on operation *Herrick*, the randomly assigned codename under which British military operations in Afghanistan were conducted from 2002 – 2014, and which cost the lives of 453 British servicemen.

As a reservist, this training would initially take place at weekends but, if I successfully achieved the standard required, I would mobilise for a period of 12 months permanent service from December 2011. The London Regiment, of which I was now part, had been tasked with providing 50 soldiers in the dismounted close combat infantry role. With over 200 volunteers there would be stiff competition for these 50 places.

As the name suggests, dismounted close combat is at the very sharpest point of delivery of UK Foreign Policy in Afghanistan. In April 2006 on a visit to Kabul, John Reid, the then Secretary of State for Defence, committed British troops to a further three years in Helmand Province. He declared: *We're in the south to help and protect the Afghan people to reconstruct their economy and democracy. We would be perfectly happy to leave in three years time without firing one shot.*

However earnestly he might have held this aspiration it has always struck me as a forlorn hope. If you send men with guns to do a job, the solution to the problem facing them is likely to involve using the tools of their trade. With the benefit of hindsight, I can be fairly certain that John Reid has regretted these words. Three years later in July 2009, with no clear exit strategy and the death toll mounting, he was forced to state in the House of Commons: *I never at any stage expressed the hope, expectation, promise or pledge that we would leave Afghanistan without firing a shot.*

A month later The Telegraph produced a report which contained the calculation that, in the three year period between Reid's first statement and his subsequent clarification to the House of Commons, the British Army had in fact fired 12,282,300 'shots' in Afghanistan. At a rate of more than 12,000 rounds every day, if this estimate was accurate, it didn't sound to me like there was a lot of time left over for reconstructing the Afghan economy or democracy.

By 2012 I don't believe we were expending ammunition at anything like this rate, but this is not to underestimate the scale and ferocity of the fighting. We still experienced skirmishes, or contacts, on a daily basis. My own introduction to Afghan combat came just a few days into our tour when a routine patrol to visit an outlying base in the very north of our area of operations came under attack from multiple firing points. Outnumbered and outgunned the patrol commander coolly requested fire support from the mortars in nearby Khar-Nikar, a base which housed a company strength group from the Royal Ghurkha Rifles. In a 20-minute period, under direction from the patrol commander, the mortars fired over 200 high explosive rounds before the enemy finally broke contact, allowing the patrol to continue on its task.

Although I'd been in contacts before, I'd never personally experienced anything like this intensity of combat. Listening to the reports coming in from the safety of the operations room, I was struck by the relative calm not only of those involved on the ground but also of the men and women in the ops room coordinating our response. I was the oldest man there by some margin, but I was surrounded by veterans of over ten years of conflict in Afghanistan and Iraq for whom this was a routine occurrence.

I was in awe at their professionalism, and more than a little anxious at the prospect of going on the ground myself. How would I react in a similar situation? With four previous operational tours under my belt, and an award for service in Bosnia in 1996, I'd always considered myself a seasoned soldier. As I watched the drama of the contact unfold the realisation dawned that, despite my advanced years and prior service, I was merely a novice. It was now clear to me why one of my instructors back in the UK had described the Upper Gereshk Valley as the University of Close Quarter Combat.

But by then there was no turning back. If I'd voluntarily enrolled on the course at that particular academy without properly studying the syllabus in advance, then I had only myself to blame. Now I could only hope to make the grade.

But, back in the spring of 2011, my main concern was how to ensure that I was one of the 50 out of 200 London Regiment volunteers who would be selected for mobilisation. Although the TA doesn't like to admit it, very few of its officers are selected for command in the close quarter combat role – and with good reason.

The TA High Command likes to boast that reserve soldiers and officers have the same capabilities as their regular counterparts but this is simply not true.

However dedicated, competent or committed a reservist might be, the fact is that he or she does not have access to the resources available to the regular army and cannot devote anything like the same amount of time to professional development and training. Accepting my limited utility in a close quarter combat role, I still needed to find a job that I could do. But with stiff competition for the limited places available there was an even more important task at hand.

I needed to convince the powers that be that I was the right man for that job.

Latitude   51.50
Longitude   -0.14
Elevation   18m
Met   Partly cloudy H:13°L:5°
DTG   141200ZAPR11

I'd never before deliberately
disobeyed a direct order from
a superior officer.

RAF: Royal Air Force
UPO: Unit Press Officer
ISAF: International Security Assistance Force
NIOC: National Information Operations Course
MPOPC: Military Psychological Operations Planners Course
PsyOps: Psychological Operations
WMD: Weapons of Mass Destruction
DCSU: Defence Cultural Specialist Unit
CULAD: Cultural Advisers
KLE: Key Leadership Engagement
LNE: Local National Engagement
FEO: Female Engagement Officer
MSSG: Military Stabilisation Support Group
DST: District Stabilisation Team
JIOTAT: Joint Information Operations Training and Advisory Team
POLAD: Political Advisor
LEGAD: Legal Advisor
STABAD: Stabilisation Advisor
TRANAD: Transition Advisor
BATUS: British Army Training Unit Suffield
COEFOR: Contemporary Operating Environment Force

Latitude:	51.50
Longitude:	-0.14
Elevation:	18m
Met:	Partly cloudy H:13°L:5°
DTG:	141200ZAPR11

IN THE WINTER of 2006 men from the London Regiment joined soldiers of the First Battalion Grenadier Guards, recently returned from the sands of southern Iraq, to form a composite company to support 12 Brigade operations in Helmand Province the following year. This unit, named Somme Company and commanded by Major Milan Torbica of A (London Scottish) Company, would go on to perform with distinction. The success of this unique pairing of a Guards Battalion with a Volunteer Infantry Regiment was the genesis of a lasting bond of respect and trust, forged over successive tours in the killing zone of Helmand's front line. London Regiment soldiers would again support the Grenadiers in Helmand in 2009, and when it became apparent that both units would be deploying in 2012, the London Regiment's Commanding Officer, Lieutenant Colonel Marc Overton worked tirelessly to ensure that his men would once more be paired with the Grenadiers.

The Grenadiers enthusiastically welcomed his advances and a number of meet and greet opportunities were quickly established. So it was that I found myself invited to lunch with the Commanding Officer and the officers of the First Battalion Grenadier Guards at Wellington Barracks in central London, a stone's throw across St James' Park from Buckingham Palace. Although the invitation was for lunch, I was under no illusion that it was anything other than a job interview. This was my opportunity to convince the Grenadiers they should take me with them to Helmand the following year. There would be many other hurdles over the course of the next 12 months, but all of these would be significantly reduced if I had a willing sponsor.

Lunch had been arranged by Major James Swanston, another London Regiment officer who had deployed with the Grenadiers to Afghanistan the year before. An immigrant Australian, his laid back style and unflappable nature had gone down well with the Grenadiers. His popularity had as much to do with his party-going antics and his contact list of beautiful young models as it did with his military skills, although both were legendary. He was going to be a tough act to follow.

We agreed to meet at a coffee shop a short distance from the barracks, where I found him nursing a double espresso and a double dose of jet lag. I was amazed to discover that he'd flown to Melbourne, Australia for 24 hours to attend a party, and had only just returned. He had spent over twice as much time in the air as he had on the ground, but he assured me it had all been worth it.

As we walked along Petty France, James gave me a potted history of the men I was about to meet. The Grenadier Guards is the most senior of the five regiments of Foot Guards and one of the oldest regiments in the British Army. Formed in Bruges in 1656 as the Royal Regiment of Guards to protect the exiled King Charles II, it has gone on to serve ten kings and four queens, including the current Queen Elizabeth II.

The regiment was renamed the 'First Grenadier Regiment of Foot Guards' in 1815, in recognition of its part in the defeat of the French Grenadiers of the Imperial Guard at the Battle of Waterloo, and has been so named ever since.

For the last decade or more my lunch had been a sandwich and a bag of cheese and onion, hastily eaten at my desk while simultaneously trying to stay on top of my email inbox. As James explained, this is not how the officers of the Queen's bodyguard choose to conduct themselves. As befits one of the most esteemed regiments in the British Army, officers assemble in the anteroom from 12.30pm and then at 1pm sharp process through to the dining room where they are served a three course lunch by the officers' mess Colour Sergeant and his staff. Once lunch is complete they take coffee in the anteroom before resuming their work schedule at 2pm on the dot.

I suspect it's a routine that has changed little since those early days in Bruges when Henry Wilmot, First Earl of Rochester commanded the battalion, except perhaps in one regard. Henry Wilmot was a popular commander who liked a drink and according to contemporary commentators *drank hard, and had a great power over all who did so, which was a great people.* The modern Grenadiers may not have succumbed to the vulgarity of a sandwich lunch, but in a concession to progress, there was no hard drink to be had.

James and I presented our MoD 90s – our British Army photo identity cards – at the barracks guardroom and were duly escorted through a maze of subterranean passageways to the mess.

Despite its historic location in the heart of London, it's an ugly concrete building of little, if any, architectural merit that conceals a rich history. Within the drab exterior the Grenadiers have decorated the walls with paintings and portraits chronicling their glorious past. Severe looking senior officers dressed in black frock coats line the walls, alongside enormous oil paintings recording magnificent, hard-won victories from a bygone age.

One such painting struck my eye.

A little smaller than the rest it seemed oddly out of place, although like so many others it depicted a fierce and violent battle. A small group of about eight or ten Grenadiers can be seen taking cover behind a low wall. As those in the background fix bayonets, perhaps preparing to fend off an imminent assault, those in the foreground are engaged in a furious firefight. Men can be seen standing dangerously exposed above the parapet firing their belt-fed machine guns at an unseen enemy, while their comrades work furiously to keep them resupplied with ammunition. The air is thick with cordite and dust, their situation looks pretty desperate. I can feel the heat of the battle, hear the crack and thump of rounds passing perilously close, smell the sweat and blood of these men as they stand firm on their position, fighting for their lives.

What made this picture so different from the others was that the paint was hardly dry. The scene it depicted was a battle not from a previous century, but from the Grenadiers' last tour of duty less than 12 months before. Standing transfixed by the painting I was once more reminded of the dangerous business I was getting myself into. I was about to sit down to lunch with veterans of this scene, or ones just like it, and wondered if I had what it took to stand shoulder to shoulder with them on the field of battle, as James had done. I didn't know the answer to that one but I did know that, if this picture was anything to go by, they'd earned the right to their anachronistic lunches.

The Commanding Officer of an infantry battalion is a supremely powerful man. He sits at the pinnacle of an organisational structure of some 500 men over whom his authority is absolute, extending well beyond what might ordinarily be expected of a civilian boss. He controls not only the minutiae of their daily working lives but also many aspects of their personal lives. He will decide when they take their annual holiday and soldiers must ask his permission before they can marry. In certain circumstances he even has the power to imprison them for up to 90 days. This level of control is considered vital to maintaining the cohesion and effectiveness of a fighting unit.

An infantry battalion is trained and equipped to protect the nation's interests through the lethal application of force and it is the Commanding Officer's responsibility to appropriately manage the violence that is at his disposal. He is responsible for the lives not only of his men, but also of his adversaries. His good judgement, his sense of proportionality and his competence as a commander will ultimately determine who lives and who dies on the battlefield and he must learn to accept that both success and failure will be measured in blood. This burden of authority is not for the faint-hearted and is entrusted only to the army's very best officers. Lieutenant Colonel Roly Walker, Commanding Officer of the First Battalion Grenadier Guards was one such.

Impossibly good looking and charming, Colonel Roly had become a poster boy for the British Army during his time in command, frequently appearing in the national press reporting on progress in Afghanistan. On return he had been awarded a Distinguished Service Order (DSO), a military decoration awarded only during wartime and typically in actual combat. Latterly, he had starred in a BBC documentary 'For Queen and Country' which follows the Grenadier Guards as they prepare to lead the Trooping of the Colour on the Sovereign's birthday parade, one of the oldest and largest military ceremonies in the world. Throughout the film Colonel Roly repeats a mantra:

There is only one standard and that is Excellent.

It's a standard that he applies equally to himself as to others and it's clear from the documentary that there is a strong bond of mutual trust and respect between the commander and his men.

Although Colonel Roly was being promoted into another job and would not be returning to Afghanistan in 2012, he still remained responsible for preparing the battalion for operations and continued to apply his exacting standard of excellence.

He would now determine my future and decide whether I could meet the criteria he required to serve alongside his beloved Grenadiers.

This was my chance to convince him that I would be a useful addition to the team. Given my background in marketing and communications, a role in army PR seemed like a good fit. Since the first Gulf War in 1991, 24-hour news coverage, and the intense public interest that this generates, had forced the military to professionalise its engagement with the media. Like most large corporate and commercial organisations, the army now had specialists in this area to protect and enhance its reputation. Every unit had its own press officer whose job was to prepare for and host media visits, and to identify and feed good news stories to the Army Public Relations team. Through discreet enquiry I had established that the Grenadiers were currently without a press officer and consequently had enrolled myself on a two week course at the Defence Media Operations Centre (DMOC) at RAF Halton in Aylesbury, Buckinghamshire.

Latitude:	51.81
Longitude:	-0.80
Elevation:	79m
Met:	Mostly cloudy, light rain H:10°L:3°
DTG:	010830ZNOV10

THE DMOC COURSE provided a fascinating insight into the army's relationship with the media. Soldiers are inherently suspicious of the press, and the course served only to reinforce this deeply held prejudice.

Through a series of classroom lectures and teaching practices we were trained to consider ourselves in a perpetual state of war with the media and to conduct operations accordingly. Defence communication priority was to:

Demonstrate real measurable progress on achieving success on current operations.

In other words: to claim that we were winning the wars in Afghanistan and Iraq. Little, if any, time was devoted to examining whether this was actually the case or not. Connecting the message with reality was not the concern of the Unit Press Officer.

I was also given the very strong impression that our adversaries, the media, had little interest in reporting the truth either. According to our instructors' collective paranoia, the press were solely fixated on discrediting the military at every possible turn. With the classroom sessions over we were tested in a series of high pressure 'hostile interviews' conducted by freelance journalists, hired in especially for the task.

The hacks appeared to thoroughly enjoy conforming to the stereotype of our instructors' prejudice and approached their assignment with creative enthusiasm. With lights, cameras and microphones thrust in our faces they methodically dismantled our arguments and ruthlessly attacked our credibility, on one occasion reducing the Adjutant of a Logistics Regiment to tears.

We then endured group humiliation sessions as, one by one, our antics on camera were played back to the class and our errors exposed for all to see. I must confess that I enjoyed sparring with the journalists, even though I fared little better than my fellow students. I didn't have a career or reputation to worry about, so the consequences of failing the course were not quite so significant for me as for others. In an ironic twist, one of the more senior officers on the course, an RAF Wing Commander was called out of the classroom to conduct a real life telephone interview as a spokesman for the UK's anti-piracy mission in Somalia. He confessed to me afterwards that the real interview had been much easier and far less stressful than any of the role playing sessions.

Latitude:	31.82
Longitude:	64.56
Elevation:	836m
Met:	Sunny H:30°L:18°
DTG:	180800DAUG12

I WOULD FREQUENTLY encounter this in-built paranoia towards the press. When Thomas Harding, The Telegraph's defence correspondent visited us in Afghanistan, he was confronted with a wall of polite and cordial silence. On an earlier visit he had used an 'off the record' comment made by a senior officer in one of his reports. This had caused some minor political embarrassment and a spat over what had or had not been said. On this subsequent visit Thomas paid for his perceived disloyalty as the army closed ranks.

His trip was carefully choreographed to ensure that there was no news to report. Soldiers were briefed in advance of his visits to avoid engaging him in conversation. Commanders were warned not to let him out of their sight. As an extra precaution I was instructed to join him on the pretext of some other task as he visited two of our patrol bases.

Thomas had worked with the army long enough to know I was a stool pigeon from the moment of our first meeting, but was kind enough to humour me and maintain the pretence.

There was no hostile interview as in our training at RAF Halton, but there was one slightly comedic moment as I briefed Thomas on the improving security situation. Perhaps exaggerating the situation a little, I explained that the area was now so quiet that the International Security Assistance Force (ISAF) were taking a step back, leaving most of the security presence to the Afghan army and police forces. Warming to my theme I had just suggested that it might soon be possible to go jogging quite safely outside the camp perimeter, when an enormous firefight kicked off about 1500 metres away. Raising my voice I cracked on with my brief as best I could, trying to ignore the increasing tempo of the gun battle behind me and the stray rounds whistling overhead. I was eventually silenced when a US Marine Corps AV8B Harrier Jump Jet screamed past at about 500ft before delivering its payload onto the enemy positions with an enormous explosion and a huge cloud of dust and smoke.

Thomas has been reporting on the war in Afghanistan since its inception and is no stranger to combat, but he was clearly not operating at his journalistic best that morning. He interrupted my monologue to ask simply *What was that?* Trying to sound as nonchalant as possible, I unconvincingly informed him that it was *probably just a show of force.*

A month or so later, as we prepared to leave Afghanistan at the end of our tour, a Taliban raid destroyed six AV8Bs as they sat on the tarmac in Camp Bastion. The Squadron Commander, Lieutenant Colonel Chris Raible was killed while leading a counterattack on the raiders in what was described as the worst loss of US airpower in a single incident since the Vietnam War. It was a severe blow to the ISAF mission. We had all relied on US 'close air' at some point or other to get us out of trouble and it was always reassuring to hear the pilots' distinctive American accents on the radio as they came on station to support us. I was shocked and saddened to learn of their loss.

Latitude:	51.50
Longitude:	-0.14
Elevation:	18m
Met:	Partly cloudy H:13°L:5°
DTG:	141300ZAPR11

BACK IN WELLINGTON Barracks, as the clock struck one, we sat down to lunch at the long dining table. I had been placed on Colonel Roly's left and now had exactly 60 minutes to convince him that I would make a good Unit Press Officer. There was precious little time to enjoy the three course meal I was being served and it went largely untouched.

I took the Colonel through a brief potted history of my civilian career, bigging myself up as best I could without sounding too boastful, and finished off by informing him that I was a recent graduate of the media course at RAF Halton. Colonel Roly listened politely, throwing in the odd question along the way, but I could see from the look on his face that he remained unconvinced.

Eventually he stopped me. *I can see you have the technical expertise but you don't know the battalion. For this job you need to know where all the bodies are buried – so the press don't find them. You need to have a good understanding of all the personalities in the battalion – who will give a good interview and who won't and above all you must have the force of character to make things happen. These things only come with years of service in the battalion.*

It was not the response to my sales pitch that I'd been hoping for but I could also see that he was right. A lesser commander might have been blinded by my credentials and commercial experience, but at the heart of it I would be just as much a stranger to the battalion as the visiting press team.

What I need to decide is whether I keep you to myself or pass you up to higher headquarters. If you can, I'd like you to come and train with us in Canada over the summer as our Information Operations officer and we'll take it from there.

I'd never heard the term Information Operations before and had no idea what this entailed but I was grateful the Commanding Officer was still holding the door open for me. I assured him I would try to clear my diary, knowing that there was precious little to clear but not wishing to sound too desperate.

As James had predicted, the Grenadier officers collected their berets and belts and departed the mess promptly at 2pm. James and I were left alone in the lobby and I debriefed him on my conversation with Colonel Roly. He assured me that I should not be disappointed by the outcome. The trip to Canada would be a great experience and an opportunity to get to know the battalion. In his opinion, Information Operations (Info Ops) was a much better job than Press Officer, although he was a little hazy about what it entailed, something to do with communicating with the local Afghans and winning hearts and minds.

I made a mental note to find out more.

Three months later, along with 20 or so other London Regiment soldiers I would rejoin the Grenadiers for a six week field training exercise in Canada. In the interim period the Grenadiers relinquished their public duties role and relocated to a new barracks in Aldershot from which to conduct their training and preparation for deployment to Afghanistan the following year.

For my part, in addition to Guy Locke's *Live Firing Tactical Training* exercise in Sennybridge, I used the time to gain a better understanding of Info Ops, enrolling myself on two courses; the National Information Operations Course (NIOC) at the Defence Academy in Shrivenham, Wiltshire and the sinister sounding Military Psychological Operations Planners Course (MPOPC) at the Defence Intelligence and Security Centre in Chicksands, Bedfordshire.

Latitude:	52.03
Longitude:	-0.36
Elevation:	28m
Met:	Good, partly cloudy H:8°L:4°
DTG:	280830ZNOV11

THE MILITARY DEFINES Psychological Operations (PsyOps) as *planned, culturally sensitive, truthful and attributable activities directed at approved target audiences within the Joint Area of Operations in order to achieve political and military objectives.* Any other organisation would call this Marketing and Communications.

In keeping with the dodgy name and windy definition I was underwhelmed by the military's capability in this area. Considerable emphasis was placed on target audience analysis – identifying and understanding the group of people that the message is aimed at – but little, if any, investment was made in the quality or types of data used in this analysis. Nor was there much investment in the actual communications, which seemed to be confined to radio and loudspeaker broadcasts or printed materials of various types. Throughout the course a plethora of badly designed posters and leafelts were presented as shining examples of our PsyOps capability. I shouldn't have been surprised. To the best of my knowledge, there is no graphic design module on the syllabus at the Land Warfare Centre in Warminster, Wiltshire.

But perhaps there should have been. I couldn't help but wonder at the reaction of my own clients if I had presented work of this lamentable quality.

I privately concluded that the PsyOps team needed to take a walk down London's Oxford Street. I was no fan of the barrage of free newspapers, magazines, leaflets and 2-for-1 vouchers to which they would be subjected but it would at least give them some higher benchmark against which to assess their own work.

Latitude:	31.82
Longitude:	64.56
Elevation:	836m
Met:	Good, partly cloudy H:18°L:7°
DTG:	101030DAPR12

MY EXPERIENCES IN Afghanistan would do little to improve my perception of the PsyOps team. For all the emphasis on target audience analysis back in Chicksands, the PsyOps planners seemed reluctant to engage with their target audience in the Upper Gereshk Valley. I would frequently receive reports generated somewhere in the rear headquarters that bore no resemblance to reality on the ground.

Perhaps even more alarmingly, they seemed to lack any grasp of the basic principles of data collection and analysis. Initially I read their reports with some incredulity and then quietly suppressed them within the battlegroup for fear of the reputational damage they would do to the wider Info Ops community of which I was now a part.

However, towards the end of my time in Afghanistan I did circulate some of the more far-fetched analyses to a discreet and trusted audience – purely for their comedy value.

My absolute favourite report asserted in bold headlines that 90% of Nahr-E-Saraj residents favoured Radio Tamadoon – the PsyOps group's own radio station – over any other. This was evidently a piece of ridiculous self-aggrandisement. The report was generated based on 15 respondents to a radio show phone-in, hardly representative of the 90,000 or so residents of the district. It also conveniently overlooked the fact that some 37,000 of those residents lived outside the range of the radio's antenna. Respondents needed to own both a radio (which in fairness we may have given them) and a mobile phone in order to be able to participate in the survey. In one of the most impoverished districts in Afghanistan such possessions were rare among the general population, many of whom didn't even have a pot to piss in.

On another occasion I received orders to collect data for a survey on attitudes to transition of security from ISAF to Afghan security forces. This piece of work was intended to inform commanders on progress, and to assist in future planning to achieve this aim. This struck me as an important project. I put my mind to figuring out how I might collect data in a sufficiently robust and reliable manner to be statistically significant and genuinely represent attitudes within the district.

This was not going to be easy. I reasoned that in any scenario where men with guns start asking questions, most people will try to second guess the response the gun-toting market researchers want.

Good afternoon, my heavily-armed friends and I wondered if you would mind participating in a survey we're conducting…

Furthermore, large areas of the district lay outside the ISAF protected community. If I did not include surveys from these locations then clearly my results would be skewed, but neither did I want to put our people in harm's way purely to prove a statistical point to which I thought I already knew the answer. I wrestled with this conundrum for a few days before eventually calling the officer commanding the PsyOps Group to discuss the problem. To my amazement my concerns were dismissed. It seemed that neither the quality nor the reliability of the data were important. What was needed, I was informed, was a total of 40 surveys, all of which could come from within the protected community, the majority of which could be generated from radio show phone-ins.

I once again tried to point out the extreme short comings of this approach, but the officer commanding was having none of it – concluding that any survey was better than no survey. I was ordered in no uncertain terms to get on with it with a deadline of a week to deliver. Our conversation was followed up a short while later by an email from a Staff Sergeant in the PsyOps Group. It informed me where I needed to send the data and in what format, but it seemed to me that there was a subtext to the message; if I failed to comply with this instruction the originator would personally take great pleasure in inflicting extreme pain upon my person.

Based on my low opinion of the group, I doubted this Staff Sergeant was up to that task, but I did spend a few sleepless nights worrying about what my next move would be. I'd never before deliberately disobeyed a direct order from a superior officer, but I wasn't about to comply with this one.

In the end I did nothing. Knowing that the officer commanding had only a few weeks left in theatre I decided to hold out for their replacement – hoping that they would take a more enlightened view of supplying potentially misleading information on which important command decisions might be made.

It may not have been Iraq, or WMD, but the principle was the same and I wanted nothing to do with this dodgy data.

The deadline passed and I ignored increasingly strident messages from PsyOps HQ. Only when I knew for certain that a new boss had taken over did I return these calls. The new commander did his best to give me a good bollocking over the phone but I could tell his heart wasn't in it and the survey was quietly dropped.

Latitude:	51.60
Longitude:	-1.65
Elevation:	90m
Met:	Sunny, some light cloud H:22°L:12°
DTG:	120830ZSEP11

THE NATIONAL INFORMATION Operations Course was altogether different, although it was no wonder that James had been a little woolly about what it entailed. The written definition of Info Ops was even more verbose and impenetrable than that of PsyOps. The doctrinal manual dedicated to the subject states that its aim is:

To achieve effects against the will and understanding of a complex variety of actors whether hostile (adversaries), neutral (indigenous populations and civilian agencies) or friendly (allies). This should be a planned and coordinated effort designed to contribute to the political and military objectives within a campaign. Within COIN (counter-insurgency) operations the affected population is seen as 'the prize' and it is paramount that the counter-insurgent gains, retains and builds the people's consent and trust so that they reject the insurgents. This includes targeting decision makers; altering their intended course of action by affecting, directly or indirectly, their available information or perception of it.

To further complicate matters, as if they weren't complicated enough already, Info Ops was also called 'Influence' and in some quarters 'Engagement'. In an attempt to restore some order, these titles were amalgamated to form 'StratCom', short for strategic communications. But the new name was short-lived and was later changed to the snappy 'Information Activities and Outreach' (IA&O), before being almost immediately amended to 'Information Activities and Capacity Building' (IA&CB).

Whatever it was to be called, I concluded that I'd spent the last 15 years preparing for this role.

Despite my growing disaffection with the relentless rise of consumerism, my role within it to persuade people to buy even more stuff they didn't need perfectly placed me to *achieve effects against the will and understanding of a complex variety of actors.*

Latitude:	31.82
Longitude:	64.56
Elevation:	836m
Met:	Mostly sunny H:8°L:-3°
DTG:	060900DFEB12

THE BRITISH ARMY may not have got its act together with regard to Info Ops, but it was apparent that, despite the impenetrable jargon, some very clever people in competing staff branches had figured out that it was potentially a game changer, or 'force multiplier'. Everyone was trying to get a piece of the action.

My paranoid old friends from Defence Media Ops at RAF Halton clearly felt they owned influence. So did PsyOps, despite their dodgy data and lamentable leaflets. They were not alone. The Defence Cultural Specialist Unit (DCSU) were relatively new to the battlefield and purported to be *specialists in the fields of anthropology, psychology, sociology and influencing skills.*

Their contribution was to provide Cultural Advisers, or CULADs. So far as I could tell, CULADs were a small bunch of clever soldiers and officers who had attended an 18 month language course to become more or less fluent in Pashtu or Dari. Perhaps not wishing to think of themselves simply as interpreters, they had positioned themselves as specialists in Key Leadership Engagement (KLE), and Local National Engagement (LNE), and as such wandered round our battlespace discussing who knows what with who knows whom.

I met our first CULAD, an RAF Flying Officer, only in his last few days in theatre. He'd been assigned to a Danish Headquarters who, uncertain what to do with him, had left him to his own devices. By all accounts he'd gone almost entirely native and at great risk to his own personal safety had been living amongst the local people – something which would never have been allowed under a British commander. Having produced a series of detailed papers and reports based on his experiences he then failed to tell anyone where he'd filed them at the end of his tour. They were lost for nine months until I rediscovered them as I was tidying up my own files in preparation to return home myself. All his efforts and the great risks he'd taken had been largely wasted.

In addition to the CULADs we also had a Female Engagement Officer (FEO). She had a different title not because of any overt sexual discrimination on the part of the British Army, but in a flawed attempt at cultural sensitivity which, to my mind, revealed the true extent of the expertise on offer at the DCSU.

Some DCSU bright spark had theorised that, in a country where gender segregation is strictly enforced, possessing a vagina would somehow demonstrate solidarity with local women and empower the FEO to engage with them. In practice, in the deeply conservative rural areas in which we worked, women were largely imprisoned in the family compound and were forbidden to speak with infidels of any gender, even if they did possess the Gates of Heaven.

Incredibly, this had been considered such a wizard idea that some FEOs were rushed into theatre having conducted an abbreviated three month language course and were subsequently assigned a male interpreter. While this made up for the shortfall in the FEO's language skills it also added an inconvenient appendage to the mix.

Of course, the real throbber was the DCSU boffin, male or female, who'd come up with this solution in the first place.

The CULADs and FEOs were all undoubtedly brave and routinely put themselves in harm's way but I honestly saw little evidence of any specialist training in the fields of *anthropology, psychology, sociology and influencing skills*. I was concerned that these people were the British Army's spokespersons with the local population. Some of them struck me as naively idealistic. What concerned me even more was that, although they had been tasked with Key Leadership Engagement, they had been given little if any direction on the message they were supposed to deliver, and no real authority or access to resources with which to back this up. As BBC World Service Correspondent, William Reeve said in 2009:

Afghans are used to being promised many things that never materialised.

The British Army has, rightly, been criticised for making promises it could not keep in Afghanistan. I suspect that much of this failed expectation lay at the hands of CULADs who were simply not empowered to deliver on their assurances.

There was however one CULAD who was the exception that proved the rule, Royal Marines Captain Owen Davis. Just as the diminutive rock rabbit that proliferates on Table Mountain improbably shares its DNA with the mighty African elephant, Owen – a Welshman by birth – was similarly genetically linked to a brick shithouse. The online urban dictionary describes such a structure as: *A huge badass motherfucker with gigantic muscles that could fuck up anyone that doesn't take steroids and go to the gym six days a week.* This pretty much summed up Owen's physical presence.

But unlike most of the other badass motherfuckers that I'd met, Owen had brains and a personality too. A brilliant linguist and raconteur, he joined the Royal Marines only after a career as an Olympic rower was cut short by a back injury. Tasked with turning around a failing Afghan police unit in the strategically important village of Rahim Kalay, he would become an invaluable asset to our battlegroup and our paths would frequently cross in the months ahead.

Yet another unit vying for space in the influence field was the Military Stabilisation Support Group (MSSG) which claims to be a *unique defence organisation that provides the UK with an array of skills and knowledge, that can be used to provide military support to the civilian efforts to stabilise countries around the world that are either emerging from conflict or are at risk of sliding into chaos.*

The MSSG tended to focus on infrastructure improvement projects such as clean water, roads and bridges which directly impacted on the quality of life for local nationals, but they worked independently of the chain of command, reporting instead to civil servants from the Foreign and Commonwealth Office's Stabilisation Unit. This relationship they jealously guarded.

In our little corner of Helmand Province, Stabilisation Unit representation came in the form of the District Stabilisation Team (DST) who mostly concerned themselves with projects to improve governance and justice. They appeared to be a dysfunctional little bunch who resented working alongside the military and constantly frustrated me with their lack of ambition. My frustrations were vindicated when, part way through our tour, a new DST team leader, Michael Steinfeldt arrived and promptly sacked or moved on all but one of his staff.

Latitude:	51.60
Longitude:	-1.65
Elevation:	90m
Met:	Sunny, some light cloud H:22°L:12°
DTG:	121030ZSEP11

BACK AT THE Defence Academy in Shrivenham, Lieutenant Colonel James Hancock our senior instructor at the Joint Information Operations Training and Advisory Team (JIOTAT), did his best to convince his students that, as Information Operations Officers, we were the *primary coordinating function* to deliver *influence effects*. He likened us to the conductor of an orchestra, repeatedly using this metaphor to illustrate how we would bring together competing elements to support the Commander's plan.

It all sounded wonderful in theory but, despite the good Colonel's assurances, I doubted whether it would quite work in practice. Info Ops, or whatever it was called this week, was getting increasingly crowded.

Along with PsyOps, Media Ops, DCSU, MSSG and the DST, there was an additional host of 'Influence Advisors' to contend with. Such as the POLAD (Political Advisor), LEGAD (Legal Advisor), STABAD (Stabilisation Advisor) and TRANAD (Transition Advisor). I privately hoped that the TRANAD, when I met him or her, would prove to be a cross dresser. In the meantime it seemed to me that it was getting to the point where Commanders would require an ADVAD (Advisor Advisor) to help them determine whose advisory services they should call upon in any given situation.

I guessed, correctly as it turned out, that there were going to be a lot of big egos to contend with in Info Ops.

I just hoped there would be enough room to accommodate my own.

Latitude:	51.27
Longitude:	-0.74
Elevation:	80m
Met:	Sunny, some light cloud H:20°L:11°
DTG:	131200ZJUN11

SOME THREE MONTHS after my first meeting with Lieutenant Colonel Roly Walker, on the eve of our departure to Canada to participate in live firing and field training exercises, I was once again summoned to lunch with the First Battalion Grenadier Guards. Although in slightly less salubrious surroundings, the lunch time ritual remained unchanged.

Having arrived a little ahead of time, I buried my head in a newspaper in a corner of the anteroom and waited for the officers to assemble. Amongst the first to arrive was a bullet-headed, moustachioed man, well over six feet in stature, who bore an uncanny resemblance to a vintage caricature of a circus strongman. It had been 23 years since I'd last seen this man but I recognised him instantly. Deep in conversation with his colleagues, my presence went unnoticed. But for my part I was powerless to prevent the instinctive reflex action to brace up sharply in my chair while simultaneously clenching my fists and thrusting my hands along the tops of my thighs towards my knees until my elbows locked.

Many parents invoke a bogeyman of some sort to ensure compliant behaviour from their children. Although Harry and Alfie knew almost nothing else about my prior military service, they knew about this man. As they could tell you:

His authority was absolute.

He was to be obeyed without question.

His wrath was terrifying to observe.

His name was **The Colour Sergeant**.

Latitude:	51.33
Longitude:	-0.74
Elevation:	80m
Met:	A couple of showers H:18°L:11°
DTG:	041700ZSEP88

I BECAME AWARE of his presence before I actually set eyes upon the Colour Sergeant for the very first time. Viscerally, I knew I'd properly fucked up well before I knew the reason why. The year was 1988 and I was trying to extract an ironing board from the back of my MGB GT, a vehicle not best suited to the carriage of such an unwieldy item. It was my first day at the Royal Military Academy, Sandhurst where I was embarking on a six month leadership training course which, if successful, would culminate in a commission as a Second Lieutenant in the British Army.

On arrival I had been directed to a car park some distance from my new home in Victory College, and instructed to get my kit unloaded and up to my new quarters in double quick time. In addition to the ironing board now stuck between the rear parcel shelf and the seat backs, the kit list of requirements had been extensive, running to several pages of curious back to front wording which transformed seemingly mundane items such as trousers and shoe polish into *trousers, civilian w. turn-up* and *polish, shoes, black.*

Getting this kit into my little car had been a gargantuan task in itself and I did not look forward to the multiple journeys to and from the car park that it would take to unload it all. In a flash of initiative that I reckoned would serve to highlight my suitability for commissioning, I resolved to bring Mohammed to the mountain and drive my car to an empty car park I had observed directly adjacent to the college. This would more than halve the unloading time.

Having put this unilateral change of plan into action I quickly completed the task, with the exception of the ironing board, which refused to budge. In an attempt to identify the cause of the obstruction I had somehow managed to squeeze my torso into the space between the parcel shelf and the seatbacks when I became aware of the Colour Sergeant at my back.

I inelegantly extricated myself from the vehicle. His towering presence loomed over me. It was obvious that I had transgressed in some way and was about to experience the wrath of the Colour Sergeant.

Immaculately dressed in blue tunic with red sash, brandishing a highly varnished wooden pace stick, the Colour Sergeant opened and closed his mouth a few times as he struggled to find the words to adequately express the full depth of his rage. The effect was like that of a pressure cooker about to explode. His arms and shoulders began to rise and fall in a series of short violent movements, but still no words emerged from his soundless lips. In an effort to diffuse the situation I stuck out my hand and attempted to introduce myself. The Colour Sergeant appeared truly affronted by this gesture, recoiling as if I had slapped him hard across the face. His impressive moustache twitched alarmingly and he finally found his voice.

I know who you are, Sir. What are you doing on my parade square?

He managed to make this prior knowledge of my existence sound deeply sinister. It was clear from his intonation that the 'Sir' was not intended as an honorific. Unsure how to answer without enraging him further it was my turn to be lost for words. The Colour Sergeant filled the void.

Are you an amoeba, Sir?

Are you pond life, Sir?

Have you recently crawled out of a nearby swamp, Sir?

Are you not aware of the difference between a car park and a parade square, Sir?

Can you get anything right, Sir?

I was dumbstruck. I had no idea how to respond. After a further few moments of uneasy silence the Colour Sergeant appeared satisfied that he had made his point.

Cut away, Sir, cut away.

And he walked briskly off in the direction whence he had come.

The Colour Sergeant was none other than Richard 'Skid' Dorney who would be my principal instructor at the Royal Military Academy, Sandhurst for the next six months. He would rule with a rod of iron and on one memorable occasion I found myself incarcerated in the Academy cells for the heinous crime of harbouring fluff in the turn-ups of my civilian trousers. In truth, I was not the best student to pass through the Academy gates, and it was largely because of rather than in spite of Skid's efforts that I was eventually commissioned in the spring of 1989.

In the intervening years Skid had enjoyed a meteoric career, rising to the rank of Lieutenant Colonel and becoming something of a living legend within the Brigade of Guards and the wider army. Once it became known that he had been my Sandhurst instructor it served as a great ice-breaker. Frequently introduced as one of his former students, I was able to bask in his reflected glory. The very fact that Skid had eventually forgiven me my transgression on his parade square and allowed me to commission provided a marker by which others could judge me. The younger officers in particular enjoyed learning of my criminal record and the story of my trouser turn-ups seemed to follow me wherever I went.

For his part Skid was very supportive of my ambition to serve alongside the Grenadiers. Although I was never quite able to break that instinct to brace up sharply in his presence, as we'd been drilled to do all those years ago, he was always utterly charming and generous with his time.

My children would not have recognised this wise and kindly senior officer as the fearsome figure of **The Colour Sergeant**.

Latitude:	50.27
Longitude:	-111.16
Elevation:	771m
Met:	Mostly sunny H:28°L:15°
DTG:	191200GJUN11

BATUS, THE BRITISH Army Training Unit Suffield, is located on the vast Canadian prairie north-west of the small town of Medicine Hat in the Province of Alberta, Canada.

British troops were first stationed here during the Second World War when it was used as a chemical weapons testing facility and to this day parts of the prairie remain out of bounds as a result. Since 1971 it has been utilised as an armoured warfare training centre and, although it is still used for this purpose, in more recent years it has become central to the training of soldiers in counter-insurgency (COIN) operations prior to mobilisation to Helmand Province, Afghanistan.

For the most part it's an inhospitable place, subject to unpredictable and extreme weather events. In twenty two days on the prairie we routinely experienced freezing night-time temperatures followed by daytime highs well above 30°C/86°F. We also witnessed dramatic electrical storms, tropical downpours, hail and even snow. These conditions, which can turn the prairie from dustbowl to quagmire in a matter of moments, made living conditions very arduous and were an ever present backdrop to the exercise itself. But the real enemy on the prairie is not the terrain, nor the climate.

It's the mosquitoes.

I'd been told by someone in the know that the mosquitoes alone *would break a civilian* and he was not wrong – it even broke one or two soldiers who had to receive medical treatment following adverse reactions to the bites. Although British soldiers have been training here since the 1940s no one, as yet, has thought it necessary to issue troops with insect repellent or mosquito nets, which ironically are widely available in Afghanistan – where there are no mosquitoes to speak of.

Each dawn and dusk we would be subjected to marauding clouds of these haematophagous insects that made our lives utterly miserable for an hour or two before disappearing again, leaving us itching and scratching in their wake. Great ingenuity was invested in killing these creatures which, given their vast numbers was largely pointless, but hugely enjoyable. One such device was the battery operated fly swat which not only squashed the offending creatures but also exposed them to a small electrical charge. Mosquitoes trapped in the electrified wires would fizz and smoke in a most satisfying way. Perhaps inevitably, the Grenadiers found a number of other uses for this device, the most popular being to zap unsuspecting, often sleeping, comrades. The resultant reaction generated great mirth and amusement from spectators, and a series of expletives and a wry smile from the victim.

Of all the training I participated in to prepare me for Afghanistan this was the most realistic. Not just because of the similarity in terrain and climate, but because the army has taken great care to create a facsimile of rural Helmand in this remote corner of Alberta Province. Troops in training are required to live in fortified Forward Operating Bases (FOBs), just as they would do in Afghanistan. Whole villages or kalays have been specially constructed in incredible detail, complete with mosques, bazaars and other structures which bear a striking resemblance to those in Afghanistan. To further add to the realism a small army of Afghan expatriates is employed to participate in the exercises, playing roles as Key Leaders, Local Nationals, Interpreters, Indigenous Security Forces and, of course, Insurgents.

Known collectively as the Contemporary Operating Environment Force (COEFOR), all of these Afghan actors have their own story as to how they come to be in the desolate wilderness of the Canadian prairie 6,500 miles from home, but there is a common thread. They have all been displaced by a war they now prepare others to fight. They all yearn one day to return to their homeland.

True to his word Colonel Roly assigned me as his battlegroup Info Ops officer and he frequently tasked me to conduct *influence patrols* and *shuras*[1] with these actors, something I always looked forward to. These events usually took place in some shady spot and often revolved around a meal, just as they would do in Afghanistan. I would be treated to mouth-watering chicken kebabs and other delicacies, cooked in front of me on an open fire. These fresh foods were a welcome respite from pre-packed army rations.

[1] **Shura**: an Arabic word for "consultation" often used by ISAF troops to describe a meeting between ISAF and Afghan security forces or local nationals.

There was only so much role playing make believe that could go on at these meetings before we slipped back into real life and I would quiz them on their back stories and their new lives in Canada. I found their responses tragic and fascinating in equal measure. It also helped that their 'handler' was a beautiful and feisty young Canadian woman, although all my attempts to arrange an illicit date with her were rebuffed.

Before I flew to Canada, Skid had given me the manuscript of a book he was writing about the Grenadiers' first tour of Helmand Province in 2007. I felt incredibly privileged to be reading this not yet published account which, despite my best efforts, became increasingly battered and dog-eared as it travelled with me stuffed into a Tesco's carrier bag in the top of my bergan[1].

The Killing Zone was a fascinating read. Where the oil painting hanging in the officers' mess at Wellington Barracks had given me a general sense of what I was getting myself into, Skid's manuscript was a detailed and painstakingly reconstructed account of frequent and intense combat with a fierce and determined enemy. Subsequently published by Ebury Press, it is a rollercoaster read that would capture any reader. But for me it had a special meaning and resonance.

In his introduction Skid notes that: *Military history always records the names of generals and politicians, but the soldiers who make and break their reputations are rarely adequately documented.* Skid had set out to redress this imbalance, to *record their heroism.* As far as I was concerned he had succeeded in his aim. I was reading spine chilling tales of incredible bravery about men alongside whom I was now living, sharing banter and brews and generally enduring the privations of life on the prairie. On more than one occasion I would be introduced to someone only to read about them days or even hours later and discover they had played a pivotal role in some action recorded in Skid's book. It was a humbling experience.

A few days before we returned to the UK, Colonel Roly came to find me. The exercise was all but over and the battlegroup had come together one last time on an otherwise featureless sun-baked expanse of prairie before heading back to civilisation. Dressed in just shorts and flip-flops, I was hiding from the fierce rays of the midday sun in the thin

[1] **Bergan**: A large rucksack, supported by a frame.

sliver of shade cast by the Land Rover in which I'd been travelling. He sat down beside me in the dust, resting his back against the rear wheel, and we swapped a few pleasantries. Eventually, not in so many words, he informed me that I had met his exacting standard and he was now satisfied that I could deploy with the Grenadiers the following year to Afghanistan.

Sitting in that dusty, desolate spot Colonel Roly had just determined my destiny.

We would not meet again.

Latitude:	51.42
Longitude:	-0.08
Elevation:	62m
Met:	Some light cloud H:24°L:12°
DTG:	220900ZAUG11

BACK IN THE UK I had, by now, managed to let out the Dulwich property and had moved in with my sister, Edwina who owned a small flat a few miles away in Gypsy Hill. Not her main home, the flat was essentially a place to rest her head on those days when she was working in London. I was grateful to her but the flat was nonetheless a constant reminder of just how far I'd fallen. In contrast to the opulence of our Dulwich home the property was very run down, the furniture tired, the carpets threadbare and moth-eaten. Even the ancient television that Jane had abandoned and I had rescued finally packed up, unable to cope with the digital switch-over.

It was not a place where I could bring my kids for more than a day or two at a time. On those rare visits they would share my bed while I slept on the floor beside them. Despite my obvious failings as their increasingly absent father they remained touchingly loyal. I would wake most mornings to find one or both of them asleep beside me on the floor.

It was about this time that Harry innocently announced that Mummy had a new boyfriend.

I wasn't surprised that Jane had found a new partner. With her model good looks she'd never been short of male admirers and, inevitably, wasn't going to be on the market for very long. But I was surprised by my reaction.

I felt nothing. No rage, no jealousy, no anguish. Nothing.

I carefully examined my emotions to see if I was suppressing my innermost feelings, even from myself, but my heart was cold. Where previous relationship break-ups had left me hopeless and devastated, my love for Jane was now an empty vessel.

Up until this moment I had naively assumed that the decision I had made, all those months ago, to seek adventure in the service of my country was in some way reversible. That somehow I could hit a rewind button and return to my conservative and unremarkable suburban existence.

This imaginary umbilical to a past life was now severed.

For all the heartfelt wishes of our children, I could never rekindle my relationship with Jane, not because of her infidelity – I wouldn't have been the first partner to forgive such indiscretions – but because of my own empty heart.

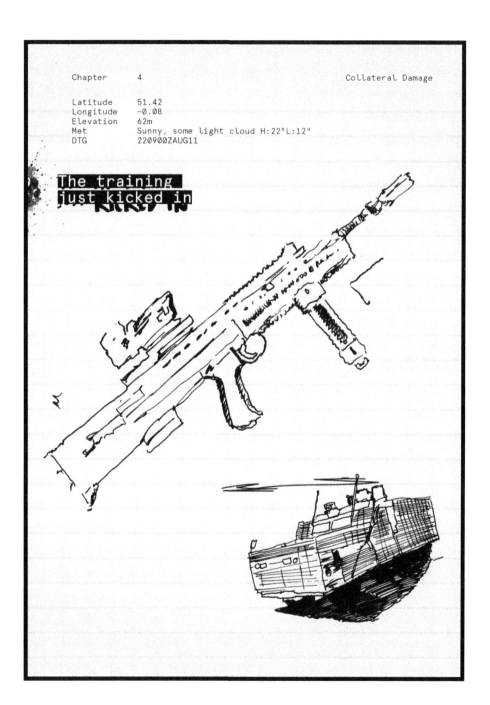

Latitude   51.42
Longitude   -0.08
Elevation   62m
Met   Sunny, some light cloud H:22°L:12°
DTG   220900ZAUG11

The training just kicked in

OPTAG: Operational Training and Advisory Group
SNAFU: Situation Normal, All Fucked Up
PT: Physical Training
ACOG: Advanced Combat Optical Gunsight
RPG: Rocket Propelled Grenade
PID: positively identify
RCO: Range Conducting Officer
STANTA: Stanford Training Area
MBE: Member of the Most Excellent Order of the British Empire
FOB: Forward Operating Base
MTP: Multi Terrain Pattern
AO: Area of Operations
BGHQ: Battle Group Headquarters
IPB: Intelligence Preparation of the Battlefield
VP: Vulnerable Point
ML/MD CoA: Most Likely and Most Dangerous Courses of Action

Latitude:	51.42
Longitude:	-0.08
Elevation:	62m
Met:	Sunny, some light cloud H:22°L:12°
DTG:	220900ZAUG11

MY FUTURE NOW lay with the Grenadiers on Helmand's front line.

Although I'd worked hard and sacrificed a lot to get this far, it was not the finishing point, nor even the line of departure. My seat on the plane with Colonel Roly's men remained conditional. I still needed to convince the Operational Training and Advisory Group (OPTAG) that I was up to the task by successfully completing a series of individual and collective training assessments.

OPTAG would have the final say on whether I was fit to deploy or not.

While all those who serve in Afghanistan receive the same operational service medal for their efforts, the army recognises three deployment categories with different training standards and requirements for each.

Category 1 applies to those who will remain inside the security perimeter at Camp Bastion. It consists mainly of a series of briefings on the dangers of overexposure to UV rays, where to find the coffee shops and fast food outlets in this vast and sprawling tented metropolis in the desert, and advice on the best place to buy your *Taliban Hunting Club* t-shirt for bragging rights in the pub back home.

Category 2 is for personnel whose duties require deployment 'outside the wire'. It includes, amongst other things, training in how to counter Improvised Explosive Devices (C-IED), patrolling skills, weapons handling drills and cultural awareness.

Category 3 is the most demanding of all and is for those in the dismounted close combat role. In addition to the Category 2 training it includes time on heavy weapons systems and other more complex and dangerous fighting activities, such as compound clearance drills.

The majority of the Grenadiers would be 'Cat 3' but thankfully someone had concluded that I really was too old to be clearing compounds and I was thus deemed a 'Cat 2+', a hybrid somewhere in between.

Over the course of the next few months I travelled the length and breadth of the UK visiting a series of training establishments set up for the specific purpose of preparing soldiers for deployment to Afghanistan. On presenting myself for training my instructors would routinely size me up and down, take in my grey hair and less than athletic physique, and ask me to confirm my Cat 2+ status. Their pens would hover in anticipation over their nominal roll, assuming my presence was some clerical error that required correcting. I was treated to some sceptical looks on confirming that I was not, in fact, an administrative SNAFU[1].

Although I'd successfully passed the mandatory physical fitness tests required for service with the London Regiment, I'd learned in Canada that the combination of heat and sheer weight of equipment carried by the modern infantry soldier could sap the strength of even the fittest of men. Just like every other Cat 2 or Cat 3 soldier I would need to be able to cope with these heavy loads in the fierce heat of an Afghan summer. In spite of, or perhaps because of, the sceptical looks of my OPTAG instructors I was determined not to be the weakest link and set about improving my fitness.

Unlike regular soldiers who have access to excellent sports facilities and for whom physical training (PT) is part of their daily work schedule, reservists are expected to keep fit in their own time and at their own expense. This was a problem for me. To try and make ends meet, I'd relinquished my central London gym membership months before.

Fortunately the TA centre had an ancient and rusting multi-gym which groaned and squealed alarmingly but was just about serviceable, and my local park in Norwood had recently installed an outdoor gym. I was able truly to excel in this environment because my new gym buddies were mostly drug addled rough sleepers breakfasting on Tenants Special Brew, or septuagenarian ladies who, despite their birdlike frailty, would fearlessly shoo away the hapless, foul-mouthed addicts.

Over time I became quite proficient at sit-ups, pull-ups and press-ups. Although I never regained the six-pack of my youth I could claim a reasonably discernable 'two-pack'.

I also added running to my fitness schedule. Not without good reason, the army sets great store in running, especially running with weight.

[1] **SNAFU**: Situation Normal, All Fucked Up

Every soldier from the Chief of the General Staff to the newest recruit is required to complete an annual combat fitness test. This consists of an eight mile speed march on an undulating cross country course while carrying 25kg, and must be completed in under two hours. However, in keeping with Colonel Roly's demand for excellence, the Grenadiers required much higher standards. I'd also read in a Headquarters Land Forces (HQLF) directive that:

Physical fitness is an indispensable aspect of leadership.

It was clear that if I was to have any credibility as a reserve officer in a regular army unit which imposed upon itself high levels of physical fitness I was going to have to shape up.

Edwina kept a small amount of exercise equipment in the flat which included a set of kettle bells. I took to running with the largest of these padded inside my big green army sleeping bag and stuffed inside a backpack I'd bought ten years earlier for a successful summit attempt of Mont Blanc. Over the ensuing weeks and months I attracted some strange looks from members of the public as I toiled up and down College Road, Gypsy Hill and the environs of Crystal Palace, gasping and spluttering for breath.

But I noticed that I was not entirely alone. Every so often I would come across other runners, all at least a decade younger than me, similarly burdened with a weighted backpack. More often than not we would nod in silent acknowledgment of our mutual endeavour and I could not help but wonder if they too were bound for Afghanistan. Perhaps the little part of south-east London in which I now lived was home to a disproportionate number of young men who had volunteered for duty in the service of their country. Despite the padding, I developed a pressure sore in the small of my back which did not fully heal until after I returned from Afghan. I bear the scar to this day, a small personal reminder of my service that I wear with pride.

Latitude:	51.49
Longitude:	-0.10
Elevation:	13m
Met:	Sunny H:21°L:12°
DTG:	291030ZJUN13

TEN MONTHS AFTER returning from Afghanistan I attended an Armed Forces Day parade at which I found myself standing next to two hugely overweight TA captains from another unit. To me they looked ridiculous, bulging out of their uniforms, Sam Browne belts straining to contain enormous bellies, rolls of fat flowing over their shirt collars. By this time I'd been conditioned by the Grenadiers to take an instant dislike to any man in uniform whose appearance might indicate an inability to meet mandated fitness requirements. These two were so vast they would struggle to find Taliban Hunting Club t-shirts in their XXXXL size.

Given the occasion, and in the interests of inter-unit cohesion, I bit my tongue and introduced myself. Ignoring my rank seniority they looked me up and down and resumed their conversation. Standing beside them I could not help but overhear their discussion. Unchecked by my presence they were making offensive and deeply critical comments about a female senior officer who was leading their unit's marching contingent. It was clear they both felt that a *lumpy jumper* was not up to this task and that they could do a better job themselves. Since they were not only obese but also overtly and crudely sexist, I was unable to resist the invitation I felt they'd just given me. I interrupted them, asking which part of the HQLF directive on physical fitness they had failed to understand.

They looked at me blankly.

Come on fellas, I said. *Take a look at yourselves. When was the last time you pulled on a pair of shorts and went for a run? No one's going to let you lead a parade while you both look like Mister fucking Blobby.*

Both men wore Afghanistan medals, along with a clutch of others that indicated many years service in the reserves. For all I knew they performed some vital role, repairing shattered lives in the Bastion hospital perhaps. It was possible they had once been flat-bellied, steely eyed killers who had let themselves go – although this really was stretching credulity. I should certainly have exercised better judgement myself, admonishing them for their inappropriate comments rather than countering with a few of my own, but HQLF is right. Physical fitness is an indispensable aspect of leadership. These two, however crucial their individual efforts were in the defence of the realm, had long ago relinquished the right to lead or command soldiers, even on a public parade in central London, let alone anywhere near the sharp end of British foreign policy.

Their stunned reaction to my outburst was to be short-lived. I observed them a couple of hours later merrily stuffing their faces at the buffet lunch laid on by the local authority to *celebrate the outstanding contribution made by our Armed Forces*. I knew I was a victim of my own prejudice, just as they were of theirs, but I couldn't help but feel resentment that these two were cashing in on the heroism of others. I uncharitably reckoned that their outstanding contribution had most likely been to Pizza Hut revenues at Camp Bastion.

Later that day, as a media trained officer I was tasked to give a television interview to Ria Chatterjee for ITV London. Ria is a very attractive young woman and I was a little distracted by her beauty. I stumbled through a series of rambling responses to her questions, full of 'ums' and 'ers', all of which I knew would be unusable in the two minute segment she was preparing. Concealing her frustration at the incompetent spokesperson with whom she'd been saddled, Ria eventually asked me why Armed Forces Day should be important to the people of London. I told her it was an opportunity to show some solidarity with the men and women of the armed forces – who put themselves in harm's way to keep others safe. It wasn't a perfect delivery but it was a good enough answer and Ria used it to close out her report.

Even as I spoke the words I couldn't find it in myself to apply them to the two chauvinist Blobby's gorging themselves in the marquee behind me.

Latitude:	50.93
Longitude:	0.87
Elevation:	4m
Met:	Overcast H:16°L:9°
DTG:	292030ZSEP11

THE STOCK IN trade tool of the modern British Infantry soldier is the SA80 A2 L85 assault rifle. It is a 5.56mm selective fire, magazine fed, gas-operated design manufactured by Heckler and Koch in a 'bullpup'[1] configuration with the magazine and firing mechanism behind the trigger group.

In Afghanistan it is fitted with a Trijicon Advanced Combat Optical Gunsight (ACOG) and a 4-sided picatinny rail[2] for the mounting of a vertical fore grip with bi-pod and a flashlight.

Like every other soldier deploying outside the wire I invested hundreds of hours and fired many thousands of rounds on rifle ranges up and down the country getting to know the SA80. Although I never felt the need to name my weapon, as many soldiers do, I knew it intimately enough that by the time I arrived in Afghanistan in January 2012 it had become a familiar and welcome extension to my right arm. Its constant presence became so normal that for many months after my return I would occasionally experience a sudden rise of panic at its absence and have to check myself. While it was perfectly acceptable - indeed mandatory - to tool up for a day out in downtown Rahim Kalay, the same does not apply to a trip to Sainsbury's in Dog Kennel Hill, except perhaps in the run up to Christmas.

It seems this experience is not uncommon among soldiers returning from duty. In July 2013, ten months after his return from Afghan, Major Andy 'Mo' Morrison, a Royal Artillery Officer attached to our battlegroup made the following Facebook post:

[1] **Bullpup**: A firearm with its action behind its trigger group. This configuration permits a shorter overall weapon for a given barrel length. This maintains the advantages of a longer barrel in muzzle velocity and accuracy, while improving manoeuvrability and reducing weight.

[2] **Pikatinny Rail**: (also known as a MIL-STD-1913 rail or tactical rail) is a bracket on some firearms that provides a standard mounting platform for accessories and attachments such as vertical pistol grips, bipods, electro-optical sights, image intensifiers; flashlights and laser sights.

I woke up this morning from a nightmare in which I had lost a pistol. For you civilians, that's the equivalent of losing the keys to your car.

With your baby inside it.

And the car is on fire.

His post drew a flurry of empathetic comments from friends and colleagues.

Like Mo, I was also trained in the use of the semi-automatic P226 Sig Sauer pistol which would be my secondary weapon system and my constant companion. I even took to sleeping with it tucked into an inner pocket inside my sleeping bag. Although I would fire many rounds on the ranges and get to know this weapon just as well as my primary shooter, the SA80, I was never to use it in anger.

Weapons training is progressive. It begins with a series of static shoots, where the user remains on a fixed firing point, and becomes increasingly more complex as the firer's proficiency and confidence grows. The most complicated shoots are scenario based and seek to recreate real life situations that the soldier may experience in theatre. These include convoy shoots, in which soldiers fire from moving vehicles, section and platoon attacks like those we had conducted in Sennybridge, and defended perimeter shoots.

In this last scenario we were required to defend a compound which had more than a passing resemblance to the abandoned District Centre in Sangin where, in 2006, British forces had been totally surrounded and outnumbered by the Taliban. It had been the scene of some of the most fierce and desperate fighting of the Afghan campaign. On more than one occasion, with ammunition low, the British troops were almost overwhelmed by superior numbers. Guy Lock, the London Regiment's Training Major had fought there and was subsequently wounded in a clearance operation.

The compound was a two storey partially constructed building with sandbagged defences including a 50-calibre machine gun position on the roof surrounded by a 12 foot high adobe wall. Although it looked exactly like many of the half finished, low-tech buildings we would find in Afghanistan, in reality it housed a complex and sophisticated electronic range management system, run from a control room concealed at the centre.

Having occupied the compound at last light we were given orders to remain in place until the following morning. As we set about establishing our routine in defence, identifying sentry and 'stand-to' positions, making up range cards, agreeing 'stag' or guard duty rosters, sleeping and administrative areas and so on, we were treated to the typical sounds of an Afghan village at dusk.

Dogs barking. The call to prayer from the local mosque. The occasional motorbike whizzing past. Children playing in the street. It was all very realistic but was being piped into the compound through hidden speakers in the walls, helping to set the scene for what was to follow.

It was fully dark and I was dozing in my bed space when word came through that some males of fighting age had been seen acting suspiciously outside the compound. This was followed by the news that insurgent radio chatter had been intercepted, which appeared to suggest that an RPG[1] had been called forward and that an attack on the compound was imminent. 'Stand-to' was called and we all silently occupied our prearranged positions.

Shortly afterwards it all kicked off big time.

Two loud explosions were followed up by long bursts of friendly fire from the 50-cal machine gun on the roof. Someone put up a series of a dozen or so flares and by their ghostly light we could see shadowy figures popping up and down beyond the compound perimeter.

We had all been trained in the need to *positively identify* (PID) targets as insurgents before opening fire. This meant we had to be certain they were carrying weapons, which was extremely difficult in the smoky haze of the flares. One or two of the lads, with younger eyes than my own, reckoned they'd seen enough to PID some enemy fighters and started calling in target indications:

2 enemy at 2 o'clock, 100 metres, base of lone tree two fingers left of corner of compound.

Enemy! Right of high feature at 12 o'clock.

---

[1] **RPG**: Rocket Propelled Grenade

Pretty soon the whole platoon was putting down suppressive fire. I couldn't really see anything but, guided by the tracer from the 50-cal and the target indications, I started putting down some rounds of my own in the general vicinity. The compound began to fill with cordite smoke, further adding to the gloom, as between us we expended thousands of rounds. Even with specially moulded ear plugs to protect my hearing the noise was deafening.

Eventually the return fire sound effects, played through the hidden loudspeakers, petered out to be replaced by more barking dogs and the wailing of women. This went on for some time, the occasional round of incoming fire being met by a short flurry of outgoing rounds, until eventually all was quiet.

Some way off to our left I could see a fire, started no doubt by one of the parachute flares, begin to take hold in the short, dry brush.

Without warning the compound was bathed in harsh white light from overhead gantries as OPTAG staff appeared out of nowhere and started giving orders to unload. Blinking in the sudden light I cleared my weapon and waited for an instructor to double check the chamber before allowing the working parts forward and firing off the action.

The training serial had been cut short due to the brush fire and we were despatched with beaters to put it out. I learned later that a similar facility had recently burned to the ground, at huge expense to the tax payer, and the range staff were not taking any chances with this one.

The fire safely dealt with we returned to the compound for a debriefing. The Range Conducting Officer (RCO) was not happy. The sophisticated range management system electronically records every round that strikes a target and although we had successfully seen off the enemy we had also hit an unarmed man and a woman in a burkha.

There was no way of knowing who had fired these errant rounds, but I had to guiltily accept that I might well have been the rogue shooter.

The RCO gave us all as good a bollocking as I've ever received in my time in the army. So thorough and effective was his reproof, so eloquently laced with invective and expletives, that even The Colour Sergeant would have been impressed.

He was right to do it too.

In August 2009, in an effort to reduce the numbers of civilian casualties in the conflict, General Stanley McChrystal, the senior American General in Afghanistan at that time, introduced a policy of 'Courageous Restraint'. McChrystal stated that *destroying a home or property jeopardises the livelihood of an entire family – and creates more insurgents* and that *large-scale operations to kill or capture militants carry a significant risk of causing civilian casualties and collateral damage.*

In the early years of the campaign, towns and villages had been reduced to rubble by air-to-ground munitions fired from aircraft called in to target insurgent snipers hiding in buildings. Collateral damage was extensive and an unknown number of civilians were killed. Those who survived were left homeless and in towns like Sangin the entire civilian population was displaced as the town's infrastructure was razed to the ground.

However well intentioned, the policy was not popular among ISAF troops. The Taliban were quick to exploit the new guidelines to their own advantage. Our own soldiers felt they were being forced to fight with one hand behind their backs and when McChrystal was dramatically sacked by President Barack Obama for insubordination in June the following year, Courageous Restraint was quietly dropped.

This did not mean that soldiers had carte blanche to open fire indiscriminately. Throughout our training the need to PID targets was drilled into us over and over again.

But this had not always been the case.

On many of the range practices I attended I spoke with soldiers who were preparing for their second and even third tours, and these men highlighted the change in attitude. On one occasion as I sat at the back of a range sharing a brew with a senior Warrant Officer while waiting my turn to shoot, two civilians carrying shovels on their shoulders walked past us. Every range complex employs a civilian team to maintain the facility and presumably these two were off to carry out some repairs on another part of the range. As they passed us my brew companion stared into his mug, then tossed the dregs onto the ground beside him and said in a low growl, intended for my ears only:

Those two would have got it on my last tour.

I didn't understand his meaning   until he pointed out that they were both males of fighting age, they both had beards and they were both carrying what, from a distance, might appear to be a long-barrelled weapon on their shoulders.

I might have dismissed his remarks as black humour, typical of the British squaddie. But I was to hear many similar observations and stories. Enough to conclude that air strikes had not been the only cause of civilian casualties in Afghanistan.

However, by 2012 great emphasis was being placed not only on the need to PID targets but also to respond proportionally. In the months ahead I would find myself defending compounds as we had been trained to do on that night of the brush fire. Even though we would come under sustained and deliberate attack from multiple firing points, the thousands of rounds we had fired in training were reduced to just a few hundred as we sought to avoid collateral damage. For my own part I never again fired rounds in the general direction of the enemy as I had done that night.

There's nothing like a well-timed bollocking to change attitudes and imprint new behaviours.

Latitude:	58.97
Longitude:	-1.04
Elevation:	12m
Met:	Clouds and sun H:13°L:7°
DTG:	221645ZOCT11

JANE AND I were hardly talking but at least we weren't shouting – not in front of the children anyway.

As often as was possible I would make my way to York to visit Harry and Alfie who by now were aware that I was going to Afghanistan. For the most part, Alfie was pretty pleased about this as I think it helped to explain my absence from his life. He no longer pleaded with me to get back together with Mummy, although he still frequently and tearfully expressed the wish that we had not split up in the first place. Drawing on his earlier assertions that I was not in the army at all but merely *helping the real soldiers,* I explained to him that I was going to Afghanistan to help the Grenadiers – the real soldiers – to stop the bad guys from doing bad stuff. This seemed to satisfy his curiosity although, despite the supporting role I'd described to him, in pictures he would draw for me I would always appear in the thick of the action. More often than not he would visualise me astride a tank surrounded by heavily armed soldiers, with helicopters, fighter planes and space ships in the skies above us, taking on a greatly outnumbered and poorly equipped enemy. It was clearly a cakewalk and we were all obviously enjoying ourselves enormously. Even the bad guys, many of whom lay dead at our feet, were grinning from ear to ear.

Harry was slightly more circumspect about the prospect of his Dad going to war. Always a deep thinker, he had a number of 'what if' questions for me.

What if I didn't come back?

What if I got hurt, or even killed?

What if I got captured?

I didn't want to think too hard about that last one but I tried to answer his questions as honestly as I could while simultaneously reassuring him that I would be very careful and it was unlikely to happen. I was deeply touched by his fears for my safety.

Although I downplayed Harry's concerns, just like everyone else in the battlegroup, I hoped for the best and planned for the worst. In view of the very real and obvious dangers inherent in dismounted close combat I took out life insurance with the MoD's approved provider. I wasn't entirely certain if I was insuring myself against the risks of death or injury in the service of my country, or against the inadequacies of the long-term care I would receive from the State in this second eventuality.

After more than ten years of conflict and a willingness by successive British governments to commit soldiers to combat, it is still a shameful reality that soldiers wounded in the service of their country are not adequately cared for by the State. They must rely instead on the generosity of the public through charities such as Help for Heroes to provide not only resources for their immediate rehabilitation as they recover from their injuries, but also for the long-term care that many will need throughout the rest of their lives.

It was most unedifying to learn of the personal greed of our political masters in the Parliamentary expenses scandal that engulfed British politics in 2009–10. At this time, according to official statistics released by the MoD, eight British soldiers a month were dying in Afghanistan. A further 13 were very seriously wounded, sustaining injuries that would change the course of the rest of their lives. It is notable that our political leaders at almost every level of governance will show public support for the men and women of the Armed Services – yet still drag their heels when it comes to ensuring that those who make the ultimate sacrifice receive adequate financial support from a grateful country.

In addition to taking out insurance I wrote my last will and testament, leaving my *estate, effects and everything I can give* in trust to Harry and Alfie. But my greatest wish required delicate negotiation with Jane. I was anxious that, should I not return from Helmand, Harry and Alfie would continue to have a relationship with my own father, Stuart. This was made complicated by the fact that he and Jane had fallen out some years before.

Dad had been tragically widowed long before Harry and Alfie were born and had filled the void left by my mother's death through service to the small rural community in which he lived. To some extent the animosity between Jane and Stuart had rubbed off on the boys and this, combined with Dad's own busy schedule, meant that visits were infrequent and often strained. In   contrast Jane's parents were ever present in the boys' lives and much loved by them both. I reasoned with Jane that it was in the boys' best interests to continue to have access to Grandpa Stuart; that all children deserve their grandparents and vice versa, but she was having none of it. Even when I persuaded a mutual friend to intercede on my behalf, Jane still refused to make any such assurances.

I was painfully discovering the collateral damage of my marriage break-up.

The consequences of not returning from Afghanistan would leave those I loved the most separated from each other in their grief.

Latitude:	52.49
Longitude:	0.76
Elevation:	36m
Met:	Partly sunny H:9°L:-2°
DTG:	060600ZDEC11

I WAS WOKEN by the alarm on my smart phone which told me it was 6am. The touch screen briefly illuminated my surroundings before I reflexively stabbed the *dismiss* button and was once again plunged into darkness. I lay on my back, disoriented by sleep, momentarily uncertain of my surroundings. It was bitterly cold and as my eyes grew accustomed to the gloom I could see my breath condensing above me. I was tempted to roll over and go back to sleep when an enormous bald head came into view. The enormous head was attached to an enormous neck which in turn was attached to an enormous torso and two enormous, heavily tattooed arms. The head spoke, revealing enormous tombstone teeth:

Sir, you snore like a fucking bastard. If it wasn't so fucking cold last night I would've got up and fucking strangled you.

I didn't doubt him for a moment. The man mountain was Glenn Haughton, the Regimental Sergeant Major of the First Battalion Grenadier Guards. Glenn appeared part human part beast, caught in a perpetual semi-transformative state between Dr Bruce Banner and The Incredible Hulk, at the point where his clothes no longer fit his outsize body but just before his skin turns green. I'd first met Glenn in Canada the year before and I knew he had a temper to match. *Don't make me angry. You wouldn't like me when I'm angry.* I was prepared to go to enormous lengths to avoid antagonising the big man and made a mental note to find alternative lodgings as soon as possible.

The Regimental Sergeant Major (RSM) is a key figure in any regiment or battalion and as the senior Warrant Officer is primarily responsible for maintaining standards and discipline. As the RSM of the First Battalion Grenadier Guards, the senior infantry regiment in the British Army, Glenn belonged to a small and exclusive club of men who had served in this capacity. Like all its members Glenn was an outstanding soldier, the best of his intake, and had reached the pinnacle of his career. As a young Guardsman he had first seen service in 1991 in the first Gulf War and had served with the battalion in the Balkans, Iraq and Afghanistan. Known simply as the 'Sarn't Major' Glenn's personality was as huge as his physique. Despite his ferocious temper he was liked and respected by all.

It was December 2011. I had driven up from London in freezing fog the night before to the Stanford Training Area in Thetford to join the Grenadiers for the last phase of their collective training. This would be the final OPTAG assessment before the headquarters team, of which I was a part, would deploy to Afghanistan in January 2012. It would also be my first opportunity to meet the new Commanding Officer, Lieutenant Colonel James Maurice Hannan Bowder, MBE.

The Stanford Training Area (STANTA) in Norfolk, made famous as the scene of the opening credits to *Dad's Army*, was originally established in 1942 as a battle training area and required the evacuation of the villages of Buckenham Tofts, West Tofts, Langford, Stanford, Sturston and Tottington. Villagers were summoned to meetings and told they had just three weeks to move out. Known collectively as the 'ghost villages' little remains today. Some were adapted for military use, others deliberately demolished or simply abandoned to the elements. Four historic churches alone have been preserved. They now appear strangely out of place; fenced off behind crude barbed wire, which prevents access to any would-be parishioners.

However, the area is now home to a new village. Specially constructed at a cost of £14 million to the tax payer, this village is designed to replicate its Afghan equivalent and is populated with more Afghan actors like those I had met in Canada. The long silent bells of St Mary's in West Tofts have been replaced by the *Adhan*, the call to prayer of the *Muezzin* from the mosque at its centre. It would be in this setting that the Grenadiers would be put through their paces one final time by the OPTAG instructors.

It was gone midnight when I reported to the guardroom at Wretham Camp. From there I was driven to Smokers Hole FOB, a purpose built Forward Operating Base on the training area which housed the battalion operations room and would be my home for the next few days. I was shown to a large tent, already occupied by a dozen or so somnolent figures, and invited to make myself comfortable. Inside the tent it was well below freezing and pitch black. With encouragement from some of the anonymous figures in the dark to *shut the fuck up*, I did my best to silently extract my sleeping bag from my bergan and find a space to get my head down.

After my encounter with the Sarn't Major the following morning, sleep was beyond me and so I quickly   pulled on my combat trousers and

Helly Hanson fleece top in an attempt to conserve body heat. As I fumbled with the laces of my boots with fingers numbed by cold I noted that since my last outing with them the Grenadiers had been issued the new multi-terrain pattern (MTP) uniforms which were now being worn in Afghanistan. I would not be issued with the new clothing, which was a much lighter shade of green than my own, for another couple of weeks. In the meantime I was going to stand out like a sore thumb, further highlighting my reserve status amongst these full-time soldiers.

Wash and shave kit in hand I went in search of the Puffing Billy, otherwise known as the M67 Army Liquid Fuel Immersion Heater. This is a genius piece of kit, originally of US design, dating back to 1943. Nicknamed the 'Kitchen Mortar' by US troops it consists of an old metal dustbin filled with water to which is clamped a diesel fired drip fed immersion heater with an enormous chimney. The Puffing Billy can produce a good quantity of hot water suitable for washing and shaving purposes, albeit with a greasy slick of diesel on the surface, but it takes a brave man to light one.

The preferred method being to throw a lighted match down the chimney and run like hell.

Sadly there was to be no hot water that morning. Not because there was no man brave enough to throw the match amongst these battle hardened soldiers but because it was so cold the diesel had started to wax and would not flow. I resigned myself to a cold shave and wandered over to a bowser where a man was breaking the ice on its surface to get to the water below. We both collected a bowl of frigid water and shared a wooden trestle table to wash and shave in silence. The ground on which we stood was still white with frost but this did not deter my companion from stripping to the waist to complete his ablutions. I felt no desire to follow his example. Keeping my Helly Hanson zipped to the neck, my own administrations were far less thorough. It was only when the stranger beside me pulled on his shirt that I noticed the distinctive Crown and Bath Star rank slide that denoted his status as the Commanding Officer.

It was my new boss.

Colonel James had joined the regular army in 1996, the same year that I had left. He had ascended to the rank of Lieutenant Colonel in double quick time and was clearly destined for the very top of the army. This was to be his third tour of Afghanistan and he had received operational awards on both his previous deployments. From the ten thousand or so soldiers on each rotation in Afghanistan only 100 to 150 are recognised in the Operational Honours and Awards list. To be recognised once is an achievement; to be recognised twice was exceptional.

As I would discover in the weeks and months ahead, Colonel James was a hard man to read. He liked to play his cards very close to his chest. While it was sometimes possible to see the cogs whirring behind his thoughtful face, I often found it difficult to know what he was really thinking. Although I would spend many hours in his company it was always strictly business. Beyond the usual pleasantries, we never got to know one another or discuss our personal lives. I would discover from others that he was married with four young children.

Leadership can be a lonely business, especially in the dangerous enterprise to which we were committed. If Colonel James appeared inscrutable and aloof I believe it was because he was profoundly engaged in the responsibilities of his command and had reached deep within himself to confront these issues. As the Commanding Officer of an infantry battalion on the front line of the most dangerous place on earth he knew, as we all knew, that not all of our number would return home alive and many others would be forever scarred by our experiences.

Most of us, myself included, locked these thoughts away in the dark recesses of our minds and hoped for the best. Colonel James, on the other hand, had to confront the knowledge that men would die on his orders, that wives would become widows, sons would predecease their parents and children would be orphaned. Rightly or wrongly he shouldered alone the burden of this responsibility. This emotional self-sufficiency didn't make him an easy man to get along with.

But I had nothing but admiration for his courage and devotion to duty.

I recalled some advice my father had given me many years before; it doesn't matter if your boss is a difficult man, he's still the boss and it's therefore your job to get along with him and make the relationship work. I'd been too young and hot-headed to listen to this advice when it was first offered and rather spectacularly got myself into a lot of trouble. That had been over 20 years ago. Given a second chance, I was finally able to heed my father's wise words.

The Forward Operating Base at Smokers Hole centred on an old farmhouse which had been transformed into a fully functioning operations room similar to that which we would use in Afghanistan. The building itself was little more than a shell but the ops room inside resembled the bridge of the starship Enterprise. Disappointingly it lacked transporter technology, but in all other respects was every bit as high tec as a Starfleet bridge and performed much the same function. From this point the Commanding Officer and his duty officers had direct communications with all units, and from here he would direct and oversee all operations. As on Enterprise the focal point of the ops room was a bank of flat-screen TVs which, thanks to ever-present unmanned aerial vehicles overhead, beamed in live pictures from any part of the area of operations (AO).

Coordinating the activities of the ops room was one of the most high pressure jobs in the battlegroup headquarters. It required a cool head to manage and synchronise all the various activities of a busy AO, especially when troops were in contact with the enemy. None came cooler than Captain Tom Gardner.

I'd met surfers on Redondo Beach who were less chilled than Tom.

From almost our first meeting he referred to me simply as 'Dude', not something anyone had ever called me before. Over the course of the next nine months we would frequently enjoy a smoke and a chat round the back of the ops tent in Afghanistan. I'd given up smoking more than a decade before – it's a young man's game – but I always enjoyed doing a bit of passive with Tom. He had a unique and unusual talent for grumbling about everything in an amusing and good humoured way. Listening to him complain about anything from the price of fish to the time of day and everything in between never failed to raise my morale.

Given his high pressure role, Tom would be scrutinised more than most by the OPTAG team over the course of the next few days but if he felt the stress of their presence he certainly didn't show it. I found him on this cold and frosty morning, cigarette in hand and cheeky chappie grin on his face, complaining happily about the lack of hot water. With him was Major Dave Kenny.

Dave was to be our Chief of Staff (COS) and the Commanding Officer's right-hand man. The battlegroup HQ is responsible for the administrative, operational and logistical needs of the unit and the COS coordinates all these different activities and is generally its hardest working man.

Dave was no exception. Over the course of our time in Afghanistan most of us would develop deep tans and bulk up from regular work-outs in the gym – referred to as 'Op Massive'. By contrast, Dave became paler and thinner with every passing week as he spent longer and longer hours in the ops room. During the summer months of the fighting season he kept up an almost permanent vigil, subsisting on a diet of cigarettes and cold rations. When the tour was over he returned home, quite literally, a pale shadow of his former self.

Like all British HQs our structure was based on the continental staff system. In this system, originally employed by the French army in the 19th century, each staff position is assigned a number specifying a role as follows:

1, for manpower or personnel

2, for intelligence and security

3, for operations

4, for logistics

5, for plans

6, for signals or communication

7, for training

8, for finance and contracts

9, for Civil-Military Cooperation or 'civil affairs'.

Since I was to be responsible for engagement with the civilian population I was assigned the number 9. Although staff numbers are not assigned according to hierarchy I was under no illusion that my role was anything other than secondary to the main business of war fighting.

In addition to a number, a letter prefix is also used to denote the type of HQ as follows:

A, for Air Force headquarters

C, for combined (multiple nations) headquarters

G, for Army headquarters

J, for Joint (multiple services) headquarters

N, for Navy headquarters.

Strictly speaking we should have been assigned the C prefix as we were to be a combined English/Danish HQ with a number of Danish officers, a Danish Armoured Infantry Company and four Danish Leopard 2 tanks under command. Inexplicably, protocol was not observed on this occasion and we were assigned the J prefix, even though we were exclusively an army HQ.

I was looking forward to reacquainting myself with the Danish military. I'd had the pleasure of working with them 22 years earlier during a UN peacekeeping tour in Cyprus. Appearances can be deceptive. Despite the unconventional barbering that most Danish soldiers seem to favour, they are highly professional and more than capable of holding their own alongside their more minimally coiffured British counterparts.

I never did find out why we were assigned this prefix, mostly because I didn't bother to enquire. However, I was to be J9, and much to my surprise I discovered that I would be working alongside a Danish officer.

Captain Thor Sommerstrand was pretty much your archetypal Viking. He didn't have a broadsword, battleaxe, wooden shield or horned helmet but if he had done I wouldn't have dared to take the Mickey. Lean, pale, intense and incredibly strong, he was a man of few words who could have been a direct descendant of Cnut the Great, ruler of the North Sea Empire and self-proclaimed *king of all England and Denmark and the Norwegians and of some of the Swedes.*

Thor's ancestors may well have raped and pillaged my own but, unlike the blood feuds going back several generations that still influenced tribal divisions in Afghanistan, I was more than happy to let sleeping dogs lie. Indeed, I was very glad we were going to be fighting on the same side.

Over the next few days the OPTAG team put us through a series of scenarios designed to test our responses and reactions, all of which were based on actual events that had occurred at one time or another over the last ten years in Afghanistan. On more than one occasion we were required to extract a casualty with multiple traumatic amputations resulting from an IED blast.

Although it was not overtly stated, as well as teaching us vital procedures that would save lives in the months ahead, this training was conditioning and emotionally desensitising us to the reality that not all of our number would return intact.

The MoD's Defence Analytical Services and Advice Unit estimated that, as front line troops, our risk of death or injury in Afghanistan was 12 times higher than that of any other army employee. According to their statistics about half our number would see someone killed or wounded, about a quarter would experience an IED detonation, and half would come under small arms fire. We now trained endlessly for these eventualities, honing our standard operating procedures (SOPs) to respond to these situations. And it worked. In the months ahead I was to hear on numerous occasions how *the training just kicked in*.

When one of the Grenadiers was randomly selected to act as the casualty in a couple of these scenarios, someone joked that he'd been unlucky enough to lose both his legs twice in as many days. This was typical of the dark humour that soldiers call upon to sustain themselves in difficult situations.

As the J9 officer I was required to deal with a scenario where burned fragments of the Qur'an were found outside one of our patrol bases by local children. Fortunately I'd read about this incident when it happened for real in Afghanistan and was able to respond accordingly. I defused a potentially dangerous situation by persuading the local Mullah to intercede on our behalf, calling for calm and accepting our assertion that the burned fragments must have been planted by the Taliban. I also arranged for books and pens to be supplied to the school. In another incident I had to deal with a complaint from a local man that one of our sentry positions overlooked his compound which was unacceptably compromising his privacy, and that of his wives and daughters. It turned out to be valuable training when exactly this situation did occur close to the end of our tour in the village of Dagian.

As well as reacting to incidents as they were thrown at us by the OPTAG team we were required to conduct our own forward planning and preparation for operations. As staff officers we were expected to produce the Operational Staff Work (OSW) that would underpin these operations. I had two tasks in this   context. The first was to prepare a Human Terrain Analysis (HTA) brief as part of the Intelligence Preparation of the Environment (IPE) in order to better understand the highly complex human environment in which operations would take place. The second was an Influence Annex that detailed the Info Ops activity that would support the main operation.

The OPTAG team were deliberately driving us hard to see where the cracks might appear. There was little time in the day to produce OSW, so we did most of our planning at night. With all staff functions crammed into the Smokers Hole farmhouse, space was at a premium and I was assigned a computer terminal in the attic. With just a few sheets of wiggly tin between myself and the elements it was bitterly cold. I tapped away on my keyboard with gloved fingers, producing shade shift[1] slides and other influence planning tools by the light of my head torch.

At least I wasn't keeping the S'arnt Major awake with my snoring.

A few days and sleepless nights later our assessment was complete. We were signed off by the OPTAG team, deemed fit to deploy. No fanfare, no high fives, no visible celebration of any kind, but it was a significant milestone. Other HQ teams had not fared so well and had been either dismissed or disbanded following an unfavourable assessment, effectively ending the careers of those involved.

Prior to departure that evening Colonel James and I shared a brew in the messing tent. As the Grenadiers were returning to their barracks in Aldershot, I would be making my way north to Nottingham to the Reserve Training and Mobilisation Centre (RTMC). We would next meet in January at RAF Brize Norton, from where we would fly to Camp Bastion. We briefly discussed our respective plans.

In a directive to his staff, Colonel James had warned against the dangers of over training. He'd observed on previous deployments that soldiers arrived in theatre exhausted from the intensity of the training cycle. This in itself had demanded long periods away from family and friends so that soldiers had not emotionally or administratively prepared themselves or their loved ones for the demands of combat operations. As the only reservist in his headquarters, I guessed that he was satisfying himself that I was adequately prepared.

---

[1] **Shade Shift**: An analysis of human terrain that acknowledges the complexity of different allegiances and interests between and amongst target audiences.

I reassured him as best I could. I was ready and had even managed to tee up some skiing in the Trois Vallees before deployment. Colonel James, as usual, revealed little of himself but joked that he was going to put on some weight in order to offset the inevitable D&V that awaited us in Afghan. Finally we shook hands.

Up until this moment I had been Colonel Roly's man, recommended and endorsed by him, but as I gripped hands with Colonel James I realised that not only the OPTAG team had been monitoring my performance. Perhaps it was merely my imagination, but it seemed to me that Colonel James held his grip and my eye for a moment longer than was necessary. We were not just saying our farewells; we were undertaking a chivalric pact. On the eve of war I was swearing my fealty to the Crown. As Her Majesty's senior representative, Colonel James was accepting my oath.

I was his man now.

Latitude:	45.34
Longitude:	6.58
Elevation:	2850m
Met:	Some sun then turning cloudy H:4°L:-9°
DTG:	201000ADEC11

I TRY TO ignore the horrible scraping sound and the damage I must be doing to the bases of my skis as I sidestep over the rocks. With pre-deployment training over, I have returned to my spiritual home in the Alps for a few days early season skiing and a brief respite from the green machine. Ironically, in the minutes ahead, it is that same green machine that will keep me and my companion alive.

This early in the season there's no snow base to speak of and despite the fifteen or so centimetres of beautiful *freshies*[1] that have fallen overnight, in this exposed and wind blown spot, every time I apply pressure to my skis they sink through the powder layer directly onto the rocks below. I shout a warning to Nicholas, my long-term ski buddy, who is similarly picking his way gingerly through the rocks a few metres above me.

If the OPTAG training team knew anything about off-piste skiing they hadn't let on. But the physical and psychological coping strategies they'd taught me to manage risk in Afghanistan applied equally well in the Alps.

It was, of course, all my fault. There was no denying that.

I had a mental image of one of my OPTAG instructors, shaking his head with furrowed brow, before noisily clicking his ballpoint pen and marking a big fat cross on his clipboard.

☐ Pass

☒ Fail

I'd been hard pressed to contain my excitement as we ascended to the drop-in point and discovered that there were, as yet, no tracks in the

[1] **Freshies**: Fresh snow on which there are no ski or snow board tracks.

snow beneath us. However, the absence of tracks is not only cause for excitement, it's also a warning that others have had second thoughts and abandoned the endeavour. It was a warning, a *combat indicator* as the OPTAG instructors would have put it, that I'd been foolish enough to ignore. I was beginning to realise that I'd made a colossal error of judgement.

☐ Pass

☒ Fail

I'd been so eager to be the first to tag the run that I'd rushed into the descent without properly evaluating the conditions. Whatever happened next my brand new Volkl Gotama skis were never going to be the same again, but just as my instructors had taught me, I pushed this thought to the back of my mind as a secondary consideration. Now I must focus solely on assessing our situation.

☒ Pass

☐ Fail

Nicholas was tracking over to the right a few metres above me and seemed to be making good progress. Following his example, I cleared the rocky section but this traverse had forced us onto a very steep pitch with an inclination well over 40 degrees.

The snow on this section was blemished with a number of little snow trails where some of the upper layers had begun to roll downhill gathering momentum as they went. It was another combat indicator, one I knew I could not ignore. The severity of the incline was making the snowpack unstable and liable to avalanche. This time I'd seen the signs and interpreted them correctly.

☒ Pass

☐ Fail

Fortunately, I'd already applied a mantra repeated over and over again by the training team and which would continue to serve me well in Afghanistan in the months ahead:

1. Hope for the best.

2. Plan for the worst.

3. Prepare to be surprised.

Before setting off that morning I'd double checked that Nicholas and I both had a complete set of emergency equipment. We both wore helmets and avalanche transceivers. In our packs we each carried a quick assembly snow probe and shovel as well as a basic first aid kit, spare warm clothing and an emergency bivouac sack. More kit, more weight to hump, but it significantly improved our odds of survival if caught in an avalanche. Finally we'd conducted a transceiver check and pre-programmed the local mountain rescue emergency number into our mobile phones.

☒ Pass

☐ Fail

Of course, none of this equipment can prevent an avalanche or the risk of burial. As my imaginary mentor reminded me before putting pen to clipboard once more, the best way to stay out of trouble is not to get into trouble in the first place.

☐ Pass

☒ Fail

Nicholas now skied down to my location and we both silently assessed our situation. If he was mad at me for leading him into such danger he didn't show it.

We have been skiing together for many years. Nicholas is technically one of the best skiers I know and skis with a grace and beauty I cannot match. His style is so unique and elegant that I could easily pick him out on the mountain from a hundred other identically dressed skiers. I've spent many hours in his company and trust his judgement and competence implicitly. This is not the first time we've taken a calculated risk together and I know he will watch my back should I get into difficulties, as I hope he knows I would do for him.

I know almost nothing else about Nicholas.

He's something big in the City and, judging from the amount of shiny new kit he brings with him on our trips, he's paid handsomely for his efforts. We meet just once a year in October or November in a pub in Victoria to discuss our skiing diaries for the forthcoming season. Younger, fitter, better looking and professionally more successful than me, the only thing we have in common is our love for snow covered mountains.

In order to select a route that presents the lowest possible avalanche danger, I conduct an intelligence preparation of the battlefield (IPB). Using the OPTAG method, I assess the terrain for *go*, *slow-go* and *no-go* areas, identifying areas of risk, vulnerable points (VPs) as my instructors would have described them. I calculate that it's not going to be possible to avoid all the VPs as we descend. We'll have to accept some risk but at least we will be alive to the threat and can plan accordingly.

Although the route will not be without hazard, I judge we can still mitigate the risk to acceptable levels by skiing the most dangerous sections one by one. I brief Nicholas that I will go first and wait for him at regular intervals away from the descent line at points which offer some natural protection and safety – assembly areas in OPTAG speak. It's left unsaid but we both understand that if one of us is buried or swept away the other will initiate a rescue.

Final preparations. I lift my skis clear of the snow and visually check the buckles on my ski boots to ensure they haven't come loose while negotiating the rocks. I pat myself down to make certain my pockets are zipped tight and adjust my gloves so they are sealed over the cuffs of my jacket. Next, I loop the straps on my ski poles over the tips of my fingers. Like many off-piste skiers I don't like to use the straps they way they teach in ski school, but nor do I like skiing with no straps at all. Taking care of our equipment, ensuring it is fully functional at all times, has been drummed into us many times over. Murphy 's Law applies and things will go wrong if given even the slightest chance. Checking and rechecking equipment in detail has become an obsession. My imaginary OPTAG mentor approves.

Lastly, I adjust my goggles and switch on the head cam that's fitted to the side of my helmet just above my right ear. OPTAG does not approve. Head cams have been banned in Afghanistan following the appearance of unauthorised combat footage on social media sites. But if this pitch doesn't kill me I want to keep a record.

I'm good to go.

I mentally rehearse the descent once more, visualising where I will make each turn. I look at Nicholas and proffer him my gloved fist. He punches me lightly with his own and I launch myself into the descent.

There are four major factors that cause an avalanche and I was ticking all the boxes. A heavy snowfall combined with wind and cold temperatures increases avalanche risk, as does untouched and steep terrain. 97% of all avalanches occur on slopes with an inclination of over 30 degrees. The final determining factor was my own presence on the slope. An avalanche can be triggered from the additional load of just one person on the snow surface. To make matters worse every time I turned I would increase the load by four or five times my own body weight. If I were to fall, the load would be increased by seven or eight times, possibly more.

Falling was not a desired outcome at this moment. But I had assessed the snowpack as a combatant and considered its most likely and most dangerous courses of action (ML/MDCoA), just as we'd been taught. In the event that I now triggered an avalanche – the MDCoA – I was as prepared as I could be.

Approaching my first turn I tried to apply pressure to my skis as progressively as I could, leaning forward and down in the direction of the turn. I was skiing with feet close together and weight spread evenly across both skis to create a stable platform. Most piste skiers will initiate a turn by transferring weight from one leg to the other in order to engage the inside edge of their downhill ski, but this technique doesn't work in powder. I was actually trying to avoid catching an edge as this can result in the ski becoming buried, causing me to tumble and fall.

The technology in my new Gotamas was also coming into its own. The Gotama is a fully rockered ski. Unlike a traditional cambered ski, which has a slight upward curve in the middle and contact points close to the ends, a rockered ski has a contact point beneath the skier's foot and is bent upwards along its length from this point. This enables it to glide extremely well in deep and tracked snow as the long gentle, upward bend prevents the tips from sinking. At this point I assessed that I had an appropriate level of competence to successfully complete the mission, and the best possible equipment for the task.

☒ Pass

☐ Fail

As I gently applied pressure into the turn the top layer of snow began to tumble away in front of me. I could hear a dull whumping sound as the snow all around me adjusted to my presence on the slope. This was the clearest combat indicator yet that the slope was in imminent danger of avalanche, but it was too late to turn back – I was already committed. Forcing myself to remain calm under pressure, just as I'd been taught, I immediately eased the loading of my presence on the slope by allowing my tips to point directly down the fall line and accelerated away, hoping the mountain was not following on behind me. But now I had another problem. I was travelling too fast for comfort and was going to have to bleed off some speed.

The only way to do this was to initiate another turn.

With my heart in my mouth, I once more progressively applied pressure. This time the rockered tips of my Gots popped out of the snow in front of me just the way they were supposed to. I breathed a huge sigh of relief. I'd kept my nerve and successfully extricated myself from danger.

☒ Pass

☐ Fail

And now this was getting fun.

I quickly established a rhythm, allowing the Gots to do the work for me as I descended knee-deep in powder, enjoying the thrill of the ride, the wind on my face and the stark beauty of the monochrome landscape all around me.

Nothing compares to the thrill of wilderness skiing.

Exactly ten turns later I've descended through the steepest and most dangerous section of the slope. I pull up on a small rib clear of the likely path of any avalanche. Looking back up I see Nicholas and wave him down. My head cam is still recording and captures his descent with all the precision and grace of his technique. To the left of the screen my own tracks are just visible and Nicholas triggers a small slip as he passes close by. In the grand scheme of things it's inconsequential and does not impede his progress, but it's a clear indicator of the slope's instability. We've been lucky and we both know it. We've been pushing the envelope, but with the help of the Operational Training and Advisory Group we've successfully navigated the most treacherous section of the route.

 Pass

☐ Fail

It's a qualified pass. I still take a bollocking from my imaginary instructor as he reminds me that my early failure to heed the obvious combat indicators had put us into a dangerous situation that could have been avoided. It's a valuable lesson. Although I don't know it yet, it's one that I will apply many times over in the months ahead.

Like guilty schoolboys we complete the rest of the run on safer terrain. It's still an awesome descent and we have the mountain to ourselves. I absorb myself completely in the sense of freedom that skiing this kind of terrain brings, feeling my own personal insignificance in this wild and barren landscape. Nothing else matters in these moments, in fact I'm not sure the outside world even exists when I'm skiing the backcountry.

Much later I turn the footage from my head cam into a short video to be replayed many hundreds of times in Afghanistan, an antidote to the heat and dust and the oppressive proximity of life inside the wire. Watching, I relive my excitement at the top of the run and the range of emotions I experienced during the descent.

For a few precious moments I tune out the daily grind of dirt, dust and sweat and return to my spiritual home in the mountains.

In addition to making skiing videos to sustain myself in Afghan, I was making a video for Harry and Alfie. This was to be my message to them from the grave should I not   return. I reasoned that if I didn't live long enough to share my love of snow covered mountains with my boys first-hand, then the next best thing would be to make a video. I tried to explain to them why I felt so drawn to the mountains and my hope that one day they would come to understand and share my passion. I also told them how much I loved them, how they were growing up to be such wonderful boys, how proud of them I was and how sorry that I would not be there to watch over them.

Finally I told them not to mourn my loss or to visit my grave – I would not be there. If they needed me in the years ahead they should come into the mountains. They would find me here on the wind as it whistles over jagged peaks, in the rays of early morning light turning the mountains pink and in the branches of pines laden with snow. Most of all they would find me in their own aching limbs after an epic powder day, in the shortness of breath that comes with thin mountain air and in the pounding of their hearts with the euphoria of a successful descent.

This is where they would find me and could be with me, for they would know then what I know now.

Latitude   58.97
Longitude   -1.04
Elevation   12m
Met   Sunny to partly cloudy H:3°L:-1°
DTG   230845ZJAN12

Get a fucking pistol as soon as you get out there mate and keep one in the chamber at all times.

THE CHAMBER AT ALL TIMES.

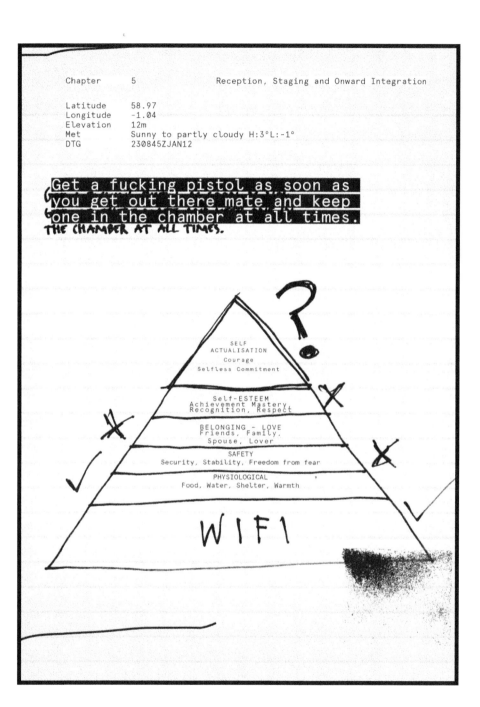

SELF
ACTUALISATION
Courage
Selflesa Commitment

Self-ESTEEM
Achievement Mastery
Recognition, Respect

BELONGING - LOVE
Friends, Family.
Spouse, Lover

SAFETY
Security, Stability, Freedom from fear

PHYSIOLOGICAL
Food, Water, Shelter, Warmth

WIFI

R&R: Rest and Recuperation
ECBA: Enhanced Combat Body Armour
RTMC: Reserves Training and Mobilisation Centre
PCS: Personal Clothing System
UBACS: Under Body Armour Combat Shirt
RSOI: Reception, Staging and Onward Integration
MOB: Main Operating Base
MCCP: Movement Control Check Point
COIN: Counter Insurgency
C-IED: Counter-Improvised Explosive Device
EOD: Explosive Ordnance Disposal
PM: Protected Mobility
HME: Homemade Explosive
ANS: Ammonium Nitrate mixed with Sugar
ANFO: Ammonium Nitrate mixed with Fuel Oil
ANAL: Ammonium Nitrate mixed with Aluminium
PPIED: Pressure Plate IED
VOIED: Victim Operated IED
MRAP: Mine Resistant, Ambush Protected
TBAU: Tactical Base Ablution Unit

MINISTRY OF DEFENCE ANNOUNCEMENT

Lance Corporal Gajbahadur Gurung. On Friday 27 January 2012, Lance Corporal Gajbahadur Gurung sustained a fatal gunshot wound while on a foot patrol to disrupt insurgent activity in the Nahr-e-Saraj district of Helmand province.

Latitude:	58.97
Longitude:	-1.04
Elevation:	12m
Met:	Sunny to partly cloudy H:3°L:-1°
DTG:	230845ZJAN12

I TRIED HARD, harder than usual, not to raise my voice as I ushered Harry and Alfie out the front door. It was Monday morning and I didn't want to be late for school. More importantly, I didn't want Harry and Alfie's last memory of their father to be of *Grumpy Dad*. We went through the usual checklist:

Book bag. Check.

Pack-up. Check.

Shoes on the right feet. Check.

Coat. Check.

We were off, joining the procession of carefree children and their parents making their way down the lane.

Past the Post Office and the tennis courts.

Over the hump-backed bridge, finishing line of the hotly contested annual village duck race.

Carefully looking left and right before crossing the road by the War Memorial.

Past the Black Bull pub, scene of Sunday afternoon coca-colas.

Up the snicket, through the five-bar gate and into the school playground.

I hoovered up every detail of the five minute journey, conscious that it might be the last few moments I would ever spend with my children. They would not see me again until I returned from Afghanistan and, although we didn't discuss it, that might well be in a wooden casket or, worse still, unrecognisably shattered and broken.

No good for climbing trees.

No good for playing footie in the park using coats for goal-posts.

No good for games of off-ground touch in the front room (don't tell Mummy).

I didn't want to think about it. I didn't want them to think about it.

In the days leading up to this moment I'd carefully explained to them that I would be going away for nine months but I would return for R&R – rest and recuperation – in just three months. In time I hoped for Alfie's birthday, although I couldn't promise this. We discussed what we would get up to in the two weeks I'd be back; this mostly involved eating junk food and watching movies. Harry and Alfie quickly cottoned on that the usual parental controls would not apply. Every time the subject came up the checklist of stuff that wasn't normally allowed grew longer.

It was an awkward wait for the bell that would signal the start of the school day. To everyone else in that playground it was a Monday morning just like any other. Children were excitedly catching up on the weekend's news and activities. Parents chatted in little groups, glancing at their wrist watches as they waited for the teachers to take charge. It was a scene being played out, no doubt, right across the country but as an absentee father it was not one in which I belonged. I felt that all eyes were on the stranger in the midst of this tight-knit village community.

I wanted to justify my absence more than my presence. They may or may not have thanked me for it but I was now keeping company with rough men standing ready to do violence in order to preserve this peaceful village idyll.

The boys and I had already discussed how we would say our goodbyes. Harry didn't want me to kiss him in the playground as it would look *babyish* and embarrass him in front of his mates. Alfie wanted whatever Harry wanted. I knew how they felt, I'd been similarly embarrassed by my own parents in the school playground, so we'd done all the mushy stuff before leaving the house. Even so it took a superhuman effort on my part not to take them in my arms one last time as the bell signalled the start of the school day.

Holding back tears as best I could, I told them to be good, to do as Mummy said, and that I'd be home before they'd even missed me. As they headed off to join their classmates, Alfie hesitated for a moment.

Daddy, he said, *is three months longer than a week?*

Over the course of the previous 12 months while training and preparing for deployment I'd spoken to many fathers about the best way to say goodbye. It's such a common issue that the army even provides advice and guidance to families on the subject, but there are no hard and fast rules. I didn't read all the literature provided in the briefing pack but I noticed that it included a charming children's book, *My Daddy's Going Away*, written by Christopher MacGregor, who is both a psychologist and an army officer. The first page reads:

> *My Daddy's going away, you know*
> *He says it's for a while.*
> *We'll miss our hugs and storytime,*
> *We'll miss his funny smile.*

I couldn't read the book to Harry and Alfie without getting a lump in my throat. There was one verse that really struck me:

> *We miss each other most of all*
> *As we snuggle in our beds*
> *But we share the same warm blanket*
> *Of stars above our heads.*

I really liked the idea that, however far away, we would always share the same canopy of stars and could reach out to each other by looking up at the night sky. We spent a number of evenings in the run up to my departure stargazing. The easiest constellation to spot was the saucepan, otherwise known as Ursa Major, the Great Bear. I'm not sure that Harry and Alfie really bought in to this idea but they certainly enjoyed running around the garden in their pyjamas after dark doing dodgy impressions of Sir Patrick Moore. However, once in Afghanistan I would routinely seek out the saucepan in the dazzling night skies. It never failed to warm my heart, bring a smile to my lips and a tear to my eye.

In another attempt to stay connected we randomly selected three pebbles from the garden. With the children's help I carefully washed each one and used a permanent marker to initial them **H**, **A** and **C**. I explained that the pebbles were   now part of a set. We would each be responsible for looking after one of them until I finally returned from Afghanistan when we would go to the beach and throw them all in the sea together.

They both seemed to like this idea and decided to place their pebbles on the windowsill in their bedroom where, as Alfie explained to me, they could act as lookouts waiting for me to return. I placed my own pebble in a small pocket in my body armour where it stayed for the duration of the tour, accompanying me wherever I went. I'm not superstitious but it became a routine part of my pre-patrol checks to ensure that I had my pebble. By the time I returned from Afghanistan it had become highly polished from my frequent touch.

Harry and Alfie's pebbles did not fare so well. As Harry later explained, *Mummy threw them away when she was tidying up.*

Latitude:	51.42
Longitude:	-0.08
Elevation:	49m
Met:	Sunny to partly cloudy H:3°L:-1°
DTG:	230800ZJAN12

WITH JUST TWO days to go before reporting to RAF Brize Norton all that was left to do was pack my kit and shave my chest.

When I'd resolved to go in search of adventure in the service of my country I hadn't anticipated that depilation would be a prerequisite. Although I'd briefly worked on the Braun male shaving and grooming account during my early career in advertising, I'd exited the sector just before it experienced 35% growth and exploded into a $20bn a year global industry. Personally, I'd never felt the need to include chest shaving in my grooming regimen. But it wasn't because I was bitter that I'd missed the male shaving gravy train.

Unlike facial hair, which has variously been encouraged, prohibited or deemed an essential part of the uniform, I was unaware of any actual military regulations with regard to the wearing of chest hair. But, like everyone else preparing to go outside the wire, I'd been issued with a medical pack that contained tourniquets, morphine, *HemCon* blood clotting bandages, first field dressings and a *Bolin* chest seal. I'd also received extensive training in their use in both self- and first-aid contexts.

The *Bolin* chest seal *is a sterile occlusive chest wound dressing for treating open pneumothorax and preventing tension pneumothorax that result from gunshots, stab wounds, or other penetrating chest trauma* - what's otherwise known as a sucking chest wound. Essentially a circular adhesive pad with a one-way valve at its centre, it allows blood and air to escape from the wound but prevents their re-entry. However, the presence of body hair can impair the effectiveness of the seal and my first-aid instructor had encouraged us to include a safety razor in our med packs for this reason.

On the basis that I probably wouldn't be up for a dry shave so soon after being shot in the chest I concluded that I was better off without the rug.

1. Hope for the best.

2. Plan for the worst.

3. Prepare to be surprised.

Packing was slightly more complicated.

In February 2010, Air Chief Marshall Sir Jock Stirrup the then head of the armed forces reported to the Chilcot Enquiry, set up to examine the UK's involvement in Iraq, that shortages of personal equipment including body armour, desert uniforms and boots had hampered the operation. Although he did not acknowledge it at the enquiry, British soldiers had died as a result of equipment shortages. Soldiers such as Sergeant Steven Roberts.

Sergeant Roberts, the first British soldier to die in Iraq in 2003, lost his life because, according to the coroner at his inquest, he had not been issued with Enhanced Combat Body Armour (ECBA). In his summing up the coroner was scathing of Ministers, saying *to send soldiers into a combat zone without the appropriate basic equipment is, in my view, unforgivable and inexcusable and represents a breach of trust that the soldiers have in those in government.*

The Ministry of Defence, somewhat missing the coroner's point, initially insisted that ECBA would not have saved Sgt Roberts' life, but eventually conceded that the coroner was correct.

Behind the coroner's words lay a further bitter truth.

Sergeant Roberts had been issued with body armour. But because there were not enough sets to go around it was taken back three days before he died to be reissued to someone who was felt to be at greater risk. In fact the army in Iraq was deficient over 2,000 sets of ECBA, largely because the Defence Secretary, Geoff Hoon had delayed for eight weeks before approving a request for extra ECBA kits in 2002.

But even this uncomfortable fact does not reveal the true extent of the tragedy.

Sgt Roberts was killed by a 7.62mm high velocity round fired from the L94A1 chain gun mounted on the turret of the Challenger 2 main battle tank in which he had been travelling. At the time of his death he had dismounted from the tank and was standing approximately 20 metres away when he came under attack from a stone throwing insurgent. Having been hit in the head and   chest, Sgt Roberts drew his ancient 9mm Browning pistol. It jammed after the first shot. When another machine gun on the tank also failed to fire the tank's crew, in a desperate attempt to protect their beleaguered colleague, brought the chain gun to bear. The L94A1 is coaxially mounted alongside the Challenger's main gun and is designed to fire in support of it, using the tank's main sight. Consequently, the weapon cannot be accurately aimed below a minimum range of 200 metres and Sgt Roberts was fatally injured.

Had Sgt Roberts been issued with a more modern and reliable sidearm, this tragic chain of events might never have occurred.

The subsequent public outcry into the extent of personal equipment shortages meant that by 2012 soldiers deploying on operations had a different problem. Shortly after our final OPTAG assessment I borrowed my father's car and drove to Chilwell in Nottingham, home to the Reserves Training and Mobilisation Centre (RTMC), where I was issued my *black bag* clothing for operations. This included items of kit such as boots, antimicrobial underpants (designed to be worn for days at a time), sleeping systems, load carrying equipment and Osprey body armour.

Some of this kit was frankly rubbish or, as The Colour Sergeant would have defined it, *locker layout only,* such as the ridiculous extreme cold weather mittens, wristlets and facemask. As a skier I knew a thing or two about cold weather equipment. This stuff wouldn't have made it onto my kit list for a day on the nursery slopes in Meribel. Even the storeman who issued them to me seemed embarrassed by these items, saying I didn't need to take them if I didn't want to.

But for the most part the kit was of excellent quality. Upgrades included the new Personal Clothing System (PCS) – a tougher, more comfortable and efficient combat uniform that can be easily adapted to suit the many different environments troops face on the front line. PCS included shorts, trousers, shirts, a windproof smock and UBACS, shirts specially designed for wearing under the new Osprey body armour that has replaced ECBA. The whole system had been well thought through and designed utilising developments in material technology to provide both thermal insulation and sweat wicking properties. It included touches like the use of Velcro instead of buttons for greater comfort under body armour, and pockets positioned so that they could still be accessed when wearing body armour.

This kit was referred to as the *black bag* issue because it included a black operational travel bag. Its 80 litre capacity was not nearly sufficient for all my new equipment. It took several trips to load it all into my father's little Citroen. Since I could take with me only what I could carry, using my rucksack and the new operational travel bag, it was not going to be possible to take everything with which I had just been issued.

It seemed to me that the pendulum had swung too far in the opposite direction. Unlike poor Sergeant Roberts, who had suffered so many kit shortages that he had told his wife in an audio diary *we know we are going to go to war without the correct equipment*, I now had so much equipment that I could not possibly take it all to war with me.

Latitude:	51.27
Longitude:	-0.74
Elevation:	80m
Met:	Sunny to partly cloudy H:3°L:-1°
DTG:	251410ZJAN12

TWENTY-FOUR HOURS prior to deploying I was required to report to Lille Barracks in Aldershot to join the rest of the headquarters group and endure one final documentation check. From there we would travel by coach to RAF Brize Norton in Oxfordshire where a trooping flight would take us first to RAF Akrotiri in Cyprus, then on to Camp Bastion. There we would undergo a week of RSOI, Reception, Staging and Onward Integration training, before flying by Chinook helicopter to Main Operating Base (MOB) Price on the south-western outskirts of Gereshk. This would be our home for the next nine months.

Sgt Herbert Sebukima of the London Regiment, himself a veteran of Afghanistan, volunteered to drive me from our regimental headquarters in Battersea to Lille Barracks. Seb and I were old friends and I had spent many hours in his company on training exercises the length and breadth of the country. We'd spoken many times about Afghanistan and I'd drawn extensively on his experiences and advice in preparing myself for this moment. It seemed fitting that he should escort me on this final leg of my journey as a reservist and deliver me into the care of the regular army.

Just before we set off I used my camera phone to take a selfie. It was not a flattering portrait but it accurately reflected my mood. I appear tired and apprehensive, pale skin drawn tight across my cheekbones, dark circles under my eyes and deep lines at their corners. There is a tightness to my unsmiling, bloodless lips that I do not recognise.

I'd spent nearly two years preparing for this moment. Now it had finally arrived I wasn't sure I was ready – or even if it was such a good idea after all. I was plagued with doubts about my capability and suitability for the venture ahead. Did I have the courage and selfless commitment, those values so highly prized by the British Army, to see this through?

The values and standards of the army are different from those of the rest of society. This is because soldiers have *the legal right to use lethal force, and may be required to lay down their own lives and risk those of their comrades.* These are big asks that rightly set

140

soldiers apart from the society they serve. Given everything I'd learned about the Upper Gereshk Valley, the nature of the operations we would be conducting, and the training we'd undertaken in preparation, it seemed probable that I was going to be put to the test. While I certainly aspired to the qualities of courage and selfless commitment, I was concerned that I would fall short.

But I wasn't about to share my last minute jitters with Seb. Distracted by these thoughts I suspect I was not good company on the drive. Perhaps recalling his own deployment, Seb made no effort to interrupt my reverie and most of the journey passed in silence.

We arrived in Aldershot to find Lille Barracks deserted. The rest of the staff, having already completed their documentation checks, had been stood down and I was greeted less than warmly by a clerk who was awaiting my arrival so that he might clock off for the day himself. It took less than thirty minutes to complete my movement control check point (MCCP), which was no surprise to me. The Adjutant General's Corp, the army's human resources specialists are of the firm conviction that documents cannot be checked too often and I'd already completed both a pre-MCCP and an MCCP rehearsal in recent days. We would be required to go through the process one more time on arrival at RAF Brize Norton. The RAF, being a different uniformed service from the army, would naturally want to do checks of their own.

There was one form however that I'd not seen before. In it I was required to complete details of height, weight, build, eye and hair colour along with any distinguishing features, such as scars and tattoos that, in the event of my death, would readily identify my body to others. I was also required to provide a *proof of life* question – a question to which, if kidnapped, only I would know the answer.

On the spur of the moment I choose the number plate of my Dad's old car – which must have been recycled into yoghurt pot tops many years ago.

For some reason I've never been able to remember the registration plates of the many cars I've owned over the years but my Dad's orange Ford Escort estate in which I'd passed my test the year Niki Lauda won his third F1 Grand Prix title has always stayed with me. This question would be used in the event that hostage negotiators required my captors to provide proof I was still alive or, if a rescue attempt was mounted, that the Special Forces rescue team would ask me to confirm my identity.

I was reminded of the question Harry had asked months before about what would happen to me if I got captured. Well now I had some answers. They weren't especially reassuring.

My MCCP complete the clerk cheerfully informed me that my next report was at 01.00 the following morning – before heading out the door at a gallop, just in case I had any other questions that might detain him further. I can't say I blamed him. It was a little after 2pm (14.00 in military speak) and I had 11 hours to kill with nowhere to go and nothing to do. The army has a maxim *Hurry up and wait* with which I was more than familiar, but this was stretching things to new limits. I went in search of some company but the camp seemed deserted.

Aimlessly wandering through the many empty office blocks I eventually came across Major Dave Groom who was catching up on some paperwork. I'd briefly met Dave on one of my previous visits to Lille Barracks but I knew him better from the pages of Skid Dorney's book, *The Killing Zone*. On that tour Dave had hitched a ride on a US convoy that came under repeated attack by the Taliban. The Humvee[1] that he was travelling in was destroyed when it detonated a hidden IED and the driver was seriously injured. Dave, badly shaken himself by the explosion, administered morphine to the driver and successfully coordinated his extraction by Chinook helicopter – but not before he'd cleared a safe lane in the minefield while still under fire, using the tip of his bayonet to gently prod the ground for further devices.

In those vital moments when lives were at stake and others around him had hesitated, Dave's actions had exemplified the values and standards of the British Army. In similar circumstances, would I be able to follow his example?

On this tour Dave would not be deploying to Afghanistan but would remain in the UK to co-ordinate the repatriation of our dead and wounded. We chatted for a few minutes but it was clear that he wanted to get on with whatever had brought him into the office in the first place. After wishing me well he dismissed me with some sage advice:

[1] **HMMWV (Humvee)**: High Mobility Multipurpose Wheeled Vehicle

Get a fucking pistol as soon as you get out there mate and keep one in the chamber at all times.

Even though this was a serious breach of regulations – British policy was not to carry weapons with a chambered round inside protected bases – I followed Dave's advice from the outset. The threat of *green on blue*, attacks on ISAF soldiers by members of the Afghan security forces, persuaded me that he was right. The consistent thread that seemed to run through the reports on these attacks was that they were unexpected, perpetrated by individuals who, for the most part, had not previously aroused concerns or suspicions. In the event that I needed to use my weapon in such circumstances I didn't want to waste vital seconds cocking it first.

Unlike the Browning, the pistol that had failed Sgt Roberts in his moment of need back in 2003, the Sig Sauer incorporates a de-cocking lever that allows the weapon to be safely holstered with a round in the chamber. There were one or two Brownings still in circulation in Afghanistan but I made sure I was issued with a Sig.

I didn't discuss Dave's advice with anyone else, but I suspect I was not the only person to flout regulations in this way.

Somehow I managed to while away a few more hours before deciding to go in search of food. The mess and cookhouse were both closed and I didn't fancy anything on offer in the vending machines outside the junior ranks club. Still dressed in my new MTP uniform I walked into Northcamp, the little run of shops that serves the military community to the north of the Basingstoke canal. I'd served in Aldershot many years before and recalled a café where we'd enjoyed many a hung-over Sunday morning bragging about our drunken exploits and conquests of the night before. The greasy spoon had gone, replaced with a smart new block of low-rise flats with boutique shops beneath. A short distance away was a small wine bar, also new, which I presumed served the residents of the flats. There was little to recommend it other than its name – 'Harry's' – but that was good enough for me.

As part of my influence training I'd studied Abraham Maslow's *Theory of Human Motivation*. Counter-insurgency (COIN) doctrine sets great store in first understanding and then winning the hearts and minds of the local population. Maslow's theory was a popular tool not only because it simplifies a complex problem but also because it's illustrated with a handy pyramid diagram. The most fundamental physiological needs are at the base of the pyramid and the more complex needs of self-actualisation at the top. In order to achieve one's full potential, Maslow argued that one must first fulfil the lower order needs. Before I could deal with the self-doubt that had been nagging at the corners of my mind all day, I first needed to meet those physiological needs, food, water, warmth, rest and free wi-fi.

It turned out that Harry's more than adequately provided these resources and I hid my uniformed self away in a small alcove at the back of the bar. I resisted the strong and sudden urge to get blind drunk - it would certainly help pass the time but might not play well with the RAF at my next documentation check. Instead, having finished my meal I justified my continued presence with coffee top-ups at regular intervals until it was closing time.

Even without all the caffeine now sloshing around in my system I reckoned it was going to be a sleepless night.

Latitude:	51.27
Longitude:	-0.74
Elevation:	80m
Met:	Partly cloudy H:3°L:-1°
DTG:	252300ZJAN12

I RETURNED TO the barracks to find a group of soldiers standing around their bergans, like so many girls at a school disco, quietly chatting and smoking, their cigarettes glowing in the dark as they patiently waited for the transport to RAF Brize Norton. A voice addressed me from the shadows:

Good of you to make it, Chris.

It was the Adjutant, Captain Rupert Stevens. Rupert had been one of the first Grenadiers I'd met almost two years ago and although he'd always been supportive of my ambition to mobilise with the battalion, that didn't mean he was averse to a bit of squaddie banter. He informed me that our trooping flight was scheduled for 07.00 the following morning but as this was 'Crab Air', army slang for the Royal Air Force, this was not a departure time but a *no move before* time. In his opinion it was anyone's guess when we might eventually take off.

Rivalry and deep cultural differences between the armed services ensured that Rupert, like all self-respecting soldiers, did not have a kind word to say about the RAF. Still there was some truth behind his comments. The RAF was trying to maintain a busy air bridge between the UK and Afghanistan using an ageing fleet of Lockheed TriStar aircraft. These had first come into service in 1978 as commercial airliners operated by Pan American Airways who subsequently sold them to the RAF shortly after the Falklands War.

After 34 years of service the TriStar was showing its age and, a bit like myself, was only just about fit for purpose.

Troops had become resigned to long delays in the journey to and from Afghanistan. It's also fair to say that the RAF, unlike the aircraft's original owner, is not a customer focussed organisation and puts little thought into the welfare of its passengers. We would all spend many hours experiencing RAF hospitality and it was never enjoyable. Disparaging comments not only helped to pass the time but also managed expectation.

Some months later a much publicised visit to Afghanistan by James Blunt and Catherine Jenkins was cancelled after the TriStar in which they were travelling was forced to abort and return to Cyprus, not once but twice, with first an air leak and then a problem with the undercarriage. James Blunt, himself a former soldier, was not impressed and wrote an uncomplimentary article in The Telegraph which delighted the rank and file but angered the top brass, who disputed his claims of military incompetence. For Rupert, who had been tasked with organising this visit and who had boasted for days about his self-appointed role as Catherine Jenkins' personal assistant, this would only serve to confirm his already very low opinion of the RAF.

Ironically, despite his obvious frustration, the RAF had actually done James a favour. So far as I could tell, Rupert had invested considerable time and effort preparing a detailed and comprehensive visit programme for Catherine in which he intended personally to take care of her every need and desire. By contrast he'd assumed 'Blunty' would doss down in the honking transit accommodation and sort himself out.

01.00 came and went with no sign of the coaches. No one seemed to mind terribly much and we continued chatting in our little groups as the grass turned white with frost around us. It was bitterly cold but since none of my colleagues, not even Tom, seemed to have noticed, I wasn't about to bring it up. Nor did they seem to share my own sense of foreboding. The group appeared relaxed, almost carefree. It would have been hard to tell that these men, only a few hours previously, had said goodbye to their families and were setting off to a war with which they were already familiar and which had claimed the lives of friends and colleagues.

Some, like Captain Paddy Rice, even bore the scars of previous deployments. Paddy, described by The Telegraph in 2009 as the *luckiest soldier in Afghanistan,* had narrowly escaped death when he was targeted by a Taliban sniper. The bullet had entered just below his left shoulder blade, travelled across his back and exited by his right ear. Paddy had calmly lit a cigarette before radioing in his own *nine liner*[1] requesting immediate medical evacuation to Camp Bastion.

---

[1] **Nine Liner**: Medical evacuation request, so called because of the nine point reporting format

A gunshot wound is an almost guaranteed ticket home and a lesser man might have chosen to convalesce in the UK but Paddy was back on duty just three weeks later. With *nothing to do all day but sit around smoking*, Paddy reckoned Camp Bastion hospital had been bad for his health. So he'd volunteered to return to his unit as soon as possible.

Eventually someone went in search of some news and a short while later an ancient Ford Fiesta screeched up. It was Dave Kenny, our Chief of Staff, who would not be deploying for another few months. He jumped out, talking urgently into a mobile phone. Looking thoroughly harassed, he explained that there'd been a SNAFU and the coach was booked for the following day. It was now close to 2am and he was trying to organise some alternative transport. Not unreasonably, everyone who might be able to assist him was tucked up asleep in bed.

He jumped back into the Fiesta, phone still clamped to his ear and roared away, wheels spinning, to return half an hour later with a couple of minibuses and two bleary-eyed drivers. Somehow, with Dave clucking about us like a mother hen, we managed to load all our gear and ourselves into these vehicles. Packed like sardines, we set off at breakneck speed.

Barrelling down the motorway in an overloaded minibus in the dead of night was not quite how I'd imagined myself setting off to war.

Latitude:	34.58
Longitude:	32.99
Elevation:	8m
Met:	Low cloud, torrential showers H:14°L:3°
DTG:	261200BJAN12

RAF AKROTIRI IN Cyprus is 2077 miles from RAF Brize Norton and 1807 miles from Camp Bastion. I know this because it says as much on a large sign on the wall of the transit lounge.

Typical of RAF hospitality the lounge is not quite large enough for all of the TriStar's 266 passengers and there are not quite enough comfy chairs and sofas for everyone to sit down. In one corner there is a 'Burco' boiler which angrily spits scalding water into meagre plastic cups for those brave enough to use it and thirsty enough to drink the bitter instant coffee on offer. A couple of vending machines and a small shop selling overpriced Cypriot souvenirs – the closest any of us will get to the real Cyprus – complete the airport retail offering. Along one wall are four or five computer terminals with internet access but not all of these work and the connection is maddeningly slow. There are a couple of disinterested RAF ground crew manning a reception desk, who periodically shout instructions across the hall that everyone else makes a point of ignoring. It smells of unwashed men. Overall I get the impression that just the bare minimum amount of effort has been made because no one really gives a shit. I'm grateful to the RAF that we've made it this far, but I feel as if we're just so much cargo.

Our journey has not been without incident. At Brize Norton there was a near mutiny when we were informed that cabin baggage would not be allowed and all bags must go in the hold. The RAF ground crew were belligerently adamant, even when one or two of our lads appealed to them, pointing out that their laptops and other personal items were unlikely to survive the journey in the hold.

No reason was provided for this decision.

The Grenadiers were unanimous in their opinion.

The RAF are all cunts.

As I handed over my cabin bag, having first emptied the contents into the pockets of my combat uniform, I was inclined to agree.

We came in to land six hours later in a torrential downpour. Air turbulence battered the aircraft as we started our approach and I stared anxiously out the window, watching the runway turn into a river before my eyes. I was convinced the pilot would have to pull up but he pressed on and dumped the aircraft onto the tarmac with a bump. We hurtled down the runway in a cloud of spray. I waited, helpless, for the aircraft to start aquaplaning, but it didn't happen.

The pilot was obviously a good one. It seems the Grenadiers are mistaken, not *all* the RAF are cunts.

Most of the rest of the day was spent confined in the transit lounge waiting for news of our onward journey. We had been scheduled to stop just long enough for the aircraft to be refuelled, but the bowser had come and gone and we had not re-embarked. Clearly there was a problem, but no one was letting on.

To escape the throng, I wandered through a door marked *No Exit from transit lounge* that had been left ajar to allow a little air to circulate. Taking a walk around the terminal building I got a few funny looks but no one challenged me and eventually I found an empty but well-appointed room that I reckoned must be the VIP lounge. I retrieved my netbook, external hard drive and noise cancelling headphones from the voluminous inner pockets of my combat jacket, kicked off my boots and stretched out on an enormous sofa to watch a movie.

Some while later I was gently woken by a kindly looking Cypriot lady of indeterminate age towing a red 'Happy Henry' vacuum cleaner. Henry, as he always does, seemed pleased to see me but the kindly cleaning lady swept her arm around the room.

You no can stay here.

Her broken English was still much better than my Greek. Coming to my senses I felt the panic rising in my gullet.

Shit! I've missed the fucking plane! Fuckity-fuck the fucking fuckers have fucking left without me. Bastard-bollocks! Fuck!

At least I was beginning to sound a little more like a soldier.

I profusely thanked the cleaning lady, who appeared unperturbed by my outburst, retied my boots and beat a hasty retreat.

To my very great relief my absence had gone unnoticed. The lounge was a little smellier, tempers were a little shorter, but the TriStar was still exactly where I'd left it on the tarmac outside the terminal building.

One of the brakes had seized on landing and, despite their best efforts, the engineers had been unable to release it. They were now waiting on a replacement part to be flown out from the UK, which would not arrive for another 24 hours. We were going nowhere anytime soon.

Hurry up and wait.

As we waited, men we were due to relieve in one of the most heavily contested parts of Helmand Province were still fighting and dying.

From what should have been my first day in Afghanistan to my last on 24 September 2012, thirty-six British servicemen would be killed in action. Lance Corporal Gajbahadur Gurung from the Royal Gurkha Rifles was the first of these brave men, killed in a gun battle with insurgents while we waited in the airless confines of the RAF Akrotiri departure lounge. His Commanding Officer said:

He died as he lived, at the heart of the action, taking the fight to the enemy and resolute in the face of danger.

Latitude:	31.86
Longitude:	64.19
Elevation:	883m
Met:	Sunny H:12°L:-2°
DTG:	282130DJAN12

TWO DAYS LATER, and almost two years after the start of my own journey, we finally begin our descent into Camp Bastion.

I find myself sitting next to Tom. This will be his second tour and he tells me that we will shortly be asked to don helmets and body armour. In the cramped aircraft this is easier said than done. The new Osprey body armour is designed to be fitted with a series of accessories including med pack, ammunition, water bottle and grenade pouches. With all this kit hanging off our bodies we can barely sit down again in our seats, let alone fasten the safety belts.

Tom cheerfully points out that we're going through this routine not because it will provide us with any meaningful protection from anti-aircraft fire, nor improve our chances of survival in the event the aircraft is brought down by a surface to air missile. In Tom's view both scenarios are highly improbable. The real reason for our discomfort, he informs me, is because the journos love writing about this moment in their dispatches from the front line. It also helps to make the REMFs[1], who never leave Camp Bastion, feel a little bit closer to the action.

A short while later the cabin lights are extinguished and we begin our descent in total black-out. All RAF trooping flights into Camp Bastion are timed to arrive and depart under cover of darkness. I'd been told this was a political decision based on focus groups and opinion polls back in the UK. These had revealed that the British public's waning commitment to the Afghan war would evaporate entirely if a TriStar with passengers and crew were shot down over Helmand. Taking off and landing in darkness helped to mitigate this risk.

There may even be some truth to this. US trooping flights are not constrained in this way. Then again Tom's theory may be just as valid. As if to prove his point, Tom falls asleep almost as soon as the lights have gone out and doesn't stir again until after we have landed.

[1] **REMF**: Rear Echelon Mother Fucker

Camp Bastion is situated in a remote desert area north-west of Lashkar Gah, the capital of Helmand Province. It is the main ISAF military base in the region and the logistics hub for military operations in Helmand. Four miles long by two miles wide, it is a vast tented metropolis with accommodation for 28,000 people and is served by a busy international airport and heliport, a state of the art trauma hospital, water bottling plant, recycling centre, fire station and police force. It even has its own bus service.

Divided into four sections, illogically titled Bastion 1, Bastion 2, Bastion 3 and Bastion Zero, each quarter has its own fast food outlets, coffee shops, restaurants and supermarkets as well as air conditioned gymnasia and internet cabins. There is even a bar called 'Heroes' where servicemen can enjoy a non-alcoholic beverage while watching Sky sports on giant flat-screen TV's.

This vast complex is located no more than 60 kilometres north of the Helmand frontline on the Kandahar–Herat Highway. Troops are protected by 40 kilometres of perimeter fencing topped with triple concertina barbed wire. Behind this sit concrete blast walls, watch towers, a sea of razor wire that is subject to an array of radars, CCTV cameras and motion detectors, all patrolled 24 hours a day by heavily armed, Oakley adorned RAF Regiment soldiers.

Troops were not required to carry weapons inside the Bastion perimeter. The vast majority would never see contact with the enemy. For many the greatest danger they would face during their tour would be a bollocking from the Camp Sergeant Major. All this was about to change, but at the time, Camp Bastion felt like the safest place in the world.

Latitude:	31.86
Longitude:	64.19
Elevation:	883m
Met:	Sunny H:10°L:-2°
DTG:	302055DJAN12

BASTION 2 WAS our temporary home for the next week as we completed the RSOI programme. There was no time to waste and, despite our late-night arrival, this started before dawn the very next morning. In a Facebook posting to friends and family a little before 9pm on 30 January I tried to find some levity in our situation:

We are currently undergoing in-theatre training before we move to our forward base. This mostly involves getting up at 5am so we can practise stumbling about in the dark for a few hours. I'm especially good at this. As the temporary accommodation we are staying in is next to the helipad we also practise sleeping while helo's take off and land in close proximity. I'm less good at this. The rest of the time we are mostly left to ourselves.

The reality was a little a different. RSOI was the final element of our preparation for operations and was designed to improve our life expectancy and our chances of returning home to our loved ones intact. Not everyone present would be so lucky.

Having conducted most of our training in a bitterly cold British winter, it was also a chance to acclimatise to the bitterly cold Afghan winter. The key point of difference for me being that I had swapped my old and bulky sleeping bag that had served me so well after Jane had cleared out the house in Dulwich for a new lightweight bag that I'd been issued at RTMC. It would be another few weeks before the mercury would begin to rise into double digits. In the meantime we regularly endured sub-zero night-time temperatures. I would don my *Jacket and Trousers thermal, reversible olive/sand with Stuff Bag*, also newly issued, before climbing into the cruelly thin bag each night but I would still wake most mornings before dawn, shivering uncontrollably.

During RSOI this hardly mattered as we were all required to be up at stupid o'clock in order to complete the crowded daily schedule. This included presentations on a range of subjects such as detainee handling and sexual health, as well as practical hands-on training in yet another specially constructed Afghan ghost village. Much of the package was a repeat of lessons   learned in Thetford and Canada but crucially our instructors and mentors were all soldiers who were coming to the end of their own tours and were therefore current on all the latest equipment and threats.

Given the strict no sex rule imposed on British troops while in theatre I was surprised to be receiving a lesson on sexual health until the presenter explained:

Don't think you're going to be getting any out here. But I know you mucky lot have all spent the last two weeks hero-shagging your way around Aldershot.

I wondered if this included the two Lieutenant Colonels in her audience.

She was a fierce looking nurse who clearly took great pride in her work. Her presentation included a grim collection of photographs of penises in various states of decay which were excruciating even to look at. Each new slide drew increasingly vocal gasps and groans of dismay from her audience.

Not all the briefings were quite so riveting and on one occasion I had to leave my seat and stand at the back of the briefing tent to prevent myself from falling asleep. From this vantage point I was amused to discover that another member of the audience had taken a different course of action. Rather than attempt to resist sleep, as I had done, he had embraced its inevitability. Invisible to presenter and audience behind some large cardboard pallets containing mosquito repellent, foot powder and sun screen, he was lying face down fast asleep on the floor.

A good proportion of RSOI was devoted to counter-IED (C-IED) training, much of which was spent on the Vallon Lane. The Vallon is the ruggedised metal detector that is used to identify concealed improvised explosive devices and, as the name suggests, the Vallon Lane is where troops conduct practical search training. More than once I made errors, over-confirming a device on one occasion and on another inadvertently straying out of the safe lane I'd marked.

It was sobering to realise that the next time I used the Vallon it would be for real. If I made the same mistakes again it was unlikely I would get a third chance.

The practical training was backed up by a classroom session

delivered by the EOD (Explosive Ordnance Disposal) and Search Task Force Squadron Sergeant Major. Throughout his presentation he repeatedly stressed that we had both the skills and the equipment to defeat the IED threat.

Despite his assurances, there were just too many names on the EOD memorial outside the classroom to convince me of this.

By 2012 the IED was the insurgents' weapon of choice, and the number one cause of death of ISAF troops, forcing soldiers into protected mobility (PM) vehicles and severely constraining our freedom of movement. According to a US report published in May 2012, the number of IEDs used in Afghanistan had increased by 400% since 2007. The number of troops killed by them had also increased by 400%, and those wounded by 700%.

Afghanistan, Cambodia and Angola are considered by experts to be the three most heavily mined countries in the world and many of the IEDs we would encounter were constructed from legacy mines or other abandoned munitions such as artillery shells, left behind by the Russians when they pulled out in 1989. The Taliban had become experts in repurposing these for their own ends. They had also developed their own bomb making capabilities.

Although extremely diverse in design, every IED is made up of three major components: the main charge, the trigger and the power source. Afghan IEDs also typically contained fragmentation generating objects such as nails, ball bearings and even small rocks to cause wounds at greater distances. These were referred to as *shipyard confetti.*

As well as scavenging military grade munitions the insurgents also manufactured their own home-made explosive (HME). Typically made using a nitrogen-based fertiliser such as ammonium nitrate mixed with either sugar (ANS), fuel oil (ANFO) or aluminium (ANAL). This last was a particular favourite with our EOD[1] Officer, Captain Pete Fahy who always enjoyed raising the subject of ANAL in his daily IED threat update briefings. Despite the deadly nature of his subject matter expertise, this never failed to generate a schoolboy snicker from his audience as he intended.

---

[1] **EOD**: Explosive Ordnance Disposal

In keeping with the dark humour that sustains the British Army, Pete and his team wore t-shirts that stated: *EOD Tech, if you see me running try to keep up.*

The most commonly used trigger mechanism we encountered was the pressure plate where the device is initiated by the subject creating a contact between two metal plates, referred to as the PPIED (Pressure Plate IED) or VOIED (Victim Operated IED). IEDs using a pressure plate are highly indiscriminate and are frequently initiated by local nationals or their livestock rather than the soldiers for whom they were intended. In some cases they are even inadvertently triggered by the emplacer. Pete would refer to these own goals as *self-resolving bomb-tech removal* and it never failed to raise morale when we learned that a bomber had been maimed or killed by his own handiwork. However, triggers were not confined to pressure plates. More sophisticated devices often incorporated consumer electronic components from mobile phones, pagers, clock radios and timers.

In addition to the main charge and the trigger, every IED must also incorporate a power source to initiate the device, most commonly a battery pack of some kind. The modern infantry solider carries with him many items of kit which require a power source and it was often the case that our own discarded batteries were used against us by the insurgents. In a cruelly ironic twist even the batteries used to power the Vallon mine detector had been discovered in IEDs. Despite constant reminders to dispose of batteries only at designated collection points inside secure areas, military issue batteries continued to be a feature of IEDs throughout our tour. Given that batteries were easy enough to acquire or purchase locally, it always struck me that using our own batteries against us was not a necessity but a deliberate and cynical attempt to lower our morale.

If this was the case, it certainly had the desired effect.

The IED war was ruthlessly Darwinian. As soon as we developed tactics or equipment to counter a particular threat the insurgents would alter their own IED designs to defeat them. ISAF had invested millions, perhaps billions of dollars in developing protected mobility vehicles which had undoubtedly saved many lives. But no vehicle can be 100% safe and at some point soldiers must leave the relative safety of the vehicle and move on foot.

Once dismounted we would be dependent on the Vallon mine detector, and our own 'spider senses', to protect us.

To my mind the Vallon operators were the real heroes in Afghanistan. Although every soldier, regardless of rank must be proficient in its use, these men were specialists who took considerable personal risk swinging the Vallon from left to right in front of them as they cleared a safe lane ahead of troops. All volunteers, they were often exposed and vulnerable to small arms fire as they performed this most dangerous of tasks.

It takes nerves of steel to clear a safe lane knowing that one mistake, one momentary lapse in concentration, could prove fatal.

To make matters worse, to try and outwit the Vallon, Taliban bomb makers were producing low metal content devices which were much harder to detect. The Vallon man, or 'Swinger' had to develop a highly sophisticated ear to distinguish between a false alarm caused by heavily mineralised soil and an alarm caused by a metallic foreign body which might or might not be an IED component. The consequences of incorrect identification were obvious. It was exhausting, nerve shredding work.

The Vallon men not only accepted great personal risk in performing this task but also shouldered a huge burden of responsibility to keep the rest of the team safe. It was not a job I would have volunteered for and I had nothing but awe and admiration for these men, to whom I undoubtedly owe my life and my limbs.

Many people were of the opinion that the IED was a cowardly and despicable weapon and that using them in some way diminished the Taliban's moral authority, but to my mind this was just so much propaganda. Although the use of anti-personnel mines was banned by international law in 1999, the British had included them in their weapons arsenal happily enough up until that point. Consequently I didn't feel we had any right to the moral high ground on this one.

Personally I couldn't see much difference between an IED and an Apache attack helicopter, other than money and technology. Both allow the protagonist to kill or maim his adversary while standing off at a safe distance and both periodically kill innocent victims. I reckoned the Taliban used IEDs not because they were inherently evil, but because they did not have access to a fleet of attack helicopters.

Latitude:	31.86
Longitude:	64.19
Elevation:	883m
Met:	Mostly sunny H:9°L:-2°
DTG:	020750DFEB12

DURING THE LAST few days of RSOI our Rear Operations Group (ROG), led by Major Gordon Gask began planning our move forward to MOB Price. It quickly became apparent that the anticipated transport by Chinook helicopter would not be possible as all the British Chinooks were undergoing vital maintenance and repairs.

In July 2009, an increasingly embattled Prime Minister, Gordon Brown persistently denied that British troops in Afghanistan lacked sufficient helicopters. Unable publicly to contradict his political master, the head of the army, General Sir Richard Dannatt, in an audacious PR stunt, chose to travel in an American helicopter to visit British troops in Sangin. When questioned by the media about his travel arrangements, General Dannatt replied: *Self-evidently... if I moved in an American helicopter it's because I haven't got a British helicopter.*

It was not the first time General Dannatt had put the needs of soldiers under his command before his own personal ambitions and he was a much loved and admired commander as a result. He may not actually have risked his life as Dave Groom had done to save a wounded comrade, but he had put lives before his own career in a true act of selfless commitment. One can only imagine how his subsequent meeting might have gone with the Prime Minister, whose mercurial temper and sudden mood swings have been widely documented. We will never know what was said but The Sunday Times subsequently reported that Gordon Brown personally intervened to block General Dannatt's promotion from head of the army to head of all three armed services.

Following this heavily publicised incident a hastily convened cross-party Commons Defence Select Committee reported that: *the lack of helicopters is having adverse consequences for operations today and, in the longer term, will severely impede the ability of the UK Armed Forces to deploy... Operational commanders find they have to use ground transport, when helicopter lift would be preferred, both for the outcome and for the protection of our forces.*

The committee stopped short of saying that British soldiers' lives were needlessly put at risk because of a shortage of helicopters but David Cameron pronounced it nonetheless:

A scandal.

Three years and a general election later David Cameron was now presiding over the same scandal – or so it seemed to me when I learned that we were, as the Defence Select Committee had observed, *to use ground transport when helicopter lift would be preferred.*

I was not alone in this view and was more than a little rattled by the reaction of many of my more seasoned colleagues when the news was announced. There was a palpable sense of disbelief and disquiet amongst these battle hardened soldiers. They understood the risks far better than any Prime Minister or Commons committee.

As if to add insult to injury, not only were there no British helicopters but, due to a shortage of qualified drivers, there were no British mine-resistant vehicles either. We would have to hitch a ride on a Danish convoy. Some considered this the silver lining in what was otherwise bad news, after all the Danes used MRAP (Mine Resistant, Ambush Protected) vehicles that had been loaned to them by the US Marine Corps. These were highly respected with an excellent safety record, second only to the British Mastiff[1].

The following morning, bathed in sweat and a thin coating of dust, we staggered up the dirt road with all our worldly possessions to Camp Viking, the Danish enclave within the vast desert base from where our journey would commence. With my knees buckling under the combined weight of body armour, helmet, assault rifle, Sig Sauer pistol, ammunition, 120 litre bergan and 80 litre operational travel bag, I walked under the impressive wooden arch, complete with Viking shields and longship sails, that spans Camp Viking's front gate.

There I joined Captain 'Stumpy' Keeley. A lifelong Grenadier and veteran of many conflicts, Stumpy was a legend. Having first joined the Grenadier Guards as a boy solider in 1984 he'd risen to the rank of Regimental Sergeant Major before taking a commission. In 2011 he'd been awarded an MBE in recognition of his loyal service. There was little that Stumpy had not already seen and done in his 28 years as an infantry soldier.

---

[1] **Mastiff**: A heavily armoured 6 x six-wheel-drive patrol vehicle which carries eight troops, plus two crew.

He certainly knew a bad idea when he saw one and at that moment he had *bad idea* written all over his face.

He nodded darkly in the direction of a lightly armoured flatbed truck carrying a shipping container and informed me that we would not be travelling in MRAPs as we had first thought but in a *mobile fucking shower unit.*

I instantly understood his meaning. The container on the back of the vehicle looked exactly like a Tactical Base Ablution Unit (TBAU). This contained three showers, three toilets, three washbasins and a urinal in a unit that conformed to intermodal shipping container specifications, so that it could be easily deployed to even the most remote locations. The TBAU not only significantly improved hygiene standards, reducing cases of D&V, but also indulged the British squaddie's love of often hilarious, sometimes vile, toilet graffiti. It was a vital source of Chuck Norris[1] facts but it was not, as Stumpy had so eloquently observed, the best mode of transport for the Kandahar–Herat Highway, one of the most dangerous stretches of tarmac on the planet.

David Cameron was right. This was a scandal. Although, given the fact that we would all be shitting ourselves, the toilets would certainly come in handy.

Word got around that this was to be our ride and a small but incredulous crowd of British soldiers gathered around the vehicle as its Danish crew prepared for departure. Eventually a Danish soldier climbed onto the flatbed, opened a small door at the front of the container and lowered a steel cable ladder to the ground. We took it in turns to climb the ladder and squeeze ourselves through the tiny door like so many Greeks heading for Troy.

Selfishly, I hung back to ensure that I was the last to ascend. Infantry work is best suited to men of physical stature and many of my colleagues had spent long hours in the gym preparing their bodies for the rigours of close quarter combat. A quick appraisal of that tiny door

---

[1] **Chuck Norris facts:** Deliberately absurd facts focussing on Chuck Norris's virility, manliness and all-round heroism. Major Uffe Pederson, the battlegroup's Danish Deputy Commander regularly travelled around in an unarmoured 4x4 vehicle which he would drive himself. This contravened regulations and exposed him to considerable risk from IEDs but it also drew grudging admiration and respect. The vehicle quickly came to be known as the *Chucknorrismobile*, imbuing it with Chuck Norris' invincibility.

and their strapping frames was enough to convince me that I wanted to be first in the queue for the exit if things started going pear-shaped.

At the top of the ladder, I peered inside the container and, as my eyes adjusted to the gloom, was relieved to see that I was not entering an ablution block but an armoured box. Instead of showers there were seats for everyone laid out like a miniature cinema, except there was no screen and each of the seats had a sturdy looking three-point harness. Once we were all secured, our Danish hosts closed the door and locked it from the inside. We sat in nervous silence. I had the only seat with a view, heavily distorted by thick armoured glass in an aperture no bigger than a postcard beside the door.

Things had moved on a bit since the sacking of Troy. It didn't take Stumpy's 28 years of combat experience to know this wasn't a good idea. To anyone with more than three brain cells it was obvious that going to war in a metal box on top of a flatbed truck was a sub-optimal state of affairs.

Latitude   31.80
Longitude   64.51
Elevation   834m
Met   Mostly sunny H:9°L:-2°
DTG   021100DFEB12

when senior policemen start
fucking your kids up the arse
it's time to take to the streets
in protest.

ANA: Afghan National Army
CF NES (N): Combined Force Nahr-E-Saraj (North)
WIA: Wounded in Action
NATO: North Atlantic Treaty Organisation
DFAC: Dining Facility
DG: District Governor
DCoP: District Chief of Police
AUP: Afghan Uniformed Police
GIRoA: The Government of the Islamic Republic of Afghanistan
DfID: Department for International Development
UAV: Unmanned Aerial Vehicle

MINISTRY OF DEFENCE ANNOUNCEMENT

Senior Aircraftman Ryan Tomlin. On Monday 13 February 2012, Senior Aircraftman Ryan Tomlin was fatally wounded by small arms fire from an insurgent attack while taking part in a partnered patrol in the Nad 'Ali district in central Helmand.

Sergeant Nigel Coupe, Corporal Jake Hartley, Private Anthony Frampton, Private Christopher Kershaw, Private Daniel Wade *and* **Private Daniel Wilford.** On Tuesday 6 March 2012, Sergeant Nigel Coupe, Corporal Jake Hartley, Private Anthony Frampton, Private Christopher Kershaw, Private Daniel Wade and Private Daniel Wilford were killed when their Warrior armoured fighting vehicle was struck by an improvised explosive device resulting, tragically, in the deaths of all six personnel.

Latitude:	31.80
Longitude:	64.51
Elevation:	834m
Met:	Mostly sunny H:9°L:-2°
DTG:	021100DFEB12

TWO HOURS LATER our vehicle stopped and a Danish face appeared at the little window mouthing that it was now safe to open the door.

We emerged into the sunlight relieved and delighted to be released from the confines of our metal coffin. It had been an unpleasant and nauseous experience but this was quickly forgotten in the obvious pleasure of having arrived without incident.

Nonetheless, Stumpy, who was to be the headquarters' J4 (Logistics) staff officer and whose responsibilities would include managing our transport requirements, vowed this would be the first and last time British troops would hitch a ride on the Danish death trap.

He was true to his word and I never saw the hideous contraption again. Nine months later, as we were planning our extraction back to the UK, I overheard him politely but firmly informing Colonel James that none of the Grenadiers would be travelling in *that mobile fucking shower unit*. It was a statement of intent that even the Commanding Officer would have been unwise to challenge.

We had arrived safely at Main Operating Base Price.

I clambered unsteadily down the steel cable ladder and stepped off the last rung into a fine powder of desert dust that enveloped my boots to the ankle. This dust was to be a constant feature of our lives for the next nine months. Fine as talcum powder it penetrated everything from electronics equipment to weapon systems, and quickly turned into a viscous brown slime in contact with liquids.

In the frequent sandstorms we endured in the early months of our tour the dust blocked out the sun for days at a time and we inhabited a surreal red-brown world. Nothing escaped its pervasiveness. Men would literally cry brown tears whenever their eyes were exposed for any length of time. Tom even complained that it put him off his stroke when masturbating, an activity in which we all presumably engaged, only with more discretion and possibly less frequency than Tom himself.

It didn't take me long to get to know my way around our new home. About 30 minutes to be precise. MOB Price had been built in the desert south-west of the strategically important city of Gereshk in the Nahr-E-Saraj district of Helmand Province. It was the main operating base for about 600 soldiers whose primary task was to provide security for the city and the immediate surrounding area.

Despite the large numbers living there, the base was surprisingly compact. One of the good things about MOB Price, unlike Camp Bastion, was that nothing was ever more than a short walk away.

Gereshk, or Girishk, is the district capital of Nahr-E-Saraj. Bounded to the south by the mighty Helmand River it lies some 120km north-west of Kandahar and is the centre of a rich agricultural region made fertile by a complex irrigation system fed by the Kajakai Dam 100 klicks[1] upriver.

The British are no strangers to Gereshk. In 1839, during the first Anglo-Afghan war, the city was occupied by soldiers of the British East India Company before being abandoned in 1842 following the massacre of Major General Lord Elphinstone's army, one of the worst disasters in British military history. Reoccupied in 1878 during the second Anglo-Afghan war, it was held until 1880 and the signing of the Gandamak Treaty. This restored Afghan sovereignty over internal affairs but ceded foreign relations and some frontier regions to British control.

Gereshk has a population of about 50,000, many of whom still hold a grudge against the British for occupying their city 130 years previously. A good few of them hold an additional grudge against the British for the more recent Russian occupation of the 1980s, on the basis that all infidels look the same so you can't really tell them apart. In truth the good people of Gereshk had an innate dislike and distrust of all outsiders. In this respect it was not unlike any market town of similar size in Great Britain.

According to many of the intelligence reports I read, *foreign fighters* were especially unpopular. It didn't matter which side of the conflict

---

[1] **Klick**: Kilometre

they were fighting on. British, Danish, American, Russian, Pakistani or Iranian, all were equally unwelcome. Even Afghan National Army (ANA) soldiers from the northern Dari speaking provinces of Afghanistan were considered by many to fall into this category.

Although MOB Price was basic it was still five star luxury compared to the Patrol Bases, but everything is relative. In this case the height of luxury was sharing a tent with eight others just a short walk from a TBAU but far enough away from the helipad that the tent didn't blow down every time a Chinook passed by.

But the greatest luxury of all was the laundry service. Every couple of days I would put my sweaty combats in a net bag and hand them over to a very pleasant man named Siyal Atar at the Price laundry. Siyal was one of a small number of local contractors, mostly interpreters, who accepted great personal risk working at MOB Price for the *khareji*[1] infidels. Almost all of those that I spoke to claimed to have received death threats and were understandably anxious about what would become of them when the British departed at the end of 2014 as David Cameron had directed.

Siyal's principal motivation for washing my smalls was love and I reckoned it was this higher purpose under which he laboured that accounted for his sunny disposition. As he explained to me, he was betrothed to a young woman of extraordinary beauty and talent. Before the marriage could go ahead however, her father had demanded an exorbitant *mahr,* or bride price, for his daughter. Working for the infidels was risky but lucrative and was his best chance of raising the funds he needed to win his bride before she was sold off to another suitor.

The ever cheerful Siyal would load my bag along with several dozen others into one of two enormous washing machines. 24 hours later my laundry would be ready for collection. A little damp perhaps, and over the course of time my clothes turned a homogeneous grey-green colour, as did everyone else's, but to my mind these were trivial gripes in the pursuit of true love.

Some time later I discovered that Siyal's real name was, in fact, Mohammed. When we were first introduced I misunderstood his

---

[1] **Khareji**: foreigner

cheery parting valediction, *siyal atar (see you later)* to be his name. He was kind enough never to correct me on this and so I continued to call him Siyal whenever we met.

At the centre of the base, inside its own perimeter fence, was a large tented complex accessed via two key-coded gates which housed the CF NES (N)[1] headquarters. This was the HQ we were due to take over in ten days time and was currently staffed by a Danish battlegroup commanded by Colonel Ken Knudsen. Over the course of the next few days Colonel Ken and his team would bring us up to speed in a series of handover/takeover presentations covering the tactical situation and the detailed minutiae of our daily working lives. Briefings complete there would be a period of a few days during which his team would babysit our first tentative steps in our new roles before relinquishing command and returning to their loved ones in Denmark.

The Danish army had led the ISAF effort in the district for over five years and had performed an outstanding job. Although they were all looking forward to getting home there was also an air of melancholy that Danish C2 (command and control) was coming to an end. More than a dozen staff officers would remain, together with a troop of tanks – the only tanks in Helmand – and an armoured infantry company, but still it was the end of an era for them.

During their time they had suffered 43 fatalities and 211 wounded in action (WIA). As we were to learn ourselves, giving up ground in which you have invested blood is a poignant and painful process. I regretfully suspect that in our eager haste to get on with the job we failed to empathise with our departing Danish colleagues.

However impressive the Ops complex appeared we would all quickly discover that the hub of the MOB Price universe was the Danish 'Kuffen' café, a little prefab building with some home-made decking adorned with a string of multicoloured Christmas lights. The Kuffen was run by some elderly Danish civilian volunteers who had vowed not to leave Afghanistan while ever there was a Danish soldier in need of coffee or liquorice. These, together with coarse filterless cigarettes, seem to be the main substances which sustain the Danish infantryman.

---

[1] **CF NES(N)**: Combined Force Nahr-E-Saraj (North)

Although the volunteers made it clear they didn't plan to hang around for any length of time after the Danish army had departed, meanwhile the Kuffen was open to all comers just so long as you liked your coffee the colour and consistency of crude oil.

As I grew accustomed to Danish coffee, elsewhere in Helmand Senior Aircraftman Ryan Tomlin was killed in a firefight with insurgents. I later attended his vigil service in Camp Bastion, where I heard for the first time words that I would come to memorise over the next nine months:

When You Go Home, Tell Them Of Us And Say,
For Your Tomorrow, We Gave Our Today

Latitude:	31.80
Longitude:	64.51
Elevation:	834m
Met:	Heavy showers H:8°L:-2°
DTG:	191100DFEB12

PRICE WAS A surprisingly cosmopolitan base. In addition to the combined Danish and British force of which we were part it was also home to Special Operations Task Force (West), a US Special Forces unit made up of Navy Seals and Army Rangers.

The SF guys were easy to spot due to their extreme facial hair and enormous physiques. They even managed to make Sarn't Major Glenn Haughton appear petite. It seemed it was not enough simply to pass the gruelling 26 week Navy Seal selection programme to serve with US SF in Afghanistan, a ZZ Top style beard was another essential precondition.

Protection of the base was provided by the Bosnian army. I had a lot of time for the Bosnians, after all they were keeping me safe as I slept in my bed at night. But, having served with the UN and NATO in Bosnia in the mid '90s, I couldn't help but wonder if any of the older guys had been my adversaries in that conflict.

I reasoned that it must be a sign of progress if men I'd been fighting two decades before were now my protectors.

In addition to the military presence, MOB Price was home to the Gereshk District Stabilisation Team. The DST was funded by the British Foreign and Commonwealth Office. It comprised a team of mixed nationalities including Americans, Brits, Danes and Afghans, who purported to be experts in stabilisation. To add to the cultural melange, camp logistics were run by a civilian contractor, KBR, who employed Malaysians, Indians and Filipinos amongst other nationalities.

For the most part we all jogged along together in relative harmony, but every so often tempers would flare and battle lines would be drawn on national, religious or cultural grounds. These spats were mostly pretty inconsequential and, given the close proximity in which we all lived, almost inevitable. Usually they would blow over after a day or two. But given the fact that we were all   heavily   armed   and self-medicating Lariam, they were still cause for concern. Under such circumstances we were all potential homicidal maniacs with guns, capable of a moment's stupidity and a lifetime of regret.

The cookhouse or DFAC (dining facility) was always the best barometer of social cohesion. During periods of harmony we would all sit together at mealtimes, a cheerful and noisy mix of colours and uniforms. During periods of tension we would quickly split into rival factions, muttering darkly amongst ourselves over our coco-pops or tinned grapefruit segments.

Latitude:	34.94
Longitude:	69.27
Elevation:	1481m
Met:	Plenty of sun H:10°L:-2°
DTG:	221230DFEB12

ON 22 FEBRUARY 2012, 650kms north-east of MOB Price at the Parwan Detention Facility, part of the vast US Bagram Airbase complex, over 1,500 religious texts were removed from the prison library after it was discovered that detainees had been using them to scribble coded messages to each other. The books, including 48 copies of the Qur'an, were boxed up and marked for disposal.

As at MOB Price and most other ISAF bases the primary method of disposal at Bagram is incineration – no matter where I travelled in Afghanistan it was almost impossible to escape the smell of burning excrement in the morning. Charred fragments of these books were subsequently discovered by Afghan garbage collectors. News of the terrible discovery that the infidels were burning Qur'ans along with their shit leaked from the base, sparking days of violent protests across Afghanistan. At least 41 people died, including four American soldiers.

This was the Qur'an burning incident we'd trained for at STANTA, only on an inconceivably industrial scale. It was immediately clear that a friendly chat with the local Mullah and a few school supplies were not going to resolve the problem. Even the apology of the President of the United States of America, who personally intervened within 24 hours of the incident, was not sufficient to stem the violence that ensued.

Thor, my Danish Info Ops counterpart, was initially so incredulous that he dismissed the news as an elaborate hoax. However, as the ISAF encrypted communications channels began to glow white hot his already pale face turned ashen.

Thor and I had drawn up a number of plans for incidents that we hoped to avoid but had conceded were still possibilities we might face in our J9 role engaging with the local civilian population. These included dealing with cultural misunderstandings and managing the consequences of civilian casualties. Industrial scale Qur'an burning was not amongst them. To say that we were ill prepared was something of an understatement, but at least we were not alone.

It seemed that the entire ISAF administration in Afghanistan was in meltdown.

Nonetheless Colonel James was looking to me as his principal J9 advisor for guidance on how best to deal with the situation. With multiple directives from different ISAF headquarters merely clouding the issue, Thor and I sat down with a large pot of Danish coffee and hastily produced a plan of our own from scratch.

The last of the coffee was still warm in the pot when I was summoned to brief the Commanding Officer.

Unsurprisingly given the short time frame, the plan was not a complicated one, but I hoped that it was still sound. It centred on two core activities. The first was to avoid inflaming the situation with our presence by minimising our patrols and staying well away from centres of population for a few days. This would allow the Taliban some freedom of movement, but Thor and I had concluded this was the lesser of two evils.

Fortunately the Commanding Officer concurred.

The second was to issue an apology. But it wasn't enough simply to say *sorry*. We needed to reassure the local community and those Afghans with whom we worked of three things:

1. We understood the terrible significance to the Muslim world of what had taken place at Bagram.

2. It was, nonetheless, entirely inadvertent and without malice.

3. We deeply regretted what had happened and offered our assurance that it would not happen again. Ever.

For this last point I'd taken guidance from a statement on the incident made by General John R Allen, the senior American Commander in Afghanistan. He had said: *we are taking steps to ensure this does not ever happen again.*

Colonel James was satisfied with points one and two but, showing a greater perspicacity than the ISAF Commander, insisted that we make no guarantees of future good behaviour. I was surprised at his unwillingness to echo the words of our boss and slightly dubious when he resignedly assured me of his absolute conviction that there would be similar ISAF fuck ups in the future. He had no desire to be reminded of past false promises when that moment inevitably arrived.

It seemed to me at the time that three tours of Afghanistan had jaded his view of the ISAF mission. But two months later his insight was proved correct. On 28 April 2012, Pastor Terry Jones of Gainesville, Florida was allowed to exercise his right to religious freedom and burn a copy of the Qur'an in protest at the imprisonment in Iran of an Iranian-American Pastor, Saeed Abedini.

It seemed inconceivable to our Afghan hosts and to most of the rest of the Islamist world that the United States – the most powerful military nation on Earth – was incapable of intervening to prevent this further crime against Islam.

Pastor Jones was admonished with a $271 fine from the Gainesville Fire and Rescue Department for burning books without authorisation and a $2.2million bounty from the Islamist group Jamaat-ud-Dawah for his head, on the one condition that it was first removed from his body.

The paltry fine and the hefty bounty only serve to highlight the cultural chasm that exists between East and West.

Having agreed a set of words with which to frame our apology that, thanks to Colonel James' acuity, offered no future guarantees, we next drew up a rather long shortlist of those to whom we needed to communicate it.

At the top of this list was the District Governor, Salim Rodi. In addition to his role as the official representative of the people of Nahr-E-Saraj District, like almost all GIRoA[1] appointees, he was also heavily implicated in Helmand's narcotics industry, believed to be responsible for around 75% of global opium production.

The pressures of high office in the violent international opium business, and the even more violent business of Helmandian politics, had taken their toll and he was also a heavy drinker. Rather like Jeffrey Bernard, only with perhaps greater justification, he was frequently too *unwell* to perform his gubernatorial duties.

---

[1] **GIRoA**: Government of the Islamic Republic of Afghanistan

Neither his drinking nor his role in the opium trade were condoned in any of the 48 copies of the Qur'an inadvertently reduced to ashes in the Bagram incinerators. Nonetheless the Governor was outraged at the news, although he grudgingly accepted our heartfelt apology.

The DG would later claim that he personally intervened to quell a riot when 'hundreds' of outraged citizens marched through Gereshk in protest. Since none of our ground units or reconnaissance assets reported any unusual public gatherings I concluded that the DG was extemporising. It seemed more likely to me that having failed to foment a riot himself, perhaps because he'd been too drunk at the time, he was attempting to spin his lack of incitive powers to his advantage.

Next on the list was the District Chief of Police, the appropriately abbreviated D-CoP, Ghullie Khan. Like his boss the Governor, the D-CoP was predictably involved in the narcotics business. To supplement this income he also used the Afghan Uniformed Police (AUP) department he commanded to collect illegal taxes from local citizens. There were a number of ISAF apologists who defended this unlawful activity as 'culturally normal'. I even read a paper on the subject, quite possibly published by the DCSU, the same organisation that had come up with the wizard idea of FEOs and then assigned them male interpreters.

Personally, I was deeply sceptical of this point of view. The truth was that ISAF seemed powerless to prevent the endemic corruption that pervaded every level of the AUP, and not a little ashamed that the primary source of these illegal taxes was a levy on the use of the main highways that bisected the district – all of which had been funded at great expense with international aid.

No one in ISAF was really sure how much the illegal taxation business was worth in Nahr-E-Saraj but it wasn't petty cash. Ghullie Khan had previously been a senior police officer in the neighbouring district of Sangin. He had been removed from this post after an ISAF investigation revealed that he'd been sodomizing little boys there. In the wake of this scandal his boss, Nabi Elham – the Provincial Chief of Police – naturally promoted him to be top cop in Nahr-E-Saraj, although it was rumoured that he'd first demanded a bribe of half a million US dollars.

There were ISAF papers defending paedophilia and bribery as culturally normal activities too, although I didn't waste any time reading them. Culturally normal or not, I reckoned that the citizens of those countries that had helped to fund the district's new highways would be dismayed to learn that they were now being used to line the pockets of a known pederast, drug baron and all round bad guy.

Ghullie's favourite son, Zaibiullah was a chip off the old block and had followed his father into the AUP. When a local shopkeeper failed to pay his taxes on time he tied his arms and legs together and drowned him into the Nahr-E-Buhgra canal to teach him a lesson. Such was Zaibiullah's intellect that it was possible to imagine him warning the drowning man that next time he failed to pay Zaibiullah would put a bullet in his head.

It was just as possible to imagine some obscure ISAF department publishing a paper defending drowning as a culturally normal method of deterrence in much the same way that waterboarding was a culturally normal interview technique in the United States.

Neither Ghullie Khan's parenting skills, nor his predilection for underage boys, nor any of the myriad illegal activities over which he presided as the district's chief upholder of law and order did much to temper his indignation when he learned of the Qur'an burnings.

However, unlike their Governor or their Police Chief, and despite our worst fears, the residents of Gereshk seemed unmoved by the turmoil engulfing the rest of the country. We waited with bated breath but much to our surprise there were no violent demonstrations, the bazaars remained open, and even the local Taliban's attempts to exploit the situation seemed half-hearted.

If I'd thought there was any chance I could pull it off I would have attributed this muted response to my brilliant engagement plan, but even I had to admit that this was unlikely. There were other forces at work here.

In stark contrast, a few months later angry protests ensued following a series of mysterious child abductions. The most likely explanation was that the D-CoP had resumed his paedophile activities and this was certainly what the citizens of Gereshk appeared to have concluded. Directing most of their anger towards him in a number of emergency shuras, they demanded that he return their children and bugger off, literally, back from where he came.

In MOB Price our intelligence analysts scratched their heads in wonder. What were the citizens of   Gereshk so upset about? Surely child abduction was just another one of those culturally normal activities that we Westerners couldn't get our heads around?

We were at a loss as to what all the fuss was about and lobbied hard for Ghullie Khan to keep his job. Yes, he was a terrible father; yes, he was corrupt; yes, he was a kiddy fiddler; yes, he was facilitating the illicit opium trade but his Danish Civilian Police mentors assured us he was still much better than the last guy, or than any of his potential successors.

It was about this point I came to the terrible realisation that I'd chosen to fight on the losing side in this conflict. The words of John Stuart Mill, which I'd used to justify abandoning my family in search of adventure in Afghanistan, were beginning to sound somewhat hollow. Instead of fighting a war to protect other human beings against tyrannical injustice, it appeared that we were propping up a regime already corrupted beyond redemption.

Instead of fighting a war for an honest purpose, we were aligning ourselves with a dishonest administration and deliberately turning a blind eye to its excesses by excusing them as culturally normal.

It was my job to reassure the district's citizens that we were here to restore order and good governance. The official master message I was required to peddle was: *A better life with GIRoA.* It was hard to make this sound convincing when their dipsomaniac Governor had his hands in the opium till and their Police Chief had his hands, and some other parts of his body, in their children's underwear.

Even the Roman Catholic Church and the British Broadcasting Corporation have eventually realised that covering up this sort of scandal is not a recipe for success in winning hearts and minds.

According to the Taliban's official version of events, its spiritual leader, Mullah Mohammed Omar first came to prominence in southern Afghanistan in the spring of 1994 when he rescued two teenage girls who had been abducted and raped by the Governor of Singesar. For good measure he then hanged the Governor from the barrel of a tank.

Later the same year Mullah Omar again demonstrated his determination to defend the innocence of children when he freed a young boy from the clutches of two militia commanders while they bickered over who would sodomise him first.

As a result of these actions Mullah Omar's public approval ratings went through the roof and two years later he entered Kabul and established the Islamic Emirate of Afghanistan.

His track record from this point forward is harder to defend, but zero tolerance towards paedophilia appears to have been a successful campaign strategy. It seemed possible to me that the Taliban's lacklustre response to the Bagram arsonists might have been because they were rather better attuned than we were to the opinions and priorities of the local populace.

Infidels burning the Qur'an is undeniably an outrage, but when senior policemen start fucking your kids up the arse it's time to take to the streets in protest.

I couldn't fault the logic or the priorities.

Order was restored only after General Shirin Shah, the Provincial Afghan National Army Commander ordered his troops onto the streets of Gereshk.

The ANA were certainly no angels but they were better disciplined and more respected than the police and, so far as I knew, their boss was not an alcoholic, a drug dealer or a pederast.

I knew this because on influence patrols I would frequently canvas locals for their views on the security situation. On one particularly embarrassing occasion a local farmer pointed out that security had been just fine until shortly after we'd turned up. Our presence had unfortunately attracted the attention of the local Taliban and there was now a gun battle raging around his compound.

He had a point. But in the majority of cases locals would grudgingly accept that an ISAF, or ANA, security presence might be beneficial. Of course, their responses may have been influenced by the fact that their interlocutor, although clearly no longer in his prime, was nonetheless heavily armed and accompanied by fierce looking ISAF or ANA warriors.

However, almost without exception the normally tight-lipped residents of Nahr-E-Saraj were volubly opposed to the idea of an AUP presence.

No one had a good word to say about the AUP. If the residents of Nahr-E-Saraj were to be believed, and all the evidence pointed in that direction, the Afghan Uniform Police, with one or two exceptions perhaps, were all cunts. Just like the RAF.

Latitude:	31.80
Longitude:	64.51
Elevation:	834m
Met:	Sunny H: 9°L: 0°
DTG:	261100DFEB12

HOW HAD THE international community ended up in such a mess in Afghanistan? I was certain the British had stayed on in Helmand with the best of intentions and believed John Reid had been perfectly genuine when, in 2006, he'd expressed the hope that we might deliver on the mission without firing a single shot. He'd declared at the time: *We're in the south to help and protect the Afghan people to reconstruct their economy and democracy.*

Tony Blair had also optimistically imagined we might destroy the narcotics industry as a side benefit to political and economic reconstruction but by 2012 there was little to show for these efforts in Nahr-E-Saraj. Unless you counted the corrupt Governor feathering his nest with drug money, or the new highways that were paying off Ghullie Khan's debt to Nabi Elham and funding his paedophile ring.

To make matters worse opium production had surged to record levels. Despite his noble ambitions, there wasn't much Tony Blair could have done about this – the odds were stacked against him.

Before the Russian invasion of Afghanistan cotton, not opium, had been the major cash crop in Helmand with two cotton factories in Lashka Ghar and Gereshk. During the chaos of the Russian withdrawal and the subsequent economic collapse of the country the cotton mills, literally, ground to a halt and were abandoned.

Farmers initially turned to opium poppy as a substitute primary cash crop but the Taliban, in accordance with Qur'anic texts declared opium *haram* (sinful) and banned its cultivation, cutting production by 94%.

In 1999 US agricultural experts remained optimistic that the cotton industry could still be revived in Helmand as a means of eradicating what remained of the illegal opium trade. It was not an unreasonable expectation given that, prior to the US led invasion in 2001, only 30 square miles of land were under poppy cultivation across the whole of Afghanistan.

However, shortly after being driven from power, the Taliban

had a religious epiphany. Realising that the global opium black market was not subject to UN trade restrictions, sanctions or embargoes and could therefore be a major source of income to fund their insurgency, they lifted the ban on production.

At about the same time the abandoned cotton mill in Gereshk was destroyed by a US air-to-ground missile after it was used as a firing point to target ISAF soldiers. Any remaining hopes of reviving cotton cultivation in the surrounding countryside were effectively dashed.

Twelve years later it was estimated that 600 square miles of land were under poppy cultivation in Afghanistan, with Helmand being the major opium producing province.

In 2006 John Reid had failed to understand that the Afghan economy, far from being in need of reconstruction, was already booming like never before. But it was easy to see how he might have made this mistake. Unlike their re-sellers in Moscow, Manchester or Miami, no one in Nahr-E-Saraj was driving around in a pimped out Range Rover Sport.

By 2007, according to the United Nations Office on Drugs and Crime, 97% of opiates on the world heroin market derived from Afghanistan, amounting to a wholesale value of $64 billion, the third biggest global commodity in cash terms after oil and the arms trade, and roughly the same size as the UK's entire defence budget for that year (£33.5 billion).

In contrast, Britain's aid budget for Afghanistan was just over £100 million. Rather less than the £148 million Adrian and Gillian Bayford received when they scooped the Euromillions jackpot.

What John Reid and Tony Blair had both failed to understand was that theirs were not the biggest swinging dicks in town – those belonged to the organised crime business syndicates who, quite naturally, were prepared to sink their own resources into protecting their new multibillion dollar investment. Nor need they concern themselves with such issues as human rights or the eradication of poverty as they went about their business. On the contrary, preserving the poverty trap in which the majority of Afghan poppy farmers must operate suited their requirements perfectly.

Of course, it didn't help that DfID, the organisation tasked with delivering UK aid to Afghanistan, were as hopelessly naïve as their political masters – and appeared to share their lack of humility. Unlike Mullah Omar who started out with fewer than 50 madrassah students (armed with 16 rifles between them) when he strung up the Governor of Singesar – and then proceeded to build his movement from the ground up – the DfID plan was to build a viable state from the top down.

This was called 'capacity building'. Ironically, as Sir Malcolm Bruce the chairman of the House of Commons International Development Committee rather belatedly pointed out in 2012: *It is questionable whether DfID has the capacity to build a viable state.*

Indeed, even though the aid budget had nearly doubled to £180 million a year by the time Sir Malcolm made his pronouncement, to the organised crime bosses this was still no more than petty cash. DfID's grand strategy failed before it even started because the planners overlooked the simple fact that they had a competitor with much deeper pockets who was not subject to oversight committees or ethical codes of practice and who was determined to maintain the existing state of affairs.

Afghanistan, with the tacit approval of Mullah Omar and his buddies in the Quetta Shura[1], had become a compliant narco-state with almost every GIRoA official from the President to the lowliest AUP patrolman on the payroll of the drug cartels. DfID didn't stand a chance.

To my mind, failing to understand or choosing to ignore the international opium black market's vested interest in Helmand Province was the single biggest strategic error the international community made in the whole Afghan campaign. But these were just my own personal musings, I wasn't an expert in any of this. If I was I'd have been seconded to DfID or the DCSU.

---

[1] **Quatta Shura**: A militant organization composed of the leaders of the Afghan Taliban, believed to be based within the city of Quetta in the Balochistan province of Pakistan.

Latitude:	31.80
Longitude:	64.51
Elevation:	834m
Met:	Sunny H: 9°L: 0°
DTG:	261400DFEB12

ALTHOUGH I WAS no cultural specialist, I did know a thing or two about selling and marketing. It seemed to me that in addition to overlooking the fact that the world's third largest commodity market was already heavily invested in Afghanistan, we were failing to provide a sufficiently compelling alternative offer with which to entice the Afghan people.

The international community's alternative to drugs, poverty and violence seemed to be democracy, gender equality and religious tolerance. Societal values prized by the West, but completely alien concepts to the majority of Afghans in Helmand Province.

I'd learned early on in my career in the advertising business that successful companies didn't necessarily make better products than their competitors but instead invested in market research to gain a better understanding of their customers.

Thus I'd witnessed a failing high street fashion retailer transform itself from a clothes shop into a purveyor of teenage rebellion for those that gave a fcuk, making millionaires of its founders in the process. Similarly, during a collapse in consumer confidence in the farming industry following the BSE and Foot and Mouth crises of the late 1990s, I'd had a hand in helping a posh food shop reposition itself as the source of *quality food, honestly priced*.

Unlike these companies and many others who had become market leaders in their respective industries by investing in understanding their customers, DfID appeared to understand very little about the deeply conservative rural population of Helmand Province and seemed intent on pedalling a 'stabilisation' offer that the majority of ordinary citizens did not want.

Democracy had been forced upon the people of Afghanistan because DfID knew what was best for them. It seemed to me that this was democracy with a Stalinist twist and in an unconscious nod to the 'Gardener of Human Happiness', DfID even proposed to reconstruct

Afghan society through a series of Five Year Plans.

While I enjoyed the oxymoron of enforced democracy I didn't get the impression that the people of the Islamic Republic of Afghanistan had very much faith in their elected representatives. This may have been because they hadn't elected them or because they didn't represent them. Or perhaps both.

It didn't help that the version of democracy on offer was distinctly substandard comprising as it did of rigged elections, corrupt officials and an incompetent civil service.

In a rare moment of unguarded candour, the DST official responsible for mentoring the Department of Justice in our district shared his disillusionment with me.

A law graduate from a prestigious Danish University, he'd put his legal career on hold to do his bit and try to make the world a better place. He'd arrived in Helmand bright with ambition to help develop Afghan rule of law capacity. His enthusiasm had been quickly dulled by the reality of his job. He had imagined he would be assisting the Afghan Justice Ministry to build a stable society in which all members are equally subject to publicly disclosed legal codes and processes.

But this was not at all what the Ministry had in mind for him.

The Justice Department in Gereshk was housed in the Old Fort. Its previous occupants, including the British in 1839 had not maintained the property to a particularly high standard. It was not only old, as the name suggested, but also dilapidated. The Justice Ministry did not require a legal missionary but was in urgent need of a janitor. The disillusioned official disconsolately admitted to me: *They only call me when the toilets are backed up or if the light bulbs need replacing.*

In the meantime, prisoners continued to be held indefinitely without charge and routinely subjected to physical abuse and torture until such time as an appropriate bribe had been paid. Court officials existed on the payroll but were permanently *in absentia* and judges were appointed without any prior legal knowledge or training.

None of this mattered because the courts never sat and no one actually expected the Justice Ministry to administer justice. There was really no need for this because the Taliban already operated a very effective, efficient and widely admired mobile Shar'ia court system. The existing legal model was far superior to the cumbersome, time-consuming and bureaucratic Western alternative my Danish friend was trying to advocate.

Not only did Helmand have a better legal system than the one that DfID insisted on imposing but the city of Gereshk was also a model for gender equality and required no further encouragement from Western infidels. It already had a school for girls and even allowed women to walk the streets – albeit covered with a burkha and escorted by a male member of the family. According to its menfolk, this was quite liberal enough.

Being an infidel, I personally believed that the vast majority of social problems in Afghanistan could ultimately be traced back to the absurd practice of gender segregation. I was pretty certain that nature had intended men and women to coexist and from time to time to engage in consensual sexual intercourse. But these were radical and seditious views that had no place in Helmand.

Curiously, the Ministry of Defence also imposed strict gender segregation rules on its representatives in Helmand and banned sexual congress entirely, not as some botched attempt at cultural sensitivity cooked up by the DCSU, but because *our personnel are expected to behave in accordance with the Armed Forces values and standards at all times.* It was never clear to me which of these values and standards applied to my sex life, but since this was an entirely solitary activity anyway it was not a question that ever came up, so to speak.

Despite their liberal tendencies, the male inhabitants of Gereshk still routinely imprisoned their wives and daughters in the family compound and subjected them to appalling abuse. Josef Fritzl – *Das Monster von Amstetten* – who imprisoned his daughter in the basement of his house and abused her over a 24 year period, would have been considered an upstanding member of the community. But he was already serving a life sentence in an Austrian prison for the criminally insane.

What had shocked the whole of Europe and been utterly incomprehensible in Amstetten, however inconceivable it might sound, was culturally normal activity in Helmand.

With democracy a farce and gender equality in the basement a lot was riding on the third strand of the DfID offer, religious tolerance.

None of the Afghans I met were really sold on this concept. It was one of those culturally normal infidel concepts that true believers couldn't really get their heads around. After all there is only one true God, Allah. None has the right to be worshipped but Allah; there is no partner unto Him. He has power over everything.

Anyone who thinks differently quite clearly deserves what's coming to them.

In November 2011, just a few weeks before I joined the Grenadiers for our final OPTAG assessment prior to deployment Stanley McChrystal, the US Army General so dramatically sacked by President Barack Obama, stated: *Without the participation of the people, security won by the military won't endure.*

McChrystal lost his job because his motor mouth got the better of him in the presence of a Rolling Stone magazine feature writer but he was still considered to be an authority in counter-insurgency warfare.

I was coming to believe that McChrystal was right. I had a very uneasy feeling that the majority of citizens in the district of Nahr-E-Saraj were not participating. This was partly because they were locked in servitude to the opium trade, and partly because DfID and the international community were failing to offer a sufficiently compelling alternative.

If McChrystal's pronouncement was correct, and my own assessment of the people's participation was accurate, the implication seemed clear; security won by the military could not endure.

Latitude:	31.80
Longitude:	64.51
Elevation:	834m
Met:	Showers; some sun H:13°L:-1°
DTG:	010800DMAR12

I PONDERED THESE thoughts, trying to come to terms with my deep personal misgivings about how we were prosecuting the counter-insurgency in Afghanistan. Meanwhile, the J2 (Intelligence) cell were wrestling with an issue of their own.

It was standard practice to accuse the J2 shop of looking up their own arseholes and wondering why it was dark, but on this occasion the object of their wonder was a report from one of our patrol bases (PBs) that they were struggling to verify.

It seemed a local national (LN) had visited the base to report that one of our drones had been downed. This was not an especially unusual occurrence. Despite the exotic name 'Desert Hawk' these were essentially remote controlled model aeroplanes fitted with a camera. The locals knew from experience that we would pay hard cash for the recovery of our toys or for reports of their whereabouts. However, on this occasion a quick check confirmed that all our unmanned aerial vehicles (UAVs) were accounted for.

This was perplexing for the Int Cell because it left only two other possible deductions. First: another ISAF unit had been flying a drone in our airspace without our knowledge or permission – a major violation – probably with an ulterior motive. Second: the Taliban had developed their own UAV capability and were spying on us.

Both seemed possible to me. I knew from a pre-Christmas trip to Hamley's with Harry and Alfie that pilotless aircraft capable of carrying a small camera were cheaply and readily available. Equally, it would not have surprised me to learn that some shady SF unit, which didn't officially exist in the ISAF order of battle (ORBAT), was operating in our AO without our knowledge.

The reality turned out to be even stranger.

The very basic living conditions in most of the patrol bases created numerous health and hygiene problems for the inhabitants. The PB in question was suffering from a rodent infestation. In addition to more conventional attempts to reduce the rodent population, soldiers who had to endure the discomfort of sharing their home with these unwanted guests had come up with some more ingenious, if less efficient, pest control methods of their own. One such endeavour involved aerial relocation by shamoolie.

The shamoolie, or illumination flare, consists of a small plastic tube with a pullstring at one end that fires a rocket propelled flare approximately 800m into the air. This then burns with a bright orange-red flame illuminating an area of roughly one kilometre for up to a minute as it descends under a small parachute. The flares were routinely used on night sentry duty to discourage insurgents from getting too close to the base's perimeter.

Having captured one of the unwanted rodents the unfortunate creature had been placed inside the shamoolie's plastic tube and explosively evicted from the base, almost certainly with fatal consequences. Its body then became entangled in the parachute which, carried by a gentle breeze, eventually came down in the compound of a nearby farmer.

The farmer had never been visited by a parachuting quadruped before and correctly deduced that ISAF must have a hand in these strange goings on. As everyone knew, it was relatively easy to get the infidel to part with his money, so he further deduced that this unusual happenstance would very likely have a financial upside for him and his family.

He'd arrived at his first two deductions with laser-like accuracy but his further assumptions were somewhat wider of the mark.

Like his neighbours, the farmer was familiar with the almost constant presence of the small ISAF aeroplanes which quietly buzzed overhead. He may even have watched them being launched or landed by ISAF troops from the nearby patrol base. He knew that the infidel paid good money to locals who found and returned these aircraft to the base when they occasionally crash landed.

Although he lacked one of the little planes, he deduced that he did have the little plane's little pilot - who must have ejected shortly before the aircraft went down. Unfortunately, the aviator was dead and therefore unable to corroborate this version of events.

Clearly these factors were likely   to adversely impact the fiscal gain he might derive from the situation, but it was still worth a punt. Surely the downed aircraft could not have travelled far after its furry flying officer had bailed out?

A short while later he reported the missing UAV to the base, embellishing the discovery of the rodent parachutist in his compound with a convincing eyewitness account of how he'd watched the aircraft, clearly in mechanical trouble, lose height as it passed over his home before the pilot ejected and it disappeared from view.

The soldiers at the base thanked him for the return of the vermin they'd tried so hard to expel, and duly reported the missing UAV up the chain of command in accordance with standing orders.

I hope they also rewarded the farmer with a few well earned US dollars for his story-telling panache and the pure comedy gold he'd just handed them.

I never did discover if this was a true story or a work of fiction intended to wind up the J2 shop – most probably it fell somewhere between the two. In the through-the-looking-glass world we now inhabited where presidents were in the pay of criminal gangs, policemen presided over paedophile rings, judicial experts served as janitors and where Josef Fritzl, *Das Monster von Amstetten*, might live in respectable obscurity, anything seemed possible.

Latitude:	31.80
Longitude:	64.51
Elevation:	834m
Met:	Heavy thunderstorms; some sun H:10°L:-1°
DTG:	060800DMAR12

THE STORY OF the rodent aviator was so good that I heard it recounted a number of times, including on one occasion in the Commanding Officer's morning briefing where it was received with much merriment and good humour.

The levity was short lived.

Later that same day six British soldiers were killed when their Warrior armoured vehicle triggered a massive IED blast at Durai Junction on the border of our AO, less than 10 klicks east.

It was a devastating blow to morale.

Latitude   31.80
Longitude   64.51
Elevation   834m
Met   Sunny H:17°L:4°
DTG   072309DMAR12

I didn't want to think this
might be because his testicles
were wired up to the Torchlight
generators.

BE BECAUSE, HIS TESTICLES,
UP TO THE TORCHLIGHT GENERATORS.

SAS: Special Air Service
MIB: Men in Black
TF: Task Force
FCO: Foreign and Commonwealth Office
UKSF: United Kingdom Special Forces
MoIA: Ministry of Interior Affairs
DPHQ: District Police Headquarters
RMP: Royal Military Police

Latitude:	31.80
Longitude:	64.51
Elevation:	834m
Met:	Sunny H:17°L:4°
DTG:	072309DMAR12

IT WOULD BE another two weeks before we could mourn the loss of Sergeant Nigel Coupe and his Warrior crew – the *Warrior Six* as they came to be known. We were about to embark on our first battlegroup level operation in support of the Afghan National Army to clear a contested rural area to our south. The mission took priority. We would pay our respects to our fallen comrades on our return.

In a late-night Facebook post I wrote simply: *Not a good day for TFH[1] but not a day to lose our resolve.* This was intended as a cryptic message to friends and family to let them know I was all right. It was, of course, a massive understatement and did not reflect how I truly felt. I was overcome with a complex range of emotions. Initial shock and dismay at the news became suffused with relief, and then with guilt. Relief that it wasn't me or anyone I knew. Guilt at the heavy price others must pay to satisfy my relief.

I sat at my desk in the J9 cell and tried to get a grip of myself, to reason with my emotions that I shouldn't feel guilty about being alive. Everyone who went outside the wire accepted exactly the same risk as Sergeant Coupe and his crew. It wasn't my fault that it wasn't my turn.

The logic may have been sound, but every time one of our own was killed or seriously injured I would endure a period of self-loathing at my cold-hearted analysis that statistically this improved my own chances of returning home unscathed.

Despite the uncomfortable realisation that DfID's plan to build a viable state from the top down was failing, I still genuinely believed what I'd written in my post: it was not a day to lose our resolve. Mr Spock, First Officer of the starship Enterprise, would have been perplexed at my illogicality.

According to Spock, the Warrior Six, together with the 398 British servicemen before them, had laid down their lives for a cause that was

[1] **TFH**: Task Force Helmand

already lost. Everything I'd seen of the Gereshk DST indicated to me that they lacked the resources, the intellectual capacity and the determination to build a better life for the Afghan people. But this didn't alter my feelings. I was determined that we should fight on, even though I knew this course of action would inevitably incur further loss of life – including, quite possibly, my own.

Of course it didn't actually matter what Spock or I thought. It was unlikely that either of us could have any meaningful impact in shaping UK strategy in Afghanistan. Mr Spock was a part-Vulcan fictional character who didn't exist and I was a part-time soldier so far down the chain of command that I barely existed either. As far as the policy makers were concerned The Colour Sergeant had been right all those years ago, I was an amoeba.

I couldn't fault Spock's logic, but neither could I concur with it and I was not alone. Almost everyone I spoke to in MOB Price, including members of the DST, would privately express their disquiet and frustration that the military mission was not being backed up with credible stabilisation effect, but no one was ready to quit.

We all knew this was going to be a punchy op. The area to be cleared was a known insurgent stronghold centred on the Yakchal bazaar. The insurgents used the bazaar as a nexus of shadow governance and economic control in the region and several previous attempts to enter Yakchal had gone kinetic[1]. If that wasn't enough to guarantee trouble the surrounding countryside was given over almost exclusively to opium poppy cultivation. Only a month before harvest, these crops would be destroyed by our tracked Warthog[2] vehicles as we sought to dominate the ground. The J2 shop assessed that local farmers, already sympathetic to Taliban governance, would join forces with the insurgents in a bid to protect their only source of income.

This would be the first time we had stepped outside the security bubble created by our patrol bases and challenged the Taliban in their own backyard. No one was quite sure how it would play out. We didn't expect the Taliban to stand toe-to-toe with us – they were much too intelligent to get involved in a fight at a time and place not of their choosing – but we knew that they would not capitulate entirely. Partly

---

[1] **Kinetic/Kinetic military action**: Military action involving the use of lethal force.

[2] **Warthog**: an armoured twin chassis articulated tracked troop carrier

because they needed to demonstrate their authority to the local people, partly because this was their home and they had nowhere else to go.

As we prepared for battle Colonel James, perhaps sensing my crisis of confidence or maybe thinking that I was getting windy, stood me down from the operation. I was to remain behind in battlegroup HQ while Thor would go forward with the Danish armoured infantry company.

Dismayed that I would not be going on the op, I tried to conceal my disappointment as I helped Thor prepare the loudspeaker system he would use to communicate with local nationals using a series of pre-recorded messages. These claimed that we were in the area to bring peace and stability and that a better life awaited with GIRoA. The truth behind the propaganda was that we could not do a great deal for the residents of Yakchal. GIRoA had little, if any, influence outside the protected community of Gereshk and, despite it being just a few kilometres outside the city boundary, the Taliban denied all access to international aid, education or healthcare support.

The clearance op would stir up a hornets' nest, making Yakchal a dangerous and unpleasant place to live in the process, but there was no plan to hold the ground for more than a few days once it had been cleared. The insurgents would quickly return once we had departed.

When I briefed the DST members on the plan they looked at me blankly. I had naively assumed they would want to exploit the temporary security bubble our presence would create to deliver some positive stabilisation effect. A polio vaccination programme perhaps, a shura to engage with their elected representatives, some infrastructure project such as dredging or repairing the complex irrigation system that was the only source of water so far from the Helmand River.

Anything that might add some truth to the fiction that a better life lay ahead with GIRoA.

Bruno, the DST leader looked confused, but some of the other team members visibly flushed with anger and stamped out of the briefing room. Bruno explained: *We don't really get involved with what the military are doing and have our own projects and priorities.* I'd managed to seriously upset some of his colleagues by daring to suggest that we might work together for the common good.

So much for the *Comprehensive   Approach* as defined in the joint doctrine manual on 'Security and Stabilisation'. As with so many of the doctrine manuals I'd read, the authors appeared to have gone to great efforts creating complex definitions to describe relatively simple concepts. In this case:

The comprehensive approach is broader than cross-government, it is also a multi-agency and usually a multinational response. Mutually-supporting cross-departmental and multi-agency effort should enable comprehensive tactical activity to deliver overwhelming campaign effect. The military will set the security conditions and lead on aspects of Security Sector Reform (SSR) such as military capacity-building. Civilian state and non-state institutions lead on: governance; engagement and reconciliation; police and justice sector reform; restoration of basic services and infrastructure; economic and financial development; and longer-term social and infrastructure development.

In 1933, Colonel (later Field Marshal) Irwin Rommel stated: *The British write some of the best doctrine in the world; it is fortunate that their officers do not read it.*

I'd read a lot of doctrine as I'd prepared for Afghanistan and couldn't agree with his assessment of the quality. Much of it seemed impenetrable and verbose to me. But at least I had read it. It appeared that my colleagues in the DST had not.

This was to be a recurring theme of my time in Afghanistan. Whenever we mounted a major operation I would appeal to the DST to follow up with some governance, engagement or infrastructure activity *to deliver overwhelming campaign effect,* but this was always considered to be too difficult or not a priority for them. Even though some of the DST members were to become my friends, by the end of my time in Helmand I was barely able to conceal my contempt for their organisation's woeful contribution to the mission.

If I was concerned that I would be redundant in my stay-behind role in the operation, I needn't have worried. Within hours of the battlegroup's departure I unexpectedly found myself at the centre of an entirely different set of events.

Latitude:	31.81
Longitude:	64.55
Elevation:	837m
Met:	Sunny H:11°L:-1°
DTG:	100645DMAR12

HAJI GUL'S DAY started much like any other. It was still too cold to sleep outside in the courtyard, as was his custom in the summer months, but even though he could not see it with his own eyes he still woke as the sky lightened just before sunrise. He roused himself from his bed as the sounds and smells of the dawning day began to intrude on his senses. The smell of freshly baked bread competed with the diesel fumes that seemed to permanently cloak the city. The sweet scents from his flower garden in the courtyard outside could not completely conceal the foul smell from the incinerators at the infidel base a few kilometres away.

Haji was a man of means, one of the city's wealthiest citizens, but he still liked to keep some livestock in his compound. Goats and a cow, rabbits and a clutch of chickens. The cow and the goats were hobbled but all the animals ranged freely within the compound's 12 foot adobe walls. Some chickens eyed him warily as he wandered into the courtyard and the rabbits quickly made themselves scarce. He cleared his throat noisily to let the womenfolk know he was up and wanted his morning chai.

Although the city had a small hydroelectric power station the turbines had ceased turning some years ago. Haji had invested in a powerful diesel generator that not only provided electricity to his home but also pumped cool, fresh, crystal clear water directly from the aquifer 30 metres or more below it.

Thanks to the generator there was no need for him to walk down to the Nahr-E-Buhgra canal to complete his morning ablutions as so many of his neighbours were required to do.

Like almost everyone else in Gereshk, Haji owned a mobile phone but unlike many others his was also connected to a network provider – Roshan – who also supplied him with a reliable internet connection. The majority of mobile phone owners used their devices to swap data files using Bluetooth connectivity and for many this was its primary function. Despite strict Muslim rules governing female modesty, some of the content included raunchy film clips of partially clothed young ladies gyrating Bollywood-style to Hindi music.

As he waited for his chai, Haji used his phone to call his brother Ajip and they agreed to meet at their shop in an hour for breakfast. This was their normal routine but Haji always liked to confirm the arrangement in advance.

The two brothers were successful *hawaladars*, money lenders, who ran their business from smart premises in the Old Quarter of the city not far from the District Centre and the Governor's Residence. The District Governor, Salim Rodi was an important client who had used their services to transfer some of the wealth he was accumulating into safe havens outside Afghanistan.

Ever since the Taliban had reversed its policy on opium poppy in 2001 the brothers' business, along with many others, had boomed. Their success was founded on their discretion and their international network of fellow hawaladars, some of them in countries such as India and Pakistan where the informal system of money transfer known as *hawala* is widespread but illegal. To maintain this network they were both frequent international travellers, although they did not always apply for visas or pass through customs and immigration control in the normal way.

Their business had received a further boost shortly after British and Danish troops had arrived in the district and international aid money began flooding in to fund large infrastructure projects such as the blacktopping of the main highways. The infidel and his money were easily parted and these projects were generally awarded to the contractor who offered the biggest kickbacks. Much of this money was reinvested into property development schemes in Dubai, and the Gul brothers had been quick to forge business connections in the Emirate to exploit this lucrative opportunity.

Although Haji and Ajip were both illiterate, each and every one of these many thousands of transactions was painstakingly annotated by hand in ledgers running to several volumes by their trusted, one-eyed clerk. These were the only record that existed of trades amounting to many millions of dollars. Although it lends itself perfectly to the facilitation of money laundering, tax evasion and the anonymous movement of wealth, the hawala system is based on a trust and honour code between hawaladars that has changed little since the Middle Ages.

Haji and Ajip did not concern themselves with how their clients accumulated their wealth or with how they chose to divest it – they simply helped them move their money to and fro according to their wishes and charged a modest commission for the service. They were well aware that their own success was indirectly linked to the illicit opium trade and the siphoning of international aid for personal gain, but they never asked questions. In accordance with the ancient code of hawala practice, their clients answered to Allah, not to the Gul brothers.

Gereshk is an important commercial hub in the region and not all the transactions the brothers dealt with were illicit. Perfectly legitimate transactions were also recorded in the ledgers alongside those of more dubious origin and the brothers' services were relied upon by farmers, shop keepers, traders and businessmen from all walks of life. Unlike their contemporaries in Western banks and financial institutions who were largely reviled after their deceit and avarice were exposed following the financial collapse of 2008, the Gul brothers were highly respected and trusted members of the community. Indeed, trust was their primary capital without which their business would quickly fail.

They were not only successful and respected businessmen, but also generous benefactors. As their faith demanded the brothers donated 2.5% of their accumulated annual wealth in the form of *zakat* to ease the economic hardship of other Muslims and were also generous contributors of *sadaqat,* voluntary charity.

Haji could easily have afforded a powerful Japanese 4x4 to rival the Governor's official vehicle but he chose instead to walk to work. He felt perfectly safe and at ease in the city in which he had lived all his life. He knew everyone and had no reason to fear anyone. As he approached the old bazaar he nodded and *salaam*'ed his way through the throng of traders setting up their stalls for the day, and reached his own shop to find his brother had arrived a few minutes ahead of him. They embraced as they always did each morning before Ajip went next door to buy sugared almonds and more sweet cardamom chai, leaving Haji to open up the shop. The two brothers were not only business partners but also soulmates.

Haji sat at his desk, worrying absentmindedly at his lapis lazuli[1] prayer beads while he waited for his brother to return, already salivating at the

---

[1] **Lapis lazuli**: A deep blue semi-precious stone prized since antiquity for its intense colour.

thought of the sweet treats they would share as they discussed their plans for the day. His reverie was interrupted by some sort of commotion going on in the street outside. As he came around his desk to see what all the fuss was about several armed men burst through the door screaming and shouting at him unintelligibly.

The lead man, a pale skinned, wild-eyed heathen with a ragged, unkempt beard knocked him to the floor and pinned him there with a knee in the small of his back and the barrel of his gun pressed to the back of his head. As currency traders in Afghanistan's cash based economy the brothers' stock in trade comprised a mix of US dollars, Pakistani rupees and Afghan afghanis. These were kept, together with their precious ledgers, in a safe at the back of the shop and now another man, speaking in Pashtu, demanded the keys.

Haji and Ajip had never felt the need for anything other than the most basic of security measures. They had so many powerful friends and allies that only a very foolish man would dare to steal from them. Haji's first reaction, even with his face pressed into the dusty Persian carpet in front of his desk, was defiance. But now he was hauled to his feet by two men who twisted his arms painfully behind his back and above his head to hold him in a vice-like grip, forcing him to bend forward at the waist. He was powerless to resist as the Pashtu speaker roughly searched his *shalwar kameez*[1] and extracted his key fob. Moments later the other men began emptying the contents of the safe into several large black canvas bags.

As he recovered from the initial shock and speed of the robbery Haji was astounded to discover that his assailants were infidel soldiers. Like all the residents of Gereshk, Haji was familiar with the different uniforms worn by the unbelievers and could readily identify British, Danish and American soldiers. These men were British, although their unkempt beards and American assault rifles marked them out not as regular troops but as special forces.

For the first time since these men had so violently intruded upon his life of privileged comfort, Haji's outrage began to turn to dread. ISAF special forces soldiers had a fearsome reputation – these warriors were known for their toughness, their complete lack of fear, and their ruthlessness. As everyone knew, they were not subject to the usual

[1] **Shalwar Kameez**: A long tunic (kameez) worn over a pair of baggy trousers (shalwar).

codes by which the infidels conducted themselves. They routinely performed 'kill-capture' missions in Helmand which tended to favour the former over the latter outcome.

Haji knew that his status within his own community granted him no special rights or advantages with these men and would afford him no exclusive immunities or exemptions. His powerful friends and allies could not help him.

The Pashtu speaker amongst them now identified himself as a representative from the Government of the Islamic Republic of Afghanistan's Ministry of Interior Affairs (MoIA). He informed Haji that he was under arrest for allegedly donating money and providing financial services to the Taliban in support of the Taliban's narcotics and terrorist operations. Haji was dumbfounded. The hawala code – which predates the Prophet Mohammed himself – dictates that money lenders cannot be held responsible for the actions of their customers, yet this man was now arresting him for aiding and abetting the Taliban. Haji's mind was racing. These were clearly trumped up charges but what could be the motive?

In his fearful state Haji could come to only one obvious but devastating conclusion. This was a robbery, plain and simple, and these men now meant to abduct him from the scene of their crime and quietly do away with him to cover their tracks.

This was not as far-fetched as it might sound. It certainly would not have been the first bank robbery in Afghanistan conducted with the connivance of American and European officials. In September 2010 nearly $1bn disappeared from Kabul Bank under the noses of Western consultants on six-figure salaries paid by the US government. Supposed to raise standards among their Afghan colleagues, they instead allowed the money to vanish in a series of mysterious insider loans.

According to Dr Mike Martin, an ex army captain who resigned his commission to publish a critical book on British involvement in Helmand, nor would it have been the first time that British troops had been duped into unwittingly supporting factional rivalries that *exacerbated the conflict, perpetuated it and made it more violent — precisely the opposite of what was intended.*

Haji pleaded for his life but was powerless to stop the men from cuffing his hands in front of him and forcing a pair of blacked-out ski goggles over his eyes. Blinded and incapacitated he was roughly bundled outside. A noisy crowd of incredulous traders and their early morning customers was being contained by more ISAF soldiers supported by AUP men. Amaurotic behind the ski goggles, Haji could not see his trusted clerk at the front of the throng, who silently observed, with his one good eye, the events unfolding around him.

In full view of the clerk, Haji was unceremoniously thrust into the back of an armoured truck. There he was forced to lie on the floor on top of the canvas bags containing the records and proceeds of his life's work and the source of his current calamitous situation.

As the vehicle sped away Haji was grateful that Allah had spared his beloved brother, Ajip from capture. He felt certain he would never see him again, at least not in this lifetime.

Latitude:	31.86
Longitude:	64.19
Elevation:	887m
Met:	Sunny H:11°L:-1°
DTG:	211000DFEB12

THREE WEEKS BEFORE Haji Gul's abduction I'd been summoned back to Camp Bastion for an Info Ops conference. There we received a top secret briefing from Task Force 196, a British special operations unit based in Helmand Province comprised mainly of SAS soldiers – the UK's Tier One special forces.

Tier One, as the name suggests, are the highest level of special forces and are national assets that bypass the normal military chain of command. They receive orders directly from top commanding Generals or Defence Ministers. In some instances missions can be so sensitive that the final *go/no go* decision rests with the Prime Minister.

I was intrigued not only because I'd never been invited to a top secret briefing before but also because one of the presenters was a former London Regiment officer. This was going to be interesting.

Disappointingly, my first highly classified briefing did not take place in an underground bunker hidden deep below the Camp Bastion runway. Nor was it accessed via a complex security system that utilised state of the art retinal scanners and voice recognition technology. Instead it was conducted in the rather more prosaic environs of the Camp Bastion library – a facility run by the Education Corps rather than the MIB[1]. I didn't even require a library card to gain admittance.

Perhaps because the Ed Corps were not used to hosting classified special operations forces meetings, only a thin sheet of plywood separated us from the library reading area. While this effectively screened the presentation from public view it did little if anything to prevent the briefing team from being overheard. The presenters were forced to compensate for this oversight by speaking in stage whispers, while periodically checking the other side of the partition to ensure that Mullah Omar had not coincidentally chosen that day to return his overdue library books.

---

[1] **MIB**: Men in Black. A fictional secret organisation that supervises extraterrestrial life forms living on Earth and hides their existence from ordinary humans.

In this unintentionally slapstick manner we were informed of a top secret campaign, spearheaded by the US Treasury Department, to starve the Taliban insurgency of its finances and which TF196 had been tasked to support.

According to the briefing team, the Taliban earned about $100 million annually from the illegal opium poppy industry but this was by no means their only source of income. We learned that over the previous 12 months the Taliban had raked in about $400 million from other sources that included donations, illegal taxation and extortion.

In those areas where Taliban shadow governance predominated, illegal taxes were imposed on the local population which included a 10% tax on their harvests and a 2.5% tax on wealth. They were even taxing services such as water and electricity, although they had no control over the supply, and in some areas were also charging a small business tax at 10%. This local taxation amounted to about 30% of the total figure raised and was primarily directed to support local insurgency operations.

However, the bulk of the revenue was raised through the extortion of nationwide enterprises such as mobile telephony, mining, transportation and construction. Another lucrative source of income was the foreign funding of aid and development projects, with the Taliban demanding a cut or agreeing protection money from the successful contractors. It was estimated that as much as 20% of Taliban income came from aid contracts funded by the United States and other overseas donors, a percentage roughly equal to that raised through illicit narcotics production and trafficking.

The US Treasury had concluded that the best way to squeeze the cash pipelines that pay for fighters and weapons was to go after the hawaladars – the money lenders at the centre of Afghanistan's cash based economy.

It was the hawaladars' lack of bureaucracy that had drawn them to the attention of the US Treasury Department in the first place. The Western banking system requires careful oversight and stringent legislation because bankers are primarily motivated by greed and avarice and cannot be trusted. By contrast, hawaladars are men of honour, bound by an unwritten but centuries old code of ethics. Ironically, in the murky world of corruption, extortion and violence which surrounded them, it was this trust based system that made the hawaladars appear inherently untrustworthy to officials in the Treasury Department.

I was as keen as the next person to starve the Taliban of funding if this meant that fewer people were either inclined or resourced to try and kill me. But it soon became clear that our TF196 briefers were uncertain how the hawala system actually worked, and whether or not the hawaladars themselves were complicit in any crimes.

There was no paper trail to follow. Deals were done on a telephone call and a handshake. Hawaladars did not feel the need to work out of high tech glass tower blocks designed by the world's foremost architects, or to entertain their clients in lap dancing clubs with Louis Roederer Cristal champagne. There were no trips to Vegas or lavish hot tub parties in the company of topless, silicon-enhanced hostesses. Or if there were they were far more discreet about it than their Western counterparts.

Rather than attempting to understand a system far superior to anything on offer in the West, it seemed the US Treasury Department had decided it would be simpler to overlook the fact that it was the banking system of choice for almost all Afghans and to close it down entirely.

In a spectacular display of double standards, the US Department of Justice cut a deal with HSBC for laundering billions of dollars for Mexican drug cartels, imposing a fine that amounted to less than 10% of the bank's $20.6 billion profit for the year. When Assistant Attorney General Lanny Bauer announced the settlement at a press conference he explained why the US Government decided to go soft on such criminal behaviour:

Had the U.S. authorities decided to press criminal charges, HSBC would almost certainly have lost its banking license in the U.S., the future of the institution would have been under threat and the entire banking system would have been destabilised.

It seemed that similar considerations would not be applied to the Afghan banking system in the pursuit of Taliban finances.

Given the simple fact that TF196 was staffed neither by criminal investigators nor by accountancy professionals, it wasn't especially hard to figure out how they planned to support the US Treasury Department campaign. As the presentation went on it became clear that they already had their sights firmly set on two hawaladar brothers in Gereshk. The evidence against them was, apparently, so highly classified that it could not be divulged to the audience in this particular top secret briefing, not even in a comedy stage whisper.

This would not be the last time that TF196 would seek to exonerate themselves with this *need to know* line of reasoning. It's a logic that works well in James Bond movies, but it struck me as out of place in the middle of a counter-insurgency campaign in which we were trying to secure the hearts and minds of the population.

The US Treasury Department's double standards and TF196's apparent lack of accountability would, in the eyes of most ordinary Afghans, make us all appear little better than the cunts in the AUP.

Latitude:	31.81
Longitude:	64.55
Elevation:	837m
Met:	Sunny H:16°L:-1°
DTG:	10845DMAR12

FORTY-FIVE MINUTES AFTER Haji's abduction Niels Vistisen, the DST's Danish Political Advisor received a phone call from the District Governor, Salim Rodi. Niels, who was well aware of the DG's late-night drinking sessions, was more than a little surprised to receive a phone call at this early hour from the man he was employed by the Foreign and Commonwealth Office (FCO) to advise. He immediately sensed trouble.

Niels was more used to managing the DG's expectations with regard to his expenses claims than to his political responsibilities. He had recently informed the Governor that the international community would not fund the purchase of 12 dining chairs for his personal residence at a cost of $1,000 each. It therefore seemed unlikely that the DG would rise this early to make a speculative £1,645 claim for a floating duck house.

Still, Niels was more than a little surprised to learn from the Governor that British special forces had just conducted an audacious armed bank robbery in broad daylight in the city centre, making off with the bank's Chief Executive and several million dollars in hard currency. And what was Niels going to do about it?

Niels assured the Governor that he would look into it as a priority and hotfooted it round to the J9 cell to see if I could shed any light on this outlandish and improbable tale. Unfortunately I could.

After the briefing in the Bastion library I expressed my misgivings about shutting down the hawala banking system in Gereshk. I pointed out that this would run counter to John Reid's aspiration to help the Afghan people reconstruct their economy.

In addition, I was concerned that snatching off the streets people who may or may not have committed a crime did not strike me as exemplary conduct in the smooth running of a democracy. Unless of course we were seeking to implement an Argentinian model. In this case 'disappearing' political dissidents, trade unionists, students, journalists, and presumably bankers, would be perfectly constitutional. However, given the bad blood that existed between the British and Argentinian governments, I was confident that neither Tony Blair nor John Reid had this model in mind.

It seemed impolite to point out that while Western banks such as HSBC, Western Union, Bank of America, JP Morgan, Citigroup and Wachovia, amongst others have all received heavy fines in the US for laundering billions of dollars for terrorist organisations and drug cartels, not a single bank or banker has been convicted of a crime, violently abducted from their place of work by special forces soldiers or held without trial or recourse to legal representation. While there are many who might feel they deserved nothing less, this would never happen in a democracy.

My concerns were instantly overruled. I was not party to the US Treasury Department's classified evidence, or the interview techniques by which this information may have been obtained. Nor was I a Tier One soldier with a licence to kill that bypassed both the military chain of command and the rule of law.

In a further echo of the Perón regime it was even hinted that my opposition to these tactics was unpatriotic. Later in the tour I was again to fall foul of TF196's intimidation when I challenged them over the slaying of three farmers in Rahim Kalay. But this was my first taste of their seeming lack of consideration for the broader campaign strategy and objectives in Helmand, and of their total lack of accountability. It was a dismay to discover that this elite force, which I had formerly held in high regard and no small amount of awe, in their eagerness to exercise their lethal talents were only compounding the problems we faced in Afghanistan.

This was not exactly how I explained things to Niels. I was able to confirm that Haji Gul, a hawaladar based in Gereshk, had been detained by British forces that morning on suspicion of aiding and abetting terrorist operations and that he was now assisting the British with their investigations. I could not comment on when he might be either released or charged.

I wasn't being obstructive as, I think, Niels suspected. I simply didn't have a clue. No one in TF196 had any intention of sharing their plans with me. After all, as The Colour Sergeant had identified all those years ago, I was pond life. Nor did they really give a shit if the Gereshk economy ground to a halt, nor stop to consider the impact this might have on the city's 50,000 residents.

They were all pond life too.

Latitude:	31.77
Longitude:	64.68
Elevation:	847m
Met:	Sandstorms H:16°L:2°
DTG:	110800DMAR12

OVER THE COURSE of the next few days the battlegroup became fixed in Yakchal, not as we had expected by the enemy, but by the weather. Sandstorms blocked out the sun in a 'brownout' that reduced visibility to a few metres and grounded aircraft and UAVs. With no eyes in the sky, no air-to-ground fire support and, crucially, no medical dust-off capability *Patrol Minimise* was ordered and the operation ground to a halt as the blokes hunkered down and weathered the storm.

This frustrated everyone, but none more so than Thor. He'd been forced to return to MOB Price after the vehicle in which he was travelling struck an IED, one of five IED strikes in as many days without a single casualty. It's a testament to the quality of the new generation of protected mobility (PM) vehicles that we'd been so fortunate. But Thor now had a personal score to settle. He stalked the J9 cell impatiently, in full body armour, his Diemarco C7A1 assault rifle locked and loaded, waiting for the storm to lift. His frustration was evident and we gave him a wide berth as his mood darkened with every passing hour. I felt almost sorry for the Taliban. They'd crossed a line by blowing him up. If Thor had anything to do with it, they would now be lucky to make it to year end and if they did they were not going to be on his Christmas card list.

As Thor waited for the storm to pass, Haji's family and friends were busy drumming up support for the beleaguered hawaladar. No sooner had TF196 departed the scene than Haji's brother Ajip made haste to the DG's residence where he appealed for sanctuary. He remained the Governor's house guest for the next few weeks – too fearful for his own safety to undertake the short walk home.

This explained the unusually early telephone call that Niels had received from the Governor. Curiously, my contacts at TF196 seized upon it as evidence of Ajip's complicit guilt. According to their twisted logic, if Ajip had nothing to hide he would not object to being violently abducted and held indefinitely without trial just like his brother. Furthermore, if the District Governor was providing safe refuge for the hawaladar it could only be because he too was aiding and abetting the Taliban.

This last assumption seemed entirely credible. The DG may have been an elected official in the GIRoA administration but in Helmand Province friend and foe are inextricably conjoined by the huge profits to be made from narcotics and the mismanagement of international aid projects. Haji and Ajip, not being servants of a corrupt and discredited administration, did not possess the same *get out of jail free* card as did the Governor.

24 hours after Haji's abduction Niels received a visit from the District Communications Advisor, Sultaan Khan. Since there was no free press, and no media channels in the district, the DCA did not spend a great deal of his day providing communications advice. He did, however, speak passable English and was used by the Governor as a go-between with the DST. Sultaan was irrepressibly cheerful and laughed off the obvious dangers of being the DG's intermediary with his trademark girlish giggle. On a number of occasions I would meet him to conduct various influence tasks in the district. My presence would require at least three armoured vehicles and a dozen or so heavily armed soldiers in full combat gear providing close protection. Sultaan would arrive on his Honda CG125 motorcycle with a little Russian made Makarov 9mm pistol tucked into his waistcoat. He would frequently tease me for being such a cowardy-custard and on more than one occasion offered me a backy on his Honda, an offer he knew I would decline, thus confirming my pusillanimity.

It was hard not to like him.

On this occasion Sultaan hand delivered a formal looking document from the DG, countersigned by Ghullie Khan, the District Chief of Police which stated that Haji Gul was not guilty of any crimes and should be released from British custody immediately. Despite working for the British Foreign and Commonwealth Office, Niels neatly sidestepped the issue by playing his Danish joker. I was duly summonsed to the DST offices to explain what the British were up to.

No one was telling me anything, but UK policy required that I neither confirm nor deny the presence of UKSF. Unable to pass the buck I stuck to my original line: *Haji Gul has been detained by British forces on suspicion of aiding and abetting terrorist operations. He is now assisting the British with their investigations. I cannot comment on when he may be either released or charged.*

Niels let me squirm as Sultaan impressed upon me the seriousness of the situation. Haji was a pillar of the community, a personal friend of the Governor, and a key business leader. The British were exceeding their authority in the district, as they had done once before back in 1842. Sultaan reminded me that things had not ended well for the Angrezi[1] on that occasion. In order to avoid a repeat performance we must now act on the DG's direct and explicit instructions or risk retaliatory attacks on British troops and patrol bases.

I counselled against attacks on British bases, which I assured Sultaan would be robustly defended, and pointed out that an official from the Ministry of Interior Affairs had been on hand at the time of Haji's detention. I recommended that the DG take this up with his own administration, which had clearly sanctioned the arrest.

Sultaan dismissed the MoIA's attendance as blatant rubber-stamping and informed me that the British were being duped by the DG's political rivals in Kabul who were fabricating evidence to settle personal scores. This was a claim I was to hear repeatedly over the course of the next few days.

Message delivered, Sultaan good naturedly patted me on the shoulder and apologised for the grilling he'd just given me: *I'm sorry Chris, I know it's not your fault but you must tell General Jim and he will fix this.* It took me a few moments to realise that the *General Jim* Sultaan referred to was in fact the Commanding Officer. But Colonel James was trapped in the storm somewhere in the Landae Dashtah, the desert area south of Highway One to the west of Yakchal.

The Gereshk business community also mobilised in support of Haji's plight. Shortly after Sultaan had departed into the storm on his motorcycle a delegation of business leaders arrived at the camp gates demanding to be taken to our leader. For reasons of operational security no one was about to tell them that the boss was currently out of the office and Thor was still in no mood to socialise, so I was summonsed once more.

In a society which respects the wisdom and experience that comes with age my juniority in rank was compensated for by my seniority in

[1] **Angrezi**: English

years. Although I was unable to match the resplendent white beards of our guests, I still sported sufficient grey hairs to satisfy them that I was a suitable recipient of their delegation.

These elders were all important businessmen in the Gereshk community. But they didn't wear bespoke business suits, expensive silk ties or handmade dress shoes. Nor did we have a business class lounge where we could serve them up a cappuccino with a selection of little pastries. Instead these venerable gentlemen were forced to stand in the dust at the camp gates, dodging the occasional armoured vehicle as it roared past spewing diesel fumes, while the Bosnian guard force biometrically enrolled them.

This painstaking process took about 45 minutes after which time we were escorted to a battered and broken picnic table hidden behind some Hesco bastion[1] over which someone, many months before, had slung an ancient camouflage net. The place was clearly being used as an emergency toilet for anyone caught short while on guard duty. It reeked of stale urine.

If we had set out deliberately to isolate ourselves from the community we sought to protect by demeaning and humiliating their business elite, we could hardly have done a better job.

I listened as attentively as I could while trying not to gag on the stench of piss but by now I was familiar with the story: the British were being tricked into doing the dirty work of shadowy figures in Kabul; Haji was innocent, indeed it was ridiculous to accuse him of being a terrorist; why were the British detaining respected businessmen while terrorists were in plain sight?; what had Haji ever done to the British?

I could do little to appease these men and they began to despair at my lack of authority. The best I could do was to reassure them that Haji was being treated with dignity and respect and that if he was innocent of any crime he would, eventually, be released. I privately hoped this was true. I couldn't really be sure what went on in 'Torchlight' – the temporary detention facility at Camp Bastion.

---

[1] **Hesco Bastion**: a Modern gabion used for flood control and military fortification and the name of the British company that developed it in the late 1980s. It comprises a collapsible wire mesh container and heavy duty fabric liner which is filled with sand, soil or gravel and used as a temporary to semi-permanent dike or barrier against explosions or small-arms. It has been widely used in Afghanistan and is routinely adapted by soldiers to fashion rudimentary furniture to make living accommodation a little more comfortable and homely.

I pressed them for the names of the shadow men in Kabul but they mumbled into their beards and were not forthcoming. It seemed likely to me that they were referring to Malim Mir Wali, a parliamentarian in Kabul who had formerly been a powerful tribal leader in the district. In the past he had duped both British and American troops into supporting his own tribal power struggles with weapons and money, simply by denouncing his rivals as Taliban. In the search for a quick solution no one had done overly much to check the factual accuracy of his assertions. Now a member of the political elite in Kabul, he remained influential in Gereshk. He was an opponent of both the District Governor and the Chief of Police because they were not from his own Barakzai tribe.

Finally, after more dark threats about violence in Gereshk, the delegation appealed to me for the return of the hawaladars' ledgers so that business in the city might resume. They impressed upon me the anxiety of ordinary citizens whose livelihoods were dependent on the honouring of transactions recorded in the ledgers and without which they might face financial ruin. They didn't use scholarly terms such as *economic collapse*, *hyperinflation* or *banking sector systemic destabilisation*, but I got the picture. They also requested the return of $3 million in mixed currencies that they claimed had been removed from the hawaladars' safe along with the ledgers. I agreed to look into this and get back to them, but could make no promises. Realising that this was the best I could offer them, and doubtless as eager as I was myself to escape the foul smell, they departed.

I returned to the J9 cell to write my report. It was not entirely complimentary. I reiterated my concerns that dismantling the hawala banking system ran counter to broader campaign aims to rebuild the economy, and that snatching people off the streets was not especially democratic. I further reported the second and third order effects of Haji's arrest. These amounted to a local perception that the British had either conducted an armed bank robbery, were settling scores dating back to 1842, or were again being tricked into supporting Malim Mir Wali in his on-going struggle for power in the district.

It didn't matter whether these perceptions matched reality or not, the net effect was to alienate the British from the population we sought to protect. In an attempt to salvage the situation I recommended that we return the hawaladar's ledgers and cash as soon as possible so that the local economy did not stall, and that a senior figure in the MoIA speak with Salim Rodi to confirm that the ministry had sanctioned the arrest. I also suggested that it would be sensible either to charge or to release Haji Gul as soon as practically possible.

Of course, we did none of these things.

However, my unfavourable report did reach senior figures in the ISAF chain of command and some awkward questions were asked. While the rest of the battlegroup continued to endure the sandstorm in the desert, I now found myself at the centre of a shit storm.

The first I knew about this was the following morning when I received a telephone call from the TF196 team leader who had led the kill/capture operation to seize Haji Gul. He was not a happy bunny. It's not every day that a Tier One special forces soldier calls you up to give you a bollocking. I think I managed to give a reasonable account of myself.

I stuck to the line taken in my report that the arrest had been unnecessarily heavy-handed, painting the British in a bad light, and that the consequences damaged the broader campaign strategy of reconstruction. The team leader countered by not unreasonably pointing out that it hadn't been my boot knocking down Haji's door or my life on the line in so doing. It had never been my plan or intention to kick down doors in Afghanistan, but several months later I was to find myself in just this situation while conducting an operation with Afghan special forces in the Dasht-E-Siminar, the desert area to the north of Gereshk. It's a nerve-wracking experience bursting through a door, full auto selected, safety catch off, finger through the trigger guard not knowing what is on the other side – a hail of bullets, a suicide bomber, or an IED. In this case I was confronted by an innocent young boy of about Harry's age, an unarmed cow and a clutch of defenceless chickens.

They may have been innocent, unarmed and defenceless, adjectives that might equally have been applied to Haji Gul himself, but they still managed to scare the shit out of me.

Point made the team leader went on to inform me that Haji was *singing like a canary*. I didn't want to think this might be because his testicles were wired up to the Torchlight generators. Or because of some other *enhanced interrogation technique* of which I was unaware. That would contravene the Geneva Convention and the Laws of Armed Conflict. But it might be simply because he genuinely feared for his life having been violently abducted at gunpoint from his place of work before enjoying the hospitality of his Torchlight gaolers.

It was soon clear that the TF196 team leader and I were not going to be able to resolve our differences of opinion. It may have been a personality clash, or because I was a part-time soldier daring to criticise our country's elite forces, or because I was tarnishing an operation that TF196 were billing as a resounding success. After all, they'd got their man and he was singing like a canary. I couldn't really blame the team leader. He'd been tasked to do a job and he'd done that to the best of his ability in the manner in which he'd been trained to do it. However, he managed to seriously piss me off by implying that my dissent made me some kind of Taliban apologist.

I responded that if Haji really was a Taliban financier then I'd gladly see him locked up. But there was no compelling evidence to support this assertion, or at least none that could be divulged. The manner of his arrest, and his subsequent detention without charge or access to legal process, was not the right way to go about this. Nor was it sensible to destabilise the local economy by confiscating his ledgers, potentially provoking a violent reaction against British soldiers.

We went round in circles for a few minutes. I was grateful this was a telephone call from an undisclosed location rather than a face-to-face meeting. Sultaan was right, I am a cowardy-custard. As my colleagues delighted in reminding me I was also getting on a bit. Plus the relentless dust storm was making me wheezy. I didn't fancy my chances in a fist fight with this flat-bellied, steely eyed killer.

His was not the only call I received that morning. The general consensus seemed to be that my report was unpatriotic and I should wind my Taliban-loving neck in. It wasn't turning out to be an especially carefree day but I did manage to persuade my antagonists that the hawaladars' ledgers should be returned. A small but significant victory, although it would be another week before they were restored to the attentive care of Haji Gul's one-eyed clerk in a ceremony at the District Police Headquarters.

Latitude:	31.77
Longitude:	64.68
Elevation:	847m
Met:	Sunny H:22°L:7°
DTG:	171200DMAR12

DPHQ IS TYPICAL of buildings in the city that have been funded by the international community. A two-storey concrete structure sited on open ground on the city's west side, part of an urban sprawl along Highway One, the main east-west arterial through-route. The build quality is poor, perhaps reflecting the fact that the contractor has had to pay kickbacks to both GIRoA and Taliban officials, as well as line his own pockets, before investing in construction materials.

Concrete decay has set in after only a few years. Poorly installed corroding rebar[1] pockmark the walls. Broken glass in most of the windows, pools of water on the floor. Paper thin doors sag from their hinges. The AUP who occupy the building do not employ a Facilities Manager. Fixtures and fittings are cheap rather than cheerful. Furniture is of the plastic garden variety, the sort that looks good in the Garden Centre brochure but which barely lasts the summer. All around a sea of mud churned up by the armoured vehicles that come and go is now slowly baking hard as the seasons change. Perhaps the construction specification did not include a car park or perhaps there was no money left over for hard standing after everyone had taken their cut.

A collection of broken down and abandoned Ford Rangers and Humvees in AUP livery litter the perimeter wall. The vehicles have been donated by the US taxpayer but the AUP don't employ a Fleet Manager either. No one thought to provide a spares and maintenance package with the vehicles, so when they break down or become damaged they are dragged to one side and left to rot.

Outside the front gates a mange-ridden three-legged dog with a litter of equally pathetic puppies somehow scratches a living on the waste ground. I first observed these pitiable creatures with disgust, but over time, without lifting a finger to help or throwing even a scrap of food to sustain them, I began to keep an eye out for them. Willing them to live,

---

[1] **Rebar**: Reinforcing bar, a steel bar or mesh of steel wires commonly used as a tension device in reinforced concrete and reinforced masonry structures, to strengthen and hold the concrete in compression.

to survive, not to escape to a better life, but because their presence here makes this shithole complete.

My unfavourable report into the abduction and illegal detention of Haji Gul must have struck a chord somewhere. Although Task Force Helmand Commander, Brigadier Patrick Sanders does not attend in person, he deems the matter sufficiently important that his deputy, Colonel Johnny Bowron is detailed to attend the formal ceremony at DPHQ in which the hawaladar's ledgers are to be returned to his loyal clerk.

I spent the 48 hours prior to this event searching for the ledgers after they were lost in transit. Initially shipped by the geniuses at Torchlight in an unmarked cardboard box without any shipping notes, they had been mislaid in the tonnes of cargo that passes through the Bastion helipad each day. With the help of the Grenadier's Administrative Officer, Captain Rich Seargent, who personally searched through several piles of 'lost' consignments, the ledgers were eventually located, repackaged and dispatched by Chinook to MOB Price - but still failed to arrive. It turned out they'd been accidentally kicked off the tail ramp of the aircraft at another patrol base. In the end I commandeered a couple of Mastiffs to go and collect them in person. It was a completely unnecessary road move which put soldiers' lives, my own included, at risk. A further example of the stupidity and arrogance of those who should have known better but seemed not to care about the significance and value of the ledgers to the people we sought to protect.

The handover ceremony is to be witnessed by District Governor Salim Rodi, Chief of Police Ghullie Khan and Niels Vistisen, the DST's Political Advisor. Haji Gul remains incarcerated at Torchlight. His brother Ajip, unsurprisingly, has declined our invitation to attend the ceremony. I have managed to persuade an RMP Staff Sergeant to play Master of Ceremonies and he more than rises to the challenge by turning up with reams of official looking paperwork which he insists is signed in triplicate by everyone present – the District Governor is ecstatic, signing each of the papers with a broadening grin and a flourish of his pen.

On arrival at DPHQ I also find a bearded Danish soldier who must be almost seven feet tall hanging around in full combat gear. It's not entirely clear what he's doing here, but since he looks like a cross between *Conan the Barbarian* and a character from *Call of Duty 4: Modern Warfare* I persuade him to act as *Escort to the Ledgers.*

He performs this unexpected role brilliantly, standing motionless throughout the ceremony beside the wooden box we've found for the ledgers, staring menacingly through his ballistic glasses, while his finger rests sinisterly across the trigger guard of his assault rifle. As soon as the RMP Staff Sergeant is satisfied that all the paperwork is in order and that the ledgers are now returned to the custody of the clerk, he disappears whence he came, never to be seen again.

My self-appointed role in the proceedings is to act as photographer. With all that I know about Ghullie Khan I'm briefly tempted to pull my Sig and convert him into a 9mm colander. But this would almost certainly get me killed and as Sultaan has already identified I'm a coward at heart. So I stick to shooting him with the camera instead, together with the rest of the ceremonial party.

After the handover is complete I return to MOB Price with the Deputy Commander in the back of a Danish MRAP. Colonel Bowron, who has looked tired and distracted throughout the ceremony, tells me he is heading home in a few days for a family skiing holiday. We keep the shred alive[1] for a few brief moments, swapping stories of powder days in mountains a world away from here as we trundle down Highway One in the back of the hot, dusty vehicle. I tell him of a crazy Swiss ski instructor who has founded a ski club in Bamiyan Province and is trying to promote tourism in the area by holding a backcountry ski race that is due to take place in a few weeks time. The blurb on his website warns participants:

The mountains of Afghanistan are not the Alps nor the Rocky Mountains. There is no mountain rescue service nor avalanche warning systems in place and local medical facilities are basic. Mobile phone service is patchy at best and non existent in the mountains. Although the province of Bamiyan is known as one of the safest in Afghanistan, the current political situation across the country is far from stable. We strongly advise all participants to arrange insurance before entering the competition and consider suitable personal security measures if desired. All participants take part solely at their own risk.

I'm secretly hoping that the Deputy Commander will instruct me to put a team together to participate. My fantasy is that a Black Hawk helicopter is seconded to the task and we spend a few days heli skiing

---

[1] **Keep the shred alive**: the pure pleasure, freedom and exhilaration that comes from skiing, snowboarding or skateboarding to a high standard of proficiency.

in the high mountains of the Hindu Kush. Mountains that are almost twice the height of the Alps with descents that have never borne the tracks of skis or boards on their pristine, powdered surface. It's a skier's wet dream. But Colonel Johnny doesn't take the bait.

In December 2008 General David McKiernan, the senior military commander in Afghanistan issued a tactical directive in which he stated: *The way [international forces] act, the techniques we use, and the means we employ must serve to protect and defend the Afghan public and reinforce their confidence in [the government of Afghanistan] and the forces fighting on their behalf.*

Four years later it seemed that these rules still did not apply to TF196. They were never required to account for the abduction of Haji Gul, who was released without charge or apology 25 days later. It's hard to imagine Fred Goodwin, the disgraced and de-knighted former Chief Executive of the Royal Bank of Scotland, or Stuart Gulliver, Chief Executive of HSBC which laundered billions of dollars for Mexican drug cartels, being subjected to such treatment.

The claim that up to $3 million in mixed currencies was taken from Haji's business premises at the time of his detention was denied by TF196, who countered that the only money removed was a small amount of change he was carrying in his pockets. We will never know the truth but, even allowing for some Afghan opportunistic exaggeration, it seems highly improbable to me that a hawaladar, whose stock in trade is hard currency, would not maintain a cash reserve of any kind in his safe.

Even if the cupboard had been bare on the morning of Haji's abduction, it made little difference to the citizens of Gereshk. They had witnessed armed men make off with several black canvas bags which they rightly or wrongly presumed contained the missing cash. There wasn't a single kafir in Afghanistan who could convince them otherwise.

To my mind the manner in which TF196 had set about supporting the US Treasury Department's top secret campaign, a campaign which in itself was deeply flawed and hypocritical, had served only to set the population against us. This was no way to win a counter-insurgency.

Back in the world, before I'd departed for Afghanistan, I'd explained to Alfie that I would be helping the good guys stop the bad guys from doing bad stuff. I wasn't getting   off to a very good start. The black and white world I'd described to Alfie didn't exist, no more than did the one he'd drawn for me where the forces of good easily overmatched the bad. The tangled and depressing reality of Helmand Province was frying my brain and testing my sanity. I needed to give my head a rest and go and lie low in one of our patrol bases for a while. By great good fortune a perfect opportunity to do that had just presented itself. We had a press photographer coming to town.

Latitude   31.77
Longitude   64.68
Elevation   847m
Met   Sunny H:17°L:3°
DTG   210510DMAR12

1.   Hope for the best.
2.   Plan for the worst.
3.   Prepare to be surprised.

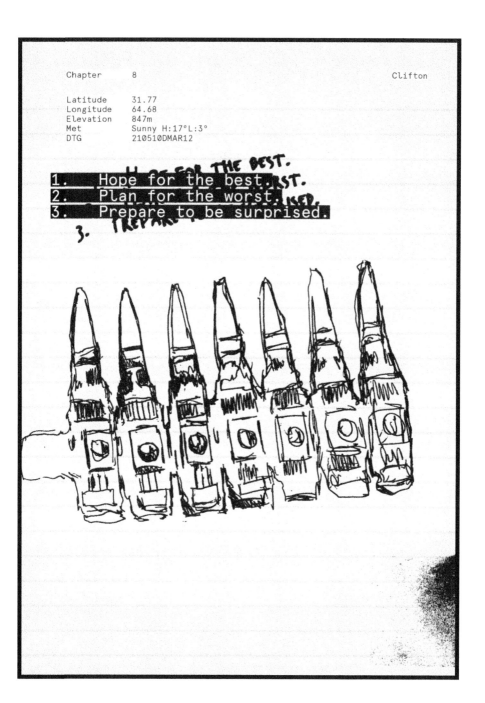

PB: Patrol Base
AFV: Armoured Fighting Vehicle
SAF: Small Arms Fire
CNO: Casualty Notification Officer
PTSD: Post-traumatic Stress Disorder
REMF: Rear Echelon Mother Fucker
DCA: District Communications Adviser
FLET: Forward Line of Enemy Troops
UXO: Unexploded Ordnance
GPMG: General Purpose Machine Gun
UGL: Underslung Grenade Launcher
4B:1T: Four Ball: One Tracer
MERT: Medical Emergency Response Team

MINISTRY OF DEFENCE ANNOUNCEMENT

Captain Rupert Bowers. On Wednesday 21 March 2012, Captain Rupert Bowers was killed in the blast from an improvised explosive device while leading a patrol to clear a position of insurgents in the Nahr-e Saraj district of Helmand province.

Sergeant Luke Taylor and **Lance Corporal Michael Foley.** On Monday 26 March 2012, Sergeant Luke Taylor and Lance Corporal Michael Foley were shot and killed at the main entrance to Lashkar Gah Main Operating Base in Helmand province.

Latitude:	31.77
Longitude:	64.68
Elevation:	847m
Met:	Sunny H:17°L:3°
DTG:	210510DMAR12

THE FIRE ALARM went off at 05.10. Its piercing tone could not be ignored, which was just as well because fire could rip through the tented city in which we lived at frightening speed. But I didn't respond. The smoke detector in our eight-man tent was prone to false alarms, it may even have been triggered by one of Major 'Mo' Morrison's thunderous and obnoxious farts.

I lay in the dark listening out for the sounds that must surely accompany a genuine alarm, running feet, raised voices, roaring flames, and mentally rehearsed the five or so paces it would take me to reach the exit, but I heard nothing. Satisfied the alarm was crying wolf once more, I rolled over and tried to go back to sleep.

At 05.30, as dawn's rosy fingers began to lighten the morning sky, I admitted defeat and headed for the wash tent. Despite the early hour, I had to wait in turn to use one of the eight communal sinks. Colonel James and Sarn't Major Glenn Haughton, safely returned from Yakchal with the rest of the battlegroup just the day before, joined the queue behind me.

There are no privileges of rank when it comes to daily ablutions.

The Sarn't Major somehow managed to squeeze his huge frame beside me behind the narrow metal sink. Thoroughly intimidated by his enormous, tattooed presence I shaved in silence to lessen the risk of offending him in some way.

Having successfully completed my own lavation without incurring the wrath of the Big Man, I dropped my laundry with Siyal before popping over to the welfare centre to check my Hotmail and Facebook accounts. Welfare Centre was a somewhat grand overstatement for the dusty shipping container with its half dozen computer terminals but it was, nonetheless, our indispensable link to the lives we'd left behind.

Being a man of upper middle age, I hadn't really got the point of Facebook before Afghanistan. Now it had become a lifeline to a world without Hesco. A world where people, in the normal course of events, were not routinely and painstakingly planning to kill each other.

Instead they were posting pictures of the places they'd visited at the weekend, of their kids winning prizes at school, or even of the maddening commute to work they'd endured on Monday morning.

Sitting down at one of the battered and bruised keyboards I enjoyed my allotted 30 minutes of internet time, living vicariously through the delicious morsels of normality that my friends and family served up from all over the globe. With a like, comment or share, I was able to join them in that moment, and in doing so let them know I was alive and well.

Facebook now made perfect sense but, ironically, it could not bring me news of my own family. *Unfriended* by Jane, I assume to avoid sharing with me any potentially embarrassing pictures of her new life with her new partner, she had also denied me further news of Harry and Alfie. To make matters worse, although I'd now been in-country for almost two months, I had yet to receive a letter either from her or from the boys. I wasn't holding out for love letters from Jane, but with every mail consignment that reached us I could not suppress the hope that, somewhere in the pile, there would be a picture or drawing from my boys.

Months later, after the tour was over, I discovered a stack of blueys I'd written to Alfie lying unopened in a drawer in his bedroom. Although I never confronted Jane about this, it seems that her bitterness towards me was such that she could not bring herself even to read my letters to our son.

By the time I found out it was too late to feel devastated so I just let it pass.

My 30 minutes up, I headed for the D-FAC, short for Dining Facility, the ridiculous 21st century name for the cookhouse. The only problem with the food at MOB Price was that there was too much of it. Somehow I managed to avoid the temptation of a full English, and settled for tinned grapefruit segments.

After breakfast I wandered down to the helipad to meet Press Association photographer, Ben Birchall. He was visiting the battlegroup for forty-eight hours and I'd volunteered to be his media escort. The British Army's innate dislike and distrust of the media meant that I faced no competition for this task. I saw it as my passport to escape the Looking Glass for a few days.

Ben was my March Hare, my ticket out of MOB Price to the relative sanity of PB Clifton. Closer to the front line and the dangers of close quarter combat, further from the self-deceiving madhouse of counter-insurgency operations. My brain needed a rest.

But Ben's first task, before our departure, was to cover the vigil service to be held later that day in memory of Sergeant Coupe and his Warrior AFV crew. The rest of Task Force Helmand had already paid their respects, but the service at Price had been delayed by the clearance operation in Yakchal and the sandstorms.

News headlines in the UK continued to be dominated by the loss of Sergeant Coupe and his crew, and it seemed likely that our delayed vigil would be deemed still topical by broadsheet and tabloid photo-editors alike.

As counterpoint to the tragedy I had two good news stories for Ben. Less than 24 hours earlier Warrant Officer Richard Burton[1] miraculously escaped uninjured during an SAF[2] contact when an enemy round passed so close that it drilled a hole through the map pocket of his trousers. On the same day, in a separate incident, Sergeant Mark James walked away unscathed from an IED strike directly beneath the cab of his vehicle. Both men had been incredibly lucky.

I briefed Ben over freshly brewed coffee in the J9 cell. I'd grown accustomed to the Danish preference for coffee like crude oil, but I could see Ben struggling with the viscous brew. Coffee over, we went in search of Sergeant James. Despite yesterday's incident he was already back at work in the MT[3] section, preparing to lead another road move to Camp Bastion. It turned out he was a natural in front of the camera and Ben was able to get a number of really good shots which were subsequently picked up by a variety of regional newspapers back in the UK.

---

[1] **Richard Burton**: Not his real name.

[2] **SAF**: Small Arms Fire

[3] **MT**: Mechanical Transport

While Ben was filing his story I found Warrant Officer Burton enjoying a crafty smoke round the back of the Ops tent. He was no longer wearing his *lucky* trousers, which were now reserved for special occasions. I was struck by how matter of fact he was, chiding the poor marksmanship skills of his adversary.

A miss is as good as a mile, he said cheerfully, as if discussing some targetry on the ranges rather than his own flesh and bone. But he also revealed to me that his wife and family were under the impression that he'd spent the last six months in a cushy job in the rear headquarters. With less than a week to go before completing his tour, he was understandably reluctant to talk to the press and expose the reality of his service in Afghanistan to his loved ones. We agreed that Ben could not tell his story. I secretly suspect that no one outside the immediate circle of soldiers who have served alongside him will ever learn the truth.

As Ben and I made our way down to the D-FAC for lunch the tannoy system hiccupped into life with a series of muffled clicks and *Standby for broadcast* echoed across the camp. My heart sank when I heard the words that followed: *Op Minimise, Op Minimise, Op Minimise.*

A comrade had been killed or seriously injured.

I wracked my brain to recall which callsigns were currently out on the ground and therefore who the casualty might be. I resisted the temptation to run back to the Ops room. If troops were still in contact, or casualties were being extracted, then I would just be in the way. My morbid curiosity would have to wait until after the duty staff had dealt with the incident.

The codeword *Minimise* refers to a restriction of normal communications until next of kin have been notified. It means that the telephone and internet cabins in the main bases will be closed, and the sat phones at patrol bases will be withdrawn, until some poor soul back in the UK opens their front door to find a Casualty Notification Officer on their doorstep. I can't imagine how that conversation goes.

Nor can I imagine how Jane would react to a visit from the CNO.

As far as I knew she wouldn't break out the bunting, or high five the poor bloke, but I couldn't see her acting the grieving widow either. So instead I've nominated my 79 year old father as my Emergency Contact. I knew that Dad would take the news stoically, but he had already endured the loss of his wife and a grandson, and I felt guilty about potentially putting him through this.

Op Minimise would be called many more times over the coming months and my reaction was always the same, a dreadful sinking feeling followed by a mental attempt to guess who it might be, based on our patrolling activity at the time. Then an anxious and sometimes long wait to find out the details. I hated this ghoulish wait. I felt guilty because my need to know was based mainly on a desire to eliminate those I knew personally from the list of potential victims. If I didn't know the name or the unit of the victim I would breathe a sigh of relief that would instantly turn to remorse. Whether I knew him or not, this was someone's son, someone's husband, someone's father.

Somewhere back in the UK an unmarked service vehicle was pulling over to the curb outside someone's house. Curtains across the street twitching as the stranger double-checked the address against his notes, opened the gate, and walked up to the front door to impart the tragic news from Afghanistan.

Much later, when the summer fighting season is almost over, *Op Minimise* is not lifted for several days following a series of successive casualties. For some reason I've returned to Camp Bastion and while I'm sitting in the Bastion D-FAC I overhear a number of young soldiers at an adjacent table complaining that the internet and phone cabins are still shut. They have lost sight of the reason why and are solely concerned about their inability to call or Facebook their mates back home.

Despite the relentless banter, not everyone in the rear echelon is in fact a mother fucker. Even with unlimited access to pizza, six months in Camp Bastion is still a commitment to service and duty. It still means six months away from family and friends enduring austerity that even the Chancellor would baulk at.

But this crew are helping to give the rear echelon its bad name. Although they have never actually gone toe-to-toe with the Taliban themselves, I sourly assume they all have *Taliban Hunting Club* t-shirts in their grip bags for bragging rights in the pub back home.

I'm dining with some colleagues from the Info Ops community but I excuse myself and go over to these dickheads with the intention of giving them a good bollocking. Before I know it I'm raging at them, flecking spit over their food, generally losing the plot for a few moments. They look at me like I'm an alien from the planet Zog, but seeing my captain's rank slide on the front of my combat shirt, they wisely don't answer back.

Eventually I run out of steam and return to my seat.

I hear a few sniggers from the tables around me and resist the very strong temptation to start filling people in. I try to finish my meal, shaking so violently that the flimsy plastic cutlery breaks in my hands. My dining companions politely ignore my outburst and finish their own meals in embarrassed silence. They all think I've got PTSD, but that's bollocks.

A little on edge maybe, but I'm fine.

I think.

Latitude:	31.77
Longitude:	64.68
Elevation:	847m
Met:	Sunny H:17°L:3°
DTG:	211300DMAR12

WE LEARNED LATER that *Op Minimise* had been called for Captain Rupert Bowers, one of the *Advisor Three Zero* callsigns who live alongside and mentor 3rd Kandak[1] 3/215 Brigade in Camp Gereshk, just next door to our own base. He was killed in an IED explosion on the same day that we were honouring Sergeant Coupe and his crew. It was yet another blow to morale.

In the light of this news, Ben was concerned that he would be intruding by attending the vigil service with his camera. To allay his fears we spoke to Camp Quartermaster, Captain Mick Guyatt and to Padre Gary Scott. I didn't know Mick well, he was coming to the end of his tour and would be departing in a few weeks, but his responsibilities as Quartermaster included the smooth running of the vigils. Sadly this was not his first, and he would have a view on whether Ben should attend or not.

Gary I knew much better. We'd first met almost a year before in Canada and to my mind he was a top bloke and the best army padre I'd ever encountered by a country mile. Gary has a fascinating backstory. Before taking the cloth he started life as a semi-professional boxer. He then swapped the ring for the classroom, becoming a teacher and latterly a head teacher, before giving it all up to answer his calling. He tells a hilarious story about his early boxing career when a misunderstanding with the promoter saw him fight under the pseudonym *Gory Scrote*.

I liked Gary enormously and found it awkward admitting to him that I didn't share his faith. Ordinarily I might have avoided this confession but I felt compelled to speak to him about it shortly after my arrival at MOB Price. Rightly or wrongly, I've lived my life as an agnostic. In the event of my death I felt it would be hypocritical to receive a Christian burial.

If Gary was disappointed at my lack of faith he didn't show it.

---

[1] **Kandak**: Afghan National Army formation equivalent to a British battalion.

He neither judged, admonished, nor condemned. Nor did he warn me to seek salvation or risk eternal damnation. He simply made a note in his pocketbook and assured me he would take care of it.

Had I died in Helmand I knew, without doubt, that Gary would have fought my corner for me, in the face of his own beliefs and against the wishes of his bosses in the Royal Army Chaplains Department. He was that sort of bloke. Although I never admitted it to him, I was greatly comforted by this knowledge.

As I suspected they would be, Mick and Gary were both keen for Ben to record the vigil service. We all agreed that his presence would be announced immediately before the service began, allowing anyone who would prefer not to be photographed the opportunity to stand in the rear rank. When it comes to it, there are no takers.

Everyone who is not on essential duties attends the service. Danes, Bosnians and US troops all turn out to pay their last respects alongside their British counterparts, as well as civilian KBR staff and the volunteers from the Kuffen.

There are no REMFs[1] in MOB Price, we all spend time outside the wire. No one here will ever complain that the injury or death of another is curtailing their own social life back home. We all have to confront our proximity to mortality, to accept that we may not live to hear the next *Op Minimise* broadcast.

The only place large enough to accommodate a parade of this size is the tank hard-standing directly outside the headquarters back gate. It's where all the vigil services at MOB Price are held and a memorial has been erected in front of the concrete blast walls that protect the fragile canvas headquarters. It consists of a white painted, waist high concrete wall on which the words *In the fight for peace* have been inscribed in both Pashtu and English. Four flagpoles stand atop this simple monument giving it its name, *Four Flags.* On the blast walls behind them British and Danish soldiers who have made the ultimate sacrifice are immortalised in neat columns on brass tablets mounted on simple wooden frames. It's a long list. A list to which seven more names will shortly be added.

---

[1] **REMF**: Rear Echelon Mother Fucker

Every patrol base I visit has a memorial to the Fallen. Although these are much more rudimentary in their construction they are no less poignant. In one, white painted stones have been inscribed in black permanent marker with the names of fallen comrades and placed inside a simple wooden frame. A scaled-up version of the pebble I carry in my body armour.

Everyone begins to assemble ten or fifteen minutes ahead of time. In bright sunshine under piercing blue skies men from different units mingle and chat quietly together, waiting patiently for the senior non-commissioned officers to start forming us up into three ranks. There are no raised voices as would ordinarily be expected on a parade square. Although it has not been mandated soldiers have swapped their floppy jungle hats for regimental headdress. We're all carrying weapons of course, but slung on our backs with the barrels pointing towards the ground in a further mark of respect.

Eventually, the Sarn't Major calls everyone to attention and Gary says a few words before reading the Regimental Collects of the units to which the soldiers belong, The Duke of Lancaster's and the Yorkshire Regiment.

O Lord Jesus Christ,

Bless we beseech Thee all members of The Duke of Lancaster's Regiment and grant that we may so loyally serve our Sovereign and our native land that, having fought the good fight and risen dauntless over all difficulties in this life, we may be known by our deeds to be Thy servants and come at last to Thine everlasting kingdom;

Through Jesus Christ our Lord. Amen.

O Lord God:
The shield and buckler of all that trust Thee:
Grant to the Yorkshire Regiment in its battalions and ranks, the strength that fears no evil tidings:
No desperate endeavours:
And no foe bodily or spiritual; but advances in Thy righteousness:
Through all rough places:
Under the Captain of our Salvation:
Jesus Christ our Lord.

The names and dates of birth of the fallen are then read out. One of them, Private Daniel Wilford was   born in 1991, the year of the first

Gulf War and my first operational tour of duty.

I was older then than he is now and have already lived more than half a life. In that moment of realisation, were it possible, I would gladly trade what's left for him. Like so many others around me I bow my head to hide the tears I shed for men I have never known.

Private Wilford is just 21, the same age as Charlie Gilmore, son of Pink Floyd guitarist David Gilmour, when he desecrated the Cenotaph during student demonstrations in the capital. Daniel and others like him have died protecting our way of life, so that Charlie and others like him can enjoy a nice day out in London, exercise their right to protest and loot Top Shop on the way home.

After the two minute silence a bugler plays the last post and the Sarn't Major concludes the service with the painfully familiar words:

When You Go Home, Tell Them Of Us And Say,
For Your Tomorrow, We Gave Our Today

I wonder how many more times I will be called to this dusty corner of some foreign field to hear this exhortation spoken for men less than half my age. As tears trickle down my face and across my cracked lips I taste the bitter reality of British foreign policy in Afghanistan.

And then the service is over and we quietly shuffle back to our posts.

By now Victoria Bowers has received a visit from the CNO and learned the shocking news that her husband is dead. Their month-old son, Hugo will never know his father.

Before the last soldier has drifted away from Four Flags, someone has already started planning the next vigil service that will honour her husband's sacrifice.

The war goes on.

Later that day Ben fired up his laptop computer and showed me the photos. His compositions of light and shadow brilliantly capture the mood of the service. In one of them Gary can be seen standing, head bowed in front of the parade. His backdrop is a coil of razor wire atop the concrete blast wall above which the British, Danish, American and

Bosnian flags hang limply at half mast in a pale blue, cloudless sky.

It's a powerful image but something is missing. There is no flag to represent the nation we seek to protect or the soil into which we bleed.

Ben's photograph inadvertently exposes the self-deception that underlies our endeavours. We are claiming not to be an army of occupation, demonstrating our solidarity with our ANA colleagues by wearing little Velcro-backed Afghan flags on the front of our body armour – but this is just for show.

Where it matters, in our hearts and at the centre of our stronghold, this is not what we believe. The Afghan flag does not fly alongside the US, British, Danish and Bosnian flags, whose soldiers are our brothers-in-arms and with whom we have a mutual kinship, trust and respect. It is not a deliberate omission, it has not been a conscious decision to exclude the flag, but the symbolism of its absence provides a striking insight into our true nature.

Or maybe, looking at Ben's photo, I was just putting two and two together and making five.

But for the next few days I didn't need to worry about any of this. Tomorrow I would be escorting Ben to Patrol Base Clifton where we would join the 'Tigers', the men of C Company, the 1st Battalion the Princess of Wales Royal Regiment (1 PWRR) on the final fighting patrol of their six month tour of Helmand Province.

Latitude:	31.85
Longitude:	64.62
Elevation:	851m
Met:	Sunny H:18°L:2°
DTG:	041300DMAR12

I'D BEEN TO Clifton before for the opening ceremony of the largest single span bridge constructed by the Royal Engineers since World War Two. The bridge connects the northern bank of the Nahr-E-Buhgra canal with the Band-E-Barq road which handrails the canal's southern bank and is an important route into the city of Gereshk, protected by the ANA in a series of sangars[1] and checkpoints along its length.

Despite the ANA protection it's still the most heavily IEDed stretch of tarmac in Helmand, known to ISAF troops as *the towpath of terror*. It's a popular spot with IED emplacers because their devices do not need to breach the armour of our protected mobility vehicles. Even a relatively small explosion will be enough to shunt a vehicle into the Nahr-E-Buhgra where its occupants will most likely drown in the brown swirling waters before they are able to undo their three-point safety harnesses and open the heavy emergency hatches.

The bridge was to be opened by the District Governor to demonstrate GIRoA capacity. It was a pathetic deception that fooled no one, least of all the local people who had watched the Angrezi[2] engineers build it. As everyone knew, the District Administration was incapable of filling in a pothole, much less building a bridge.

When I explained to Sultaan, the DCA, that the bridge was a gift not from ISAF but from his own administration, he laughed to cover his confusion, or perhaps his embarrassment at my stupidity. He pointed out to me that the bridge had already been named *ISAF Bridge* by the local population. But this didn't suit the DST's narrative. We needed to demonstrate to the local community, and to the international media, that a better life lay ahead with GIRoA, not with ISAF who would be pulling out in two years time.

---

[1] **Sangar**: A small protected structure used for observing or firing from

[2] **Angrezi**: English

Incredibly we managed to deceive ourselves, our political masters, and sometimes even the media, that all was going swimmingly well. But the local population remained stubbornly sceptical.

Not surprisingly the opening ceremony was a bit of a flop as almost no one turned up. This may have had something to do with the fact that, for security reasons, we'd avoided telling anyone until the very last minute. Alternatively it may have been because the locals were unwilling to put themselves in harm's way. An event with a high probability of gunplay was hardly a fun day out for all the family.

In all over 200 ISAF soldiers were involved in providing security for the event. They were joined by an RAF Reaper MQ-9, silent and invisible, piloted from an office on a US military base more than 7,000 miles away near Las Vegas.

This was to be my first trip down the towpath of terror and I made sure I was sitting directly below the top gunner's hatch. I reckoned it was the best exit point from the vehicle if we were to get whacked and end up in the canal. Trying to appear casual, I rested my left hand on the quick-release buckle of my three-point harness. This was also part of my survival plan. The night before I'd jerry-rigged a quick release strap into my body armour. I didn't want to survive the IED and escape the flooding vehicle only to drown in the filthy waters of the canal under the weight of ballistic plates.

I normally carried my Sig 9mm pistol on the front of my body armour but for this trip I wore a dropleg holster on my right thigh. The dropleg holster looks great on Lara Croft in the Tomb Raider franchise, but it's not much good in the real world. It's almost impossible to run with a chunk of metal flapping around on your mid-thigh, plus anyone going on the ground soon learns that carrying your secondary shooter below waist level means immersing it in water several times a day as you climb in and out of irrigation ditches. Wearing a dropleg is a pretty good indicator that you don't do either of these things on a regular basis and is the mark of a base rat poseur. However, for this trip my Sig was uncomfortably chafing against my vastus lateralis because, if we did go into the canal, there would be no way to recover my assault rifle from the rack beside me, and once I'd dumped my body armour, I'd have no firepower.

I didn't want to survive the IED, escape the flooding vehicle and avoid drowning under the weight of my body armour, only to find myself defenceless in the face of a reception committee eager to

240

dress me in an orange jumpsuit before sawing my head off with a rusty penknife. I recalled a different war in a different time and place in which two off-duty soldiers were dragged from their vehicle and literally torn apart by an angry mob before being executed. Back then there'd been no social media, no internet on which to post the footage of this sickening incident, but I'd viewed it as part of my own training and conditioning for that particular conflict. It had convinced me then that I should seek to avoid this outcome, and 24 years later I hadn't revised my opinion.

1. Hope for the best.

2. Plan for the worst.

3. Prepare to be surprised.

We made it to the bridge unscathed but one of the vehicles behind us was not so lucky. A Danish tracked armoured personnel carrier strayed off the narrow strip of tarmacadam and detonated an IED. It was hard to believe that the ANA were unaware of its existence, in clear line of sight with a checkpoint less than 100 metres away. This was yet another example of the collusion between GIRoA forces and the Taliban, as locally agreed ceasefire lines and informal agreements were worked out between them at the expense of ISAF troops.

We were infidels, and therefore expendable.

Thankfully no one was seriously injured or ended up in the canal, but the road was blocked until the disabled vehicle could be recovered, an operation that would take at least 24 hours.

We pressed on to the bridge where I met Major Simon Doyle, MBE the officer commanding the Tigers. The bridge is in his AO and is a couple of klicks due south of PB Clifton. As soon as I arrived Simon gave me a quick briefing to orient me to the ground and the direction of any threats.

I tried not to show my alarm when he informed me that the FLET[1] was about 300 metres to our east. This was indeed worrying as it meant we were well inside the effective range of the AK47, the weapon of choice for most self-respecting insurgents. Back in the UK I'd assured friends

---

[1] **FLET**: Forward Line of Enemy Troops

and family that I would be so far behind the lines that I would need to send my laundry forward. If the enemy were only 300 metres away it seemed I would be calling on Mullah Omar to take care of my dirty washing. I could only hope that he would be as irrepressibly cheerful and accommodating as Siyal.

But the opening ceremony passed off without further incident. Although there were almost no locals to witness this auspicious event the District Governor, looking even more hung over than usual, imaginatively named the bridge *Azadi Pull,* Freedom Bridge, and cut the ribbon Sultaan had strung across its southern entrance. He then walked across the span in the company of several local dignitaries, soldiers and policemen to shake hands with Colonel James who was standing on the northern bank. I was guilty of having choreographed this piece of pointless symbolism. Ironically, I'd struggled to get approval for the $200 I'd given Sultaan to decorate the bridge and source drinks and nibbles for the VIPs.

According to some estimates, the cost to the taxpayer of British military involvement in Afghanistan was running at £15 million a day. The operation to provide security for this little sham must have run into several hundreds of thousands of pounds. But my request for $200 was initially turned down as too extravagant. It required the intervention of Colonel James to be authorised.

The ceremony over, we were all eager to get home. With the Band-e-Barq road closed by the disabled Danish APC, this entailed a lengthy and uncomfortable detour through the *dashte* (desert) to circumvent Gereshk. This was treacherous landscape, extremely difficult terrain for our vehicles, an unforgiving mix of axle-shattering bedrock, steep ravines, sand dunes and sinkholes. To add to the complex geography it was littered with Russian era UXO[1] and more modern IEDs. No one fancied driving around the dashte in the dark so we said a hasty farewell to Simon and saddled up.

The return journey quickly descended into chaos as vehicle after vehicle became buried in soft sand. No sooner was one dragged free than another became stuck. At one desperate point all our vehicles were buried to their axles, wheels spinning, engines screaming as their drivers frantically tried to release them from the desert's embrace. By

---

[1] **UXO**: Unexploded ordnance

now the sun had set. Ignoring the threats, we dismounted and began to dig ourselves out.

As the Sarn't Major's stress levels began to exceed safe limits he finally completed the transformation to Incredible Hulk. I did my best to stay out of his path as he raged around the stricken vehicles. Having survived the towpath of terror I had no desire to fall victim to an enormous, indestructible and very angry comic book character with stupendous strength he can barely control.

It was the early hours of the morning before we eventually extricated ourselves and continued our odyssey. Somewhere off to our left illumination rounds eerily lit the night sky, followed by the distant criss-cross of red and green tracer as combatants exchanged fire. I was grateful that the insurgents had been busy elsewhere while we'd been trapped, exposed and vulnerable in the sand.

A gold-throned dawn finally heralded our return to MOB Price and the rewards of a full English breakfast.

Latitude:	31.85
Longitude:	64.62
Elevation:	851m
Met:	Sunny H:9°L:6°
DTG:	230845DMAR12

BEN AND I arrive at PB Clifton with the mail, courtesy of an RAF Chinook. This immediately makes us popular. After the Chinook has departed, sand-blasting us all as it struggles for lift in the thin desert air, we help load the several sacks of welfare parcels and blueys onto the back of a quad bike before wandering over to the Ops room where I introduce Ben and Simon.

The patrol is due to depart in 15 minutes. Simon has just time to brief us on the plan. For the last fighting patrol of their six month tour, before handing over to the Grenadiers of Inkerman Company, Simon has decided to pay a visit to the *kalay,* or village, of Kakoran which lies behind the FLET and is a known insurgent stronghold.

A fighting patrol, as the name suggests, accepts combat as a likely or even desirable outcome in order to achieve its aims, and is planned and conducted with this in mind. In this case, Simon's aim is to disrupt insurgent freedom of movement and to dominate the ground forward of the patrol base. If we can destroy or kill the enemy in the process this will be an added bonus.

As Simon calmly explains that patrols usually come under fire when they reach a point roughly 150 metres west of the village, and pretty much remain in contact from that point on, I realise I've forgotten to bring my laundry with me. He also warns us that all the tree lines, ditches, hedges, tracks and paths are heavily seeded with IEDs and we will need to stay in the safe lane even when we come under fire.

Although neither Ben nor I bring it up, it's impossible to overlook the fact that he says *when* not *if.*

Briefing over we have just a few minutes to get ready. As Ben's media escort my sole responsibility on this patrol is to look after his welfare and ensure he returns safely. If I fail to complete this simple task I will find myself at the centre of a media storm. I will also be extremely unpopular with Ben's mum and with the Ministry of Defence. In addition, there will be a large amount of paperwork and explaining to do, which I'm eager to avoid. All this apart, since I've grown to rather like Ben, I'm taking the job seriously.

I'd noticed the previous day that Ben's admin was all over the place. Coats, bags, cameras, laptops, other tools of his trade, were quickly strewn across the desk we'd given him to work from. But, checking him over before the patrol, I'm impressed. He hasn't weighed himself down with too much kit, has sufficient water for the duration and is correctly wearing body armour, helmet and personal protection equipment, including gloves, knee-pads, pelvic protector (a.k.a. combat nappy), protective glasses and ear defenders. He's also rigged up two cameras onto his body armour in such a way that he can easily shoot from both while keeping his hands free when necessary.

Given the nature of the patrol everyone, except Ben, is heavily armed. Between us we're carrying an array of weapons: assault rifles; combat shotguns – designed for close quarter compound clearance; Minimi light machine guns; GPMGs – another machine gun but with a heavier round and more stopping power than the Minimi; L129A1 sharpshooter rifles – designed to engage targets with accurate fire out to 800 metres; LASM 66mm anti-structure rockets, L9A1 51mm mortars; L109A1 HE fragmentation grenades and L17A1 UGL 40mm grenade launchers.

All these weapons will be only so much dead weight if we run out of ammunition so, in addition to the eight fully bombed 30-round magazines I'm carrying on my body armour, together with the three spare clips for my Sig pistol, I have a spare bandolier of 150 5.56mm rounds in my bergan. At the last minute I'm given a belt of 7.62mm 4B:1T[1] ammunition for the GPMG. It's common practice to spread the load of spare ammunition for the heavier weapons across the patrol. My advanced years don't excuse me from this additional burden.

The combined weight of body armour, weapons, ammunition, water and other equipment adds up to about 52 kilos, 65% of my bodyweight. It's a burden that stretches sinews and cartilage to breaking point. It's no wonder the Taliban, who go to war unencumbered by health and safety legislation, call us *donkey soldiers*. The British seaside donkey code of best practice recommends that donkey loads do not exceed 25% of an animal's

---

[1] **4B:1T (*Four bit*)**: Four Ball: One Tracer. The standard configuration of tracer to ball rounds in UK 7.62mm belted ammunition for use with the GPMG machine gun.

weight. No such guidance exists either for donkeys, or for British soldiers, in Afghanistan.

I make ready at the loading bay with the rest of the patrol and hard target through the front gate and into a scene from Monty Python's 'Life of Brian'. Men in *shemaghs*[1] and *dishdashes*[2] stare at us with blank expressions from the corners of compound walls while herds of goats scratch around in the bare earth looking for something to graze on. As we pass a gaggle of children Ben throws the youngest of them a bag of sweets. He's immediately pounced on by his mates who try to rip them from him, but he's not giving them up without a fight and a tremendous struggle ensues.

Patrol Base Clifton sits atop high ground just outside the green zone overlooking a rural community which has not changed much in the last 500 years. Families live in walled compounds made of mud and straw, side by side with their livestock. They have none of the creature comforts we take for granted in the West. Despite these privations it has a certain rustic beauty. Fields are carefully tended, watered by a delicate and intricate irrigation system which provides an ever-present, soothing soundtrack of flowing water. Whitewashed compounds are shaded by magnificent mulberry trees which stave off the relentless heat of the Afghan summer.

In stark contrast to the dashte in the north, the land is fertile. The favourable climate and an abundance of water enable three growing seasons each year. Farmers harvest poppy in April, wheat in June and maize in September. Poppy, however, is the main source of income and this illicit trade binds the community to an insurgent narco-nexus which facilitates the movement of wet opium to markets in Gereshk, and as far afield as Pakistan and Iran.

Lying as it does outside the protected community of Gereshk, GIRoA has made little if any investment in this population over the years. As a result of inadequate security, a general lack of access to services, and widespread corruption, the people have become increasingly disenfranchised. Taliban shadow governance dominates and deliberately isolates the community still further from GIRoA. Possession of a *tashkiera*, a government identity card, will result in a

---

[1] **Shemagh**: A traditional Middle Eastern headdress designed to protect the wearer from sand and heat, typically worn by men.

[2] **Dishdash**: Long one-piece tunic worn by men.

beating and a heavy fine, cell phones are banned and night curfews commonplace.

It is also a place where the risks and rigours of everyday life far exceed any acceptable norms of our own society. Despite it being a heavily contested area, pregnancy rather than insurgency is the main cause of premature death. Polio and cholera remain prevalent and poverty is widespread.

ISAF are not welcome. Over the past six months Simon has made numerous attempts to gain access to Kakoran and its sister kalay of Narqiel a few clicks further south. All have resulted in 'kinetic activity' – the military euphemism for the use of lethal force. Further east in the kalay of Adinzai insurgents have been observed routinely gathering at a tea shop in the local bazaar, openly carrying their weapons without fear of reprisals. This group of young bandits is known to be especially wild and fond of violence and is informally labelled the *Crazy Gang* by our J2 (Intelligence) cell.

Back in the UK Captain Alex Bayliss, our Intelligence Officer had described this area to me as the 'Heart of Darkness'. It's a place where brown underpants are a sensible precaution.

We continue to patrol down into the green zone where we go firm on the side of a dirt road beside an ANA checkpoint which is surrounded on all sides by poppy fields. The ANA lads look bored, wandering around in flip-flops and t-shirts, pretending to ignore what we're up to. Someone is preparing a meal while another man splits logs with a lump hammer and a metal stake. I notice also that no one is manning the machine gun or carrying weapons.

A battered white Nissan pulls up and five or six lads get out. Although they're in civvies they're obviously part of the gang. There's lots of hugging and fast talking. I'm curious to know how an ANA soldier can afford to own a motor vehicle but I keep that thought to myself. In the distance I see men labouring in the poppy fields in a slow, measured way that suggests they're pacing themselves for a lifetime of hard manual labour. Nothing much has changed here for centuries it seems, so there's no great rush to get anything done.

It's obvious that everyone is watching us and waiting to see what our next move will be. Up to this point Ben has not taken a single photograph because, he tells me, this is quintessential Afghanistan and there are already a thousand   images just like the one we're in right now. He's right; I've seen so many of them before myself.

After about 30 minutes we're given the order to move and head out across the fields towards some compounds about 200 metres distant. We're following a safe lane cleared by a Vallon operator and marked by his number two with blue spray paint. It's a slow but essential process; IEDs are the insurgents' weapon of choice and the number one source of 'Category A' casualties amongst ISAF and ANA soldiers. A Cat A is defined as a life threatening injury which requires urgent medical attention within 90 minutes.

In Helmand the Medical Emergency Response Team take pride in providing life saving surgery in under half that time, literally on the battlefield, or more accurately above it. The MERT is a mobile surgical ward, complete with surgeons, anaesthetists and theatre nurses, which deploys in the back of a Chinook helicopter as close to the point of wounding as possible, often while troops are still in contact.

The incredible bravery and skill of the MERT teams, and their American counterparts PEDRO, means that even the most severe blast injuries involving multiple traumatic amputations are survivable, but the consequences are of course life changing. It is such a prevalent risk that every soldier in Helmand has to embrace the possibility that they may return home without one or more of their limbs. I've lost count of the number of conversations I've had about the best and worst types of amputation. I'm by no means alone in trying to project what life might be like without legs.

At first the going is pretty straightforward but as we move deeper into the green zone the ground becomes heavily waterlogged. Progress gets tougher and tougher as mud oozes over the tops of our boots, then up to our knees. It's almost impossible to mark a safe lane in this sea of liquid mud but I take consolation from the fact that it would be equally near impossible to maintain the integrity of a battery pack, an essential component of any IED, in this volume of water.

By the time we reach the tree line I'm blowing hard and covered in filth – there's a dodgy stench about me that may or may not be human excrement, which the locals routinely recycle onto their fields. I try not to think about it. Grateful for the camelback I was issued at the Reserve Training and Mobilisation Centre in Chilwell, Nottingham, I suck down some deliciously cool water through the drinking tube clipped to the front of my body armour. Somehow Ben has managed to keep his cameras free of mud and at last is busy clicking away.

We go firm in the tree line and scan our arcs. There are plenty of local nationals who have come out to watch the show. For us it's a good sign because it suggests that the insurgents haven't warned them to stay away, but we're not letting down our guard. A number of shifty looking blokes of fighting age are having a bit of a chin wag about 300 metres away. One of them is clearly talking into a mobile phone. A couple of motorbikes are also whizzing up and down a track on our left and appear to be keeping tabs on our movements.

In order to get a clearer picture of what's going on we decide to push forward across another field, but first we have to cross an irrigation ditch. It's full of waist deep murky brown water with steep banks on either side. There's no way to jump across with all the kit we're carrying. In any case it's a vulnerable point which will have to be cleared by the Vallon.

The insurgents are experts at identifying likely crossing points such as this and placing IEDs in the banks to catch unwary soldiers as they climb in or out. Ben is ahead of me as we clear the ditch but the guy behind me struggles to find a foothold on the slippery bank. I lend him a hand and he nearly pulls my arm from its socket as he hauls himself out. Unbalanced, I take a step backwards and stumble before falling headlong down the other side of the bank. I try desperately to stay in the safe lane but to no avail. We've been told that 90% of IED casualties are caused by straying out of lane. This time my luck holds but my underpants are going to require an intensive wash cycle.

In the short time it's taken us to clear the ditch the atmospherics have changed. Women and children can be seen fleeing from the two compounds immediately to our front, herding their livestock in front of them. The likely lads we saw earlier have now split into two groups. One of our blokes sees what he thinks is a long-barrelled weapon being taken into one of the compounds. These are all sure fire indicators that we're about to be taken on and we now assess these two compounds to be the most likely direction of any threat.

In a procedure the Tigers call *advance to ambush* we continue to move towards the compounds, expecting to come under fire at any moment. I repeatedly check the safety catch on my assault rifle with the index finger of my right hand but resist the temptation to slip it to 'off'. Unless I'm unlucky enough to be hit by the initial burst of fire, in which case it'll make no difference anyway, there'll be plenty of time to depress the safety as I sight the weapon.

In these moments my focus on the compound is absolute. I no longer register the smell of human excrement encrusted on my combat trousers or the pain of blisters forming inside my waterlogged boots. I am unaware of the weight of my backpack compressing the blood supply to my left arm or the constant chafing of ballistic plates over my salt-rimed skin.

I have forgotten my role as Ben's protector.

My existence has narrowed to a set of binary choices: Live or die; hunt or be hunted; kill or be killed. These moments are the culmination of hundreds, if not thousands of hours of training. Training which began in the outdoor gym in Norwood Park, working out with the grannies and the meth heads, and which has consumed almost every waking hour of my life for the past 18 months. It is for these few precious minutes that I've turned my back on a lucrative career, abandoned my comfortable suburban existence, my beautiful wife, my trophy house, my exotic bi-annual holidays.

I'm not disappointed. The simplicity is exhilarating.

I'm taking a long hard look at the compound wall, trying to identify any likely firing points or murder holes, when there is a huge explosion. My first thought is that one of us has initiated an IED but then I see smoke billowing from the compound. Perhaps it's an IED own goal.

But less than 30 seconds later I hear the distinctive sound of rotor blades and turn to see an Apache attack helicopter approach from behind us at about 500 feet. It has fired a Hellfire missile right through the open window of the compound's main building. Now it follows up with a long burst of 30mm cannon. I take a knee and watch as the building appears to disintegrate into a cloud of dust in front of us.

After the intensity of the preceding moments I feel strangely impassive but, given that we are between the Apache and its target, it crosses my mind that now would not be a good time for the pilot to sneeze. This clearly hasn't occurred to Ben. He has left the safe lane and is standing in the open at the corner of the field, capturing it all on a video camera I hadn't even noticed he was carrying before this point.

Ben hasn't once complained about the mud and the shit. He's got some big balls to join us on this patrol into an insurgent stronghold, armed only with his cameras. I admire him. Nevertheless his balls will go the same way as his legs if he doesn't stay in the safe lane. It may be my job to look after him, but there's no way I'm risking my own gonads by straying out of lane, so I call him over to me instead. He looks a little sheepish when he returns, and apologises, but I tell him it's the children he hasn't yet conceived to whom he needs to apologise.

We learn later that, undetected by us or by the likely lads, the Apache pilot had come on station a few minutes earlier. From his vantage point, unseen and unheard five klicks behind and above us, the pilot had been able to see what we could not see from less than 150 metres away on the ground. He had positively identified two shooters about to open fire and under ISAF rules of engagement he had permission to make a pre-emptive strike on the basis of *imminent threat to life*. In this case our lives.

The Apache remains on station for another 20 minutes during which time life returns to normal. Less than five minutes after the Hellfire missile has been fired I watch a man come out of his compound pushing a wheelbarrow and begin to tend to his crops. Kids appear from nowhere to stand and stare. Curiosity even gets the better of one or two women dressed in head to foot burkhas who come out to watch the show.

Once it's clear that no one is moving in the destroyed target compound someone, presumably Simon, makes the decision that we've done enough fighting for one day and we pull back towards the patrol base. Everyone remains vigilant on the return journey. Insurgents frequently *shoot and scoot* at returning patrols. But we arrive back at Clifton without further incident and are greeted by a cheering crowd as we walk through the gates. Simon and his Tigers have successfully completed their last fighting patrol and their mates are on hand to celebrate their safe return.

Latitude:	31.85
Longitude:	64.62
Elevation:	851m
Met:	Sunny H:9°L:6°
DTG:	240930DMAR12

THE FOLLOWING DAY I bumped into WO2 'Bullet Magnet' Barrow, another London Regiment soldier who had just completed his first week in theatre and already acquired a new nickname. He landed the job of Inkerman Company's Intelligence Warrant Officer and was involved in its first significant contact of the tour. The experience did not seem to have dampened his enthusiasm. He gathered together half a dozen other London Regiment soldiers who had also been assigned to Inkerman, and there was just time for a quick chat and a brew before a Chinook arriveed to take Ben and me back to Bastion.

The lads still had the slightly wide-eyed, fresh-faced look that marks out all 'newbies' to theatre. They were eager to hoover up any insights I could give them. I quizzed them on how they were settling in with the Grenadiers, and told them what I knew about the district and where their own AO fitted into the bigger picture. In parting I urged them to take it easy in their first few weeks. Statistically, casualties are highest at the beginning and end of tours. Initially soldiers lack battlefield awareness, experience and knowledge. Towards the end they start to switch off and wind down.

I would return to Clifton just a few weeks later to discover these lads had become seasoned warriors with some incredible tales of their own.

Ben and I were catching a ride with the last of the Tigers, and as the aircraft took off there were cheers and high fives all round. It was clearly an emotional moment for them and the RAF Loadie[1] knew better than to interrupt the celebrations.

It was my turn to feel the newbie. I still had another seven months to push.

Back in Bastion I dropped Ben off at the Media Operations cell, which is hidden away behind the fire station in Bastion One. We joined a number of other journalists who were enjoying a cold drink on a

---

[1] **Loadie**: [Loadmaster]. An aircraft crew member in charge of loading and unloading cargo.

shaded veranda. I couldn't help but note that the hacks had rather better accommodation than our own, but this was to be expected. We were, after all, trying to create a favourable impression.

I listened as Ben recounted the tale of our fighting patrol to his colleagues. I could tell they were envious. He had some good content. A strikingly beautiful, blond-haired woman with searching blue eyes, who had hitherto been languorously curled up on one of the sofas with a laptop balanced on her knees, sat up and began to listen intently. She introduced herself to me as Deborah Haynes, The Times defence editor and engaged me in conversation, clearly fishing for a story.

We chatted for a short while until some of the army media ops team arrived. They were taken aback to find me there having an unauthorised and unmonitored conversation with Deborah and the other journos, in a flap that I might have said something 'off-message'. I enjoyed their discomfort. But I hadn't given Deborah a front page splash.

That came much later.

Eventually, to the very obvious relief of their handlers, I said my farewells to Ben and the others. It had been a real pleasure working with him and we exchanged email addresses and promised to stay in touch. I headed off in search of a bus that would take me to the Grenadiers' rear headquarters in Bastion Two to seek out some good banter and a bed for the night.

Latitude:	31.77
Longitude:	64.68
Elevation:	847m
Met:	Sunny H:19°L:6°
DTG:	261500DMAR12

ON MY RETURN to MOB Price I learned of the deaths of Sergeant Taylor and Lance Corporal Foley. The Merlin helicopter in which I was travelling had briefly touched down in MOB Lashka Gah just prior to the green on blue incident in which they were both killed. A disgruntled ANA sergeant became agitated when he was directed to wait outside the base. He tried to force his way in, opening fire on Sergeant Taylor, Corporal Foley and another soldier who was wounded but survived, before being shot and killed himself.

As a retail marketing consultant back in civvy street I'd obsessed about the importance of first impressions on a customer's purchase decisions. I'd been commissioned by retail property giants to work alongside leading architects and designers to create award winning retail experiences. I'd even been invited to present my work at industry conferences such as the International Council of Shopping Centres. After my meeting with the Gereshk elders who had remonstrated for Haji Gul's release, I couldn't help but observe that anyone visiting our bases was most likely to be forming an unfavourable opinion of ISAF, at odds with our ambition to win their hearts and minds.

I set about trying to convince the powers that be of this fact but, in a botched attempt to demonstrate my credentials in this space, I stupidly used language such as *customer journey*, *brand engagement*, *sensory experience* and *mystery shop*. None of these terms appear in any of the Joint Doctrine Publications. My proposals fell on deaf ears. This was partly because there was no budget to implement any of my recommendations but mostly because, with hindsight, I was talking namby-pamby civilian nonsense to hard bitten combat soldiers.

The coroner would judge that Sergeant Taylor and Corporal Foley's killer *was believed to be acting on his own with a personal grievance rather than with insurgents … This was a shocking, appalling, unexpected thing to happen.* I had no desire to say *I told you so* after these deaths. I could only reflect that had I judged my audience better and made a more compelling case to improve the *customer experience,* this tragic sequence of events might have been avoided.

The wonders of the digital age delivered Ben's pictures back to the UK even before the RAF delivered me back to MOB Price. Long before Ben himself completed the gruelling journey home via Minhad and Episkopi. The news of Sergeant Taylor and Corporal Foley's deaths dominated the headlines but Ben's pictures were still picked up by news desks at The Daily Mail, The Telegraph and the Metro, as well as several regional newspapers and websites. I appear in one of them, stepping gingerly through a gap in the razor wire outside the ANA base at the start of the patrol into Kakoran. I'm looking nervous, staring hard at the path directly in front of my feet. My nerves are well-founded; friends and colleagues will lose limbs on this ground in the weeks and months ahead.

In a short space of time Ben has managed to vividly capture the highs and lows of combat operations in Afghanistan. His photos paint a heroic picture of stoic British squaddies putting up with austere living conditions in a foreign land where they bravely confront our Nation's enemies. Ben's pictures, and others like them that illustrate the war in Afghanistan, have won the public's respect and admiration for our Armed Forces and the difficult, dangerous job they do.

I'm grateful to him and his colleagues for their bravery in bringing these images into the homes of the British public to win their support, if not for the war itself then for those that fight it. However, it seemed to me that Ben, knowingly or not, was colluding in the national self-deception that we could win this war.

Military superiority is no antidote to a failed state and a failing counter-insurgency campaign. If ten years in Afghanistan had taught us anything it was that there was a seemingly inexhaustible supply of young men willing to take up arms against ISAF. The two young fighters we'd killed in Kakoran would be replaced easily enough.

Granted, the $3,500 PKM[1] machine gun with which they had intended to take us on and which had been demolished in the compound would be harder to replace, but it was still considerably cheaper than the $58,000 Hellfire missile that had destroyed it.

---

[1] **PKM**: Gas operated, belt fed, air cooled, automatic only, machine gun. Originally designed and manufactured in Russia in the late 1960's copies are still in production in Bulgaria, China, Iran, Poland, Serbia.

Some months later I would return to Kakoran and spend a tense couple of nights in the compound next door to the one destroyed by the Apache. It remained an abandoned ruin. With the departure of the soldiers Ben and I had accompanied on that day, the engagement had been long forgotten in the collective ISAF memory.

I recalled the words of General Stanley McChrystal: *destroying a home or property jeopardises the livelihood of an entire family – and creates more insurgents.* I had no way of knowing what had become of the family that had once lived there, or even if they'd joined the insurgency, but it seemed likely to me that the destruction of their home by the infidel invaders would be bitterly recalled for generations to come.

Even in the picturesque kalay of Kakoran I could not escape the complexities of counter-insurgency warfare. Our fighting patrol had inadvertently triggered a sequence of events in which our eagerness to deliberately pick a fight with the insurgents had resulted in the displacement of innocent civilians.

All too often the effect we sought to achieve, in this instance to disrupt insurgent freedom of movement, had unanticipated side effects.

I'd been quick to criticise the DST and TF196 for their efforts. Now I had to acknowledge my own part in the displacement of a family to whom we'd promised security and *A better life with GIRoA*. It felt as if we might be losing the counter-insurgency one family at a time, and on this occasion I had to shoulder some of the burden of responsibility for that failure.

Latitude   31.77
Longitude   64.68
Elevation   847m
Met   Sunny H:19°L:6°
DTG   270750DMAR12

Less Afghan Face,
more Afghan Ass.

RCSW: Regional Command South West
USMC: United States Marine Corps
AFM: Army Field Manual
SO1: Staff Officer, Grade One
NGO: Non-governmental Organisation
RMO: Regimental Medical Officer
RAP: Regimental Aid Post
ALP: Afghan Local Police
AISPO: Italian Association for solidarity among people
H4H: Help for Heroes
BATUS: British Army Training Unit, Suffield
BFBS: British Forces Broadcasting Service
ANSF: Afghan National Security Forces

MINISTRY OF DEFENCE ANNOUNCEMENT

Corporal Jack Leslie Stanley. On 8 April 2012, Corporal Jack Leslie Stanley died in hospital in Birmingham from wounds sustained in Afghanistan when caught in the blast from an improvised explosive device and seriously injured.

Sapper Connor Ray. On 18 April 2012, Sapper Connor Ray died in hospital in Birmingham from wounds sustained in Afghanistan where he was seriously injured in an IED strike.

Guardsman Michael Roland. On Friday 27 April 2012, Guardsman Michael Roland was fatally wounded during an exchange of small arms fire while deployed with his company on a three-day operation to disrupt insurgent activity in a contested area in the north of Nahr-e Saraj district.

Latitude:	31.77
Longitude:	64.68
Elevation:	847m
Met:	Sunny H:19°L:6°
DTG:	270750DMAR12

BACK IN MOB Price I was now on the countdown to R&R (rest and recuperation). Thanks to the generosity of Rupert, our Adjutant, who delayed his own leave so that I could return to the UK in time for Alfie's birthday, I was due to fly to Minhad Airbase in the United Arab Emirates on 9th April. From there, the RAF would organise my onward journey to the UK via Cyprus. Even allowing for technical mishaps with the ageing TriStars, I was confident the RAF could manage to get me back in time to celebrate my son's fifth birthday on 19th April. If needs be I could always do a bunk at Minhad or Episkopi and make my own way home.

I had just over ten days to push. Then I would return to Camp Bastion to complete pre-leave administration before going back to the World for two weeks. This would involve the inevitable reverse-MCCP, the handing over of my weapon systems, ammunition and morphine for safekeeping, and a mandatory viewing of a short film on the perils and pitfalls of R&R.

The film warned us not to overdo the alcohol, to stay out of bar fights wherever possible, and not to assume that our wives or girlfriends would necessarily be waiting for us in their underwear when we knocked on the front door. I already knew that Jane wouldn't be waiting for me in her underwear. But the film also warned us that young children might be uncommunicative and suffering from a sense of abandonment. I hoped this wouldn't be the case with Harry and Alfie. But since I hadn't spoken to them or received a letter from them in all the time I'd been in Afghan, I had to admit it was possible that they would not be looking forward to our reunion quite so much as I was myself.

I resolved to count down the days safely out of harm's way behind my desk in the J9 cell. I could easily busy myself with report writing and operational staff work. But there was another task that I had been putting off and which now required my urgent attention.

Task Force Helmand, the British military mission in Afghanistan forms part of a multinational division commanded by a United States

Marine Corps (USMC) General. Prior to our deployment in January, Major General CM Gurganus, the commander designate, had visited our headquarters team at the Command and Staff Training facility in Warminster, Wiltshire.

The perfect stereotype of a Marine Corps General, Gurganus is a huge bear of a man with a grizzled, careworn face that has fearlessly stared down the enemies of the United States for almost four decades without the benefits of meterosexual moisturiser. With a tough uncompromising manner and a John Wayne drawl to match he had three main points to impress upon his audience. Firstly, he reassured us that, despite an impending drawdown in US troop numbers, the USMC would continue to protect our flanks. Secondly, he articulated his determination to maintain the pace of transition of security responsibility to indigenous forces, using the memorable phrase *Less Afghan Face, more Afghan Ass.* Lastly, he acknowledged that in previous years military operations had defined the *narrative* in Afghanistan. But he had now been convinced by his *communications guys* that the narrative must instead come first, in order to define the shape and scope of the military mission.

Colonel James seized upon this last point and concluded that we should have a narrative of our own. He directed that we must envisage what successful transition would look like in Nahr-E-Saraj in 2015, work backwards from that point in order to understand our mission in 2012, and construct a narrative to achieve that aim.

Preparing for Afghanistan I'd observed that the word 'narrative' was a popular one in contemporary military operations, especially in the context of counter-insurgency. It had even been enshrined in UK military doctrine in Army Field Manual (AFM) Volume 1:10, which states:

Each counter-insurgency campaign requires an agreed single vision of the future for the host nation that is consistent across any coalition or alliance. The 'vision' is a competing 'narrative', the statement of what the UK with allies and civilian partners is trying to achieve. The narrative should be stronger than the insurgents' message, should seek to persuade rather than coerce, should emphasise security and development within its text and should be reflected in the UK Information strategy.

However, after more than ten years of counter-insurgency warfare in Afghanistan, while the need for a narrative was almost universally recognised, the term was still not well understood. No agreed single vision existed as doctrine demanded. Successive British deployments had sought to produce narratives but, as General Gurganus had stated, these had not endured.

Over the course of the next few months both the Regional Command and Task Force Helmand would produce narratives but these were laughably amateur, demonstrating a lack of commitment to the concept, despite its perceived doctrinal importance and General Gurganus' convictions.

Perhaps I should not have been surprised. Information Operations was still a developing and often confused staff function within the military. Unlike marketing roles in a commercial environment, which tend to be highly sought after and require a minimum degree-level professional qualification, the UK military seconds staff to this function from every branch of the services following a two week training course. Furthermore, employment outside mainstream military roles is largely considered a foul for career-minded soldiers and officers, something to be avoided. Major Dave Kenny, our Chief of Staff who had recently pink listed and was awaiting promotion, admitted to me that he dreaded being picked up as SO1 Info Ops – the senior information operations job in Task Force Helmand. The very fact that he might be considered to lead this staff function, despite having no prior experience, perfectly served to highlight the army's lack of investment or understanding.

He looked deeply sceptical when I pointed out that this would be akin to being Chief Marketing Officer at Apple, McDonalds or Volkswagen, all of which are hotly contested, pivotal roles at the heart of their respective businesses. There was arguably much more at stake, lives rather than livelihoods on the line, billions invested. Nevertheless Info Ops remained a career limiting sideshow.

Colonel James had made it clear that I was to produce the Nahr-E-Saraj narrative and that this was to be ready by the time the rest of the battalion arrived in theatre at the end of March. The deadline was fast approaching and he had scheduled a meeting to discuss progress. To add to the pressure I felt certain that my return to *Angrezistan* would be postponed should I fail to deliver the goods on time.

As a marketing consultant I'd done this sort of thing many times before and was familiar with the process. But this was different. Everything

I'd seen over the last two months had convinced me that the UK strategy in Afghanistan was deeply flawed.

The breathtaking hubris of DfID's nation-building ambitions, combined with the superficial resources at their disposal and an absence of competence with which to execute the plan, were a recipe for disaster. Unfortunately, there was no plan B, and no one brave enough to put the brakes on this particular runaway train. By 2012 the international community were pinning their hopes on a corrupt Karzai regime in Kabul while failing to take into account the influence of the international opium black market.

Joint Doctrine Publication 3-40 Security and Stabilisation: The Military Contribution broke the mould of verbose British doctrine when it simply and bluntly stated: *Failed States fail their people.* There was no doubt in my mind that the GIRoA government was failing its people. Propping up this dysfunctional administration was at best prolonging the failure, at worst it was amplifying the catastrophe.

Success was further hampered by the refusal of the Foreign Office to work alongside the Ministry of Defence in accordance with the *Comprehensive Approach* doctrine in order to achieve *overwhelming campaign effect.* Following my experiences first with TF196 and then on patrol into Kakoran I was also concerned that the daily reality of our operational activity did not reflect the words or aspirations of our most senior military commanders.

In September 1941 Joseph Goebbels wrote: *The essential English leadership secret does not depend on particular intelligence. Rather, it depends on a remarkably stupid thick-headedness. The English follow the principle that when one lies, one should lie big, and stick to it. They keep up their lies, even at the risk of looking ridiculous.*

It may or may not have been true at the time, but Goebbels' assertion now seemed pertinent to the endless stream of 'good news' that was produced to demonstrate success at a time when it was pretty clear to all concerned that the mission was failing and we were indeed at risk of looking ridiculous.

In short, UK policy in Helmand was a goatfuck. To my mind there had never been a greater need for a narrative, but I questioned my own professional capability to unfuck the goat when so many others had clearly failed. In any event I was so far down the ISAF food chain that I doubted I could have any strategic impact on the Helmand mission.

I was a rabbit, or possibly a goat, staring into the headlights of my meeting with Colonel James at which he would find me intellectually empty-handed. He was not a man to suffer fools lightly. I wasn't looking forward to his reaction to my lack of productivity.

I wandered disconsolately up to the J9 cell. Past the gently twinkling fairy lights outside the Kuffen, mis-selling the coarse Danish coffee that lay within. Past the giant, squatting forms of the Leopard 2 main battle tanks, their brutish presence reinforcing the oxymoronic message of the *Four Flags* memorial: *In the fight for peace*.

If I was looking for inspiration from these seemingly self-contradictory symbols of our life in Main Operating Base Price, none was forthcoming.

Latitude:	31.77
Longitude:	64.68
Elevation:	847m
Met:	Sunny H:19°L:6°
DTG:	270758DMAR12

DURING THE FEW days I'd been away at Clifton, I discovered that in my absence someone had 'cocked' the notepad I'd been foolish enough to leave in plain sight on my desk.

Cocking was an obsession in the headquarters, a symptom of the sexual repression under which we all laboured. Both British and Danish commands imposed a strict no sex rule in MOB Price, which for the most part was observed. This abstinence was not the result of a commendable adherence to military discipline. Had an opportunity to engage in sexual congress presented itself I'm pretty certain that most of my colleagues, like me, would have set aside all considerations of military discipline and good order – but opportunity did not present. Price was a predominantly male, heterosexual community most of whom had wives or girlfriends waiting for them back home.

Sex, or the lack of it, was a constant preoccupation. So much so that at one of our decompression briefings in Cyprus at the end of our tour a female officer from the Royal Army Chaplains Department felt it necessary to remind us that sex involves two (or possibly more) people. By then I could hardly wait.

For the dozen or so women in Price, mostly medics and dog handlers, life in this sexually charged, testosterone fuelled environment must have been a minefield. On one occasion a female reserve officer was admonished for running wearing running shorts. This came to the attention of the chain of command who deemed it dangerously erotic. She was ordered to cease and desist immediately. In her case I had to admit they had a reasonable point, but the officer in question was incensed. When she came to seek my counsel it seemed inappropriate to compliment her on the comeliness of her gluteus maximus, so instead I offered a sympathetic ear, and tried to impress upon her the uncertain benefits of voluminous army issue shorts.

For men at their sexual peak – and even for those of us who had already passed that particular milestone – this enforced abstinence inevitably had its frustrations which were expressed in a number of ways. Cocking was one of them.

As far as I am aware this is an exclusively male obsession and involves the covert drawing of phallic imagery. This is nothing new of course. Such representations have been found dating back to the Ice Age around 28,000 years ago, and appear in many ancient cultures and religions. But the art reached new heights in MOB Price. Penis imagery would mysteriously appear on notebooks, notice boards, signage, PowerPoint presentations and operational staff work. An unusual geographical feature to the north-east of PB Clifton was even referred to on our maps as 'cock and balls'.

On one occasion I attended a packed briefing session in which a senior officer scribbled a note intended for Colonel James, who was sitting across the room, and handed it to the man next to him to pass down the table. By the time it reached its destination it had passed through the hands of a dozen or so officers and warrant officers, many of whom had surreptitiously cocked it. Although it was impossible to overlook the images with which it was now adorned, Colonel James accepted the note without so much as a raised eyebrow.

The towering penis that had been drawn on the front cover of my notebook was magnificent. It was a detailed and anatomically precise representation depicting an erection I'd have been justifiably proud of in my twenties and could only dream about in my forties. Phallic imagery varied considerably according to the imagination of the artist. I noticed, for example that Tom's notebook had been illustrated with a lovingly drawn image of Winnie the Pooh being improbably penetrated by his diminutive sidekick, Piglet.

Judging from their absurdly oversized erections, which more closely resembled ancient Greek and Roman depictions of the deity Priapus than the sketches of AA Milne, they were both clearly enjoying the experience in a way that their creator had never intended.

Oh, D-D-Dear! said Piglet.

Back in civvy street, probably even back in barracks in the UK, Victorian prudishness and political correctness would not have tolerated phallic observance of this nature. HR departments would be called in, enquiries held, perpetrators reprimanded or even sacked. But in MOB Price phallophoric celebration of the Lingam, and to a lesser extent the Yoni, went unchecked.

The sexual health nurse who briefed us on RSOI had been right. None of our mucky lot was getting any and it was clearly preying on our minds.

Latitude:	31.77
Longitude:	64.68
Elevation:	847m
Met:	Sunny H:19°L:6°
DTG:	271700DMAR12

MY MEETING WITH Colonel James was scheduled for 17.00. In the absence of any original thought I'd thrown together a presentation of past successes to facilitate a dialogue about project direction, look and feel. This delaying tactic had worked reasonably well for me in the past. It carried the not so subtle implication that if I could just pull my finger out and do some work, my prospective clients might enjoy similar success to the illustrious, market-leading companies I named in the presentation. The delays and missed deadlines would all be worth it in the end.

I learned this tried and tested method of placating frustrated clients from a former boss and Tony Blair speech writer, one of the architects of the New Labour landslide in 1997. A copywriter by trade who had famously applied the words *Hello Boys* to images of a Czech supermodel dressed only in her underwear, he had perfected the verb-free sentence which littered TB's early speeches, expressing aspiration but making no commitment to delivery: *our streets, free of crime; for every child, opportunity; in old age, tranquillity; for counter-insurgency, narrative.*

These noncommittal promises of future performance had served me reasonably well in a business context where I'd enjoyed moderate success. Unfortunately, Colonel James Maurice Hannan Bowder, Commanding Officer of the Queen's bodyguard and most prestigious infantry regiment in the British Army, did not strike me as a likely New Labour devotee.

As I put my credentials together it became glaringly obvious that applying commercial experience to military problems was uncharted territory. Name-dropping brands in the automotive, retail and fashion industries seemed a less persuasive strategy when the intended recipient had main battle tanks parked outside his office and a vast arsenal of deadly military hardware at his disposal.

To say I was nervous about the outcome of our meeting was something of an understatement.

It was impossible to judge Colonel James' mood as I meandered laboriously through my presentation. He seemed preoccupied with other, more important issues but periodically interjected with an observation or point of clarification. I was dutifully jotting down his feedback when he unexpectedly complimented me on my erection. I was a little taken aback until I realised that he was referring to the rampant illustration adorning the front cover of my notebook rather than to any goings-on in my combat trousers.

We briefly admired the portrait, trying to guess who the artist might be, before the Commanding Officer abruptly ended our meeting. He thanked me for my presentation, going so far as to declare that he'd learned something new — although at this point he may have been referring to the illustrator's impressive anatomical accuracy — before reminding me that I had just a few more days to complete the narrative.

Priapus the protector of livestock, bees, fruit plants, gardens and male genitalia, through the more earthly hand of the mystery cock-artist, had interceded on my behalf to win a stay of execution. I was extremely grateful to them both.

In every notebook, a penis.

Latitude:	31.77
Longitude:	64.68
Elevation:	847m
Met:	Sunny H:21°L:6°
DTG:	280845DMAR12

MAJOR KARA WATTERS was unprepared for the patient brought in to her morning surgery. 'Walk-ins' were not uncommon at MOB Price. Locals knew that the ISAF base had much better medical facilities than were available at the Gereshk district hospital – known locally as the *Italian* hospital because it received funding from an Italian NGO.

Run by a combination of Bangladeshi and local national staff, they did their best to treat the 8,000 patients they received each month, but were resourced for less than half that number and lacked both medical expertise and adequate supplies.

Even in the short time we'd been in-country Kara, our Regimental Medical Officer (RMO) had seen more than her fair share of the casualties of war. Our own most seriously wounded soldiers were airlifted by the MERT or PEDRO from the point of wounding direct to the hospital in Camp Bastion and did not pass through Kara's Regimental Aid Post (RAP). But she was frequently required to treat and stabilise local young men from the ANA and AUP, and from the ALP – Afghan Local Police, the non-uniformed militia that purported to provide security to rural communities outside the protected areas. Often close to death, with serious injuries that Kara lacked the facilities to treat, they were brought to her by desperate colleagues when treatment by an infidel Angrezi woman became the option of last resort.

Despite her best efforts, Kara could not save them all.

Kara's patient that morning was not a grievously wounded man of fighting age but a young girl of about six, accompanied by a desperate father. Ameena had not been caught in crossfire or, like so many other child victims of the conflict, inadvertently initiated an IED intended for ISAF troops. She was nonetheless a casualty of war.

The girl had suffered terrible burns to her hands, arms and chest when she'd fallen into an open cooking fire while playing at home. Her injuries would leave her with permanent scars but, with almost half of all emergency, non-battle related   paediatric hospital admissions in

Afghanistan the result of domestic burns, the regional hospital in Lashka Gah had both the experience and the resources to treat her wounds. It was to this unit that the staff at the Italian hospital had directed her father when he'd initially taken Ameena to them for treatment. But there was a problem – Ameena's father worked as an AUP patrolman in *Lash.* He could no more attend the hospital there than I could have done myself. Many of the medical staff, either through sympathy to the cause or through coercion, also treated Taliban casualties. Out of uniform and unarmed he could not risk being identified; taking his daughter to the hospital in Lashka Gah would put his own life in jeopardy.

Unable to access the specialist care she needed, Ameena's father persuaded the staff at the Italian hospital to treat her. Lacking both the expertise and the sterile gauze required, they bound Ameena's wounds directly with sticking plaster. It was in this state, several days later, with the injuries now showing signs of sepsis beneath the plaster, that she was delivered to Kara for treatment. Kara knew instantly that the child was in mortal danger. But she too lacked the sterile environment and the anaesthetic required to remove the sticking plaster and clean the wounds. Without hesitation she called the hospital in Bastion and requested Ameena be airlifted to them for priority treatment.

To her shock and dismay her request was turned down.

For many of the people who worked there and who never left its confines, Camp Bastion was the sum of their experience of Afghanistan. They knew nothing of life in the desert beyond the concrete blast walls, and it was all too easy to forget why the British taxpayer was funding our £15 million a day mission in Helmand Province. Consequently, a hospital administrator, having consulted the manual on admissions criteria, cold-heartedly ruled that Ameena was not eligible for treatment because her injuries were not the direct result of military action.

Technically he was right, of course, although this overlooked the fact that Ameena was unable to access treatment as a consequence of her father's employ in the AUP, an entity in which the international community was investing considerable effort and resource to try and enhance its capacity and credibility in the run-up to transition.

It was also a decision that failed to recognise that while we could lose the counter-insurgency one family at a time, as General Stanley

McChrystal had identified and as I had witnessed first-hand in Kakoran, conversely we might also win it one family at a time.

This was not such a ridiculous proposition. It was after all exactly how Mullah Omar had come to power after he executed the Governor of Singesar. However, I suspect that the dim-witted administrator had never left Bastion, and did not consider that he was a combatant in a counter-insurgency. Fighting and even daring to win the war in Afghan was somebody else's business. His area of expertise was the smooth running of a hospital. This would have been just fine if the hospital in question was in Reading. To my mind it was inexcusable in Afghanistan where we all exerted influence on the outcome of the war.

Rather than such strategic considerations, I suspect it was basic human compassion and decency that drove Kara to put her Hippocratic oath before the edict of some pen pushing bureaucrat. There was no question of turning Ameena away. If the Bastion hospital would not treat her, then she would do so herself.

Kara knew only too well that she was taking a huge risk. The Price medical centre was little more than a few prefabricated consulting rooms. There was no sterile operating theatre, no paediatric medicines, and crucially no paediatric anaesthetic. She would have to improvise, diluting adult dosages as best she could, while relying on her dedicated medical team to turn one of the consulting rooms into a spotlessly clean operating theatre.

Whatever the risks she was Ameena's last and only hope.

Latitude:	31.77
Longitude:	64.68
Elevation:	847m
Met:	Sunny H:21°L:6°
DTG:	281830DMAR12

IT TOOK KARA most of the day to painstakingly remove the sticking plaster from Ameena's burns. She was still operating when the rest of the headquarters staff assembled at 18.30 for the daily Commander's Update Briefing, which was where I first learned of Ameena's plight.

Fearful that an overdose of anaesthetic might have fatal consequences, Kara used just the barest minimum. Despite her most tender of touches, Ameena's cries of anguish were heart-rending. Kara and her team were all tough cookies used to treating appalling injuries, including gunshot wounds and multiple traumatic amputations. Inevitably, they had become conditioned and to a degree desensitised by these experiences. But when I spoke with them later that evening they were all clearly exhausted and close to tears.

Kara had successfully removed the sticking plaster and replaced this with her complete stock of special burns dressings. She was treating the infection with a combination of oral and intravenous antibiotics.

Time would now tell if she had done enough. Soon enough.

Ameena remained under close observation in the med centre, mildly sedated and in the most sterile conditions possible, for the next few days. She was a fighter. Slowly but surely she recovered, and she began to trust the strangers who soothed and reassured her in a language she could not understand. With the help of the antibiotics she first beat the infection then, thanks to the special burns dressings that Kara changed daily, her wounds began to heal.

However, the specialist dressings so fundamental to Ameena's recovery betrayed Kara to the Bastion administrators.

The MOB Price med centre was demanding a large quantity of these items but was not reporting any burns casualties in their daily reports. Perhaps Bastion guessed at the truth. An investigator was dispatched to conduct an unannounced spot check. Fortunately Kara had allies in the Bastion hospital, surgeons who would willingly have treated Ameena if only the administrators had allowed, and who were surreptitiously providing Kara with professional advice and guidance. Now they warned her that an inspector was in-bound by helicopter, giving her a 20 minute lead on his arrival to put a deception plan into place.

Everyone rallied round to confound the inspector.

The physiotherapy department, which was housed in a different part of the base, insisted on a lengthy and detailed audit, buying further vital minutes for Kara to temporarily relocate her unauthorised patient and disguise any traces of Ameena's presence. The Danish medics who worked alongside Kara momentarily forgot they spoke perfect English. An interpreter had to be found to answer the inspector's questions, adding further delays. Finally a few favours were called in with the Army Air Corps. The inspector's return flight was mysteriously and unexpectedly called forward, forcing him to return early to Bastion, before he could solve the mystery of the missing burns dressings.

Kara, with a little help from her friends and colleagues, had pulled off the deception. But it couldn't last and in any event Ameena's condition had now stabilised and she needed specialist treatment to help her regain some of the mobility in her hands and fingers for the best possible outcome. Kara had discovered a specialist paediatric hospital with a burns unit in Herat, run by the Italian association for solidarity among people (AISPO). She had managed to speak with the hospital director who had agreed to take Ameena as their patient. But she had, as yet, no idea how to get her there.

Herat is the third largest city in Afghanistan and capital of the province of the same name. It lies 450km north-west of Gereshk, far enough away from Lashka Gah that Ameena's father would feel safe there. Getting Ameena and her father there safely was the problem.

The Kandahar–Herat highway forms part of Highway One, which itself is part of the southern section of a 2,200km ring road inside Afghanistan connecting the cities of Mazari Sharif, Kabul, Ghazni, Kandahar, Farah, and Herat.

Originally constructed by the Soviets in the 1960s, hundreds of millions of dollars of international aid, mostly from the US, Saudi Arabia and Japan, have been invested in its reconstruction following ISAF intervention in the country. In 2005, then US ambassador to Afghanistan, Zalmay Khalilzad called the highway *a symbol of Afghan renewal and progress.* But in some quarters it is also known as the *Highway to Hell.*

Anyone wishing to travel the highway must pay illegal tolls, not only at the many ANA and AUP checkpoints along its route, but also to armed gangs and brigands, some of whom claim to be Taliban, who control its more remote stretches.

Kidnappings and killings of those unable or unwilling to pay are common, as are attacks on both military and civilian ISAF convoys that use the route. The road is heavily cratered in places and littered with burned out trucks, further hazards for the unwary traveller. In addition to logistics convoys, locals working with the government, aid agencies, and those connected to Westerners are also frequently targeted and killed.

Travelling at night is not recommended. Some sections of the highway have solar powered street lighting installed, but the photovoltaic panels have been stolen long ago. Lone headlights attract the attention of local bandits. Approaching one of the many ANA checkpoints after dark is likely to attract automatic gunfire from nervous soldiers who, with good reason, fear suicide bombers.

Driving to Herat from Gereshk was not for the faint-hearted and not a journey to be undertaken lightly. But it was the only way for Ameena to get the long-term care she now needed.

Kara and I discussed this problem and concluded that however risky it might be, this was still the best course of action. We couldn't put Ameena and her father on a military convoy for obvious reasons. In any event British convoys did not travel as far as Herat. The best solution seemed to be to engage the services of a local taxi driver to undertake the gruelling six hour journey.

This also was complicated. Although there were plenty of taxis in downtown Gereshk, as a general rule there wasn't much call for taxis in MOB Price and consequently no taxi rank outside the camp gates. Nor did I have any local numbers conveniently saved on my mobile phone, mainly because I'd left my phone, along with other personal effects, back in Camp Bastion before deploying forward.

What to do? In the end I wandered over to the US special forces compound to see if I could recruit my friend Chris to the cause. Chris was a Navy Seal I'd got to know   soon after my arrival in Price. Like pretty much everyone else he teased me about my advanced years, but his own personal gripe with me was that despite his hard-won status as a member of one of the world's most elite fighting forces he was still getting less *trigger time* than an old Limey part-timer.

Chris was a real family man with five kids of his own back home and I reckoned he'd want to help Ameena if he could. But it turned out that he was not around and no one could say what he was up to or when he would return. I assumed he was addressing the issue of his lack of trigger time. I explained my predicament to one of his colleagues whom I'd never met before. He conformed to the US special forces stereotype – six foot or more of lean hard muscle, dressed in shorts and flip-flops, topped off with a baseball cap over an unkempt beard.

Chris's colleague, who somehow never told me his name, didn't hesitate to help. Telling me to wait where I was he disappeared, to return a short while later in a fancy dress costume which he obviously considered to be incognito civilian garb. To me he looked more like a Walt Disney version of Ali Baba, complete with turban and pointy-toed shoes.

By this time I'd met a lot of Afghans. None of them looked or dressed anything like this.

Undeterred by the lack of authenticity his disguise afforded him, Chris's anonymous colleague hoisted his huge frame onto a little Honda 125 motorcycle and headed into the Gereshk bazaar to recruit the services of a taxi driver. On those occasions when I visited Gereshk myself it was a major undertaking involving a minimum of three mine-resistant vehicles, supported by a dozen or so heavily armed combat soldiers. Even with these security measures in place I was always a little apprehensive. The idea of popping down to the Gereshk bazaar in fancy dress costume was simply incomprehensible to me.

However, less than 30 minutes later I found myself standing in the dust bowl just outside the camp gates haggling over the price of a taxi to Herat. With a little help from Ali Baba it had been as simple as *Open Sesame*.

I'm not renowned for my financial negotiating skills but I managed to beat the driver down to $300 from his opening bid of $1,000. I've no idea if this represented a good deal for the British taxpayer or not, it was simply all the cash I could get my hands on without having to raise some awkward paperwork and reveal the true purpose of the expenditure.

It may seem excessive compared to the $150 a month salary that Ameena's father officially earned as an AUP patrolman, especially when you consider that he actually received considerably less than this after paying off the kickbacks his chain of command extracted from him.

Everything is relative, however, and I reasoned that it was still extraordinarily good value for money when compared to the £15 million a day the British government was investing in our Afghan adventure.

The way I saw it Kara had not only saved Ameena's life, she had also secured the on-going support of at least three generations of her extended family. Ameena's father's gratitude was obvious to see and might also inspire him to be a better policeman. Better policemen were desperately needed if the AUP was ever going to reform itself into a credible force.

Ameena herself would never forget the loving care she'd received at the hands of strangers whose empathy and compassion had transcended the need for a shared language. It was an experience she would almost certainly recount to her brothers and sisters, cousins and friends. In time the story would be told to her children and perhaps even her grandchildren. If the residents of Gereshk could hold a grudge against the Angrezi dating back to 1842, it seemed entirely possible that an act of kindness might similarly be remembered for generations.

Kara's legacy would remain long after ISAF troops had withdrawn.

Kara's defiance of the hospital administrators would not earn her a mention in the *Herrick 16* operational honours and awards list. Even so, it may have been the single most effective contribution the entire battlegroup made to the counter-insurgency during our time in Helmand. It was certainly more effective than anything the DST ever accomplished.

General Chrystal's words echoed in my head: *destroying a home or property jeopardises the livelihood of an entire family – and creates more insurgents.* Kara and her colleagues inspired me to think that the opposite could also be true.

For the most part I'd been a bystander in Ameena's plight. Witnessing her story and its potential ripple effect on her family and the local community provided me with the insight at last to complete the narrative for Colonel James, producing something he would later describe as *the cornerstone of our approach.*

Ten days later, as I waited impatiently for my flight out of Camp Bastion, 3,580 miles away in Selly Oak, Birmingham Corporal Jack Stanley died from his wounds.

Latitude:	51.75
Longitude:	-1.58
Elevation:	84m
Met:	Partly cloudy H:10°L:2°
DTG:	111500ZAPR12

IT WAS A pleasure to see Rob, although I wouldn't have blamed him if he'd never wanted to see me again. He was kind enough to maintain that I'd saved his life, but probably closer to the truth to say that I'd nearly killed him in the first place. Either way the last time I'd seen him was back in January, hooked up to an array of monitors in a French hospital.

Rob, a chemist by trade, has a great sense of humour, a seemingly endless bank of jokes and stories – Harry once referred to him as *the funny scientist*. He was still trying to crack jokes just hours after his ribcage had been surgically cracked open but to be honest, through the morphine fog, they weren't his best material and he didn't look too chipper.

Rob and I first met in 2003 when he skied off a cliff in white-out conditions in the Grands Montets area of the Chamonix Valley, a mecca for off-piste skiing in the French Alps. In those days we were both just getting into off-piste. Neither of us had any specialist equipment or even understood the risks and hazards of backcountry skiing, although with the benefit of hindsight I now realise that these had been considerable.

We just made it up as we went along.

Most of the time this was a lot of fun but every now and then we had a mishap. On that particular occasion Rob somehow avoided serious injury, although he did lose some fancy prescription glasses for which loss he still, inexplicably, holds me accountable.

Over the course of the next decade I joined Rob on many of his annual 'long ski weekends', which often extended to six days or more. Rob's partner, Roslyn endlessly teased him about his definition of weekend. Sadly it was these same trips that Jane would cite as evidence of my 'excessive skiing' in her divorce petition.

On this occasion Rob had clearance for a five day weekend in the Trois Vallées, travelling out on New Year's Day 2012 and, of

279

course, I went along for the ride. We spent most of the next two days above 2,500 metres in the Mont du Vallon backcountry. Snow conditions were a little challenging but that's to be expected so early in the season. We were skiing hard, covering a lot of ground and having a great time.

Right up to the point when Rob had a heart attack.

Rob must have a tremendous threshold for pain because his self-diagnosis was merely 'indigestion'. But when he started complaining of shooting pains in his arms I knew something was up. A combination of physical exertion with exposure to high altitudes and low ambient temperatures is known to increase the risk of myocardial infarction, and although Rob was atypical of cardiac patients he had nonetheless succumbed. This was almost certainly my fault because, when it comes to skiing, Jane was quite right about me – I'm incredibly selfish.

Nothing else matters when I'm in the mountains. I have little time for those who can't keep up. Rob had been skiing with me long enough to know that if he was having a bad day it would be a waste of breath telling me about it. I wouldn't be listening.

So it was pretty incredible not only that Rob had agreed to pick me up from Brize Norton, but also that he and his partner Ros had offered to put me up for the duration of my R&R in the guest wing of their fabulous home – Gooseberry Hall. When Jane point-blank refused to drop the boys, Ros even made the two hour journey north to collect them so they would be waiting for me when I arrived. I was overwhelmed by their generosity.

It was a perfect spring day and Rob picked me up in his fancy open top two-seater sports car. It's a car I've always coveted. When the visibility closed in that day in the Trois Vallées, grounding the rescue chopper, and it was becoming apparent that Rob might not make it off the mountain alive, I suggested he might like to bequeath it to me. He retorted by assuring me that he would be skiing the following morning and kicking my ass too, but as it turned out he was still in the hospital in Annecy when I departed for Afghan three weeks later.

With the roof down and the wind in our hair we flew north along the A429 under azure spring skies, through pristine Cotswold countryside dotted with ancient limestone villages and market towns with quintessential English names; Stow-on-the-Wold,

Moreton-in-Marsh, Stretton-on-Fosse. It was all in perfect contrast to the dry barren dashte which makes up so much of Helmand Province.

Britain was flirting with me that afternoon, displaying her beauty, tantalising me with her delights, proving – if proof were needed – that she was worth defending, even if it meant fighting a war over 3,500 miles away.

At my request, we stopped for a pint at the *Virgins and Castle* in the historic town of Kenilworth. Built in the fifteenth century, about the same time as the siege of Herat, it first became a pub in 1563, when Britain was still burning Protestants at the stake for heresy.

At that time Jalaluddin Muhammad Akbar, *Akbar the Great*, the third and greatest ruler of the Mughal Dynasty controlled the Gereshk valley and much of the rest of Afghanistan. Little has changed in the largely rural district of Nahr-E-Saraj in the intervening four and a half centuries, except that under Akbar the Mughal Dynasty was a model of religious tolerance, encompassing Islamic, Hindu, Christian and Buddhist faiths.

In truth I needed a bit of Dutch courage before being reunited with Harry and Alfie. I hadn't spoken to them since we'd said our goodbyes in the school playground back in January. Although I'd written to them every couple of days, I hadn't received any return mail. I'd missed them terribly and thought of them often but, after watching the R&R DVD in Bastion, I had to steel myself for the possibility that they might be less eager to see their Dad than their Dad was to see them.

Gooseberry Hall lies to the north of Kenilworth Castle in the heart of the Warwickshire countryside and is about as far removed from MOB Price as it's possible to be. There are no main battle tanks parked on the magnificent lawn. Its walls are not adorned with Lads Mags pin-ups or mimetic cock art. There are no Apache helicopters flying overhead.

To my very great delight it seemed my fears had been unfounded. I didn't even make it to the front door before Alfie threw himself into my arms, clinging to me in a fierce embrace as I was nearly knocked off my feet by his brother Harry.

It was indescribably good to see them, hear them, smell them, touch them. I held them both tight for as long as I was able until they finally felled me like an old tree, collapsing onto the lawn in a bundle of giggling, laughing, writhing limbs.

Afghanistan serves as a constant reminder of the fragile and tenuous grip with which all life clings to planet earth – something it's easy to forget in our cosseted lives in the west. Even without the armed conflict being waged inside its borders, it is a harsh and unforgiving place.

Average life expectancy is just 44 years. Pregnancy rather than insurgency is one of the primary causes of premature death. According to the World Health Organisation, one Afghan woman in 11 will die of causes related to pregnancy and birth during her childbearing years. In neighbouring Tajikistan, that figure is one in 430, while in Austria, it is one in 14,300. It's a figure that dwarfs the estimated 21,000 deaths resulting from the conflict since 2003.

Being reacquainted with life's cruelty and suffering heightens the appreciation of simple pleasures. Rolling around on Gooseberry Hall's manicured lawn with my kids was an unforgettable reunion, a moment of pure, unrestrained joy that I will treasure my whole life and take with me, smiling, to my grave.

As my anxieties melted away we were joined by the rest of the Gooseberry Hall Gang (GHG), a chaotic, happy-go-lucky collective of kids and pets who all call Gooseberry Hall home and who filled the air with noise and laughter as we played in the sunset.

It was a beautiful evening and the perfect homecoming.

For the next two weeks I did not let my boys out of my sight.

But Afghanistan was never far from my thoughts as we toured the country visiting friends and family. I even tuned the car radio to BFBS, the British Forces Broadcasting Station on the basis that they would be first with any news.

I'd experienced on previous tours this inability to switch off completely during R&R, when the conflicts I'd been fighting had been all but invisible to the British public. Back then, I'd wanted to stop strangers in the street and berate them for not realising there was a war being fought on distant, or not so distant, shores on their behalf.

But not this time.

Immediately following the 9/11 Twin Towers atrocity in 2001

there had been broad public support in the UK for the use of military intervention in Afghanistan, with a clear majority in favour of an invasion to defeat al-Qaeda and the Taliban regime which sheltered it.

A random telephone survey of over 1,000 adults, commissioned by The Guardian newspaper and conducted between 14th and 16th September 2001, revealed that 66% of voters backed the use of military force in Afghanistan. However, between 2007 and 2010, public confidence changed as the mission changed, as more and more American and British troops were killed and as the cost of the war increased.

Eleven years later in September 2012, The Guardian reported on the findings of an annual transatlantic trends survey conducted by the German Marshall Fund of the United States. This indicated that public support for the Afghan war on both sides of the Atlantic had collapsed. Fewer than 50% of people in most European countries believed the ISAF intervention had been worthwhile. 52% of Britons surveyed favoured an immediate and complete withdrawal.

However, despite the collapse in public support for the war, those fighting it had never been held in such high regard. Perhaps the clearest evidence of this was the staggering success of the Help for Heroes (H4H) charity launched on 1st October 2007 to provide better facilities for British servicemen and women wounded or injured in the line of duty.

In its first year H4H raised £14.2 million. But four years later in 2012, when The Guardian was reporting that public support for the war had all but collapsed, it raised a staggering £40.6 million – adding to a total of £166 million in just five years. An incredible accomplishment, but also a measure of the British public's support for its troops.

Back in 2011, returning from BATUS after Colonel Roly had given me the green light to join the Grenadiers in Afghanistan the following year, I'd felt a fraud when the Canadian public had stopped to applaud as we passed through the departure lounge at Calgary airport. I'd done nothing to deserve their display of support. The greatest danger I'd faced had been the marauding prairie mosquitoes.

Eighteen months later I hadn't felt quite so abashed accepting a can of cold lager on the flight from Minhad, donated by a grateful British public through the Beer For The Boys charity.

Beer For The Boys is an idea conceived and developed by the personnel of 216 Squadron at RAF Brize Norton, who operate the ageing TriStars that maintain the air bridge between Afghanistan and the UK. Its principle aim is to provide a free can of beer to servicemen and women flying home from Afghanistan. Supported by UK breweries, private companies, clubs, associations, charities and private individuals, it's run entirely by squadron personnel who manage the fund, distribute the beer and fundraise in their spare time.

Since its inception in 2007, it has served over 187,000 cold beers to thirsty troops. This not only highlights the huge public support for the armed services, but also proves beyond any reasonable doubt that, despite the relentless banter, not all the RAF are cunts.

On Alfie's birthday, as we drove to Norfolk to celebrate with family and friends, BFBS announced the death of Sapper Connor Ray. Connor had been caught in an IED blast on the day that Rob picked me up from Brize Norton. While I'd been fooling around on the lawns at Gooseberry Hall, he'd been fighting for his life. A battle he fought heroically for seven more days before succumbing to his wounds.

The familiar feelings of guilt and dismay washed over me.

Latitude:	52.36
Longitude:	-1.58
Elevation:	97m
Met:	Partly sunny H:19°L:6°
DTG:	211600ZAPR12

IT WAS TIME for me to return to Afghanistan.

The following morning I was to drive the boys back to their home in York before returning to Brize Norton for the long journey back to the war in which I'd invested so much.

Our last day together at Gooseberry Hall, though tinged with the inevitable pain of the coming separation, was a joyous affair culminating in a game of British Bulldog on the lawns. As the sky reddened in a sunset that would have delighted even the most sceptical of shepherds the GHG charged up and down the manicured turf to a delightful sound track of squeals and laughter.

The perfect antidote to the stress of the war in Afghanistan. And to the conflict of my deteriorating relationship with Jane.

In the two weeks I'd been back in the UK we'd not spoken to each other even once.

That night, not wishing to relinquish a precious moment of the time we had left together, I sat and watched Harry and Alfie as they slept. Like all proud parents I marvelled at their physical beauty; they shared the same flawless skin, perfectly proportioned limbs and unruly mop of tousled, sun-dappled hair. But they had their differences too. Harry's thoughtful, almond-brown eyes were the perfect contrast to Alfie's mischievous, pale blue peepers.

I had literally thousands of photos of them both but the images I treasured the most were in my head, not stored on digital memory cards. These were a much more satisfying and complex synthesis of sight, touch, sound and smell, indelibly burned onto the receptors of my brain to which I now added these carefully studied images of their sleeping forms.

Then, just for good measure, I took out my smart phone and added a few dozen more digital photos to my collection.

Leaving them once again and returning to Afghan was not going to be easy. But the combination of some rest and relaxation, together with the inspiration provided by Major Kara Watters, had filled me with renewed hope and optimism. As I waited at Brize Norton for the flight to Minhad I emailed an update to Lieutenant Colonel Marc Overton, the Commanding Officer of the London Regiment, in which I wrote:

Most of VIMY [the London Regiment company attached to the Grenadier Guards] *will have completed RSOI while I have been on leave and H16[1] will begin in earnest when I return.*

I feel incredibly motivated by the task and really excited that "influence" is actually driving rather than supporting operations in some of the least permissive areas of Afghanistan where shadow governance leads and GIRoA, ANSF[2] and ISAF have hitherto had almost no presence.

The extra few months in theatre in advance of the main body have been hugely beneficial and mean that I have a real in-depth understanding of the issues to guide and support the sub-units as they find their feet. I think this will pay dividends in the months ahead.

My *in-depth understanding* would not help Guardsman Michael Roland, killed on the day I returned to MOB Price at a place we called 'The Garden', less than half a kilometre north of Kakoran where Ben and I had patrolled. He'd arrived in Afghanistan just a few days before I'd departed on R&R.

---

[1] **H16**: HERRICK 16. Herrick is the randomly assigned codename under which all British military operations in Afghanistan have been conducted since 2002. Herrick 16 covered the period March – September 2012.

[2] **ANSF**: Afghan National Security Forces

```
Latitude    31.77
Longitude   64.68
Elevation   847m
Met         Sunny H:21°L:8°
DTG         290750DMAR12
```

There were only two priority effects applied to the names on this list. Kill or capture.

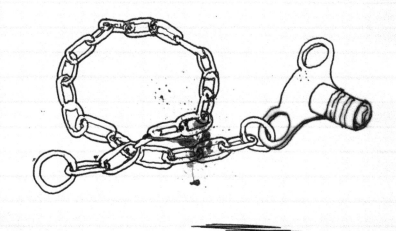

FTTT: First to the Truth
RIAB: Radio in a Box
POG: Psychological Operations Group
DCC: District Community Council
HPRT: Helmand Provincial Reconstruction Team
DfID: Department for International Development
GOVAD: Governance Advisor
D&AD: Design and Art Direction
MSSG: Military Stabilisation and Support Group
NCO: Non-commissioned Officer
JPEL: Joint Priority Effects List
BDL: Bed Down Location
VSO: Village Stability Operations
SOF: Special Operations Force
OSW: Operational Staff Work

MINISTRY OF DEFENCE ANNOUNCEMENT

Corporal Andrew Steven Roberts and **Private Ratu Manasa Silibaravi.** On Friday 4 May 2012, Corporal Andrew Steven Roberts and Private Ratu Manasa Silibaravi were killed in an indirect fire attack on Forward Operating Base Ouellette, in the northern part of Nahr-e-Saraj district.

Corporal Brent John McCarthy, RAFP and **Lance Corporal Lee Thomas Davies.** On Saturday 12 May 2012, Corporal Brent John McCarthy and Lance Corporal Lee Thomas Davies were killed by small arms fire near Patrol Base Attal in the Lashkar Gah district of Helmand province.

Captain Stephen James Healey. On Saturday 26 May 2012, Captain Stephen James Healey was killed when his vehicle was struck by an improvised explosive device while conducting a patrol in the northern part of Nahr-e-Saraj district.

Corporal Michael John Thacker. On Friday 1 June 2012, Corporal Michael John Thacker was hit by small arms fire while manning Observation Post 'Tir' in the Nahr-e-Saraj district of Helmand province.

Private Gregg Thomas Stone. On Sunday 3 June 2012, Private Gregg Thomas Stone was fatally wounded in the Nahr-e-Saraj district of Helmand province while apprehending a group of insurgents who had abducted a member of the Afghan Police.

Lance Corporal James Ashworth. On Wednesday 13 June 2012, Lance Corporal James Ashworth died as a result of enemy action while on patrol in the Nahr-e-Saraj district of Helmand province, Afghanistan.

Corporal Alex Guy. On Friday 15 June 2012, Corporal Alex Guy was fatally wounded in an insurgent ambush in the Nad 'Ali district of Helmand province while trying to relieve a group of Afghan soldiers who were pinned down by enemy fire.

Warrant Officer Class 2 Leonard Thomas, Guardsman Craig Roderick and **Guardsman Apete Tuisovurua.** On Sunday 1 July 2012, Warrant Officer Class 2 Leonard Thomas, Guardsman Craig Roderick and Guardsman Apete Tuisovurua were attacked and fatally wounded following a shura in the Nahr-e-Saraj district of Helmand province, Afghanistan.

Latitude:	31.77
Longitude:	64.68
Elevation:	847m
Met:	Sunny H:21°L:8°
DTG:	290750DMAR12

OUR DANISH PREDECESSORS in the J9 cell had built a shaded terrace at the back of the ops tent complete with outdoor furniture, open air cinema and barbeque pit. Many of these makeshift chill-out areas existed in Price, made largely from recycled defence stores by the ingenuity of the camp's occupants. Professional soldiers go to considerable efforts to transform even the most basic accommodation into something a little more comfortable and homely and take great pride in their work. In my youth I'd spent a cold and uncomfortable Christmas in a trench system in the Bosnian mountains overlooking Sarajevo. In keeping with the festive season a string of sparkly lights, liberally adorned with the flimsiest of ladies underwear, festooned the dugout. In one corner a tinsel covered tree, straddled by a scantily clad Barbie doll, took pride of place. The decorations didn't provide any protection from Serb mortars but they did improve morale.

The intervening 20 years had not dimmed the British squaddie's desire to improve his living quarters and inevitably there was a competitive element. Afghan 'Grand Designs'. In an ambitious attempt to outclass their rivals the three man Army Air Corps team responsible for running the busy MOB Price helipad even attempted to install a plunge pool and jacuzzi into their accommodation. Regrettably an error in their plans or, more likely, the absence of any plans other than some hastily scribbled notes on the back of a cigarette pack, resulted in several hundred gallons of water flooding the HLS[1]. Fortunately they had chosen the height of the summer for their flawed hydro engineering project and the soggy mess dried out soon enough. Kevin McCloud would not have been impressed.

The J9 loggia, which we had been lucky enough simply to inherit, surpassed all these other attempts and since it seemed churlish to claim rights of ownership over something we had not ourselves created it was widely used by all the HQ staff. There was however, one essential but grim task for which it was perfectly suited but which I doubt its creators had anticipated.

[1] **HLS**: Helicopter Landing Site

Less than 24 hours after Guardsman Michael Roland was tragically killed by a Taliban bullet, a Royal Military Police investigative team arrived in MOB Price to conduct an inquiry into the circumstances leading up to and immediately following his death. The two men and one woman in the team would painstakingly and carefully take detailed statements from all those who had been present on the ground at the time to construct a comprehensive picture of events.

The shaded and soothing space so lovingly created by the departed Danish J9 team seemed an ideal location for men who would have to remember and relive the harrowing experience of losing a comrade in combat. I did not hesitate to offer it for this purpose.

We all tried not to intrude on this distressing process, but I witnessed a succession of pale and dejected young men troop through the J9 tent to the makeshift interview area beyond. The RMPs gently coaxed statements from Michael's colleagues as they sat in the dappled shade of overhead cam-nets, holding their heads in their hands, chain smoking, staring at their feet as they repeatedly flicked imaginary ash from locally purchased Korean 'Pine' cigarettes onto the dirt floor.

Up until Michael's death the Grenadier Guards battlegroup had been extraordinarily lucky to avoid serious injury or loss of life with countless near misses, partial detonations and lucky escapes. Chance would continue to play an inexplicably benign role in our fortunes, but even she could not deny mathematical laws of probability. This painful scene was to be repeated several times over the coming months.

These statements, taken just hours after the incident, would be made available at the inquest into Michael's death at Nottingham Coroner's Court, held almost two years later. They provided vital first-hand accounts of the events and assisted the Coroner in returning a narrative conclusion that Michael was *killed on active duty in the service of his country.*

Perhaps just as importantly for Michael's family, they also revealed the Herculean efforts of his friends and brothers-in-arms as they desperately tried to save his life during an intense two hour gun battle. After the inquest Michael's father stated:

We have taken comfort hearing of his comrades' attempts to treat and evacuate Michael while under fire, and I would like to thank them for this.

Although we'd trained together in Canada, I couldn't say that I really knew Guardsman Roland, but that didn't matter. From the moment Colonel Roly took me on as the battalion's Information Operations officer I became an associate member of the Grenadier Guards. I would never be granted full membership, nor did I aspire to achieve this status, but nonetheless I felt strongly that I now belonged to the same unit as Guardsman Roland and this made his death personal.

In an MoD statement released to the press, Colonel James said: *He will be missed hugely by the battalion and the regimental family as a whole.*

It was a family of which I was now a part.

As with all major incidents the J9 Cell was responsible for communicating the ISAF version of events to the local population. I was required to produce a statement which confirmed that an ISAF soldier had been killed and provide a sanitised outline of the events leading up to Michael's death. Once approved this would be translated into Pashtu and transmitted across the district in regular news bulletins via the MOB Price RIAB, radio-in-a-box.

Great importance was placed on the speed of reporting in order to be the first to fill the *information vacuum* following an incident. This was referred to as being *first to the truth, FTTT,* or in the lexicon of the phonetic alphabet Foxtrot Triple Tango.

It wasn't always entirely clear to me which was the priority, being truthful or being first.

In the relentless quest for good news and the blind insistence that everything was going swimmingly well, even when this was quite obviously not the case, it seemed to me that the truth was not always the overriding consideration.

As long ago as 1758 Samuel Johnson observed: *Among the calamities of war may be justly numbered the diminution of the love of truth, by the falsehoods which interest dictates and credulity encourages.* Little had changed, it seemed, in the intervening 250 years.

The radio-in-a-box was exactly that. A rather large and cumbersome box which contained ruggedised tape and CD decks, together with sophisticated recording and broadcasting equipment. Requiring only the addition of electrical power, an antenna and a willing DJ, it contained all that was needed to set up a new radio station.

I'd been introduced to the RIAB on the PsyOps course I'd attended at the Defence Intelligence and Security Centre in Chicksands, Bedfordshire. Due to the very high rates of illiteracy in Afghanistan, or perhaps due to the very low number of Pashtu speakers amongst ISAF soldiers, radio was considered an essential communications tool by both British and American forces.

RIABs had first been used in Afghanistan in 2005 at a time when the Taliban were assessed to be winning the public relations battle. At the time ISAF had no means to counter Taliban propaganda or to communicate anti-Taliban and anti-al-Qaeda messages of its own. The RIAB was the answer, enabling ISAF to broadcast its version of events to a large, often remote audience.

By the time I arrived in Helmand the RIAB was the *psyopers*[1] weapon of choice and a network of radio transmitters had been set up across the province using local Afghan DJs to broadcast information and host call-in shows. The psyopers liked to call their creation 'Radio Tamadoon', but all the Afghans I ever met called it what it was, *Radio ISAF*. To complement the transmitters, wind-up radios had been handed out to local nationals. Although I was not prepared to vouch for the reliability of the statistics, it was alleged that 92% of Helmand Province's 1.5 million inhabitants listened to the radio every day.

Certainly thousands of radios had already been distributed and I gave away hundreds more on my FFUI[2] patrols, but I never saw any of the locals actually using the radios or listening to *Radio ISAF*. All the locals who eagerly accepted the free radios I handed out assured me that they tuned in every day, but I was sceptical. I'd grown used to locals telling me what they thought I wanted to hear so I took to carrying one of the wind-ups in my pack and attempting to tune into the RIAB on my patrols. To my surprise, despite maps of the province produced by the PsyOps Group which outlined antenna reach and indicated almost

---

[1] **Psyoper**: A psychological operations practitioner

[2] **FFUI: Find, Feel, Understand, Inform.** In January 2010, Major General Michael T. Flynn USA wrote an influential paper titled *Fixing Intel: A blueprint for making intelligence relevant in Afghanistan*. His paper recommended *sweeping changes to the way the intelligence community thinks about itself – from a focus on the enemy to a focus on the people of Afghanistan*. This involved modifying the five components of the kinetic targeting approach: find, fix, finish, exploit and analyze into a non-kinetic social engineering construct: find, feel, understand, inform.

total coverage in our AO, I discovered that reception outside Gereshk was patchy at best and non-existent in many areas.

In contrast it was easy enough to tune into BFBS Radio, the English language station for UK troops, almost everywhere I travelled. BFBS was of course staffed by civilians, all of whom were professionals in the broadcasting industry, while the RIAB was staffed by soldiers, like me, with little if any prior experience.

Nonetheless, Thor and I invested a lot of time trying to improve the station programming and make it less blatantly an ISAF propaganda tool by inviting GIRoA officials, ANA commanders, Mullahs and other local dignitaries to conduct radio shows. We even had a go at healthcare and agricultural advice programming, but neither of us had any experience in running a radio station and there was no budget to produce these shows. Our efforts, while initially enthusiastic and well intentioned, were amateurish at best and we quickly ran out of goodwill and content to fill our ambitious schedule.

It was claimed that some RIAB DJs had as many as 50,000 listeners, but I guessed that poor reception and dodgy scheduling was having a negative impact on our figures and I started scanning the phone-in reports produced after each show. Despite the statistics being bandied about by the PsyOps Group, I discovered that most of the calls we received came from the same half dozen callers. Even Sultaan, the irrepressibly optimistic District Communications Advisor became disillusioned with the RIAB and stopped turning up to host the weekly live phone-in show that Thor and I had given him.

When I discussed my reservations with Owen, our Royal Marines Cultural Advisor and one of only a handful of fluent Pashtu speakers in Task Force Helmand, he helpfully pointed out that one of my supposedly local DJs was in fact from another part of Afghanistan where they spoke a different dialect from the Helmandis. This embarrassing oversight may have had something to do with our rather poor performance.

But there was another even more compelling reason. I'd read in an intelligence report that ownership of an ISAF radio could be injurious to human health. In the contested area in which we operated locals risked a severe beating from the Taliban if they were found to be in possession of one of the free wind-ups we were handing out, although I'd observed that these were still eagerly accepted in all but the most hard-line areas. All my evidence   may have been circumstantial but it still pointed to an obvious conclusion. Our woeful reception and lamentable programming were quite simply not worth a beating. Although I couldn't prove it, I rather suspected that the majority of the radios I handed out ended up, still in their original packaging, in the markets and bazaars of other more permissive districts.

Perhaps the RIAB was not quite as effective a weapon in the communications war as the PsyOps Group were claiming. It seemed perfectly possible to me that the POG were psyoping the home team by overstating the role and value of the RIAB to the counter-insurgency.

Latitude:	31.77
Longitude:	64.68
Elevation:	847m
Met:	Sunny H:22°L:8°
DTG:	282315DAPR12

NAHR-E-SARAJ IS ONE of 14 districts which make up Helmand Province. Each is governed by a council of elected officials known as the District Community Council (DCC). This was an entirely Western institution conceived by the Helmand Provincial Reconstruction Team (HPRT[1]) and overseen by the DST. Founded in 2010, elections were to be held every couple of years when each of the mosques in the district would be entitled to select three men to represent them. These representatives would then form an electoral college who would vote on the 20 or so from their number who would actually serve as DCC councillors.

Gereshk being a shockingly liberal city, the Nahr-E-Saraj DCC was unique in Helmand Province in having a small number of female councillors. This was something the DST had insisted upon at the initial election and which had been grudgingly accepted by the district's menfolk. To get around the obvious problems of actually allowing women a free vote, or the possibility that a female might defeat a male election candidate, such women as were permitted to do so by their husbands held a separate vote to select only the female councillors. On election, these token women councillors were not allowed to join their male colleagues at the council table and were authorised to debate and vote only on women's issues. No one seemed entirely clear what these gender specific issues were, but this didn't matter because they were never discussed.

Despite these rather obvious flaws, the DST took great pride in its female councillors. To my mind, rather than representing progress towards gender equality, they highlighted the lack of it.

It was not only women who lacked representation on the Community Council. Many of the outlying areas in the district did not have a councillor to represent them. This was because these areas were

---

[1] **HPRT**: Helmand Provincial Reconstruction Team. The HPRT was a multi-national, multi-department team funded by DfID dedicated to Helmand Province. It was established in Sep 2004, and ceased operations in Dec 2013.

under the control of the Taliban who had not conveniently signed up to the PRT's plan to bring democracy to Helmand Province. In fact the Taliban had so actively discouraged participation in the DCC that a few would-be councillors had died of democracy as they slept in their beds. Somehow, the PRT managed to find the silver lining even in these assassinations by declaring that this demonstrated the *resilience* of the DCC institution.

In reality, while the DST looked the other way, Balool Khan the DCC's venerable Chairman, a former Mujahideen fighter, gifted these vacant seats to his friends and tribal allies without the need for troublesome elections and they, in turn, re-elected him as Chairman. This way Balool retained control of the Council and ensured that his own tribesmen were first in line for any handouts from the District Development Fund. This purported to be a state fund managed by the Ministry of Finance in Kabul. It was in reality a multi-donor international aid package less an undisclosed percentage skimmed off by Ministry of Finance mandarins. This was how democracy worked in Afghanistan and by these standards it worked very well in Nahr-E-Saraj.

Perhaps I should not have been surprised. The PRT was, after all, trying to overlay democracy onto a regime of tribal patronage that had been in existence long before the birth of democracy in Athens around 510BC. Balool Khan was a wise old bird and I was pretty certain that as far as he was concerned the DCC's only purpose was to part the infidel from his money. It was fair to say that he easily out-smarted any of the DST officials, and I had to admire his ability to run rings around them. It seemed inevitable that he would revert to the old patronage system as soon as the funding dried up.

Naturally, the Helmand PRT glossed over these failings and relentlessly communicated progress in expanding governance and the delivery of basic services, when no such progress existed. As early as 2010, in a frankly delusional Annual Report, the PRT claimed that:

- *Security improvements have enabled Afghan government officials, civilians, and goods to travel more safely through the Central Helmand River valley, improving access to government services and markets.*

- *The ability to travel safely within districts has increasingly allowed districts in central Helmand to elect district community councils with representatives from across the district.*

- *Freedom from insurgent intimidation and control has enabled access to trusted dispute resolution systems, primarily community-based dispute resolution; the fledgling statutory justice system started functioning at the district level in 2010.*

- *Although opium production remains substantial, the provincial government's sustained counter narcotics programmes have delivered steady reductions in poppy cultivation since 2008.*

- *The network of paved roads has been expanded, increasing local commerce and stimulating business confidence.*

- *Health and education infrastructure has been largely restored to pre-Taleban levels.*

The PRT's claims were astonishingly inaccurate and wholly divorced from reality. Once again it seemed that *falsehoods which interest dictates and credulity encourages* were getting in the way of the truth.

In 2012 the House of Commons International Development Committee produced a report entitled *Afghanistan: Development progress and prospects after 2014* in which it stated:

A serious problem for DfID in Afghanistan is the difficulty in monitoring its programme since security conditions prevent DfID staff visiting projects. We appreciate that working in Afghanistan is extremely difficult and commend DfID staff for the job they have done. Nevertheless, we are concerned about the high turnover, resultant loss of capacity and knowledge, weak institutional memory and, at times, a lack of staff with adequate training and skills.

To my mind there was very little reason to commend DfID staff for the job they'd done but, reading between the lines of political correctness which constrained the IDC, their report chimed with my own view that DfID staff were poorly trained in the first place, had no notion of reality on the ground, and lacked any real ambition to make positive change. At best they were enthusiastic amateurs ill-prepared and equipped for the task their masters in the Foreign Office had set them. At worst, some of them at least must have been professionally negligent for knowingly producing reports that satisfied their political masters but which were largely devoid of any shred of truth. Some, by their own admission, were simply taking the inflated salary offered to civil servants for service in Afghanistan, sitting tight inside their mortar-hardened accommodation as they paid off their mortgages back home.

In one respect, however, the PRT's claims may have been accurate. One morning over breakfast in the MOB Price D-FAC I risked engaging Glenn Haughton, the Grenadier's Regimental Sergeant Major in early morning conversation. I judged the big man's mood to be more in keeping with Doctor Bruce Banner than his alter ego The Hulk, and so I enquired if he could identify any progress in the district from his previous tour of Nahr-E-Saraj in 2007. Glenn contemplated my question while consuming a very large quantity of boiled eggs before eventually informing me that the roads were now much better than they had been.

Following billions of dollars of investment the roads were indeed much better, although Glenn's analysis overlooked the fact that travelling on them had become a life threatening activity. Taliban attacks, IED emplacements, police corruption and extortion, and robbery by armed gangs were commonplace activities which made road travel a very high risk mode of transport.

It didn't surprise me that Glenn had not considered a democratically elected council a sign of progress. As the Grenadier Guards' senior non-commissioned officer responsible for maintaining standards and discipline, it was his role to preserve democracy rather than to practice it. However, having imposed the DCC construct on the province two years earlier, an election was now due. Between the DST's incompetence, Balool Khan's contrivance and the Taliban's intimidation the Nahr-E-Saraj DCC had failed from the outset to represent the people of the district but this was an ideal opportunity to redress this parlous state of affairs. I believed that, in keeping with our Transition Narrative, giving residents the opportunity to vote for their chosen representatives and thereby gain some influence and control over their own future might just compel them to support the GIRoA administration.

The PRT was responsible for running the election and made it very clear from the outset that they did not require, or desire, military assistance in this matter. Much to my surprise residents of the district were to be given just ten days notice of the impending election. When I raised my concerns about the brevity of this timeline, the Helmand PRT's Governance Advisor helpfully explained to me that this was intentional. His team would not be   able to cope with large numbers of citizens actually turning out to vote. In a revelatory late-night conversation in the J9 cell he further elucidated that it was important to create the semblance of an election without going to the trouble of actually holding an election. In his opinion this would be unnecessarily bothersome and might even result in candidates considered undesirable by the PRT getting elected.

I was stunned. In part by the suspiciously racist manner in which the GOVAD appeared to view the populace of Helmand. In far greater part by the implication that American, British and Danish soldiers were risking, and losing, their lives in the district so that the PRT could create the semblance of an election.

The following morning I relayed this conversation and my disquiet to Colonel James. His annoyance and frustration were palpable and I took the opportunity to suggest that we might get around the DST's objections to military involvement by recruiting Sultaan to the cause. As the District Communications Advisor he might reasonably be expected to communicate the election as far and wide across the district as possible and we, in turn, could hardly refuse his request for assistance in this endeavour. Colonel James hesitated for just a moment before giving me the green light to proceed on this basis. I saluted smartly and exited his office before he had the opportunity to reconsider.

Later the same day I briefed Sultaan. He initially appeared sceptical but, with typical enthusiasm, quickly embraced the novel idea of performing a task that matched his job description. It seemed that, to him, it was an equally novel idea to hold an election in which we were actually going to encourage people to vote. This was not how democracy was generally conducted in this part of the world but it sounded like it might be fun and Sultaan was always up for a laugh – or in his case a bit of a giggle.

Knowing by this time that we had only a dozen or so listeners to the RIAB we decided not to rely on the radio to communicate our election campaign. Instead we opted for a combination of posters and leaflets.

Conventional ISAF wisdom dictated that high rates of illiteracy in Helmand rendered print campaigns ineffective, but I was less certain. It was my personal experience that the majority of locals who came to speak to me at the regular walk-ins and shuras I conducted would bring a handwritten list of demands with them which they would pass to my interpreter. I concluded that   it was routine practice to engage the services of a scribe and reckoned the process probably worked equally well in reverse. If we handed out flyers they would be taken to the local scribe for an explanation. I was further encouraged in my thinking by the frequency with which the Taliban used posters of their own to communicate with locals in the more hard-line areas of our AO such as the Yakchal bazaar. Needless to say I was never able to convince the PsyOps Group of this line of reasoning. It seemed they had already invested too much in the RIAB to question its efficacy.

By 22.00 that evening, using Sultaan's laptop, we had created a poster showing a line of brightly coloured amorphous figures queuing patiently behind a ballot box with their voting papers. To this we added a headline, a few lines of explanatory copy and in the top left corner a GIRoA logo. It was never going to win a D&AD Yellow Pencil, the prestigious UK Design and Art Direction award for excellence in the creative, design and advertising industries, but Sultaan was pleased with our efforts and by the next morning he had secured the approval of Salim Rodi the District Governor.

We now had an approved artwork, but no means with which to print it.

Latitude:	31.83
Longitude:	64.68
Elevation:	847m
Met:	H:22°L:7°
DTG:	10245DAPR12

EVEN AS HE slept, Haji Jalander was alerted by the barking of distant dogs. Instantly awake he stared up at the night sky oblivious to the spectacular beauty, undimmed by light pollution, of the Milky Way above him. One of his many grandchildren stirred beside him in the large courtyard bed, a common feature of the region where summer night-time temperatures made sleeping outdoors preferable to the airless confines of thick adobe walled rooms baked hard by the sun. Haji listened intently, his senses on red alert. Beneath the yelping and howling of the dogs he detected the lower tones of a helicopter several kilometres to his west.

Haji Jalander was a widower, a family patriarch who shared his home with his two sons and a daughter, together with their respective spouses and offspring. He was a loving and much loved grandfather but he was also a former Mujahideen fighter whose instincts had kept him alive through a decade of conflict with the Russian Army. He now lived in Zumbalay, an insurgent stronghold to the east of Gereshk under Taliban shadow governance. Here his extended family made a good living farming poppy in the spring, wheat in the summer and maize in the autumn. He had no strong ideological ties to the Taliban but he had become disaffected with the GIRoA administration many years before and, like most of his countrymen, distrusted foreigners. Rooski, Angrezi, Pakistani or Irani, they were all the same to him and so he preferred to live outside the so-called *protected areas*.

As a former *Muj* who had killed many Russians he was respected, revered even, by the young men who now took up the fight against the infidel. Although content to leave the fighting to others, he knew many of this new generation of Jihadists and their leaders. Men like Mohammed Momin, a Taliban commander from the Deh Adam Khan region to the north of Zumbalay who would often seek safe refuge, good company and wise counsel in Haji's home. His own son-in-law occasionally supplemented his income as a poppy farmer by borrowing Haji's AK47 and participating in attacks on ISAF and ANA bases north of the river.

In Haji's opinion these were largely pointless gun battles in which both sides would often expend thousands of rounds but which achieved little else. Such duels with the infidel seldom resulted in more than a handful of casualties on either side and had little or no impact on the strategic direction of the war. However Haji had to concede it was an easy and relatively harmless way to earn $10USD a day – funded from the Taliban war chest. As an extra precaution he had taught his son-in-law how to hide in the shadows, moving fire positions frequently to avoid detection. His daughter's husband was a sensible and cautious man. Haji was confident she would not be widowed by his freelance activities.

Beneath the matchless night sky, Haji monitored the aural progress of the helicopter. It was not uncommon to hear them in the distance as they shuttled between the infidel's main bases in the west and their patrol bases north of the Helmand River, but they seldom flew directly overhead. Haji had witnessed first hand the terrible destructive power of the Russian HIP[1] and HIND[2] attack helicopters. Even now, all these years later, the noise made his heart beat faster.

To Haji's consternation, the dull thump of rotor blades pounding the night air grew louder and as it did so became distinguishable as not one but two helicopters. Local dogs began to take up the cacophony of barking from their more distant neighbours. Haji had heard enough. He roused those of his grandchildren who had chosen to sleep in their courtyard bed, urging them to go to their mothers. Quickly.

Sleepy-eyed children looked at him in bewilderment as the noise grew to a howling crescendo, drowning out all other sound. The downwash of rotors whipped up dust storms, tearing thatch from the roofs of the buildings and causing terrified livestock to stampede around the compound. Suddenly night turned to day as the courtyard was bathed in a light so bright that Haji was temporarily blinded and forced to shield his eyes. He did not see the dozen or so soldiers fast-rope into his compound from one of the helicopters now hovering overhead.

---

[1] **HIP (Mil Mi8)**: A Soviet-designed medium twin-turbine helicopter. Among the world's most-produced helicopters, numerous versions were built including an armed gunship variant (Mi8TVK) used by Russian forces in Afghanistan from 1979-89.

[2] **HIND (Mil Mi24)**: Russian designed and built armed assault and attack helicopter operated by the Soviet Air Force and its successors since 1972. Known to pilots as the *flying tank* it is a combination of armoured gunship and troop transport and was greatly exploited by airborne units of the Soviet Army during the 1979–89 Soviet war in Afghanistan.

As his eyes adjusted to the helicopters' searchlights he willed himself through sheer force of personality to ignore the sensory overload of the events unfolding around him and think. His first instinct was to run into the main building where he still kept his AK47 hanging on the back of the door, in plain sight of his many grandchildren. All of them could look but were forbidden to touch the weapon with which their gentle and loving grandfather had made his name as a ferocious Mujahideen fighter.

Haji reasoned with himself that the moment for armed resistance had already passed. This course of action would not only get himself killed but put the lives of his family in jeopardy. Two of the heavily armed soldiers now swarming around his compound began moving towards him, weapons raised in the firing position, both men staring through close quarter battle sights that project a red dot onto the intended target. Haji had no doubt that in that moment he was the target. But he also knew that the infidels from Europe and America lacked the ruthlessness of their Russian predecessors. Certainly his life was in danger, but he was still alive and could remain alive so long as he was utterly submissive and compliant. Determined not to show the fear swirling around in his belly he slowly placed his hands behind his head and sank to his knees with as much dignity as he could muster.

Almost immediately the men were upon him, binding his hands with plasticuffs. Still on his knees he was half dragged, half carried across the compound and placed in a group with his daughters and their children. They had been separated from their husbands and some of the older boys who were being contained in another corner of the compound. Haji realised the infidels were separating the potential combatants from non-combatants – women, children and old men. He was unable to conceal the flash of anger and humiliation he felt at the realisation that he had been categorised as a non-combatant and silently vowed revenge on the men who had so underestimated him.

Once the infidels were satisfied that all the compound's occupants were accounted for, they began searching the buildings and outhouses. Haji's AK47 was quickly discovered behind the front door and placed in an evidence bag together with several hundred rounds of loose 7.62mm ammunition. Haji surmised with annoyance that these must belong to his son-in-law who had brought them into the house without his permission. It was not long before Haji's ledgers which recorded his dealings with farmers' merchants were also discovered, together with a small quantity of US dollars, Pakistani rupees and Afghan afghanis. These too were   sealed in evidence bags. Finally, to Haji's dismay, a football-sized quantity of brown opium resin wrapped in white muslin cloth was unearthed from its hiding place in one of the animal enclosures. This represented Haji's life savings, his healthcare plan and his pension.

Like many other farmers Haji retained a small quantity of raw opium each year which he set aside for the unexpected: drugs to ward off sickness; food to compensate for a poor harvest; the services of a midwife to ensure the safe delivery of another precious grandchild. As the search continued Haji watched his sons and the eldest of his grandsons being questioned by an infidel interpreter. He was demanding to know who owned the AK47 and whether there were any other weapons in the house. He also wanted to know the whereabouts of Mohammed Momin. It had been several days since the Taliban commander had visited and no one was about to reveal the true owner of the AK47. The interpreter's questions were met with blank looks and sealed lips.

Less than 15 minutes after the soldiers had arrived Haji's son-in-law was separated from the other men, blindfolded and led from the compound to a patch of open ground just outside. One of the helicopters landed and collected the infidels, together with their prisoner and the evidence bags containing Haji's most important possessions. Within moments it was airborne again.

Haji continued to stare in the direction of the retreating aircraft long after he could make out their forms in the inky blackness of the night sky or hear the beat of their rotors. Eventually even the distant dogs that had warned him of his persecutors' imminent arrival quietened.

All he could now hear was the hushed sobs of still terrified children behind him, barely audible above the deafening roar of rage and humiliation inside his head.

Latitude:	31.77
Longitude:	64.68
Elevation:	847m
Met:	Sunny H:21°L:8°
DTG:	080750DJUL12

PRIOR TO DEPARTING on R&R, inspired by Major Kara Watters, I'd managed to persuade Colonel James that our narrative – which we dubbed the *Transition Narrative* – should take its lead from General Stanley McChrystal's statement: *without the participation of the people, security won by the military won't endure.* From this we concluded that the best opportunity for successful transition in Nahr-E-Saraj would be to compel local nationals in sufficient numbers to reject the insurgency and to accept GIRoA governance.

In truth it had not been hard to convince Colonel James that this was our best course of action because it was what he himself had directed us to do when the headquarters had first trained together in sub-zero temperatures on the STANTA training area in Thetford. To envisage what transition in 2015 would look like and to work backwards from this point in order to understand our mission in 2012.

Colonel James, like so many of his generation of professional soldiers, had spent a good portion of the previous decade studying, training and fighting in Afghanistan. His experience had taught him not to expect too much from the Afghan administration. As a career soldier he was way too smart to say this outright and risk criticising our political masters. Instead he was indirectly ordering us to set our sights fairly low.

For all DfID's state-building hubris on the pillars of democracy, gender equality and religious tolerance, we were not going to achieve Libertopia in Helmand in the next two years. What we needed to do was to unfuck the goat just enough to prevent a swift and embarrassing descent into civil war the moment we turned out the lights in Camp Bastion for the final time.

However, taking into account everything I'd subsequently learned about Governor Salim Rodi's incompetent, corrupt and narco-compliant administration, even these lowly ambitions struck me as a near impossible task. The uncomfortable truth in Nahr-E-Saraj was that local GIRoA officials had no interest in serving the community they purported to represent. Their   sole interest was personal gain. It seemed unlikely to me that this was a sufficiently compelling reason to convince local residents to accept GIRoA governance.

There was, in fact, some evidence to suggest that the Taliban were not winning the war in Helmand Province but, perversely, that GIRoA was losing it.

About this time, the boffins in Regional Command South West, Task Force Helmand's US Higher Headquarters produced a perception trend report based on aggregated monthly surveys conducted over the previous 12 months. After my experience with the PsyOps dodgy data I was more than a little sceptical of these kinds of reports. This one, at first glance, appeared to conform to the standard pattern of self-deception with which I had by now become familiar. According to this report, dubbed The AP-A Atmospherics Word on the Street, everything in Helmand Province was coming up roses.

The data had been presented in a graph that plotted Atmospheric Values – whatever they were – over time. According to the graph, public perception of the Taliban was very low, represented by a red line knocking along the bottom of the horizontal axis. Perceptions of GIRoA, a bold green line, were several points higher somewhere in the centre of the graph. Naturally, given this was a US report, perceptions of ISAF were highest of all, a striking cobalt blue line running along the top of the chart.

I was pretty certain that none of the respondents in the survey had been canvassed on the streets of Kakoran, or any of the other places I'd visited recently. But, this aside, something else about the slide caught my eye.

The Regional Command eggheads had applied some linear regression to their data points to smooth the red, green and blue lines running across their chart. While this helped to illustrate their point that perceptions of GIRoA were significantly higher than those of the Taliban, I also observed that there was a slight downward trend to the GIRoA data set.

I decided to redraw the graph, extending the timeline out to December 2014, when British forces were due to depart Afghanistan. I then extrapolated the Taliban, GIRoA and ISAF trend lines based on the Regional Command linear regression and discovered that while perceptions of the Taliban continued to bump along the bottom of the graph, at some point around June or July 2014, assuming current trends remained constant, perceptions of GIRoA would be as low, if not lower, than those of the Taliban.

This did not augur particularly well for successful transition. But it did, perhaps, provide the insight we required to unfuck the goat in 2012 as Colonel James had directed.

My analysis was admittedly rather crude but necessarily so. Since I didn't have the original data set to work from I'd simply extrapolated from the Regional Command graph, but I felt certain I'd done enough to warrant further investigation.

I showed my redrawn chart to Colonel James who dismissed it with a wry smile. It wasn't telling him anything he didn't intuitively know already. I then fired it back to the Regional Command boffins for their comment. I didn't have to wait long. First came an anonymous reply from a shared email address which, in not so many words, told me that I was a dumbass infantryman and couldn't possibly understand the complexities of applied mathematics and statistical analysis. I should leave the number crunching to the number crunching experts and get back out there and kill more bad guys.

As a parting shot the anonymous boffin smugly informed me that it was not possible to use the data for forecasting purposes as I had done. Spotting an obvious flaw in his intellectual superiority line of reasoning, I replied by pointing out that the linear regression he'd originally applied to the data was generally used for exactly this purpose. He retorted by stating that 12 months data was not enough to produce an accurate forecast. I agreed, and asked him to send me all the data for the previous five years.

At this point email communication ceased.

I took to the telephone and tried to track down the mystery boffin in his ivory tower a long, long way away from anywhere hostile and dangerous but no one wanted to take my calls. My several messages were not returned. A short while later I received a call from a British colonel in Task Force Helmand who discreetly informed me that I was not *on message* and, while he conceded that I might have a point, this was not helping Anglo-American relations. He was utterly charming but equally adamant that I was to stop by-passing the chain of command and harassing the Regional Command boffins. He also made it very clear that I was not going to receive the data I'd requested and I was to drop any further attempts at linear regression analysis.

It seemed that my *off message* forecasting of GIRoA perception trends was being buried *by the falsehoods which interest dictates*. Although this was a much more genteel and civilised dressing down than the one I'd received from TF196 it was a bollocking nonetheless.

Latitude:	31.77
Longitude:	64.68
Elevation:	847m
Met:	Sunny H:21°L:8°
DTG:	031315DMAY12

I WAS ALONE in the J9 cell when the secure telephone I shared with the other dozen or so occupants starting ringing. As soon as I picked up a guttural voice announced without preamble: *Iz Man at Gate.*

It was a member or the Bosnian Guard Force informing me that we had a walk-in visitor at the front gate. This was a reasonably frequent occurrence and in most cases would be a local national come to make representation to ISAF on some matter, most commonly to seek compensation for damage to property. It was well known that ISAF would reimburse citizens for any damage to crops, property or livestock for which it was responsible. In the early days of the Afghan campaign commanders would carry a quantity of hard currency with them on operations and pay out according to their own individual assessment.

Carrying large amounts of cash on the battlefield presents some obvious problems and as the campaign wore on the British professionalised their approach to the payment of compensation. Instead of cash, commanders began carrying claims forms which they passed to locals for presentation at any of the main British bases where the Military Stabilisation and Support Group (MSSG) would assess their claim and pay, where appropriate, at a predetermined but still generous rate.

Naturally the Afghans stepped up their game in response, and enterprising individuals, much like ambulance chasing law firms in the West, could be hired in the Gereshk bazaar to help citizens with their claims. These 'consultants' provided a range of services, including basic help with the filling out of forms, the taking of digital photos to help support claims and even representation at the weekly 'Compensation Clinics' run by the MSSG.

Like everyone else in theatre the MSSG assessors rotated every six months or so. This created an opportunity for those less fortunate citizens who lacked a genuine claim for compensation to jump on the Angrezi gravy train. Some less scrupulous consultants offered for sale in the bazaar photographs from historic cases which could be resubmitted in support of a fresh claim to a new assessor. I'm sure these claims consultants were obliged by their regulatory body to advise their clients that past performance was no guarantee of future success. I'm also sure that they demanded from their clients a premium for this particular service, while implying the near certainty of a payout. But this was not always the result. A number of the MSSG operators I spoke to, while grudgingly admiring this Afghan enterprise, routinely rejected claims from multiple different claimants that relied on identical photographs as supporting evidence.

I was not authorised to assess claims. If the visitor was seeking compensation there was little I could do for him other than advise him to attend a compensation clinic. However, since I was alone in the J9 cell, it fell to me to see what he wanted. The balance of probabilities suggested that this particular visitor was unlikely to be a suicide bomber, or a Taliban assassin, but I laboriously donned my body armour and checked chamber on my Sig 9mm pistol just in case.

1. Hope for the best.

2. Plan for the worst.

3. Prepare to be surprised.

The mantra had kept me alive so far and with the number of attacks at shuras and other engagements on the increase I wasn't about to get complacent.

The smooth surface of the percussion cap on the chambered round gleamed reassuringly from the dark confines of the Sig's working parts. I was confident that, if called upon to do so, the weapon would perform the task for which it was intended. Things had moved on a bit since my first few, nervous days in theatre. I'd not yet fired the Sig in anger but I'd been called upon to use my primary shooter, the SA80 Mark 2 assault rifle, sufficiently often that I was equally confident that operator error would not be an issue.

I spent a few frustrating minutes locating the duty interpreter whom I eventually found playing table football outside the Kuffen with his mates. We wearily headed up to the front gate, both of us irritated, no doubt, by this unscheduled and probably fruitless interruption to our day.

Standing in the dust just outside the front gate was a straight backed, hook-nosed, white bearded gentleman in a grubby *shalwar kameez*. A disinterested nod in his direction from the Bosnian guard on duty indicated that this was *Man at Gate*. Judging from the number of deeply etched lines running from the corners of his eyes, across his cheeks and into the dense white thatch of his beard he clearly exceeded DfID's assessment of average life expectancy in the province.

Although the guard was doing a good job of pretending otherwise, it was impossible to ignore the penetrating glare of his obsidian eyes, undimmed either by age or the harsh light of the Afghan sun.

After a brief exchange of rapid-fire Pashtu my interpreter informed me that our visitor was a former Mujahideen fighter from Zumbalay called Haji Jalander who was seeking information regarding a missing person.

Zumbalay was only 15km as the crow flies from where we now stood, but it might as well have been on another planet. Deep in insurgent held territory it was a place I'd never visited and a place where both ISAF and GIRoA were most unwelcome. To the best of my knowledge ISAF troops had not challenged this state of affairs since Danish forces had unsuccessfully attempted to establish a platoon house in the *Witches Hat* area of Zumbalay in 2009.

It was most unusual to receive visits from local nationals living outside the so-called protected areas. I took Haji Jalander's unwavering stare and his claim to be Mujahideen as thinly veiled code for Taliban. Even if my assumptions were incorrect his visit would almost certainly have been sanctioned by the local Taliban neighbourhood watch who were not in the habit of encouraging fraternisation with ISAF. If not, Haji Jalander was taking a very grave risk in presenting himself at our front gate. News of his visit would almost certainly filter back to the insurgents who had eyes on the base 24 hours a day through a network of informants and dickers[1].

Haji made little if any attempt to disguise the deep disgust and disdain with which he viewed me and the traitorous interpreter through whom we spoke. Outwardly he appeared ferociously calm, but I noticed

---

[1] **Dicker**: A term originally coined in Northern Ireland to describe low level, usually unarmed informants, often children, who follow patrols and hang around outside military bases providing basic intelligence on troop movements and dispositions to the enemy.

threaded through his fingers a slim brass chain with a radiator key at one end which he flicked unconsciously back and forth across his hand.

Haji was not as fearless as he wanted us to think.

I couldn't help wondering how he had come by the radiator key. I was pretty sure that he wouldn't have central heating installed in his compound. There wasn't much call for it in Afghanistan.

The old Mujahideen fighter gave me the distinct impression that he would not hesitate to kill me if circumstances allowed. But I judged that this was not the purpose of his visit. Perhaps on some other day, but not today. Nevertheless I made sure he was thoroughly searched before admitting him onto the base.

I guessed this was not going to be a routine case of casual claims embezzlement.

Once Haji had been thoroughly searched he was also bio-enrolled. This process included collecting a DNA swab from the subject's cheek as well as retinal and fingerprint scans using a device that looked similar to the old Polaroid instant print cameras from the 1970s. Haji's fingers were so worn and calloused that the scanner was unable to detect a fingerprint, something I'd never come across before, but there was no such problem with the retinal scan of his piercing black pupils.

If Haji had been up to no good there was a reasonable probability that he would already be on the ISAF database, in which case I would hand him over to the RMPs for an interview without coffee. But there was no record of his bio-data.

Next I sat down with one of the NCOs in the J2 (Intelligence) cell to see if they had anything on Haji. A quick name search of their database drew a blank but when we studied a list of all the known residents of Zumbalay we discovered a close match, Ajip Yallander.

Ajip Yallander was a former Mujahideen fighter now resident in Zumbalay who had come to the attention of the intelligence community as a known associate of Mohammed Momin. The only photograph of Yallander on file was a very low resolution, out of focus shot of a man with a long white beard. It might have been Haji. It might have been Santa Claus.

The photograph was inconclusive but it seemed possible, if not probable, that Haji Jalander and Ajip Yallander were one and the same. If this was so then the man I'd just invited onto the base was not keeping good company. Mohammed Momin was so well known to ISAF that he'd been assigned a codename and placed on the Joint Priority Effects List (JPEL).

Although the title might seem to have suggested otherwise, there were only two *priority effects* applied to the names on this list. Kill or capture.

ISAF wanted Momin dead and was actively seeking this outcome. I already knew a great deal about him because I had, by coincidence, sat on a targeting board that had reached this conclusion only a few weeks earlier.

At the time I'd unsuccessfully argued that killing Momin might have unintended consequences. Momin was one of six brothers who had been born and raised in Deh Adam Khan, a prosperous and largely peaceful rural location on Gereshk's eastern outskirts. It was where we always took the international media when we wanted to show the world what a wonderful job we were doing. Momin was the black sheep of the family and his five brothers, by contrast, appeared to be upstanding, law-abiding pillars of their community. Killing Momin, I argued, might upset this balance and turn his brothers into insurgents, potentially destabilising a pacified, pro-GIRoA area – of which there were precious few.

The board had initially responded positively to my argument with several supportive nods around the table. However, this quickly dissipated when Major Uffe Geckler Pederson, the senior Danish officer in the headquarters, passionately and persuasively countered that Momin was known to have killed at least three Danish soldiers and was implicated in dozens of other attacks. Uffe argued that Momin had chosen to live by the sword and should be prepared to die by the sword – as we should be ourselves. As a known combatant who would continue to target ISAF and GIRoA forces, Momin could not and should not be protected by the unsubstantiated possibility that his brothers might then take up arms against us. He had a point. The board certainly thought so and Momin was voted for targeting on an 8:1 majority under the codename Objective Beninghaus.

Beninghaus was known to exert some influence over the *Crazy Gang,* a bunch of violent and unpleasant hoods terrorising the Adinzai Bazaar, just a few klicks north of Zumbalay. Intelligence indicated that he was thought to be using Zumbalay as a transit route to commute to and from Adinzai and that he routinely used Ajip Yallander's compound as a bed down location (BDL).

For the time being at least, it seemed reasonable to assume that Haji Jalander the *Man at Gate,* and Ajip Yallander the known insurgent facilitator were one and the same.

According to an October 2011 study by the Afghanistan Analysts Network simply being a facilitator was enough to be assigned a codename and subjected to *priority effects.* The report examined the effectiveness of controversial ISAF night raids aimed at *decapitating the Taliban on the battlefield by removing their commanders.* This was a tactic much favoured by General Petreus who had replaced McChrystal after his motor mouth got the better of him. It revealed that the words *leader* and *facilitator* were sometimes used interchangeably in ISAF press releases, although *facilitator could just be someone whose house an insurgent group was thought to have used.*

The study also revealed that these night raids were not exactly a precision tool. For every leader killed eight other people also died. Since ISAF was very careful not to kill civilians I presumed these other eight must all be insurgent facilitators. American Special Forces were particularly adept at avoiding civilian casualties.

In the first few weeks of our tour I'd been approached by a US Navy Seal team running a Village Stability Operation[1] in Parschow, an area just south of MOB Price. The Seals had been in contact with the enemy when they witnessed a young boy being callously gunned down by insurgents as they fled the scene. The Seals were keen to be first to the truth with the news and wanted to use the MOB Price RIAB to communicate the brutal and heartless disregard for human life which the Taliban had displayed.

Since isolating the insurgents from the population is a cornerstone of counter-insurgency operations, this seemed like a good idea to me and

---

[1] **VSO**: Village Stability Operations. A US SOF initiative the aim was to provide *enhanced security, governance, and development in strategically important rural areas critical to the Afghanistan campaign but beyond the effective reach of the Afghan government and U.S. conventional forces.* It was perhaps insightful that the Parschow VSO was just 3 km due south of Gereshk, the seat of GIRoA District Governance and home to the District Police Headquarters, the main Afghan National Army base and ISAF's Main Operating Base Price yet still beyond the reach of the Afghan government and US conventional forces.

I readily agreed, asking only that the Seals provide me with a few more facts before I could produce a transcript. I also explained that I would need approval from Task Force Helmand for broadcast, which needn't be a problem but was a factor in determining the speed with which we could get the message into the public domain.

The Seal team leader seemed reluctant to submit to a British chain of command but promised to get back to me with more details. When he returned a short while later, he revealed that it might in fact have been a stray American round that tragically killed the boy after he was caught in crossfire. The incident, as with all incidents involving civilian casualties, would now be subject to an internal review. All reporting on the subject would be postponed until this had been completed. I inwardly breathed a sigh of relief that I'd not been tempted to step outside the TFH reporting chain in order to assist the Seals. In the light of these new details it would have shown appallingly poor judgement on my part which, quite rightly, would have cost me my job.

The next morning I again bumped into the Seal team leader outside the DST office. He cheerily informed me that there was no longer any need for an enquiry. The casualty was not after all an innocent young boy but a baby-faced Talib fighter whose body had been recovered along with an AK47 rifle. He now wanted me to report a great victory in which ISAF had protected the people of Parschow from vicious insurgents, one of whom had been killed in the battle. Promising to look into it, I made myself scarce.

While I'd been doing my research Haji Jalander, or Ajip Yallander, had been kept waiting under the watchful eye of the Bosnian guards in the same spot where I'd met with the Gereshk business leaders following Haji Gul's abduction by TF196. Despite my lectures on customer experience it was still being used as an emergency urinal. Haji and the interpreter were clearly not getting along in my absence. They sat across the table from each other in uneasy silence.

I apologised to Haji for the wait and suggested that he might tell me the purpose of his visit. I was not expecting his account of the night raid in which he'd been relieved of his son-in-law and of his life savings.

According to Haji this had all taken place a few weeks earlier and he'd heard nothing since of the whereabouts of his daughter's husband. Haji assured me that this was a good man and a good father who'd never done anything wrong and did not deserve to be dragged from his bed and abducted in this way. Haji himself was now destitute with no means of paying his debts to the farmers' merchants from whom he had bought seed and fertiliser. He now had many mouths to feed and not enough hands to bring in the harvest. His daughter was inconsolable, as were his grandchildren. Finally, Haji reminded me that he was a former Mujahideen who had fought the Russians when the Americans had asked him to. Was this how the Capitalists meant to repay him for defeating the Soviets?

Of course, Haji neglected to tell me that his son-in-law was a freelance gun for hire, occasionally employed by the Taliban on a zero-hours contract. Nor did he feel the need to specify the illicit commodity in which he'd invested his life savings, nor the names and identities of his house guests although, if his story was true, this undoubtedly accounted for the visit from the Special Operations Force.

It was an extraordinary tale but not an improbable one. Night raids were commonplace in Afghanistan and Haji was not the first person, nor would he be the last, to receive a visitation from Special Operations Forces in the middle of the night. As with everything in the secretive world of SOF it was difficult to know precise details. But a US military source told researchers for the Open Society Foundation in April 2011 that as many as 40 raids were being carried out every night. Jon Nagel, a former member of Petreus' staff described them as *an industrial strength counterterrorism killing machine.*

This sounded most impressive but Mr Nagel appeared to be fighting the wrong war. We were supposed to be conducting a counter-insurgency not a *counter-terrorism* campaign. Perhaps I was splitting hairs but Mr Nagel really should have known the difference between counter-terrorism and counter-insurgency, because his own boss had rewritten the counter-insurgency manual to great acclaim and fanfare. In it Petreus had mandated: *Legitimacy is the Main Objective.* Impressed, no doubt, by British military doctrine writers' ability to use a dozen words where half that number would have sufficed he went on to state:

The best counter-insurgency campaigns integrate and synchronise political, security, economic, and informational components that reinforce governmental legitimacy and effectiveness while reducing insurgent influence over the population. COIN strategies should be designed to simultaneously protect the population from insurgent violence; strengthen the legitimacy and capacity of government institutions to govern responsibly and marginalise insurgents politically, socially, and economically.

There was no mention of an industrial strength killing machine in any of the manual's 242 pages. Unsurprisingly night raids singularly failed to reduce insurgent influence over the population or to demonstrate the legitimacy of our cause.

In fact there was plenty to suggest that they were having the directly opposite effect. Towards the end of our tour a night raid in Rahim, conducted by a joint TF196 and Afghan Special Forces team, resulted in three brothers being gunned down in their compound in front of their wives and children.

Again I found myself in conflict with British Tier One Special Forces. TF196 insisted the men were insurgents, but this claim seemed highly improbable to me. The brothers' compound was just a short distance from one of our patrol bases and any suspicious activity would almost certainly have come to our attention. Our own J2 Shop had nothing on the men. The general consensus from our analysts was that the SAS, while ruthlessly efficient as always, had directed their special talents against the wrong targets.

When I challenged a TF196 spokesman on their version of events he played their top secret joker once more. Speaking to me by phone from an undisclosed location he said the information was classified. As a known Taliban-loving apologist and mere part-time soldier I could not be trusted and had no authority to contradict elite tier one special forces. A short while later I received another telephone call from the charming colonel in Task Force Helmand ordering me to drop my line of enquiry. Although he remained amiable I detected a hardening in his tone.

The TFH top brass had silenced me, but the Rahim *spin zhiras* remained determinedly voluble on the subject. They steadfastly maintained the brothers' innocence and were outraged at the brutal executions in front of the victims' families. Emissaries were despatched to the patrol base threatening retaliation and demanding an apology and blood money for the relatives. The PB Commander was bitterly angry that the raid had gone ahead without his knowledge, destroying the work his own men had done over the previous six months to marginalise the Taliban and protect the population from insurgent violence.

Shortly after we completed our tour the Rahim patrol base was abandoned and Afghan National Security Forces ceded control of the area to the Taliban. Perhaps these events were not linked to the slaying of the supposed insurgents but, given the long memories of our Afghan hosts, this seemed unlikely to me. Our actions had done nothing to strengthen the legitimacy of the GIRoA government as the Petreus COIN Field Manual had directed.

It didn't particularly surprise me that there were no official records of the night raid in Zumbalay that Haji Jalander was reporting, or of the subsequent incarceration of one its residents. As I'd already learned, the SOFs were not especially good at sharing their OSW with me and despite my best efforts I was unable to corroborate the proud old Mujahideen's version of events. He was not the compensation claimant I'd suspected he might be when I'd first heard the words *Iz Man at Gate*, but I was no more powerful to assist him than I'd thought I would be.

It was also perfectly possible that Haji's story was just that. An elaborate hoax aimed at extracting money from the infidel. Perhaps there had been no night raid and no missing son-in-law, just as there'd been no rodent flying officer and no downed UAV. Attempts to embezzle the infidel were commonplace and some of the tales equally extraordinary. It was just as Samuel Johnson had described it all those years ago: *Among the calamities of war may be justly numbered the diminution of the love of truth, by the falsehoods which interest dictates and credulity encourages.*

Either way Haji Jalander returned home to Zumbalay still bristling with anger, deeply frustrated by his fruitless and dangerous journey into the infidel stronghold. If he had once been ambiguous about the ISAF presence in his country his recent experiences now hardened his resolve to avenge his missing son-in-law and drive out the Capitalists, just as he had driven out the Soviets who had come before them.

His prayers would shortly be answered.

Latitude:	31.77
Longitude:	64.68
Elevation:	847m
Met:	Sunny H:21°L:8°
DTG:	101014DMAY12

ON 10th MAY 2012 at 10:14 the HPRT made the following post on its Facebook page:

The DCC (district community council) election was conducted in Gereshk, Helmand Province on 8th May. 5000 residents of the district including 1100 women participated in the election and voted in members of the DCC from a list of pre-registered candidates. The district community council for the Gereshk is comprised of 23 members including 5 women. 35 members of the DCC were elected through free election yesterday and the remaining posts such as director, deputy and other members for the DCC will be elected by the DCC members themselves. The gathering of the thousands of the civilians for the election shows that the civilian population is increasingly supportive of the government and that civilians are satisfied that their problems can be resolved through the DCC. Previous members of the Gereshk DC had also been chosen by the local residents in free elections.

The Rt Hon. William Hague MP, Secretary of State for Foreign & Commonwealth Affairs subsequently stated in his monthly Afghanistan progress report to Parliament:

The Nahr-e-Saraj District Community Council (DCC) election was held on 8 May. Of the 4,423 people that were registered to vote, 4,091 individuals actually voted, of which 1,023 were female. There were 45 candidates for 27 male seats and seven candidates for five female seats.

His statement sparked further commentary in both the House of Commons and the House of Lords which identified the Nahr-E-Saraj election as a significant and encouraging indicator of progress in the process of enabling local representation in Helmand. It was observed that: *Voter participation during 2012 for district community council elections has been impressive by comparison with levels during previous presidential and parliamentary elections in the same area.*

Naturally, the DST took the credit for this success, boasting that the election *was entirely Afghan run without any support from the International Community.*

The truth was a little different. This was Helmand after all.

The PRT's Governance Advisor was furious when he learned that I'd been plotting with Sultaan to publicise the election. He took a copy of our poster to Colonel James and tried to convince him to pull the plug on our plans.

He was particularly scathing of the visual we'd used, claiming that images of figures queuing at a ballot box to cast their vote was not an accurate representation of the electoral process, in which the district's 1,400 or so mosques would each choose three men to represent them in an electoral college from which councillors would then be selected by polling. He argued that since not everyone would be able to cast a vote by ballot our image was misleading. Ironically, as Colonel James would later point out, it was photos of men and women queuing at ballot boxes that the HPRT used to illustrate its Facebook posting, many of which were subsequently picked up by international news organisations.

Fortunately I'd been keeping Colonel James updated on progress at our twice daily meetings and he was able to defend the poster, correctly stating that it had been designed by the District Communications Advisor and approved by his boss, the District Governor.

The Governance Advisor was not happy. But there was little he could do, and not everyone in the DST agreed with him. Niels Vistisen, the Governor's Danish political advisor who had so neatly sidestepped accounting for the British abduction of Haji Gul, was quietly cheering from the sidelines. The POLAD was thoroughly enjoying the GOVAD's frustration. I suspected there must be some bad blood between them.

While Niels' support appeared to be personally motivated, I was taken aback by the enthusiastic assistance I received from members of the battlegroup. When I went cap in hand to ask the Geo cell, who designed and printed our maps, if I could use their large format printer to produce some posters, the Royal Engineer Corporal in charge not only instantly agreed but also personally supervised an overnight print run. He was bleary-eyed and tripping on caffeine when I collected the posters the following morning. Even the PsyOps Group, with whom I was more usually at loggerheads,   agreed to print a large quantity of handbills for me on their presses at Lashka Gah, which were then flown forward by helicopter to MOB Price.

Within 72 hours, thanks to the generosity of others I had amassed a huge quantity of printed materials in a variety of formats and sizes with which to promote the forthcoming election. Now we had to figure out a way to distribute them across the district. Once again my task was made easy by others' kind support. With help from the Army Air Corps detachment, whose half-baked plans for a water feature had flooded the helipad, a quantity of election materials were flown to each of the patrol bases in our district from where they were distributed into the local communities via their village *spin zhiras* or on partnered patrols with the ANA and ALP.

Sultaan ensured that posters were put up in the Gereshk bazaar and personally distributed handbills throughout the city. He even persuaded the commanders of the many police checkpoints which surrounded the town to display posters and to hand out flyers to passers-by. He suggested I might like to help deliver these in person from the back of his motorcycle but I arranged for the Danish Royal Military Police, who rode around in armoured Eagle IV vehicles, to do this instead.

The commander of the Warthog Group took it upon himself, in a highly dangerous and I suspect unauthorised mission, to distribute posters in the Yakchal bazaar – the seat of Taliban shadow governance in the district. Even the Female Engagement Officer got involved, handing out flyers at a women's meeting she attended.

By the time Election Day came around thousands of handbills, flyers and posters had been distributed across the district. Unless you happened to have been confined indoors all week, which of course accounted for most of the womenfolk, it would have been hard to avoid the news that the Community Council was up for election.

Our advertising campaign achieved sufficient popular support for the DCC election that it warranted mention in both houses of the UK parliament. The Palace of Westminster, a landmark for democracy the world over, may have been encouraged and impressed by the electoral process taking place 4,432 miles away but it did little to alter the makeup of the District Community Council. Despite the fact that only 4,091 votes were actually cast it still took two days to count them all and then declare that Balool Khan and his cronies had been returned to the Council. A few seats had changed hands but these were mostly female councillors and therefore unimportant. Everyone in the battlegroup smelled a rat, but the DST insisted everything was in order and democracy had been served.

It seemed that the Governance Advisor had got his way after all. An election to satisfy the Palace of Westminster, without remedying the lack of representation in Nahr-E-Saraj.

DfID would later proclaim: *Afghans now have an unprecedented voice in how their country is run, nationally and locally.*

Latitude:	31.77
Longitude:	64.68
Elevation:	847m
Met:	Abundant sunshine H:32°L:16°
DTG:	111100DJUL12

ON 11th JULY 2012, some six months after I'd departed the UK, I finally received a communiqué from Jane. Not a message from Jane herself but an email from a Leeds based law firm which stated:

As you may be aware we have been contacted by Jane Harris in connection with the breakdown of your marriage, Indeed we are instructed that the marriage is at an end and we are to commence divorce proceedings against you in the near future. It would be helpful if you could provide me with an address to which the papers can be sent. The divorce will be based upon your unreasonable behaviour.

Although it was pretty obvious that Jane and I were heading for a divorce I was shocked and confused by this news. We had previously agreed that we would wait until I returned from Afghan before deciding our future as man and wife. By that time we would have lived apart for two years. Knowing that Jane already had a new boyfriend, I'd promised her that I would consent to a decree being granted if this was what she wanted.

This not only left the very slim possibility of reconciliation, but also ensured that Jane would receive a widow's pension and other benefits from the army in the event of my death. I didn't understand why Jane had so suddenly and dramatically changed her mind, but I could do little more than wait to learn of my unreasonable behaviours from the York County Court.

A few days later I received a further email from her solicitors to which they had attached a copy of the court papers. Internet access in MOB Price could be maddeningly slow and was confined to 30 minute sessions on the computers in the welfare cabins. I waited several long minutes as the file downloaded but then had no means of copying or printing the eight page document, which was written in a legalese with which I was not familiar. Hastily scribbling the main headings onto a bluey – the free aerograms supplied to troops on active service – I tried to make sense of the petition.

Part 6 the *Statement of Case* outlined my unreasonable behaviours:

1. *Over the course of the last 12 months of the marriage, on occasions far too numerous to specify there were arguments between the Petitioner and the Respondent. More annoyingly for the Petitioner when there were not arguments there were prolonged periods of silence causing a very unpleasant atmosphere within the matrimonial home. The respondent could sit for hours without speaking.*
2. *Over the course of the last 12 months of the marriage the Respondent was controlling and selfish.*
3. *The Respondent would take issue with the Petitioner for boiling more than one cup of water in the kettle and wasting electricity.*
4. *The Respondent would take issue with the Petitioner for using the vacuum instead of a carpet sweeper.*
5. *The Respondent would go on 2 or 3 skiing holidays a year, without inviting the Petitioner nor the children, causing the Petitioner upset.*
6. *The Respondent would complain that house hold paper work remained unfiled.*
7. *The Respondent demanded the running of the property in his own way and was derogatory towards the Petitioner when his own way was not followed.*
8. *The Respondent on one occasion threw a pack of BBQ skewers at the Petitioner following the Petitioner having made a cooking suggestion.*

Jane was right, of course, everything she'd outlined in her divorce petition was true, I was guilty as charged. But perhaps her statement of case didn't quite tell the whole story.

We had indeed argued *on occasions far too numerous to mention*, although these arguments had principally been about Jane's refutation of our precarious financial situation, or about her point-blank refusal to rein in her expenditure, describing this to me as *demeaning*. I had indeed insisted on running the property and our budgets in my own way, but only after Jane spent the £3,500 I'd earmarked for school fees on her wardrobe. I had enquired on numerous occasions why she refused to use the energy saving 'one cup' kettle my father had kindly given us for Christmas, although I suspected I knew the reason why. I did recall sitting for hours in stunned silence after Jane had revealed to me that she'd voted in local elections for a party of the right most commonly associated with shameful immigration policies and shaven-headed, tattooed thugs. And yes, I had complained about unfiled paperwork and I had thrown a pack of BBQ skewers.

There was also the question of my excessive skiing. I'd declared my passion for skiing long before we married and we had been on several skiing holidays together. But Jane did not share my love of snow covered mountains and never took to the thrill of descending their gelid gradients. When she informed me that she no longer wished to go on skiing holidays I hadn't understood this to mean that I should no longer go skiing either.

If I were splitting hairs I might have argued that I had merely asked Jane to remind our housekeeper to use the carpet sweeper, rather than the vacuum, on our expensive Persian rugs. To the best of my knowledge, Jane neither vacuumed nor swept.

However, there was one further item that I could not accept. My hand shook as I hurriedly scrawled the final statement onto the bluey:

9. *The respondent would become very aggressive towards the Petitioner following occasions when the Petitioner merely made simple suggestions or comments. The Petitioner would view the actions of the Respondent during such periods of time as borderline abuse.*

I couldn't accept the allegation of aggression and abuse. It simply wasn't true and just rereading the accusation in my own illegible handwriting on the flimsy airmail paper felt like a betrayal that brought tears to my eyes. I hadn't expected Jane to lie. But perhaps I should not have been surprised *by the falsehoods which interest dictates and credulity encourages.*

Much later I would draw the conclusion that Jane must have been schooled by her solicitors on this point. She would never produce any evidence to substantiate these terrible claims and was always very careful never directly to accuse me of abusive or aggressive behaviour, stating instead that this was her opinion of my behaviour. Over time I think Jane came to believe her own rhetoric, and would always default to this line whenever we had a disagreement.

It seemed that Jane and I were now at war and she had achieved Foxtrot Triple Tango. Stuck as I was on the front line of the most dangerous district in the most dangerous province of the most dangerous country on the planet, with just 30 minutes of low speed internet connectivity per session in the MOB Price internet cabins, there was precious little I could do about it.

Latitude:	31.84
Longitude:	64.66
Elevation:	833m
Met:	Sunny H:37°L:10°
DTG:	291650DAUG12

MOHAMMED MOMIN WAITED patiently on the northern bank of the Helmand River, concealed from view and shaded from the afternoon sun by a thick stand of tamarisk trees. It was an idyllic spot where, in another life, he might have enjoyed a picnic with his family beneath their slender branches. The natural beauty of his hiding place was not lost on Momin but, following the ambush on the Angrezi patrol, his senses were still too heightened by adrenaline to be seduced by the soporific sound of running water or the sweet fragrance of the delicate, five-petalled flowers that flooded the trees' upper boughs.

Momin carried, concealed beneath a dark blue cloak, an SA80 Mk2 assault rifle recovered from the corpse of an Angrezi solider he'd killed in a gun battle nearly two years before. The heat of its recently fired barrel burned against the skin of his right thigh but he made no effort to move it, the discomfort was a means of sharpening his vigilance and honing his senses.

Waiting in the shadows he mentally reviewed his exfiltration route. First he must cross the Helmand River. He would be dangerously exposed for the ten or fifteen minutes it would take him to ford the fast flowing waterway but once across he could quickly lose himself in the fields of maize and marijuana that now stood taller than any man. In just a few weeks the crops would be harvested, but for now he would be invisible to the infidel spy planes and helicopters all the way to his destination. It had been several weeks since he had last seen his good friend and mentor, Haji Jalander.

After the night raid on his compound and the unauthorised visit to the Angrezi base in Gereshk, many feared that Haji had given Momin up to the kafirs in exchange for the return of his son-in-law. Momin had never doubted his mentor's loyalty, although he'd been unable to spare the old man a beating for his impetuosity. Time had now passed, trust had been restored and he was looking forward to their reunion.

Momin narrowed his eyes as he searched the cloudless sky once more for enemy aircraft. Next he closed his eyes completely and turned his head slowly through 180 degrees,   listening intently for the slightest sound that might signal the presence of his enemy. Finally, keeping his eyes closed he lifted his face to the breeze and gently sniffed the air. Engaging each of the senses separately to detect sight, sound or smell of his enemy was a trick the old Mujahideen had taught him many years before and which had served him well.

Satisfied that his path was clear, Momin removed his sandals, gathered up the loose folds of his cloak and stepped from cover. In less than an hour he would be sitting in his friend's compound sipping sweet cardamom chai, snacking on dried fruits and other sweet treats, as the older man's many grandchildren played excitedly around them.

Despite all his field craft skills Momin had made an unforced error.

Perhaps he allowed his guard to slip as his thoughts turned to home and his friend's hospitality, but as he strode purposefully towards the river the distinctive barrel of his SA80 rifle, no longer concealed beneath his cloak, was clearly visible to the RAF Reaper MQ-9 pilot in his office 7,000 miles away outside Las Vegas. Recognising the distinctive British-made weapon system, the pilot immediately queued up an Apache AH1 attack helicopter flying a holding pattern above Camp Bastion airbase.

The SA80 Mark 2 rifle revealed Momin's identity, and sealed his fate. Guided by the Reaper and with the aid of his powerful optical sights the AH1 pilot, still several kilometres distant and undetected by Momin, positively identified his target as Objective Beninghaus. As a known *bravo* or male target on the JPEL, Beninghaus was already cleared for *priority effects* and the pilot required no further authorisation before dispatching one of his payload of 16 AGM-114M Hellfire missiles. Travelling at 450 metres per second, flight time to target was a little under nine seconds and the pilot watched the missile all the way to its devastating destination. Momin was instantly atomised by the munition's 9kg blast fragmentation warhead. There was no need to review the strike using the on-board camera system. The pilot radioed control and confirmed *Jackpot*. Mission success.

Men in operations rooms in Nevada, Middlesex, Kandahar, Camp Bastion, MOB Price and PB Clifton, all watching live feeds of the strike on flat-screen TVs, raised their fists in silent salute at a job well done.

A few red misted fragments of steel, originally forged in Nottingham at the Royal Ordnance Small Arms Facility were all that remained of Momin's SA80 A2 L85 assault rifle. Having avenged their previous owner they were quickly claimed by the swirling waters of the Helmand River.

Latitude   31.82
Longitude   64.68
Elevation   859m
Met   Sunny H:37°L:21°
DTG   311425DAUG12

He says you will die here today,
the Taliban will not let you
leave alive. NOT LET YOU LEAVE ALIVE.

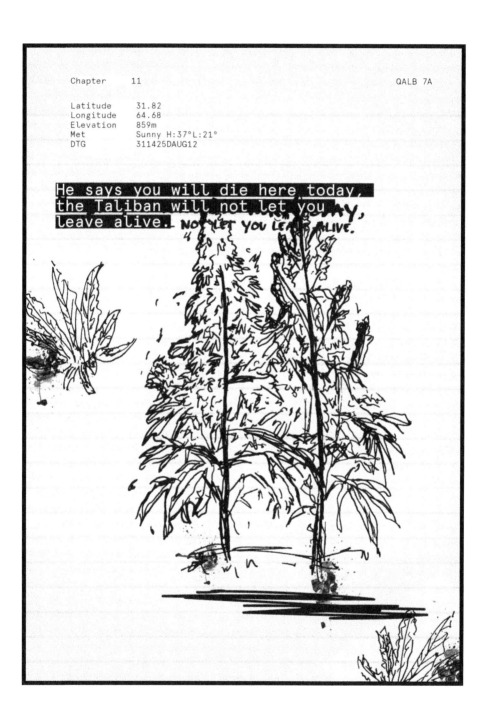

RPG: Rocket Propelled Grenade
HEAT: High Explosive Anti Tank
HVO: Hydrogenated Vegetable Oil
WAG: Waste Activated Gel
C2: Command and Control
HAF: Helicopter Assault Force
PMAG: Police Mentoring and Advisory Group
THC: Tetrahydrocannabinol
PRR: Personal Role Radio
SOP: Standard Operating Procedure
RV: Rendezvous
TCP: Temporary Checkpoint
ACOG: Advanced Combat Optical Gunsight
AO: Area of Operations
MERT: Medical Emergency Response Team
GPMG: General Purpose Machine Gun

MINISTRY OF DEFENCE ANNOUNCEMENT

Lieutenant Andrew Chesterman. On Thursday 9 August 2012, Lieutenant Andrew Chesterman was shot by insurgent small arms fire while commanding a vehicle patrol in the Nad 'Ali district of Helmand province after the lead vehicle struck an improvised explosive device.

Lance Corporal Matthew David Smith. On Friday 10 August 2012, Lance Corporal Matthew David Smith was hit by small arms fire while building a new checkpoint next to the Nahr-e-Bughra canal in the Nad 'Ali district of Helmand province.

Guardsman Jamie Shadrake. On Friday 17 August 2012, Guardsman Jamie Shadrake died of gunshot wounds when his checkpoint was attacked by insurgents in the Nahr-e-Saraj district of Helmand province.

Latitude:	31.82
Longitude:	64.68
Elevation:	859m
Met:	Sunny H:37°L:21°
DTG:	311425DAUG12

THE HEAT OF the blast wave prickled my skin and knocked me to the ground before my ears registered the detonation. It wasn't the first time I'd been in close proximity to an RPG strike but, wearing only shorts and flip-flops, it was the first time I'd failed to dress correctly for the occasion.

A second blast wave washed over me emphasising the extreme inadequacy of my wardrobe selection. Despite the energy sapping daytime temperature I was beginning to regret my decision to flout the strict dress code for combat operations in Afghanistan.

RPG! RPG!

Somewhere off to my left someone was redundantly letting us all know we'd just been whacked by a brace of RPGs.

'Mastiff Pete', who moments earlier had been watching *The Expendables* on his tablet in the commander's seat of his Mastiff protected patrol vehicle, pulled the heavy armoured door shut with a clang, effectively cutting me off from the sanctuary within.

I couldn't really blame Pete for locking down his vehicle but I'd be lying if I didn't admit to more than a little dismay at being on the wrong side of the door as the restraining bolts slid into place.

The RPG or *Ruchnaya Protivotankovaya Granata* is a World War Two era high explosive anti-tank (HEAT) hand grenade first developed by the Soviet Union. While it was easily defeated by the Mastiff's bar armour, this depended on the doors being closed. If an RPG were to penetrate the crew compartment it would ricochet around the interior at high velocity with devastating effect, damaging equipment, igniting fuel and ammunition and, most likely, killing Pete and the vehicle's other occupants.

Even if it might be at my expense, Pete had unquestionably made the right decision.

In the finest traditions of his regiment, Captain Peter Eadon of the Royal Tank Regiment, otherwise known as Mastiff Pete, was a dashing young blade. Good looking, utterly fearless, blessed with supreme self-confidence and all his own hair. We had almost nothing in common except that on the same day that my divorce papers came through he'd received a Dear John letter. I knew this because the Adjutant had raised it as an agenda item under 'any other business' in the Commander's update briefing. If Pete was distressed at his private life being made quite so public he was too gallant to let it show.

He and his men had swapped their day jobs in Germany as Challenger 2 main battle tank crews to drive the heavily armoured Mastiff troop carriers. In a headquarters with an over-supply of Captains with the same name, Pete had quickly been designated Mastiff Pete to differentiate him from Danish Pete and EOD Pete. If he'd left me to fend for myself on this occasion I could hardly complain. The Mastiffs had come to my aid on countless occasions in the past.

Just a few weeks earlier I'd conducted a series of patrols in the Northern Dashte with an Afghan Special Forces Tiger Team. The Tiger Teams were better trained and equipped than the ANA guys but they still lacked military discipline and self-control. They could be pretty feisty and often caused problems on the base, on one occasion starting a brawl in the D-FAC, on another giving poor Siyal, the MOB Price laundryman a beating when he refused to prioritise their washing. On the ground it was always a case of shoot first and ask questions later. In their defence they were a fearless bunch who never shied away from a fight. I liked many of them and enjoyed working with them.

The Northern Dashte is a harsh, mostly uninhabited desert region to the north of Gereshk. It had been largely ignored by ISAF, principally because COIN doctrine focuses on securing centres of population. Colonel James was rightly concerned that the Dashte was a blind spot for us about which we knew almost nothing, and instructed me to conduct a series of FFUI patrols to learn more. He was particularly concerned that the dry river beds running north-south through the region could be insurgent facilitation routes for bringing arms and ammunition to resupply their fighters in our AO. He was right about this; we discovered that the Dashte was not just a Taliban supply line but an unofficial freeway for anyone wishing to bypass ANA and AUP checkpoints on Highway One. For many local people this was simply a way of avoiding the illegal taxes many of these checkpoints charged. However the main user was not   local nationals or insurgents but the narco-industry. Away from the prying eyes of ISAF, yet under our very noses, the Dashte was being used as an opium trade route to ship the vast poppy harvest north.

Naturally the opium runners, who were just as well armed as the Taliban, were not best pleased to see us on their patch and attempted to dissuade us from staying. Throughout this period Pete and his Mastiff crews frequently exposed themselves to danger, in particular to the threat of IEDs, as they provided overwatch to our foot patrols with their 50-calibre machine guns.

Teaming up the Tiger Teams with the Mastiff Troop had proved so successful in the Dashte that we were now jointly supporting a Danish Armoured Infantry Company on another intelligence gathering operation into Zumbalay. The Danish infantrymen from *Batallion og 2nd Jydske Dragon Regiment,* or 2nd Battalion The Jutland Dragoons, were new to theatre. It was never mentioned in so many words, but I suspected that our role, in part at least, was to provide a nucleus of in-theatre experience to a mission heading for the Taliban badlands.

The suspicion was confirmed for me when I learned that our CULAD, Royal Marines Captain Owen Davis would be joining us. Owen was the only fluent Pashtu speaker in the battlegroup but he had also amassed a wealth of combat experience over the previous six months and as such was one of our most valuable assets. Having Owen on the team was reassuring and alarming in equal measure. While the big Welshman's language and fighting skills were legendary, his inclusion was also a clear indicator that the mission planners were expecting trouble.

At this moment their assessment was proving perceptive. The Taliban had mounted their RPG attack as we were setting up a temporary desert leaguer[1] to the south of Zumbalay from which to conduct follow-on operations. Although we didn't know it yet we were to remain almost continually in contact[2] with the enemy for the rest of the mission.

---

[1] **Leaguer** (from South African Dutch **Laager**): A temporary defensive encampment surrounded by armoured vehicles – a military term originating from the Boer War.

[2] **Contact**: An engagement with the enemy in which rounds are exchanged.

With the Mastiff locked down and nowhere else to go I crawled underneath the vehicle and snuggled up to the huge run-flat tyres of the twin rear axles.

From this vantage point I watched as the Jutland Dragoons began to sort themselves out and respond to effective enemy fire. For many this would be their first taste of combat.

There was a distinct pause in their response, characteristic of all first-timers, as soldiers who had trained for months for just this moment came to the collective realisation that the time for training had now ended and the time for action was upon them.

The lull in battle was eventually broken by the unmistakable sound of another World War Two era weapon. The Rheinmetall MG42/59 general purpose machine gun is derived from the awesome Maschinengewehr 42 universal machine gun, used extensively by the Wehrmacht in World War Two. Its design has changed little since the fall of the Third Reich.

There appeared to me to be a vicious symmetry in our efforts to kill one another using Second World War era antiques, long after the protagonists in that particular conflict had all hung up their combat boots.

The distinctive sound of the MG42/59 is a by-product of its greatest asset – its ability to produce a high volume of suppressive fire of up to 1,200 rounds per minute in the infantry role – and it was this asset which was now being put to good use.

As I lay in the sand beneath the Mastiff trying to decide whether I should return fire or don my body armour, an impossibly good looking Danish infantryman dressed only in his underpants, his feet stuffed into unlaced combat boots, and a filterless *Prince* cigarette clamped between his teeth, advanced upon the enemy position firing the Nazi machine gun from the hip.

Like a modern day Achilles, his dodgy heel safeguarded by his high-top boots, he made no attempt to protect his near naked, perfectly toned and glistening body from enemy fire. Standing in open ground in front of our position he hosed down the RPG firing point, his muscles rippling with every recoil as he held the massive weapon in one hand while feeding the 120-round disintegrating belt into the open bolt with the other.

I briefly considered jumping up and joining him in this partially clothed assault but quickly dismissed the thought in favour of a supporting fire role from the relative safety of the rear wheels of the Mastiff. This was not only a much safer option but also acknowledgement that my own middle-aged body would ripple in an entirely different and less seductive way from that of the Danish/Greek hero.

With his ammunition spent the machine gunner turned his back on the enemy, hefted the still smoking MG42 onto his shoulder and casually returned to his vehicle without so much as a backward glance. Those Taliban that had survived the onslaught clearly knew better than to take on a mythical Greek hero manifesting as an earthly Danish infantryman and made themselves scarce.

As he strode past me, cowering beneath the wheels of the Mastiff, our eyes locked for a moment. I can't be sure but I think he winked at me as he took an enormous drag on his cigarette before flicking the butt in a long, lazy arc across the sand.

It could have been a scene from the film Mastiff Pete had been watching just minutes before, except of course that most of the *Expendables* actors were even older and more decrepit than I was myself. Even so, I'd never yet seen life imitate art quite so precisely. I assumed that, like their British counterparts, the Jutland Dragoons spent their downtime consuming war movies and first person shooter games – I was always slightly bewildered to find soldiers relaxing after the rigours of a fighting patrol by playing *Call of Duty* on their gaming consoles.

The actions of this particular Jutland Dragoon may have more closely resembled a scene from a Vietnam war flick than an infantry training manual but he had certainly lived up to his regimental motto, *Fortuna Fortes Juvat* – Fortune Favours the Brave.

The contact now over, we all returned to our previous tasks. For Mastiff Pete this meant putting his feet back on the vehicle's dashboard and resuming his rudely interrupted movie.

On arrival at the desert leaguer, Pete had quickly manoeuvred his vehicles nose to tail into a tight defensive position known as the *Iron*

Triangle[1] with interlocking fields of fire from the roof-mounted 50-calibre machine guns. The confined isosceles within would be our temporary home for the duration of the operation. As had just been thoroughly demonstrated this provided ample protection from the threats we faced from the Taliban. However the less experienced Dragoons had opted for a more widely dispersed defensive position in keeping with conventional war fighting. While this mitigated against mortar, artillery and air attack (capabilities which the Taliban did not possess), it required digging fire positions around each of the vehicles into unyielding terrain baked hard by the sun.

This unnecessary labour was born of inexperience but it was no use trying to explain this to the newcomers. Inter-unit pride and rivalry demanded that any suggestion from the British would be pointedly ignored. All the same I reckoned the lesson would be quietly absorbed and the Dragoons would not make the same mistake twice.

While the Dragoons toiled in the 37°C/98°F heat to complete their positions we looked on with critical eye from the shade of a cam-net some of the crewmen had strung up between our vehicles. It was too hot to watch *Hexie*[2] *TV* and with nothing else to do it helped pass the time. I am not the first person to observe that modern warfare vacillates between brief moments of mesmerising tension and long periods of intense boredom.

[1] **Iron Triangle**: A defensive position in which three armoured vehicles park nose to tail in a triangular formation.

[2] **Hexie TV/watching Hexie TV**: Squaddie slang referring to the preparation of hot rations or boiling water using army issue hexamine cookers.

Latitude:	31.85
Longitude:	64.62
Elevation:	851m
Met:	Sunny H:37°L:18°
DTG:	181000DJUL12

SHORTLY AFTER I'D learned from Jane's solicitors that our marriage was at an end and several weeks before the trip to Zumbalay, I'd taken up residence in the temporary accommodation tent at Patrol Base Clifton. It would be my home for most of the month of July. Like temporary accommodation everywhere, it was honking.

Most of the camp cots set aside for passing visitors were damaged, broken or simply missing vital components, plundered as spares no doubt by the permanent residents. Previous occupants had clearly left in a hurry, abandoning the usual detritus of patrol base living; inedible blocks of vacuum packed sticky toffee pudding (one of the least popular items in our HVO[1]-rich 24 hour ration packs), broken flip-flops, stained and in some cases still moist back issues of 'Zoo' and 'Nuts' magazine, used WAG[2] bags, and an old and rancid loofah.

Being transit accommodation it was naturally closest to the helipad and the downwash of rotor blades filled the tent with dust and dirt every time a helo passed by, which was often. On one occasion during my tenure an inexperienced or possibly vindictive Chinook pilot managed to collapse the entire structure.

None of these things bothered me in the slightest. PB Clifton was the perfect antidote to the mounting pressure of my fractured marriage. For reasons that I never fully understood, but which I assume had some Machiavellian purpose, Jane and her solicitors were forging ahead with divorce proceedings in my absence and a hearing date had been set in the York County and Family Court a month hence.

As Jane well knew I would not return from Afghanistan until the end of September and could no more attend Court on the appointed date than I could pop down to the Adinzai bazaar for a cuppa. To make matters worse I was also required to complete a lengthy and complex financial

---

[1] **HVO**: Hydrogenated Vegetable Oil

[2] **WAG Bag**: Waste Activated Gel bag. Single use, zip close human waste bags. Literally a toilet in a bag; complete with toilet paper and hand sanitizer.

statement which her solicitors required ahead of the hearing. Without access to the relevant documentation, none of which I'd thought to bring with me to a war zone, completing the form was an impossible task.

Contacting the Court or attempting to appoint a solicitor of my own using the welfare cabins in Price was proving to be a nightmare. The great advantage of Clifton was that there were no welfare cabins. So I could ignore the problem, and hope it would somehow go away.

Inevitably, it did cross my mind that one solution might be to not return home at all. I would never go so far as to consider taking my own life. But that wasn't necessary in a district where an inexhaustible supply of young men were queuing up to kill Angrezi infidels.

It was an unshakeable and obvious solution. Given the choice between confronting my failed marriage or confronting a wild-eyed Jihadist, intent on waging Holy War on my person, I chose the Jihadist and developed a certain recklessness over the summer months. This was later reflected in my post-operational appraisal in which Colonel James wrote:

Personally courageous, he never once flinched from getting out onto often heavily contested ground with the rifle companies. Indeed, his instinct was to spend as much time as possible forward where the challenge was greatest.

Although I was deeply flattered by his kind words, had Colonel James known my true motivations, I suspect he might have taken a different view and confined me to camp. As Sultaan, the District Communications Advisor could have told him, the well of my personal courageousness was not especially deep.

Ostensibly I'd gone to Clifton not to escape from my personal problems, or to get myself killed, but to play my part in Operation Qalb 7a. This was to be a combined operation working alongside the Afghan National Army to clear the north-eastern approaches to Gereshk in an area that came to be known as the Kakoran Gap. It would prove to be one of the most demanding and costly operations of the tour.

In the early months of the year the Afghan National Army, with ISAF assistance, had conducted a similar clearance operation in a demonstration of nascent ANA capability that Colonel James was eager to consolidate but which the ANA themselves appeared to be squandering.

Having cleared the ground the ANA lacked the will and the capacity to hold and build on their territorial gains, preferring instead to retreat back to their patrol baseline, a series of check points which ran due north from the Nahr-E-Buhgra canal along Route Sephton to PB Clifton. This marked the eastern extent of the ANA's defensive belt or *kammarband* around Gereshk.

In the months following the initial clearance the insurgents, with little opposition from the ANA, had returned to the Kakoran Gap and strengthened their own positions, creating a deadly and almost impenetrable IED belt about 300 metres to the east of the kammarband.

Lacking any counter-IED equipment or training I couldn't really blame the ANA for their reluctance to patrol in what was effectively an unmarked minefield. But there were also suspicions that the local ANA Commander, Captain Abdul Manan had agreed an informal ceasefire deal with his Taliban counterpart. I met with Captain Manan on a number of occasions and he struck me as a slippery fish. More than once we agreed to conduct joint patrols in the area for which he and his men simply failed to turn up. When I took him to task on this he concocted childish excuses that ranged from *feeling sick* to *I forgot*. He never actually claimed that the dog ate his homework but I wouldn't have been surprised if he had.

I didn't like Manan one bit and I supposed the feelings were mutual. My greatest concern was that his ceasefire deal extended to passing on details of ISAF intentions and troop movements to his Taliban co-conspirators. Having discussed and agreed patrol traces and plans with him in advance it wasn't hard, when he failed to turn up, to jump to the conclusion that he'd passed this information to his new mates in an attempt to earn brownie points.

I wasn't alone in these misgivings. Major Dom Alkin, who had succeeded Simon Doyle as the officer commanding PB Clifton had similar concerns and deeply distrusted Manan.

Shortly after the DCC election I'd managed to persuade the newly appointed councillor for the Kakoran Gap, Abdul Haziz to visit the community he now served. It wasn't entirely clear to me how Haziz had been elected but, setting aside the manner of his elevation to the Council, connecting the local population with the government official purporting to represent them was a significant step forward. However, as the councillor was not actually from the Kakoran area he could no more pop down to the bazaar than I could myself without attracting the unwelcome attention of the local Taliban neighbourhood watch. A joint ANA/ISAF patrol had been planned to facilitate this visit.

To ensure everything went off smoothly Dom had organised a pre-briefing with Captain Manan and the DC Councillor at PB Clifton on the morning of the planned surgery. Manan turned up with a rather nervous looking Abdul Haziz and a motley crew of ANA soldiers dressed in a variety of different uniforms and armed with a collection of AK47s, M16s and RPGs.

As the briefing got under way the tension in the room was palpable. Captain Manan was unhappy with Dom's proposed plan and was clearly spoiling to abort the visit. Eventually, after lots of raised voices and fast talking, he stormed out of the meeting, taking his men with him and leaving a bewildered and rather fearful councillor behind.

It was one of only a handful of occasions when I felt the situation might escalate into a green on blue, so much so that I'd surreptitiously released the retaining strap on my pistol holster. I silently thanked Dave Groom for his advice to *keep one in the chamber at all times,* although with so many armed men in the room it would have been absolute carnage if things had kicked off.

A photo was taken at the time which showed Dom, Manan and Aziz poring over a map of the area. It was later widely used to illustrate improved Afghan civil-military coordination with ISAF in the run up to transition.

Nothing could have been further from the truth.

Our CULAD, Owen also shared these misgivings about Manan's loyalty. When they'd first met Owen had not declared he was a fluent Pashtu speaker and Manan had been angered to discover this afterwards from another source. Whether his anger was proof of a guilty conscience I couldn't say, but I later watched the two men have a fierce argument in Pashtu which nearly came to blows. Given that Manan was a diminutive Afghan and Owen was an enormous Welshman, I had grudgingly to admire Manan's willingness to square up to the larger man.

Although I wasn't happy about it I could see why Captain Manan might be striking a deal with our enemies, and I couldn't really blame him.

Nahr-E-Saraj may have had a better mobile phone network than Norfolk but it was essentially still a feudal society in which vassals served a lord in return for a livelihood and protection. It was a system that had worked well, with and without cellular telephony, for at least half a millennium. The insurgents and the narco-industry understood this. But we were blinkered by our own cultural conceit – our desire to win hearts and minds. Our justification for intervention in Afghanistan had remained the liberation of a downtrodden population from tyranny long after it had become apparent that the population did not especially seek or desire liberation. The proposed mechanisms for emancipation were hardly compelling – a corrupt democracy, religious tolerance and gender equality, none of which could provide either sustenance or security.

As a marketing man rather than an infantryman, I reckoned that if Manan and others were looking elsewhere for their future it was principally because our own offer wasn't good enough.

I'd once tried to explain to Sultaan what it means to be a true football fan. Supporters remain loyal to their club for life – through thick and thin, through feast and famine. I even tried to explain how the losses in the lean years make the wins so much sweeter. Like so many times before, Sultaan covered his embarrassment at my stupidity with his trademark high-pitched giggle. Surely, as every Helmandi already knows, the sensible thing to do is to align yourself with whichever team stands the best chance of winning the most trophies. This means hedging your bets each season for as long as possible and picking a side only when victory seems assured.

In our district it was not uncommon to discover families hedging their bets in just this way with one son serving with the ANSF and another with the Taliban. On one occasion I paid a visit to the compound of Mohammed Gul, an elderly gentleman whose son, Mirajdin was doing his best to kill my colleagues and me with a long range DShKM 50-calibre heavy machine gun. In an attempt to mitigate his firstborn's antisocial behaviour he produced photographs of a second son, Toryala in his ANA uniform who at the time was serving in Lashka Gah.

As Mohammed pointed out to me, with ISAF set to depart in a few years time, what was a father supposed to do? It seemed that having already declared we would be withdrawing from the tournament our trophy cabinet was looking metaphorically bare.

Setting aside the possibility that Captain Manan might be actively seeking a transfer to another club, Colonel James was determined to improve ANA confidence forward of their patrol baseline and his plan to achieve this was a bold one. It involved inserting the Grenadiers as a Helicopter Assault Force (HAF) into a series of temporary blocking positions to the east of the Kakoran Gap, deep behind enemy lines. Colonel James correctly reasoned this would be a deliberate provocation bound to bring about an adverse and violent reaction. By drawing the insurgents away from the Gap to take on the infidels who had just set up camp in their backyard, he hoped to create time and space for the ANA to reassert themselves forward of the kammarband.

Latitude:	31.82
Longitude:	64.68
Elevation:	859m
Met:	Sunny H:37°L:21°
DTG:	010433DSEP12

IT'S A LITTLE after 4.30am and I'm already weeping sweat from every pore. This is partly because for some weeks now night-time temperatures have not fallen below 20°C/68°F, and partly because the combined weight of my combat body armour, weapon systems, ammunition, water and other equipment tops the scales at just over 52kg.

Fooling around on the lawns at Gooseberry Hall with Harry and Alfie we'd perfected a manoeuvre we called *the triple* in which Alfie would sit on Harry's shoulders and Harry would then sit on mine. We would then stagger around the garden for a few minutes before eventually collapsing in a heap of bodies and a fit of giggles. Between them they weighed substantially less than the kit I'll be wearing for the next eight hours as temperatures soar into the high thirties.

When the RPG and the Maschinengewehr 42 universal machine gun first came into service in World War Two, the average fighting load of the infantry soldier was a modest 25kg. The weapon systems may not have changed much in the intervening seven decades, but with all the other 'essential' gadgets we now carry, loads have more than doubled.

Studies have shown that at 173cm in my socks, I'm the perfect size and build for the modern infantry soldier. Human joints essentially work on a lever principle. The heavier the load and the longer the lever, the weaker the joint and the more prone it is to failure. So-called short-arses like me have an advantage over our taller and longer boned colleagues, but in my case I reckon these advantages are well past their sell-by date. I'm not the only one who thinks so. Shortly after we arrived in MOB Price an anonymous colleague procured a Zimmer frame from somewhere and kindly placed this beside my desk in the J9 cell. I was touched by their concern for my welfare and mobility needs and used the AOB slot in the Commander's update briefing to publicly state my gratitude.

Woken by one of Mastiff Pete's crewmen, I have only to tighten the laces of my boots to complete my morning routine and start my day. Despite the presence of hideous and terrifying camel spiders I've slept in the sand beneath the rear doors of one of the Mastiffs. According to squaddie mythology the camel spider gorges on the flesh of ISAF soldiers by injecting them with numbing venom as they sleep.

I know this to be false but I'm still fearful of the ferocious, nocturnal arachnids, and I'm not the only one. Owen, infallibly courageous in the face of the enemy, has elected to spend an uncomfortable night on the unyielding steel floor of the Mastiff's crew compartment in order to avoid their unwelcome attention. Designed to carry eight fully equipped soldiers, it is still too small to accommodate the supine form of the big Welshman and he is forced to sleep with his legs sticking out of the open rear doors. I've spent much of the night staring up at his enormous bare feet as they twitch above me in the light of a waning gibbous moon.

I drink a litre of water, courtesy of the bottling plant at Camp Bastion, into which I mix a powdered energy drink from my 24 hour ration pack. Breakfast over I don my body armour and with Owen and the Tiger Team lads set off to find the Danish platoon we'll be joining on a pre-dawn patrol into Zumbalay.

ISAF last patrolled there in 2009 and despite the tale of abduction told to me by Haji Jalander there is no official record that anyone has returned since that time. Our mission is to search some compounds of interest, to assess the extent to which the local population are sympathetic to the Taliban and to probe and test insurgent dispositions. With everything I already know about Zumbalay from the J2 shop, and after the welcome reception we received the previous afternoon, I'm pretty certain the insurgents will be equally keen to test our own resolve and dispositions.

I'm not used to patrolling before first light because, even with night vision goggles, it's impossible to observe ground signs such as soil transference, discolouration or disturbance that may indicate the presence of an IED. However, on this mission we've calculated that the IED threat will be minimal, principally because the Taliban only place IEDs in contested areas. If the official records are correct, Zumbalay has not received ISAF visitors for over three years and the IED threat will therefore be negligible. I hope we're right.

It all makes perfect sense but old habits die hard. I'm still wary where I place my feet. I'm more than willing to confront a wild-eyed Jihadist but I'm much less eager to be dismembered by one of his improvised explosive devices.

As always I was relying on my mantra to see me through today's mission:

1. Hope for the best.

2. Plan for the worst.

3. Prepare to be surprised.

On this occasion I haven't checked chamber on my weapon systems because it's still too dark to do so. But I already know I'm *locked and loaded*. I never, *ever* go outside the wire without first making my weapons ready with a round in the chamber and the safety catch on.

The compounds of interest are about two clicks from our current location in the desert and about 800 metres inside the green zone of lush agricultural farmland fed by the waters of the Helmand River. At this time of year most of the fields are sown with either maize or marijuana and both plants stand well above head height. Our plan is simple enough. We'll cross the desert under cover of darkness and then lose ourselves in the crops. It won't be possible to conceal our presence completely – the local dogs will see to that – but we can still make it difficult for the Taliban to track us and pinpoint our exact position. After first light the Danish platoon will set up inner and outer perimeters around the compounds and Owen, the Tiger Team and I will then go and introduce ourselves to the occupants.

After a brief confab with the Dragoons' platoon commander to confirm the plan has not changed overnight, we set off across the desert for the green zone. We move in a single file of about 45 men in a formation we call the *Afghan snake*. Assessing there will be no IEDs is a calculated risk, but a risk which can be further mitigated by travelling in single file. It's rough on the lead man who has to prove the route, especially in the dark without IED detection equipment, but those walking in his footsteps are relatively safe. At least that is the theory. But Lance Corporal John Wilson was the sixth man in his patrol when he lost his legs, and Jay was 37th, so the theory is no guarantee. I strain my eyes in the pre-dawn half light to see exactly where to place my feet.

Moving in a single file reduces the risk of IED detonation but it creates problems of command and control (C2) between the front and the back of the column. Every man is a link man and it's essential to keep eyes on the men immediately to your front and your rear to ensure the *snake* does not get split up. It sounds simple enough but requires training and teamwork to maintain, and continue to operate as a cohesive fighting force. On this patrol we have Afghan, Danish and British troops who are working together for the first time. We all have different languages, equipment, communications systems and training methods, which now puts increased pressure on our C2.

I find myself towards the back of the column, behind the Tiger Team lads and in front of the Danish multiple bringing up the rear. The Tiger Team are eager to push on and get onto the objective, while the Dragoons are responsible for watching our backs and repeatedly sweep the rear of the column, which slows their forward progress. Trying to maintain the link between these two elements of the patrol with two very different tasks is proving a challenge even in open ground. It's going to get much more difficult once we move into the fields where visibility will be reduced to a few metres.

To make matters worse the young Afghan machine gunner who is my link man with the Tiger Team has taken one look at the ageing, part-time soldier watching his back and concluded that he's better off with his mates. I keep signalling for him to slow down so that we can maintain a visual on the Danes but he's having none of it. I can't say I blame him. I wouldn't want me watching my back either.

There is now a real danger that in my efforts to keep the link between the Tiger Team and the Dragoons I'm going to find myself separated from both. This is referred to as being *Man Away,* and is never a desirable outcome. Especially not here. There can be no appeal for *nanawatai*[1] or protection under the ancient *Pashtunwali* code in a place such as this. I have a pretty good idea of what will happen to me if I'm captured by the Taliban in their home base.

I'm planning not to let that happen. Although I no longer fall into the intended age demographic, I still plan to follow Rudyard Kipling's advice in his poem The Young British Soldier:

When you're wounded and left on Afghanistan's plains,

---

[1] **Nanawatai**: (Pashtu: *sanctuary*) is a tenet of the Pashtunwali code of the Pashtun people. It allows a beleaguered person to enter the house of any other person and request sanctuary or protection. This cannot be refused, even at the cost of the host's own life or fortune.

Jest roll to your rifle and blow out your brains.

If it comes to it, I'll be saving the last round in my Sig for myself. Almost subconsciously, I brush my left hand against the weapon in its habitual place on the front-left side of my body armour. I feel reassured by its presence, soothed by the knowledge that, in the last resort, it will spare me from torture and suffering at the cruel hands of others.

Latitude:	31.85
Longitude:	64.62
Elevation:	851m
Met:	Sunny H:37°L:18°
DTG:	041400DJUL12

THROUGH A SERIES of complicated builds and animations Colonel James had produced an impressive and compelling PowerPoint presentation that outlined his bold plan to create time and space for the ANA to assert themselves forward of the kammarband.

Miniature Chinook helicopters flew on and off the screen *HAFing*[1] little blue stick-men behind enemy lines. No sooner had the helicopters departed than little red stick-men, who had previously been lined up in front of the kammarband, abandoned these positions and began to swarm around the little blue men. Meanwhile, little green stick-men standing behind the kammarband surged forwards and filled the void the little red men had left behind. Just like the pictures that Alfie had drawn for me prior to deployment, everyone seemed to be enjoying themselves enormously as if engaged in an elaborately choreographed Scottish country dance. No one seemed to mind at all when the little red men began mysteriously disappearing from the screen until only one or two were left.

I sat at the back of the conference tent as Colonel James presented his plan to Brigadier Douglas Chalmers, the Task Force Helmand Commanding General and his Staff. It all looked rather lovely and effete on the presentation. But all the men in the meeting had been hand-picked by the Brigadier for their hard-won combat experience. To a man they knew first-hand the dangers and risks of operating behind enemy lines and understood perfectly well that this bold and audacious plan would be committing the Grenadiers to a ferocious fight.

As I listened to the conversation ebbing back and forth across the table I was reminded of the painting of a fierce and desperate battle from an earlier tour of Afghanistan that I'd seen at Wellington Barracks when I'd first joined the Grenadiers for lunch all those months ago. I'd wondered at the time if I had what it takes to stand shoulder to shoulder with the Queen's bodyguard in similar circumstances. I'd

---

[1] **HAF**: Helicopter Assault Force

missed out on the clearance op into Yakchal, but it seemed likely now that I was soon to find out.

Everyone unanimously agreed that the ANA needed to step up their game in the Kakoran Gap and fully supported Colonel James' plan. There was however one rather obvious but crucial flaw. The Grenadiers might create the time and space but ultimately success depended on the ANA dominating the ground forward of the kammarband. Despite their key role in the plan, no one had thought to invite any of the ANA commanders to the meeting or even to ask for their opinion. Others would later declare their deep misgivings at this critical defect, but by then it was too late.

I was reminded of a joke that had been doing the rounds when I'd worked in the corporate world which was funny because there was more than a grain of truth to it. Whenever bad news was discussed at a meeting, such as a fall in share price or a drop in sales, the key thing to do was to identify who was missing from the meeting and swiftly blame them, or their department, for the problem. With no one present to refute the allegation the meeting could then move on to other, more favourable, topics for discussion.

When the presentation was over Colonel James introduced me to the Brigadier, kindly crediting me with writing the Transition Narrative and bigging up my role in restoring order in Gereshk following the Haji Gul fiasco. His generous words must have made some kind of impression on the Brigadier. It was the only time we ever met but he later wrote of me:

Captain Green has been tested at every turn and delivered consistently with flair and innovation. He has adapted his deep knowledge of marketing to great effect and his work on the Transition Narrative was simply superb. Not just in writing it but ensuring that it was believed. His efforts ensured that it informed every tactical action. This showed real depth. Deeply impressive.

As the battlegroup's engagement officer, my role in the weeks leading up to the operation was to conduct a 'human terrain analysis' of the Kakoran Gap in an attempt to understand the degree to which the local population were dependent on shadow governance and sympathetic to the insurgency. I also had to try and identify what might compel them to change their current perceptions and to accept GIRoA as the legitimate political authority. It was on this basis that I now found myself bedding down in the temporary accommodation at PB Clifton.

As a marketing professional I'd carried out many attitudinal surveys in the past but I was still daunted by the task in hand. The Kakoran Gap, for all its bucolic rural beauty and magnificent mulberry trees was an unusually dangerous place in which to be conducting market research. It was also IED Central.

As the Grenadiers or *fighting Ribs*[1] of Inkerman Company knew only too well, living with the constant possibility that your every next step may trigger an IED slowly and inevitably degrades the human spirit. It pervades every waking moment and is a constant and exhausting factor. Every breath must be carefully savoured lest it be your last. Every footfall must be critically considered and evaluated before being placed. Each tread is committed with unyielding trepidation. The euphoria of one safe step is immediately replaced by apprehension at the next and so on and so on until …

According to Aristotle, *Fear is pain arising from the anticipation of evil.* Not being as erudite as the great Greek polymath, for me, fear is the ever-present possibility that my fellow man has carefully concealed a yellow palm oil container packed with a volatile mixture of ammonium nitrate and aluminium in the ground beneath my feet. It is the screaming anticipation that my very next step will initiate this crude mixture and a dark and powerful blast will remove my legs and my manhood and leave me bloodied and broken in the dirt.

As friends and colleagues fall victim to these devices and are forever mutilated or killed in circumstances or locations you have visited yourself, it becomes possible to reflect not that you have been lucky, but that you must be next. It's a conviction that slowly and inexorably takes hold in the darkest recesses of your exhausted mind and grows like a malignant cancer.

During the course of my patrols in the Gap I witnessed young Guardsmen so overcome with fear that they would vomit at the front gates of the base before bravely stepping off on a patrol they have convinced themselves will be their last. I have also seen men so

---

[1] **Ribs/fighting Ribs**: Inkerman Company, First Battalion The Grenadier Guards are known as the Ribs or fighting Ribs after their predecessors took part in the Anglo-Dutch Wars (1652-74) as marines, accommodated in the ship's hold amongst the ribs.

exhausted by constant vigilance that they lose all reason and stumble about blindly, no longer caring if they live or die.

Both are equally distressing to observe. But in this I was not always a mere observer.

On one patrol I was myself so overwhelmed by the certainty that I was about to take my last few steps on this earth that I became rooted to the spot unable to move either forward or back. It took the gentle and patient persuasion of a better man half my age to guide me, temporarily broken and useless, to safety.

I would hear IEDs detonated by other callsigns, sometimes less than a kilometre distant. Or I would join a platoon for a few days, to learn soon afterwards that one of their number had been grievously wounded.

One device claimed the legs of another London Regiment soldier, Lance Corporal John Wilson with whom I'd trained and prepared for deployment, another took the foot of Jay, an SF soldier whom I'd got to know. Jay had postponed his end of tour date when yet more faults on the ageing RAF TriStar fleet had delayed his replacement's arrival into theatre.

I tried to convince him that he didn't need to go back out on the ground but he ignored my advice. When the news came through that his patrol had been whacked by an IED and had a serious casualty I instantly feared it must be him, and so it proved to be. Some reckoned he'd been lucky - the device only partially detonated and his injuries could have been much worse – but I knew that Jay's luck had run out with his *chuff chart*[1].

He was not the only casualty. He and Thor, my Danish counterpart, had forged a strong bond of trust and friendship over successive patrols together. Thor had been with his friend when he was injured and something had snapped inside him. He became uncommunicative, ill-tempered and confrontational – so much so that his boss, Major Uffe Pederson considered withdrawing his weapon systems, although it never came to this. As time passed Thor became increasingly critical of the mission and of those around him, including me. Friends and

---

[1] **Chuff Chart**: A chart or calendar used by servicemen and woman to count down the days until the end of a tour of duty.

colleagues did their best to talk him round but he retreated within himself, preferring instead to spend long hours alone in the gym.

At the end of July he returned to Denmark without saying goodbye.

Latitude:	31.82
Longitude:	64.68
Elevation:	859m
Met:	Sunny H:37°L:21°
DTG:	010512DSEP12

THE DANISH DRAGOONS have perfected a novel and effective way of traversing the many irrigation ditches that criss-cross the green zone, providing the essential element from which its name is derived.

Water turns arid, barren desert into lush, green agricultural farmland. Where the water runs out the desert begins. So stark is the contrast between the two that it is possible to step from one to the other in a single stride.

Although the critical importance of water in Helmandi society was obvious to see, ISAF did little if anything to safeguard this vital resource, preferring instead to invest billions of dollars expanding the country's road network. DfID's nation building plans, it seemed, were centred on *Freedom of Movement* and progress was measured in miles of asphalt.

If the strategic significance of water was considered at all it was as a source of electricity, but plans to provide power to thousands of Helmandi families, in an attempt to win their support for the Kabul government, were badly conceived, childishly optimistic and squandered a vast ocean of Western tax payers' money.

The ill-fated Kajaki Dam hydroelectric plant, roughly 100km north of our current location, served as an unwelcome metaphor for ISAF intervention in Afghanistan. Huge military resources were committed to the project which consumed over $500m of US AID[1] funding without ever producing a single additional watt of electricity.

Meanwhile, uncontested by ISAF, the Taliban and the illicit narcotics industry adopted a low-tech, low cost and yet highly effective method of controlling water distribution in the district. Simply by leaning on the local *Mirabs*[2] or water masters, who maintain the irrigation network and

---

[1] **US AID**: United States Agency for International Development

[2] **Mirab**: (Pashtu) Water Master. Afghanistan is an agricultural society and water for irrigation is a precious resource. Historically – and in the present – villagers have not trusted each other to take only their share.

are responsible for the allocation of water, it was possible for the Taliban to bend the local population to their will. If a farmer attempted to defy Taliban shadow governance, a quiet but persuasive word with the Mirab would ensure that water was diverted away from his fields. Once bountiful soil on which the farmer depended for his livelihood would quickly turn to dust, and there would be no harvest to transport to market on the expensive road network in which DfID and the international community had invested so much.

The irrigation ditches the Mirabs maintained provided vital sustenance for the crops and pastureland on which the Helmandis survived but were a significant conundrum to the infantry soldier. Too broad to jump across in a single bound and often too deep and steep-sided to climb in and out without assistance, they slowed our movement, fixing us in exposed positions open to attack. However, to avoid them by using local crossing points or bridges would make our route predictable and potentially channel us into vulnerable points where the Taliban would lay IEDs.

While British soldiers laboriously clamber in and out of these obstacles, the Danes have adopted a different technique. By laying a lightweight 12 foot aluminium ladder over the ditch soldiers are able to nimbly traverse across without the need for immersion in foul smelling, waist deep water. It's a simple and effective solution when it works. But doing anything nimbly while weighed down with over 50kg of equipment is not an easy task, made even more difficult by the alarming flex of the ladder itself.

Despite the hostile location, or perhaps heightened by it, there's still comedy to be derived from the misfortune of others. Step between the rungs and experience a painfully slapstick fall. Lose your footing on the bucking ladder and tumble headlong into the foetid water. One or two of my comrades-in-arms suffer these indignities, along with the stifled laughter and hushed banter of their unsympathetic mates, as we make our way ever deeper into the Heart of Darkness.

By now we are well inside the green zone, moving through fields of towering maize and ganja that conceal us from view but which also reduce visibility to just a few metres. The innocent rustle of hemp or

---

The job of the Mirab is to equitably distribute irrigation water to each household, usually based on the size of their landholdings. The Mirab is paid collectively by the community and because of the importance of their job is a very influential figure.

corn leaves may signify the presence of friendly forces or just as possibly of those with hostile intent. We cannot tell which. What is certain is that our progress is being tracked.

Given our numbers it is virtually impossible to move covertly through the dense foliage. Even if we were able to conceal our presence, our alien scent has been detected by the local mongrels even before we entered the green zone. If the J2 assessment was correct, somewhere beyond the thick fronds of maize and the more delicate but equally dense cannabis phyllotaxy, the local Taliban are urgently tooling up, determined not to allow our presence in their stronghold to go uncontested.

As long as we keep moving it'll be difficult for them to fix us and mount an attack, but by now the sky is lightening and we'll soon go firm on our objective.

We are entering the most dangerous and vulnerable phase of the operation.

Latitude:	31.85
Longitude:	64.62
Elevation:	851m
Met:	Sunny H:37°L:18°
DTG:	281430DJUL12

I WAS LYING naked in a pool of my own sweat when the men of the Light Dragoons turned up. It can't have been a pretty sight but they didn't seem to notice. In the stifling heat of yet another cloudless Afghan afternoon I was sprawled on my camp cot in the transit accommodation at PB Clifton trying to remain as still as possible. Even completely naked and motionless I was still pouring with sweat in the oven-like confines of the tent, but at least I was in the shade.

Lieutenant Ed Whitten, Sergeant Lee 'Davo' Davidson and the men of Support Troop, A Squadron, The Light Dragoons formed a Police Advisory Team, part of the Police Mentoring and Advisory Group (PMAG), tasked with improving the capacity and capability of the Afghan Uniformed Police. Based on everything I knew about the AUP in our district it was a much needed but enormously challenging task. Ed and his men had been given just three months to turn things around.

PB Clifton was to be their base for the duration and with no time to waste they immediately set about transforming the transit accommodation into their new home. I pulled on a pair of shorts and marvelled at their resourcefulness and ingenuity. Within a few short but industrious hours they'd created a tented palace worthy of Jalaluddin Mohammad Akbar the Great, the third and greatest emperor of the Mughal Dynasty whose proxies had ruled the Upper Gereshk Valley in his name from an ancient fort just a few klicks from where we now stood.

All the grubby, salt-encrusted camp cots were replaced with brand new models, each sporting its own integrated mosquito net and hanging shelf. The detritus of previous occupants was swept away and replaced by electric cabling with a precious power socket in every bed space. In one corner a few canvas easy chairs surrounded a low coffee table sporting an updated collection of Zoo and Nuts magazines together with a few Penguin paperbacks for the literati amongst them. Out front they even built a little private terrace complete with a couple of Hesco bastion loungers. Ed and his men clearly knew how to live and as Davo, his second-in-command rather pointedly observed, *any fool can be uncomfortable in the field.*

It was all in humiliating contrast to the squalor I'd previously been living in and I was more than a little ashamed.

If Ed and his men had formed a low opinion of my personal hygiene standards they were nonetheless wonderful hosts and adopted me as one might adopt a mangy and ill-tempered cat left behind by a previous owner. They generously insisted that I benefit from all their equipment upgrades and included me in their daily banter. Most generous of all, they had a secret source of deliciously chilled water and would always remember to bring me a bottle whenever I was around.

As we got to know each other I discovered that Ed had attended the same primary school as Harry and Alfie and I was able to write to the boys with this exciting news. Davo was a real family man with two boys of his own and a marriage that clearly wasn't on the rocks like mine. In fact his wife was expecting their third child and Davo was over the moon. He was an incredibly proud husband and father and one of his first tasks on arrival in Clifton was to put up a wooden board in his bed space to which he pinned pictures of his family, including a scan of his unborn baby.

Ed and Davo were from very different backgrounds but they made a great team and there was an obvious bond between them. Ed was an academic who already had a first class honours degree and a diploma from the International Language Institute in Cairo to his name when he joined the army in 2010. His academic achievements had continued at the Royal Military Academy. Where I had succeeded only in incurring the wrath of the legendary Skid Dorney by parking my car on his parade square, Ed had been awarded a medal as one of his intake's top students.

Davo, by contrast, had started life as a pavement resurfacer before joining the army in 1998, the same year Ed was enjoying life as a year six student at Harry and Alfie's primary school. He'd served in Bosnia, Iraq and Afghanistan in the intervening years and was one of the most experienced and respected men in his regiment.

Ed was indisputably the boss but he gratefully leaned on Davo for advice and guidance. Davo never challenged his boss's authority but was the true power behind the   throne.

I also discovered they were both nuts about skiing. We spent many a pleasant evening watching extreme skiing films on Ed's laptop while discussing our plans for the forthcoming season. Thanks to the generosity of friends I would be heading to the Porte du Soleil. Ed and Davo were both planning ski holidays with other members of their close-knit regiment.

I'd arrived at Clifton in a state of low personal morale and endured some of the most mentally and physically demanding patrols of the tour. By the time I returned to Price with my Human Terrain Analysis complete, my faith in human nature had been restored.

I was no longer contemplating a terminal solution to my personal problems.

I had even managed to engage the help of the Army Legal Service to write to York County Court requesting a postponement of divorce proceedings on the grounds of my *uncompromising situation*.

Things may not have been exactly rosy but they were certainly looking up. If I was still in one piece it was largely thanks to the professionalism and bravery of the Ribs but it was the generous hospitality of Support Troop that had raised my spirits and dared me to look beyond my personal problems and the horizon of my last few months in Afghanistan with some hope and optimism.

And this wasn't all that was looking up. On my last day in PB Clifton before returning to MOB Price I awoke with a morning glory to rival the drawing in my notebook back in the J9 cell. A toxic combination of stress, anxiety, depression and exhaustion had all conspired to ensure that I'd not been troubled by nocturnal penile tumescence for some weeks. Albeit perfectly normal and healthy, it was a somewhat inconvenient phenomenon when sharing cramped sleeping quarters with a dozen other blokes. Renewed optimism, it seemed, had unexpected physical side effects and I was required to cover my modesty and embarrassment – but I wasn't complaining.

Over the coming weeks I would frequently bump into Ed and his troop and it was always a pleasure to see them and catch up on their progress with the AUP. Despite the enormous challenges of their task, which might have overwhelmed lesser men, they always remained cheerfully optimistic.

Latitude:	31.82
Longitude:	64.68
Elevation:	859m
Met:	Sunny H:37°L:21°
DTG:	010531DSEP12

THE LADDER BUCKS beneath my feet and I lose my balance.

In a desperate attempt to avoid a dunking in the filthy water below I rush the last few rungs, lurching wildly for the safety of the opposite bank. I land half in and half out of the water, painfully barking my shins in the process. A small fountain of blood saturates the lower half of my combat trousers.

I can hear the Danish ladder-men behind me chuckling at my misfortune. Fair enough. I can't be absolutely sure, but it's probable that sympathy lies somewhere between shit and syphilis in the Danish dictionary, as it does in the English volume.

It takes a few moments to sort myself out. Bleeding shins will have to wait for now but will quickly become infected if I don't deal with them soon. One of the joys of Afghanistan is that every little cut or nick turns septic if not treated immediately. It's one of the reasons we don't shave when in the field. I always carry a tube of antiseptic cream to deal with the inevitable scrapes that are part and parcel of employment in the infantry.

By the time I'm back on my feet the young Tiger Team machine gunner who is my link man to the forward elements of the patrol has disappeared into the tangled fronds of a soaring field of cannabis. Thinking I can make out his path in the swaying foliage I chase after him. This particular crop seems ready for harvest, the pungent aroma almost overwhelming. The bases of the leaves above my head are visibly loaded with THC[1] crystals which cascade over me as I push further in. I'm beginning to feel a little light-headed. But this is the least of my worries.

I've lost contact with the front of the patrol. They're somewhere in the ganja field. It's possible they're only a few metres away but they might just as well not be there at all. The Tiger Team are nowhere to be

---

[1] **THC**: Tetrahydrocannabinol. The principal psychoactive constituent (or cannabinoid) of cannabis.

seen. I try to raise Owen on the personal role radio (PRR) on the left shoulder of my body armour. The big Welshman must be somewhere ahead of me, but the line is dead. Unable to make comms, I search for a few futile moments before coming to the conclusion that I have no choice but to turn back and retrace my steps to the irrigation ditch. Then I can team up with the Danish multiple taking up the rear of the patrol and figure out my next move.

It cannot be more than a couple of minutes since I plunged into the field of marijuana, but by the time I return to the scene of my undignified fall from the Danish ladder the spot is deserted. The Danes have moved on. British and Danish field radios are not compatible. There's no chance I can raise them on the net.

This is not propitious.

This is not very fucking propitious at all.

I am now *Man Away* in the Taliban Heart of fucking Darkness.

This is the very same fucking place that Captain Alex Bayliss, our Intelligence Officer warned me about all those long months ago when Afghanistan was still just an imaginary place in my stupid fucking head full of mystery, adventure, excitement and promise. What a dickhead I've been. For talking myself into coming here in the first fucking place. And now for getting myself fucking lost. When was this ever a good fucking idea? I've lost count of the number of times regular soldiers have expressed amazement that I've actually volunteered for Afghan. It's finally fucking dawned on me why.

It isn't even six o'clock in the morning. I'm already having a really bad day.

I have two options. I can press on to the target compound alone using the bearing and grid reference on my map, and then rejoin the patrol. Or I can go firm and wait for the patrol to return.

The standard operating procedure (SOP) in these situations is to rendezvous at the last known point prior to separation. But this assumes I will be missed. Since I'm not part of the Danish ladder team it's unlikely they'll report me as lost. It's even less likely the Tiger Team's machine gunner is going to admit he's mislaid the ageing Angrezi. It's entirely probable that   I won't be missed at all.

My only hope is Owen. He may realise something's up when I fail to show at the target compound. But by then it may be too late. However, to ignore the SOP and crack on to the target alone isn't without hazard. There's no telling who I might bump into on the way. Although I'm pretty clear on what they'll do to me if that happens.

I reluctantly accept that my best course of action is to follow the SOP and go firm in my present location. A shallow depression at the edge of the field just a few feet from where we crossed the ditch affords reasonable cover and a good field of fire along the most likely axis of enemy advance.

First I remove my day sack and place it in front of me as a makeshift weapons platform. Next I take all my magazines from their pouches on the front of my body armour and place them in a neat row next to the day sack.

If I could just stop my hands from shaking this would make for faster mag changes when the time comes.

I also remove the speed loader and spare 130-round bandolier from the inside zip pocket of the day sack. I'll likely not get the chance to re-bomb[1] my mags, and my hands are shaking so violently that, in all probability, it'll be impossible anyway, but you never know and the bandolier is no good to me tucked away in my pack.

Finally, although I know there's already a round in the chamber, I unload and reload my Sig 9mm pistol. The Sig incorporates a decocking lever on the left side above the magazine housing that allows the hammer to be dropped, making it impossible to accidentally discharge the weapon. But experience has taught me that I generally miss with my first shot because of the extra trigger pressure required to recock. This time, once reloaded, I don't drop the hammer. I'm not on the MOB Price range. I need every round to count.

1. Hope for the best.

2. Plan for the worst.

3. Prepare to be surprised.

---

[1] **Re-bomb** *(re-bomb my mags)*: to refill magazines with ammunition

Whatever happens next, I'm as ready as I can be. My hands are still shaking.

Latitude:	31.77
Longitude:	64.68
Elevation:	847m
Met:	Sunny H:36°L:16°
DTG:	141525DAUG12

IF I'D HOPED to stand shoulder to shoulder with the Grenadiers in the manner of the painting in the officers' mess at Wellington Barracks I was to be disappointed once more. Having missed out on the Yakchal op I volunteered myself for Op Qalb 7a as soon as I returned from PB Clifton, but Colonel James thought better of deploying me forward to the temporary blocking positions east of the Kakoran Gap. The Commanding Officer, no doubt, had his reasons for excluding me from this most dangerous of missions but chose not to share these with me.

Owen, the younger, more capable man was selected for this task. I tried hard not to show my disappointment. I kicked my heels in MOB Price for a few days before eventually returning to Clifton in another futile attempt to encourage Captain Manan to patrol forward of the kammarband in accordance with the role outlined for him in Colonel James' animated PowerPoint presentation.

No sooner had I arrived than Manan disappeared on unplanned 'leave'. No one was quite sure when he would return and his men were naturally reluctant to leave their checkpoints without direct orders from their *Toran* or Captain.

In Manan's absence I attempted to engage with his boss, Colonel Hamayoon whose headquarters were a short distance from MOB Price in the desert south-east of Gereshk. Colonel Hamayoon was a colourful character with a fiery temper. A Dari from the north of the country he exuded a self-confidence that bordered on arrogance and was openly contemptuous of the Helmandi Pashtuns. He frequently crossed swords with local GIRoA officials and saved particular scorn for Ghullie Khan the District Chief of Police, whom he referred to as the *Great Bearded Robber*. Much to my own personal amusement, he also insisted on calling Ghullie Khan's British mentor, a burly officer in the Light Dragoons, the *Great Bearded Robber's Handmaiden*.

When he wasn't raging at his own government's incompetence he could be equally disdainful of ISAF and never missed an opportunity to share his opinions with his military advisors. When we were first introduced many months before, he'd insisted that I leave my weapon systems with one of his men outside the meeting room. As he well knew, this was not something I was prepared to do. An uncomfortable stalemate had ensued before the meeting was eventually reconvened outside.

Ever after Colonel Hamayoon claimed that my apparent lack of trust was insulting and disrespectful but, if he had been deliberately engineering some kind of test of character, I appeared to have passed. Although we didn't always agree, we could at least agree to disagree. At the end of my tour when I said my farewells he good-naturedly pointed to my grey hair and advised me that it was time to enjoy my wives while I still could and leave the fighting to my sons. It seemed churlish to mention that both my sons were under ten and my only wife was in the throes of divorcing me.

However, on this particular occasion he avoided the subject of the missing Captain by volubly demanding instead that we do something to improve living conditions in one of the bases we shared with his troops in another part of our AO. Every time I attempted to return to the subject of the Kakoran Gap he would simply raise his voice and talk over me. Eventually I gave up. Although he did not say as much, it seemed that Colonel Hamayoon had no more interest in Colonel James' plan than did his subordinate.

My attempts to persuade the ANA to perform the pivotal role envisaged for them in the Qalb 7a operation were proving futile. It was, after all, a plan they had not been party to and a role they had not signed up for or were equipped to perform. A number of the ANA's British military advisors, one of whom was a highly respected sergeant in the London Regiment, also privately counselled me that I was wasting my time. In their opinion the ANA would never patrol forward of the kammarband. It was not territory they wished to contest with the Taliban and they had effectively already ceded that ground to the enemy.

It was small comfort to know that Brigadier Chalmers, the ultimate custodian of the UK's £15 million a day military investment in Helmand Province, could no more convince the ANA High Command to invest in the Angrezi plan for the Kakoran Gap than I could persuade Colonel Hamayoon or Captain Manan to patrol with me there.

Much later I would reflect on my failings to engage with them both on this subject and come to the uncomfortable conclusion that the Brigadier had been wrong about me when he'd said ... *his work on the Transition Narrative was simply superb. Not just in writing it but ensuring that it was believed.* I'd utterly failed to persuade the two ANA officers to believe in the narrative and my failure would have profound consequences.

When I attempted to raise these concerns with Colonel James he cut me short, insisting there could be no deviation from the plan – the ANA must be compelled to play their part. I know I was not alone in expressing my misgivings but the Commanding Officer was not receptive to these entreaties and steadfastly stuck to his concept of operations.

I was reminded of the poem *If* by Rudyard Kipling:

If you can keep your head when all about you
Are losing theirs and blaming it on you,
If you can trust yourself when all men doubt you,
But make allowance for their doubting too;

If Colonel James was making allowances for my own doubting then he certainly wasn't letting on, but I could only admire his extraordinary self-confidence, personal conviction and strength of character.

I also had to respect his perspicacity. If the ANA were refusing to participate in the plan, the Taliban on the other hand were behaving exactly as Colonel James had predicted.

Within hours of the temporary checkpoints being established they had come into contact with the enemy.

Latitude:	31.82
Longitude:	64.68
Elevation:	859m
Met:	Sunny H:37°L:21°
DTG:	010533DSEP12

THE SWAYING OF the maize plants in the field on the opposite bank of the irrigation ditch betrays their forward movement before they break cover about 25 metres away from me.

Even before they reveal themselves I know it won't be the 7th Cavalry – all the friendly forces in the area are on my side of the ditch. I adjust my firing position slightly, raising the optical gunsight to my right eye while simultaneously adjusting the change lever from single shot to full auto with the thumb of my left hand and depressing the safety lever to fire with the index finger of my right.

Two men dressed in khaki coloured *dishdashes* emerge from the field in front of me. Both wear loosely tied turbans on their heads, one black, the other a brown check material. Both carry AK47s with folding stocks. I note that neither weapon is fitted with a rear sight. Even at 25 metres this improves my odds markedly. Unable to shoulder their weapons properly with the stock folded and without an effective sighting system they will be firing in my general direction from a standing position, whereas I will be taking aimed shots from a stable prone platform. My rate of fire will be more accurate. And I will be presenting a much smaller target for them to hit.

I take up first pressure on the trigger. The difference between life and death may now be measured as 3.12kg, the precise amount of additional resistance I will need to apply to the trigger in order to release the firing mechanism.

By the way both men carry their AKs it would appear that neither is aware of my presence. For the time being at least it seems my MTP camouflage combat uniform is doing its job. This also means that I have the tactical advantage of surprise.

Despite being outnumbered 2:1 the odds are now stacked in my favour.

Through the x6 magnification of the gunsight I can see that the younger of the two, whom I've identified as *Talib#1*, wears on his left hand an ostentatious ring set with a large red ruby. I wonder if this could be a wedding band. If so, I am about to become a widowmaker.

Judging by his grey-flecked beard, *Talib#2* is not only at least a decade older than *Talib#1,* but will also live a little longer. It takes one to know one and I reckon the older man's reaction times will be slower than his colleague. In practical terms this means simply that he will witness his friend's death and have just time to register that he is himself in mortal danger before I switch fire.

I minutely adjust my position so that the orange cross-hair of the gunsight rests on the third button of *Talib#1's dishdash.* I'm going for an *M* or *Mobility Kill* rather than a *K* or *Catastrophic Kill.* A *K Kill*, usually a head shot, kills the target instantly. An *M Kill* renders the target immobile but doesn't necessarily kill them immediately – it may take some time for them to bleed out or otherwise succumb to their wounds.

My decision is made not out of a cruel desire to inflict pain and suffering on my enemy, but a realistic appraisal of my own marksmanship skills. Outnumbered, I simply can't risk a head shot. Even at this range I might miss. The body mass is the bigger target and will do the job I need done.

At this moment my plan does not extend beyond killing the two men in my sights. It's enough to know that if I am going to die today, I'm not going to die alone. Finally, my hands are steady.

I slowly exhale, and hold my breath.

It turns out that taking life, even the life of someone intent on killing you, is not as simple as the application of 3.12kg of pressure. I hesitate. At this range I will be both architect of and intimate witness to their deaths and I already know how this will play out.

From the moment I realised I was *Man Away* I've been mentally preparing for my imminent demise, at my own hand if necessary. The Talib, unaware of my presence just a few metres away, have had no time to make the same mental adjustment from hunter to hunted. The sudden shock at their change in circumstances will be replaced by a realisation that they will initially resist with each ragged, pink-misted breath. Finally, in their last few moments of consciousness, they will reluctantly accept their fate as hopes, dreams and ambitions all slip away and their eyes dull forever.

As I waver, both men turn away from me to scan the irrigation ditch in the other direction. It doesn't say as much in our Rules of Engagement, but I've read enough *Battle*[1] comics as a kid to know I can't shoot them in the back.

I have a brief vision of Harry and Alfie asking me what I've done in the war and admitting that I killed two men while they were looking the other way.

I know they'd both be disappointed in me.

Without breathing I wait for the men to turn back in my direction but after just a few moments they head back into the maize, returning the way they came. I continue to track their progress through the swaying field as they force their way through the giant crop until all is still.

Only then do I draw another breath.

Neither man will ever know that they owe their lives to a 1970s comic book and the moral judgement of two young boys.

---

[1] **Battle:** At various times also known as **Battle Action Force**, **Battle Picture Weekly** and **Battle with Storm Force**, was a British war comic published by IPC Magazines from 8 March 1975 to 23 January 1988. Most stories were set in World War II.

Latitude:	31.80
Longitude:	64.51
Elevation:	834m
Met:	Sunny H:36°L:16°
DTG:	171607DAUG12

BY MID-AUGUST, sustaining the soldiers manning the beleaguered temporary checkpoints had become the main focus for the battlegroup and almost all our resources and energy were invested in this activity.

Supporting 90-odd men behind enemy lines was an enormous operation, the details of which were coordinated by our Chief of Staff, Major Dave Kenny.

Each morning Dave would hold a meeting around the *bird table* – a makeshift table on which a large satellite image of the district had been pasted, affording us literally a bird's-eye view of our AO. This was overlaid with various traces, showing details such as operations boxes, interdiction boundaries, no-fire lines and other information vital to military operations.

Standing around the table, Dave would receive a brief from each of the branch heads outlining the issues and concerns they were dealing with. He might then ask a few questions before giving further guidance and instructions. Unlike the Commanding Officer who never betrayed his emotions, Dave wore his heart on his sleeve and his worry and concern for the men on the ground was obvious for all to see. He rarely left the headquarters for more than a minute or two and his personal contribution to British American Tobacco revenues had reached record levels. Before our very eyes, Dave was growing pale and thin in the service of his country. The smokes, the lack of sleep and the stress were getting to him. He looked a wreck but steadfastly soldiered on without complaint.

I wondered if some of his anxiety was caused by scepticism about the plan. But if he shared my misgivings he never revealed this to me. It's possible that he raised his concerns with Colonel James in private, as I had done myself, but in front of the staff he never expressed anything other than his loyalty to the Commanding Officer and an utter commitment to the mission.

Dave didn't waver, not even when Guardsman Karl Whittle was shot

12 times at point-blank range.

The attack occurred while Karl was on sentry duty at one of the temporary checkpoints. Four motorcycle pillion riders approached Karl and, drawing weapons they'd concealed under their robes, shot him from just one or two metres away. The insurgents then attacked the main compound. They were repelled, but not before making off with the General Purpose Machine Gun (GPMG) that Karl had been manning.

Incredibly, Karl survived the attack and was able to talk to some of his colleagues before being airlifted to Camp Bastion. Described as *one of the leading lights of his Company*, Karl was a bit of a joker. He complained that his tackle was on display after the medics cut his uniform away in order to treat his wounds. He even quipped with his mates not to drop him as they carried him to the MERT.

Finally, he told them to let his fiancée know that he loved her and their baby daughter.

It was obvious that Karl must have been in a pretty bad way but we all fervently hoped he would be telling her himself soon enough. Although he fought on for a further three weeks, testimony to his great strength and lust for life, it would prove to be a forlorn hope.

It took three days for the surgeons at Camp Bastion to stabilise his condition sufficiently for the long flight back to the UK. Meanwhile his stolen machine gun became an emblem by which the success or failure of operation Qalb 7a would come to be defined.

As far as we were concerned there had to be consequences for daring to make off with the British weapon. Those consequences would ideally be fatal. For their part we knew that the insurgents would be crowing about their victory and parading their recently acquired machine gun for all to see.

We badly wanted it back. Very badly.

Every available intelligence, surveillance, target acquisition and reconnaissance asset was diverted to the search. We weren't just looking for the GPMG. Anyone who handled the weapon, assisted in its concealment, or even so much as mentioned it in conversation on their mobile phone came under scrutiny. More than once the weapon or its location was successfully   identified but on each occasion a strike could not be authorised or was called off at the eleventh hour.

As we planned to exact our revenge on Karl's attackers the Taliban, emboldened perhaps by their recent success, were making plans of their own.

Shortly after 4.00pm on 17th August, as Karl was being transferred to the Queen Elizabeth hospital in Birmingham, Guardsman Jamie Shadrake took over sentry duty at TCP 40, another temporary checkpoint not far from the one Karl had been manning.

Moments later insurgents armed with AK47s, RPGs and hand grenades assaulted the position in a ferocious attack. Jamie, who had turned 20 on the day that Karl had been attacked, didn't stand a chance. Sustaining gunshot wounds to his head and chest he died at his post. Like Karl, his assailants then made off with the GPMG he'd been manning.

The two GPMGs were but base metal when compared to the flesh and blood of these fine young Guardsmen but they were nonetheless symbolic.

In times gone by the capture of an enemy's Standard or Colour in battle was considered a great feat of arms, and a devastating blow to the vanquished. Although the Colours themselves continue to be treated with reverence, the British Army stopped carrying them into battle in 1880 following the loss of the Queen's Colour and Regimental Colour of the 66th (Berkshire) Regiment of Foot at Maiwand. This battle had been fought, and lost, just a few klicks south of where Karl and Jamie had fallen.

132 years later, the loss of the GPMGs took on a similar significance that rocked us all.

Although it remained unspoken, we also knew that with one soldier dead and another mortally wounded any political will for this most dangerous of missions would quickly dissipate.

Two days later in a press statement released by the Ministry of Defence confirming Jamie's death, Colonel James wrote: *we are determined to finish the mission that he so courageously helped to start.* I didn't doubt for a moment the heartfelt sentiment of his words but the future of the mission was no longer in his hands, or even those of the Task Force Helmand Commander to whom he reported. The decision was now a political rather than a military one. It would be made somewhere in London by men in suits sipping Fairtrade soya lattés through the plastic lids of recycled cardboard cups.

Within days the TCPs were withdrawn and operation Qalb 7a was concluded.

Although it was staring us all in the face, the operation's fatal flaw could never be divulged, not least because it would expose a more fundamental failure. The Afghan National Army, on behalf of the Government of the Islamic Republic of Afghanistan, had neither the will nor the capacity to secure and safeguard the people of the Kakoran Gap. This did not sit comfortably with our own counter-insurgency doctrine which mandated the *population as the prize.* It exposed the extreme shortcomings of the structures we were putting in place to run the province after our departure in two years time.

Such an acknowledgement might have prevented DfID from blithely declaring *real progress towards democracy.* It might even have prevented David Cameron from proclaiming *Mission Accomplished* in December 2013, seven months before the Coroner at Jamie Shadrake's inquest recorded a verdict of death by unlawful killing.

His killers and those of Karl Whittle have never been brought to justice. Nor have their GPMGs ever been recovered.

Latitude:	31.82
Longitude:	64.68
Elevation:	859m
Met:	Sunny H:37°L:21°
DTG:	010536DSEP12

THE PRESENCE OF the two Talib gunmen on the opposite side of the irrigation ditch has provided me with vital intelligence which has a bearing on my plan. They must be part of a scouting screen. Like our own reconnaissance troops, they are working forward of their main fighting force. Most likely they didn't fancy getting their feet wet in the irrigation ditch and have gone in search of a crossing point.

Based on this new information, I decide not to hang about waiting to be outflanked or, even worse, for the main body to turn up with a 12 foot aluminium ladder of their own. It seems reasonable to assume that since the recce screen is behind me, the only troops between me and the target compound must be friendly forces. My best course of action therefore is to crack on and hope that I'll rendezvous with the good guys either en route or at the target itself.

I'll still have to be careful though. There are plenty of nervous infidels in Zumbalay this morning besides myself who could just mistake my presence for that of the enemy. I also know from prior experience just how trigger-happy the Tiger Team lads can be.

But I know it's the right decision. I quickly stow my gear and prepare to move off once more. As I'm doing this, to my very great horror, I become aware of a huge figure moving through the ganja field at speed towards me. No longer in my prepared firing position, not yet quite ready to move, I freeze somewhere between fight and flight.

Even though I spent much of a happy childhood in Wales, even though I own a Tom Jones *Greatest Hits* CD and, inexplicably, know almost all of the words to *Young New Mexican Puppeteer,* I can't claim to have any special affinity with the people of Wales. But when the biggest Welshman I've ever met stumbled out of the hemp field in front of me, covered in a liberal dusting of psychedelic chemicals, I could have wept with joy. Fewer than ten minutes can have elapsed since I saw the Tiger Team machine gunner disappear into the marijuana crop from which Owen now emerges. To me it has seemed an eternity.

Never before or since have I felt quite so alone or fearful as in those few slow agonizing minutes.

Given the large quantity of THC with which he was adorned, it's possible that Owen was more than a little stoned, but what is absolutely certain is that he was a lot less pleased to see me than I was to see him. In fact he was about as incandescent as it's possible to be without giving your position away to an enemy you know to be close by.

For fuck's sake, Chris, he seethed, *keep up or you'll get us all fucking killed.*

Now was neither the time nor the place to dispute this and I followed him back into the *Mary Jane*[1] like a delirious puppy.

Safely reunited with the patrol, I saw Owen have a quiet word with the Tiger Team machine gunner, presumably telling him not to let the geriatric wander off again. We pressed on through the pungent crop, as yet more crystals cascaded down from above. I was feeling euphoric and couldn't decide whether it was the cannabinoids or my recent brush with disaster that was the root cause. Most likely it was a combination of the two.

As we pushed ever deeper into the crop the general mood of the patrol seemed to become less tense and by the time we arrived at the target compound there was an almost jovial atmosphere. Danish and Afghan soldiers sat in little groups on the ground smiling and chatting away together, sharing cigarettes and cold rations as if on some sort of breakfast picnic. It was undoubtedly a beautiful spot, the perfect place for a picnic perhaps, but the near presence of the Taliban seemed to have been forgotten almost entirely.

Once we'd safely cleared the compound Owen was keen to interview the two male occupants alone. He asked me to wait outside. I wasn't entirely happy with this. Owen was the linguist but I was the info ops officer and this was pretty much the whole reason why I'd come to Zumbalay. However, given my earlier foul-up at the irrigation ditch I decided not to press the point and instead went outside to interview a couple of young men the Tiger Team had found skulking about.

---

[1] **Mary Jane**: A slang term for marijuana derived from the Mexican Spanish meaning of the word: *Maria* (Mary) and *Juana* (Joan or Jane). Hence, *Mary Jane*.

They were in their early twenties, both extremely nervous. I couldn't prove it but they were almost certainly dickers[1] who'd been tasked with gathering basic intelligence about our numbers and intentions. I decided we should temporarily detain them so they didn't go running straight back to their insurgent masters, although not in quite the way that the Tiger Team lads had in mind. Instead I gave them a couple of Danish cigarettes and told them to sit by the corner of the compound wall.

Next I took out my patrol camera and started photographing anything I thought might be useful for the report I would be writing on my return. I'd got into the practice of doing this early on in the tour and had found it to be invaluable. Engrossed in this task I turned the corner of the compound and almost walked into Haji Jalander, the old Mujahideen I'd interviewed back in MOB Price. Somehow he'd slipped through the Danish cordon unnoticed.

Although I knew Haji was from Zumbalay it hadn't occurred to me that I might meet him here. But my surprise was nothing compared to his. The last time we'd met I was pretty sure Haji was up for killing me. I certainly wouldn't have been the first *khareji*[2] he'd put to death, but once again I had the advantage on him. I was armed with more than just a camera, while he had only his trusty radiator key on its slender brass chain.

Finding my wits I wished him *As-salaam Alaykoum,* to which he instinctively replied before he could check himself, *Alaykoum As-salaam.* Pleasantries over we stood and stared at each other for a few moments before we were joined by one of the Tiger Team lads who spoke a little English.

I waited patiently while they spoke rapid-fire Pashtu. It was clear the Tiger was getting the full backstory on how Haji and I came to be acquainted. Haji went on at length and the more he spoke the more the fierce old Muj was winding himself up. I was reminded of my soon-to-be-ex father-in-law who had a similar capacity to raise his own blood pressure to dangerous levels simply by reading The Daily Mail.

---

[1] **Dicker**: A term originally coined in Northern Ireland to describe low level, usually unarmed informants, often children, who follow patrols and hang around outside military bases providing basic intelligence on troop movements and dispositions to the enemy.

[2] **Khareji**: foreigner

Eventually Haji ran out of steam and the Tiger turned to me and skilfully translated his lengthy diatribe into four words: *You know this man?*

I acknowledged that I did and asked him to enquire after Haji's son-in-law. Had he returned? This was obviously a mistake as it set Haji off on another long stream of uninterrupted invective.

The young Afghan soldier was clearly a master of the paraphrase. Laughing a little too nervously for my liking, he translated this last tirade:

He says you will die here today, the Taliban will not let you leave alive.

Looking Haji directly in the eye, trying to sound as nonchalant as I could, I replied that I'd lived a good life and was ready to die.

It was complete bollocks of course. With three weeks left to push in Afghan, I very much wanted to live.

I had plans.

Like almost everyone else counting down to the end of their tour, these centred around getting very drunk, driving fast cars and sleeping with loose women, although not necessarily all at the same time. But most of all I wanted to see my sons and to return to my spiritual home in the mountains. Almost every spare moment in my day was now consumed in planning my reunion with Harry and Alfie, or in visualising virgin powder descents from *Les Hauts Forts* above the French ski resort of Avoriaz into the *Vallée de la Manche*.

I could only guess at how the young Tiger had translated my words but Haji seemed satisfied with my answer and nodded sagely in approval.

Our reunion was suddenly interrupted by a long burst of machine gun fire from the roof of the compound where some of the Danish troops were providing overwatch. Almost instantaneously the air was alive with high velocity rounds as insurgents returned fire from the edge of the maize fields to the north-east of the compound. It seemed Haji was not the only one who'd managed to slip through the cordon undetected.

For once my military training over-ruled my finely honed instinct for self preservation. I turned on my heel and started running towards the sound of the gunfire as fast my ageing limbs and my 52 kilos of kit and equipment would allow. I rounded the corner of the compound with the old Muj and the young Tiger in hot pursuit to find the two dickers prostrate on the ground in a state of abject terror. Haji was not impressed and wasted no time telling them exactly what he thought. I didn't need a translator to know they were getting a ferocious bollocking from the old spin zhira.

The Jutland Dragoons and the Tiger Team lads on this side of the compound, having put their picnic aside, were pouring fire into the maize field. But they were getting just as much back in return. There was no cover to be had and they were all firing from exposed standing or kneeling positions on the edge of the field with the compound wall to their backs. The enemy cannot have been more than 20 metres away, just inside the maize.

The machine gunner on the roof was still going gangbusters and now that everyone else had got involved, the weight of out-going fire was intense. It seemed impossible to me that anyone could survive it but, incredibly, we were still taking a decidedly unhealthy amount of return fire.

It was only a question of time before one of us was going to get hit.

To my left I saw a flash of movement in the maize and immediately opened up. Until this moment I hadn't fired a single shot. Now I made up for it by giving the shadowy figures a full mag in two or three long bursts. It wasn't very professional of me and more than a little hypocritical. I'd previously admonished the Tiger Team lads for firing their weapons in just such long and uncontrolled bursts. But at that moment it seemed the right thing to do. Perhaps it was the effects of the cannabis. Or perhaps the guilty secret that I'd earlier been too squeamish to kill two of our attackers when I'd had the chance.

I dropped to one knee as I changed mags and was immediately floored by one of the Dragoons. *Mortars, Danger Close*[1] he had just time to tell me by way of explanation before several explosions rocked the ground and shrapnel peppered the compound wall behind us.

---

[1] **Danger Close**: The term **danger close** is included in the request for supporting fires such as artillery or mortars when there are friendly troops or positions in close range of the intended target and inside the blast radius of the munition.

Unbeknown to me because of the incompatibility of our radios, the Dragoons had called in a mortar fire mission on the Taliban positions just a few metres from our own. We'd been *Danger Close,* inside the blast radius of the ordnance, when it arrived. The quick thinking Danish infantryman had risked his life to save mine.

I didn't even know his name.

The mortars brought a temporary lull in the battle and the Dragoons were urgently indicating that we should take advantage of the break in contact to move off. I couldn't have agreed with them more.

I was saying a hasty farewell to Haji and the still terrified dickers as Owen emerged from the compound several shades paler than when he'd gone in. Unlike me, he had received no warning of the in-coming mortars and had been firing over the top of the compound wall when they struck. Enveloped in a cloud of dust as the wall disintegrated around him, incredibly he was otherwise unscathed.

With him was the Danish machine gunner who'd been up on the roof. I didn't immediately recognise him with his clothes on, but it was the Greek hero who'd assaulted the Taliban RPG position in his underpants the day before. Once again our eyes locked. He indicated the MG42/59 in his arms and said:

This machine gun is fucking heavy. If I'm gonna carry it for the next six months I'm gonna fucking use it. I'm gonna use it a lot.

Based on our short acquaintance I had no reason to doubt him.

Latitude:	31.82
Longitude:	64.68
Elevation:	859m
Met:	Sunny H:38°L:21°
DTG:	011623DSEP12

FOR A MAN who'd just cheated the sniper's bullet by the narrowest of margins, Owen accepted the cigarette I'd lit for him with an admirably steady hand. The round had passed so close by that I'd felt the air it displaced before I'd heard the crack and thump.

Owen was manning the General Purpose Machine Gun mounted in the top gunner's hatch of the Mastiff. He ducked his head back inside the crew compartment as he inhaled almost the entire cigarette in a single drag. I watched, fascinated, as the glowing ember marched steadily towards the filter tip leaving a lengthening cylinder of ash in its wake. The big Welshman removed the spent cigarette from his lips and, through a dense cloud of tobacco smoke that filled the vehicle, stated the blindingly obvious:

That one had my name on it.

It did not seem the appropriate moment to remind him of the MoD policy that prohibits smoking in service vehicles and other enclosed spaces.

Bent double inside the Mastiff, Owen struck a somewhat comical figure of two halves. The top half of his body, which had been exposed to enemy fire in the top gunner's hatch, was dressed in full combat gear, including helmet, ballistic glasses and body armour. In contrast the lower half of his body, safely ensconced inside the vehicle, was completely naked but for a pair of disgustingly filthy underpants. Owen had seen more combat than most on this tour and it was widely acknowledged that he had some massive balls. It wasn't a pretty sight.

Despite taking heavy casualties at the target compound earlier in the day, the Taliban had continued to harass our patrol as we withdrew back to the desert leaguer. My new best friend, the Tiger Team machine gunner, had been busy with his Russian-made PKM. In addition to making sure I didn't wander off, he fired hundreds of rounds in wide sweeping arcs of our flanks as we made our way through the green zone. I got the impression he was thoroughly enjoying himself.

Eventually we requested air support but, even after a helicopter killed a further two of their number, the Taliban doggedly pressed their attack. It seemed there was an element of truth to a joke I'd heard back in the MOB Price D-FAC about the anti-bacterial hand wipe dispensers. I'd been told these were called *Talibans.* Every time you take one out, another one pops up.

Haji Jalander may or may not have been telling tales when he came to visit me in MOB Price, but his claim at the target compound had been truthful enough. The Taliban seemed prepared to stop at nothing in their efforts to prevent us leaving Zumbalay alive.

The Taliban sniper was clearly a skilled operative. He'd managed to get himself and his weapon into a firing position undetected before taking his shot and was unlucky not to score a kill when he narrowly missed Owen. However, he now faced a further test of his tradecraft. A second shot would reveal his position. Would he have the self-discipline to overcome his frustration at missing the giant kafir and remain undetected, or would he risk firing again?

The decision was his and his alone to make, but an entire armoured infantry company of the Jutland Dragoons now waited, locked and loaded, on the outcome of his deliberations.

It seemed that the sniper lacked one of the skills most vital to his trade – patience – he went for the second shot. It was a catastrophic error of judgment.

It had taken a little over 24 hours to transform the Jutland Dragoons from wide-eyed newcomers into combat veterans and there was no hesitation, as there had been the previous day following the RPG strike. The Dragoons opened up with everything at their disposal, including the Bushmaster III 35mm automatic cannon mounted on their APCs. One of Mastiff Pete's 50-cal gunners also joined the fray as did the Tigers with great enthusiasm, if less accuracy. Thousands of rounds pulverised the sniper's firing position. Nothing could have survived the maelstrom.

Due to the incompatibility of the British and Danish radios, I couldn't hear the Danish radio operator calling in the contact to the MOB Price operations room. But I could hear our Ops Officer, Captain Tom

Gardner's incredulous response:

Roger that, I read back: "Contact: 2 x rounds small arms fire. Action taken: Return fire with 5.56, 7.62, 50-cal and 35 mil." How many rounds did you fire? Over.

Roger that, I read back: "Too many to count." Was that proportionate? Over.

Roger that, I read back: "You didn't use the mortars." Return to this location as soon as possible, we need to talk. Out.

Tom had just called time on our fact finding mission into Zumbalay. I could not have been happier.

Latitude   31.79
Longitude   64.67
Elevation   852m
Met   Sunny H:37°L:10°
DTG   091117DSEP12

Top of my shopping list was a
Taliban Hunting Club t-shirt.

VCP: Vehicle Checkpoint
GIRoA: Government of the Islamic Republic of Afghanistan
JTAC: Joint Tactical Air Controller
WAG: Waste Activated Gel
ME: Main Effort

MINISTRY OF DEFENCE ANNOUNCEMENT

Guardsman Karl Whittle. On Friday 7 September 2012, Guardsman Karl Whittle died in Queen Elizabeth Hospital Birmingham from wounds sustained in Afghanistan when his checkpoint was attacked by insurgents in the Nahr-e-Saraj district of Helmand province.

Sergeant Lee Paul Davidson. On Sunday 9 September 2012, Sergeant Lee Paul Davidson was fatally wounded in the Nahr-e-Saraj district of Helmand province when his vehicle struck an improvised explosive device.

Lance Corporal Duane Groom. On Friday 14 September 2012, Lance Corporal Duane Groom was killed in action when his vehicle struck an improvised explosive device in the Nahr-e-Saraj district of Helmand province.

Sergeant Gareth Thursby *and* **Private Thomas Wroe.** On Saturday 15 September 2012, Sergeant Gareth Thursby and Private Thomas Wroe were shot and fatally wounded by a rogue Afghan Local Policeman in the Nahr-e-Saraj district of Helmand province.

Captain James Anthony Townley. On Friday 21 September 2012, Captain James Anthony Townley died in Camp Bastion, Helmand province, from wounds sustained whilst serving at Forward Operating Base Shawqat.

Latitude:	31.79
Longitude:	64.67
Elevation:	852m
Met:	Sunny H:37°L:10°
DTG:	091117DSEP12

MIRAJDIN LAY IN wait less than 250 metres from the huge explosive device he'd buried on the track junction. Inshallah, his patience and daring would soon be rewarded. He would avenge the death of his revered commander Mohammed Momin, assassinated on the banks of the river Helmand, and those of his brothers-in-arms who had perished resisting the infidels' incursion into their homelands just eight days earlier.

Assembling and positioning the bomb had been dangerous and audacious, his intelligence unreliable. Working under cover of darkness, Mirajdin had assembled the deadly components in his father's compound before digging a huge pit to accommodate the 20 yellow palm oil containers that housed the main charge of fertiliser based explosive.

As he'd been acutely aware, this had been the riskiest part of the operation. Not only was the home-made explosive mixture highly unstable but he had to avoid detection by the infidels' invisible eyes in the sky. Many brave emplacers had died positioning their devices, vaporised by their own explosives, or by the infidels' Hellfire missiles. He had required good fortune, as well as a cool head and a steady hand, and Allah had smiled upon him.

Next, he had buried the command wire with which to detonate the device in a 250 metre long trench that ran from the bomb to his current hiding place. Finally, just as his mentor Haji Jalander had instructed, he painstakingly concealed all evidence of his handiwork ensuring that none of the telltale ground signs, such as discoloration, disturbance or subsidence, remained to betray him.

Mirajdin had worked diligently and risked much for this moment and his labour had already been rewarded. An hour earlier the infidels had driven mine detection vehicles down the track but had failed to locate his device. He'd resisted the temptation to detonate the bomb under the American mine plough. A greater prize would follow.

All that was now required was patience.

Clouds of dust to the south indicated the imminent arrival of the kafir invaders as their lumbering armoured vehicles left the relative safety of the blacktopped highway and headed north on the unmetalled road into Zumbalay The infidels, cowering inside their vehicles, were coming to meet their fate.

Mirajdin had been trained in bomb making while studying at a religious seminary in the Pakistani province of Baluchistan. His device was the product of more than one country. The detonator was a blasting cap made in China, the firing cable from Iran. The main charge had been produced in a chemicals factory owned by a company traded on the derivatives markets in the United States of America.

Mirajdin's pulse raced and he prayed his nerves would not fail him. As he had done a thousand times already that morning, he committed himself to Allah's will.

Although Mirajdin invoked Allah in his endeavours to kill British servicemen his was not a Holy War. Mirajdin was a proud Muslim, but not a Jihadist nor even a Talib. He did not fight for reasons of faith or ideology.

Nor was his an intergenerational struggle against a colonial oppressor, even though his forebears had routed the British at the battle of Maiwand. As a wide-eyed toddler at his grandfather's knee, Mirajdin had listened in awe to bloody tales of the last stand of the 66th (Berkshire) Regiment of Foot at the Mundabad Ravine, not far from where he now lay.

These stories, passed down the generations by the village *spin zhiras*, had nothing but praise and admiration for the bravery of the Angrezis who'd fought to the last man in the defence of their Colours. It was said these men, surrounded by thousands, died with their faces to the enemy, fighting to the death and their courage was the wonder of all who saw it.

It was a courage Mirajdin did not recognise in the men who now came to avenge them, hiding as they did in armoured vehicles while raining death and destruction from the sky.

Although Mirajdin, along with many others, was of the firm conviction that the British had returned after 150 years to avenge their ancestors, his own motives for opposing them dated back to a much earlier time. As an Ishaqzai tribesman, Mirajdin fought to resolve an injustice imposed upon his people over two and a half centuries earlier when Ahmed Shah first united the Pashtun clans of Afghanistan and founded the Durrani Dynasty.

Prior to 1747 the Ishaqzai had been the dominant Pashtu tribe in Helmand. Under the Durrani Confederation their fortunes had waned and another tribe, the Barakzai had come to prominence. Loss of power and prestige had resulted in a loss of livestock, many lost their nomadic lifestyle, and some were also deprived of their respected status as warriors.

Impoverished Ishaqzai nomads were forced by circumstance to become farmers and earned the derogatory nickname *Sogzai* or Vegetable People. Ironically perhaps, the Vegetable People had learned to grow poppy and, under the Taliban, their fortunes had revived.

Mirajdin now fought the British not from religious zeal, or from racial hatred, but because the British, following the fall of the Taliban, had been duped by the Barakzai leadership into supporting their efforts to take control of the opium trade in Helmand. The British, and the Americans before them, had empowered the Barakzai by awarding them lucrative construction and security contracts. In return, the Barakzai had fooled the British into believing their old tribal rivals were insurgents, or Taliban.

In 2006, in the face of Barakzai intimidation, with the unwitting collusion of British troops, Mirajdin's family had been forced to abandon their home to the north-east of Gereshk and resettle in less fertile lands outside the green zone. Seen through the lens of a centuries-old intertribal rivalry, Mirajdin had endured this humiliation as a teenager and had silently vowed to restore his family and his people's honour. Six years later, lying in the dust beside the road, with pounding heart and trembling fingers, he was just moments from realising his pledge.

If God willed it.

Mirajdin was no more than an accidental insurgent. He fought the British simply because they were his rival's allies. His forefathers had contested Barakzai domination long before the arrival of the Angrezi kafirs, and his descendants would continue to do so long after they had departed.

Latitude:	31.80
Longitude:	64.51
Elevation:	834m
Met:	Sunny H:36°L:12°
DTG:	071903DSEP12

THE MEN OF No.2 Company,1ˢᵗ Battalion Grenadier Guards were a long way from Buckingham Palace. After nearly five months of almost constant combat they looked tired and haggard, their combats rumpled and dusty, as they stood around the map. Assault rifles littered every available horizontal surface and in one corner lay several sets of salt-encrusted body armour. Most of the men were sipping brews from battered thermos mugs as they listened to a series of briefings. A fug of stale body odour, farts and cigarettes suggested they'd already been there for some time.

By the very nature of their chosen profession infantrymen tend to be alpha males but there was one man, a little older than the rest, who comfortably dominated the group through sheer force of personality. Even to an outsider like myself, there was no doubting his authority. In a room full of armed and very dangerous men, Major Chris 'Sarge' Sargent stood out as the undisputed leader.

Sarge waved me over with a huge, calloused hand. Bitten and broken fingernails together with an unlit cigarette clamped between yellow-stained fingers belied his casual bonhomie. Behind the bluff, good-natured demeanour Sarge cared deeply about his men. Although he would never admit it, the burden of command in one of the most isolated and vulnerable outposts in Afghanistan was taking a personal toll.

A fearless leader, Sarge made the welfare of his soldiers his first and foremost priority, always reserving the most dangerous and difficult missions for himself. Sarge loved the army and, like all good commanders, confronted a terrible dilemma every time he committed his men to battle; risking the death of the thing he loved the most.

I'd been called to this meeting with his planning team to discuss their next mission. In a few days time Sarge would be taking the men of No.2 Company into Zumbalay where they would act as a decoy to draw insurgents away from an ANA operation in another part of the district. Our planners had assessed that putting a force back into Zumbalay for 48 hours would act as an irresistible draw to every insurgent with an AK47, thus allowing the ANA operation to go ahead largely uncontested.

I didn't envy them the task but I was more than happy to share my recent experiences. For the next 30 minutes or so Sarge and his team bombarded me with questions. I could see that my answers were helping to shape their plan. To protect against the known RPG threat, and some new intelligence that the insurgents had acquired an even more powerful SPG-9[1] recoilless rifle, Sarge opted for a compound takeover rather than a desert leaguer as the Danes had done on our last patrol. I was able to point out a cluster of compounds just south of the green zone, marked on Sarge's map as 24-41 X8C, that I reckoned would be large enough to accommodate his vehicles.

Next I outlined the problems and risks we'd encountered patrolling in the dense hemp and maize crops and the resultant extreme close quarter nature of the combat that had ensued. We'd ended up fighting the insurgents on their terms on terrain where they'd held the tactical advantage, and I reckoned we'd been very lucky not to take casualties.

I assured Sarge there was no need to take these risks in order to draw the Taliban's attention. Our presence in the desert hinterland had been provocation enough. Sarge agreed with my analysis and elected to establish a vehicle checkpoint (VCP) on the main track just outside the green zone rather than attempt framework patrolling within it. This would not only draw the insurgents, as the plan demanded, but would also restrict their freedom of movement to take on the ANA operation.

We discussed the benefits of an AUP presence on the checkpoint and agreed that an 'Afghan Face' to the operation would demonstrate a hitherto non-existent GIRoA capacity in Zumbalay. I suggested that Ed Whitten and his Police Advisory Team, who'd so wonderfully transformed the transit accommodation in PB Clifton, might be in a position to facilitate this.

As the questions began to dry up, Sarge slapped me heartily on the back and declared: *If you're not doing anything else old man, we'd love to have you on board.* He made it sound like an offer I couldn't refuse. But I had no desire to return to the Taliban Heart of Darkness and, as it happened, I was doing something else.

---

[1] **SPG-9**: The SPG-9 Kopye (Spear) is a Russian, tripod-mounted, man-portable recoilless rifle. It fires fin-stabilised, rocket-assisted high explosive and anti-tank projectiles.

When Sarge and his men were due to depart for Zumbalay I would have a little over a week remaining before my end-of-tour date. My plan was to beat a hasty retreat to Camp Bastion where I would count down the days sipping leisurely cappuccinos in the *Green Beans* café and indulging in a little retail therapy. Top of my shopping list was a Taliban Hunting Club t-shirt.

Inexplicably, I heard a voice, unmistakably my own, casually accepting Sarge's invitation as if he'd just suggested we pop down to 'The Dog and Duck' for a quick one on the way home.

What the fuck was I doing?

On reflection, it was Sarge's tremendous charisma that persuaded me, in a heartbeat, to give up my plans and join him. Like many great leaders, Sarge had the capacity to convince others to do things they would not otherwise do. I was not immune to his powers of persuasion. If ordinary men like me were capable of extraordinary things it was largely because we were led astray by men like Sarge.

The following morning I learned the sad news that Karl Whittle had died of his wounds in the Queen Elizabeth hospital in Birmingham. I needed no further reminder of the dangers of the mission we were about to undertake.

Latitude:	31.79
Longitude:	64.67
Elevation:	852m
Met:	Sunny H:37°L:10°
DTG:	091121DSEP12

MIRAJDIN LAY IN his dusty hiding place clutching the command wire in his sweaty palm. To initiate his device he needed only to place the wire's exposed end against the negative terminal of the vehicle battery beside him. It was a seemingly simple task made complex by the extreme danger of his situation and the enormity of what would follow. Mirajdin had never taken a life before. His own would never be the same after this moment.

Although he had invoked Allah's will many times that morning, Mirajdin was not unfamiliar with the teachings of the Qur'an that cherished the sanctity of human life. While he could not read the words of the Holy Book, he had recited so many of its verses as a child that they were now committed to his memory for evermore.

Al Qur'an 6:151: *...take not life, which God hath made sacred, except by way of justice and law: thus doth He command you, that ye may learn wisdom.*

Al Qur'an 5:32: *...if any one slew a person it would be as if he slew the whole people: and if any one saved a life, it would be as if he saved the life of the whole people.*

Al Qur'an 5:2: *Do not let your hatred of a people incite you to aggression.*

Al Qur'an 5:8: *And do not let ill-will towards any folk incite you so that you swerve from dealing justly. Be just; that is nearest to heedfulness.*

Mirajdin was equally familiar with the teachings that placed parents second only to Allah.

Al Qur'an 17:23: *And your Lord has decreed that you worship none but Him; and that you be dutiful to your parents. If one of them or both of them attain old age in your life, say not to them a word of disrespect, nor shout at them, but address them in terms of honour.*

And yet he had defied his father   to become a bomber. They had argued and quarrelled many times before he had departed for the seminary in Baluchistan. His father was no fool and knew precisely his motivations for attending and the lessons he would learn there.

On his return they had clashed again, this time over the company Mirajdin was now keeping. His father forbade him to associate with the Jihadis or to visit the home of Haji Jalander, the legendary old Mujahideen fighter whom they revered and who taught them tactics and fieldcraft while his grandchildren danced around his feet. It was here, defying his father's instructions, that he had met the charismatic Taliban commander, Mohammed Momin.

Momin had preached that killing the Americans and their allies was the individual duty of every Muslim who was able, in any country where this was possible. There could be no respite until the Aqsa mosque in Jerusalem and the Haram mosque in Mecca were freed from their grip, until the kafir armies had been shattered and were no longer capable of threatening even a single Muslim.

After his talk, Momin had ignored the entreaties of the other fighters, who were all vying for his attention, and instead approached Mirajdin. They chatted quietly together for several minutes. Momin reassured him that, in the eyes of Allah, he had a duty to stand up to the injustices bestowed upon his family and his people. His father might not appreciate it now, he told him, but in time would come to realise that Mirajdin was respecting not only his father as the Qur'an dictates, but also his Ishaqzai forefathers who had been humiliated at the hands of their rivals the Barakzai for centuries. In order to take up with the kafirs, the Barakzai had abandoned their faith and were apostates. For this offence against God there could be no human forgiveness. They could no longer call themselves true Muslims or even Pashtuns.

The fact that Momin chose to speak alone with Mirajdin had elevated his status amongst the young men whose company he now kept. Mirajdin had been shocked and dismayed to learn of Momin's death. Along with hundreds of others, he had travelled to Deh Adam Khan to attend his funeral. As what was left of Momin's body was committed to the earth his own resolve to act had hardened. Finally, when the infidels came to Zumbalay and killed so many of his new friends, he knew he must take action and put the skills he had learned in Baluchistan to good use.

Once again he sought the counsel of Haji Jalander. The wise old Muj had been Momin's friend and mentor. He was also a man who did not bend to the will of others. It was a quality Mirajdin much admired. Not only had he fearlessly resisted the Soviets, as everyone knew, but he had also defied Taliban enforcers to enter the ISAF fortress in Gereshk in search of his missing son-in-law. Unarmed yet unafraid, he had even confronted one of the Angrezi soldiers who'd come into the village and, it was said, chased him away with words alone.

The older man listened to Mirajdin's plan and imparted wisdom that had not been on offer in Baluchistan. He explained how to use an aiming marker to detonate the bomb directly beneath its target. He also counselled Mirajdin not to hit the lead vehicle but to hold his nerve and initiate the device under one of the larger vehicles somewhere towards the middle of the convoy. This would kill more infidels, and would split the convoy causing maximum confusion, thus facilitating his escape undetected.

Just as Haji Jalander had instructed, Mirajdin allowed the lead vehicle to pass. As the second vehicle came level with his aiming marker, dust thrown up by the convoy began to obscure his vision. Straining to see, he was forced to shift position slightly, inadvertently revealing himself to the infidel machine gunner in the top hatch of the second vehicle.

Even above the noise of the convoy, Mirajdin could hear the machine gunner's shouted warning to his comrades as he swung his weapon to face him. Their eyes locked for a moment before Mirajdin lunged for the battery pack and touched the exposed ends of the firing cable to the terminal post.

Latitude:	31.80
Longitude:	64.51
Elevation:	834m
Met:	Sunny H:37°L:10°
DTG:	090845DSEP12

AS I MADE my way down to the MOB Price vehicle park I consoled myself that this was a quick in-and-out operation. We would be on the ground for just 48 hours. This meant that I could be safely back in Bastion by Wednesday morning. All I had to do to get my personal Afghan exit strategy back on track was keep my head down.

In a break with military tradition, Sarge had decided against a move at first light and everyone seemed to be enjoying the leisurely start. Men stood around their vehicles in the morning sunshine, kicking tyres, smoking cigarettes and making last minute adjustments to their equipment. It was going to be another hot one.

I made my way over to Sarge's command group and reported in. At odds with strict regulations but in keeping with his extrovert character Sarge wore a blue patterned bandana around his neck. I went to great lengths to avoid drawing attention to myself in the field, even eschewing my badges of rank, but this was not Sarge's style. Where I tried to avoid the sniper's attention, Sarge dared him to take the shot. I did not say as much but I was glad, for my sake as well as his, that we'd significantly reduced the sniper threat on my last trip.

Sarge informed me that we were waiting for an American mine clearance team, callsign *War Hammer*, to prove the route. As soon as they gave the all-clear, he would order us to move out.

The British and American approaches to mine clearance varied significantly. The British policy was to try and out-think the emplacers by choosing unexpected routes, avoiding vulnerable points and maintaining extreme vigilance. The Americans preferred a more head-on technique.

Rather than avoiding the obvious route they would drive down it in specialist armoured vehicles equipped with flails, rollers and ploughs intended to detonate devices in their path. Although it ran counter to our own doctrine – we preferred to defuse devices rather than deliberately initiate them – it was an effective method of dealing with ordnance that relied on some kind of pressure plate to initiate the primary charge. It was less successful with other trigger methods, such as command pull or command wire devices, but the Americans assured Sarge they would take care of these as well.

With *War Hammer* in charge of route clearance, the plan was to drive down the main dirt road that linked Zumbalay to Highway 1. It was the same route the Jutland Dragoons had used ten days earlier but with one crucial difference. Prior to the Danish op, ISAF hadn't officially been anywhere near Zumbalay in over three years. The Danes had therefore taken a calculated risk that there would be no IEDs to contend with. This had proven to be correct and allowed us an unusual freedom of movement that had been a critical factor in the mission's success. It was now an equally safe bet that, having given the insurgents a bloody nose, the route and surrounding environs would have been heavily mined in the days after our departure.

Mastiff Pete was so convinced of this that he raised it as a concern on a number of occasions, but the *War Hammer* team seemed unfazed so, in the end, we let them get on with it.

Waiting for the order to move out was turning into something of a reunion. Mastiff Pete and his crews were there of course, as were Ed Whitten and Davo Davidson with their AUP mentoring team. I assumed Ed, like me, had been talked into coming on the op by Sarge. Although I didn't let on, I felt a twinge of guilt that I'd recommended him and his men for this one.

I spotted a few of the Jutland Dragoons I recognised and wandered over to say hello. They were briefing a small cluster of their British counterparts on what to expect in Zumbalay. I could tell their audience was either new to theatre or had not yet deployed outside the wire. It wasn't just their wide-eyed demeanour that betrayed them but their pristine body armour and unblemished knee pads. One or two were even wearing dropleg holsters. I smiled inwardly, recalling that the Danes had themselves been combat virgins only ten days earlier.

There were also a half dozen London Regiment soldiers going on the op, including PB. We'd last met, many months before, on the ranges in Sennybridge. At the time he'd called me a *fucking cunt, sir* when I fell on him from a great height, but he wasn't one to bear a grudge and we shook hands warmly. We chatted for several minutes. He tried to play it down, but I could tell he'd had a pretty crunchy time of it.

Finally the word came to mount up. As I departed to find my ride one of the London Regiment lads said:

See you on the other side, Sir.

At the time it struck me as a little dramatic. I fervently hoped this was going to be a straightforward VCP op. I'd done dozens of these over the last nine months and they'd all gone off without mishap. Just two days from now I'd be sitting in the *Green Beans* café, enveloped in the warm, dusky aroma of fresh-roasted coffee. After months of Danish crude oil, I could already taste the soothing, bitter-sweet, velvet cappuccino.

Latitude:	31.79
Longitude:	64.67
Elevation:	852m
Met:	Sunny H:37°L:10°
DTG:	091121DSEP12

SERGEANT DAVO DAVIDSON was taking no chances. Despite assurances from *War Hammer* that the route was clear, he was standing in the cupola of his Ridgeback patrol vehicle scanning the route ahead for ground sign. He ignored the sandblasting effect of the dust thrown up by Lieutenant Ed Whitten's lead vehicle 20 metres in front as he looked for the telltale signs of IED emplacement. The fingers of his left hand rested gently on the pressel of his radio. If he saw anything even remotely suspicious he would call a halt to the convoy and go forward with the Vallon to investigate.

As the Ridgeback approached a cluster of abandoned compounds Davo's sixth sense went into overdrive. The absence of local nationals going about their daily lives was a known combat indicator and Davo could see clear evidence that these particular compounds had been abandoned in haste. In addition to scanning the track ahead for IEDs he now began to scan the compounds for likely firing points. He briefly discussed his concerns over the intercom with his driver as they inched forward.

Lieutenant Whitten's vehicle had just cleared the last of the compounds when Davo spotted movement about 250 metres off the road in a narrow alley between two buildings. It was a perfect firing point and instinctively Davo flicked the safety catch of the GPMG as he traversed the weapon on its swivel mount to face this new threat.

As he did so a massive blast ripped through the Ridgeback, effortlessly flipping the 20 tonne vehicle onto its roof. Incredibly, the explosion failed to breach the hull and its other occupants, although gravely injured, would all survive the blast. Sergeant Davo Davidson, exposed in the top-side hatch, was not to be so lucky.

Davo, superb soldier, top bloke, loving husband and father, who had so proudly decorated his bed space in PB Clifton with pictures of his family, including a scan of his unborn baby, never regained consciousness. He died from his wounds before reaching Camp Bastion. He was the 427th British serviceman to die in Afghanistan. But he was the only one I knew personally.

Much later, at the inquest into Davo's death, one of the *War Hammer*'s American officers, stopping short of admitting they'd blundered, acknowledged they'd failed adequately to assess the risks and check for command wires, as they had promised they would.

Typically, there was no such prevarication from Sarge. He took full responsibility saying: *I made the call wrongly, but I made it in good faith.*

Davo was killed at the hands of an accidental insurgent engaged in a centuries old dispute in which the British had temporarily and inadvertently embroiled themselves. But his fate had been sealed before *War Hammer* gave the all-clear or Sarge ordered us to mount up.

Davo died that day because, 36 hours earlier, I'd not only suggested an *Afghan Face* to the operation but had also specifically recommended the excellent Police Advisory Team at PB Clifton for the task.

Latitude:	31.79
Longitude:	64.67
Elevation:	852m
Met:	Sunny H:36°L:10°
DTG:	131153DSEP12

AFTER DAVO'S DEATH 48 hours turned into 72, then 72 into 96 before I stopped counting. The *Green Beans* café was now but a dim and distant memory. Finally, 18 months after I'd first set eyes on the painting in the Grenadier Guards officers' mess, and with my chuff chart fast running out, I found myself in the company of Grenadiers, standing firm, holding ground, unwavering and resolute. When I'd first seen the painting I'd wondered if I had what it took to stand shoulder to shoulder with men of this calibre on the field of battle.

Now I knew the answer. All it had taken was a split-second lapse of my instinct for self-preservation. When I'd accepted Sarge's casual invitation to return to the Taliban Heart of Darkness I'd overlooked everything I'd learned on my previous visit. It should have been obvious to me that this was never going to be a straightforward VCP operation. With my days to go in single figures it would have been the easiest thing in the world to have declined. I was, after all, present at the briefing only in an advisory capacity. No one would have thought any the worse of me for it. But I'd accepted and here I was. Having failed to adequately plan for the worst I was now hoping for the best and praying there would be no more unpleasant surprises.

Ed Whitten, the young troop leader who commanded the Police Advisory Team at PB Clifton, was inspirational in the immediate aftermath of the bomb that killed Davo Davidson, his more experienced mentor, confidant and friend. It cannot have escaped him that he'd lived while Davo had died only because the bomber had, unaccountably, elected to detonate his device under the second rather than the lead vehicle in the convoy.

Perhaps the Chinese blasting cap had not activated at the first attempt.

Perhaps the Iranian firing cable had not delivered sufficient electrical charge across its 250 metre length.

Perhaps the American funded ammonium nitrate fertiliser had not triggered immediately.

Or perhaps the young bomber's trembling fingers had betrayed him.

Ed must have put any such thoughts to one side. He calmly took control of the situation, securing the perimeter and calling in helicopters to extract his mortally wounded friend and the vehicle's other casualties. There were many others who rallied round, risking their own lives to protect and save the wounded, but it was Ed who coordinated and inspired these activities, regaining control of a desperate situation before continuing on task.

Later that evening, after we'd established a secure bed down location for the night, I was able to speak briefly with Ed in the gathering gloom of his longest day. He remained calmly detached and determined to see the mission through. Sergeant Davo Davidson, who by now we knew had met his warrior's fate, would have been truly proud of him.

For my part, Davo's death was different from all the others. Whenever we had a KIA my initial shock and dismay at the news was always quickly replaced by relief, then with guilt and finally with a terrible self loathing. Relief that it wasn't me or anyone I knew. Guilt at the heavy price others must pay to satisfy my relief. Guilt that men half my age had been taken when, surely, I should have been ahead of them in the queue. And finally self-loathing at my cold-hearted analysis that their deaths statistically improved my own chances of returning home unscathed.

With Davo it was different. I knew Davo. We had shared banter and brews together. He had talked endlessly about his family and never wasted an opportunity to show off carefree happy snaps of his wife and kids. I knew those smiling, well-loved faces would soon appear on the front pages of national newspapers dressed in black and masked with grief. And I knew they had to bear this terrible pain, this devastating loss from which they would never fully recover, because I had recommended Davo and his team for this mission. However fervently I wished it so, nothing I could do would bring him back or relieve their suffering.

The day after Davo's death I found myself bedding down in a squalid outbuilding with a military dog handler and his charge, Soya, a beautiful fox red Labrador. Somehow, Soya's master had become separated from his kit and had no rations either for himself or his dog. We divided one of my own meagre ration packs between us and, with stomachs still rumbling, chatted quietly long into the night. After the events of the previous day only Soya, it seemed, could find solace in sleep, periodically farting heinously into the already foetid night air.

The following day all three of us were tasked to accompany a patrol to a nearby compound of interest. From the moment we stepped off we came under the unwelcome scrutiny of the Taliban. As the thermometer rose, so too did the intensity of the gun battle between us. Finally we were pinned down by a long range DShKM heavy machine gun.

The *Dushka*, or 'Lover' as it's affectionately known in Russian, has a fairly low rate of fire but each round can punch a hole in all but the very thickest of armour. The human body could not survive being struck by such a round and our foot patrol had nothing to match either the range or the lethality of the big gun. The Talib team manning the Lover knew this and made no attempt to conceal their location as they rained fire down upon us.

It was time to call in the Fast Movers.

As we hunkered down behind a compound wall our Joint Tactical Air Controller (JTAC) talked two American F16 pilots onto the enemy position. Moments later they appeared, as if from nowhere, seemingly skimming across the ground in a heat haze of their own making, before rolling up their target.

The Lover was silenced.

As the F16s screamed overhead, firing chaff countermeasures, something snapped in poor Soya's eager doggy brain. Unable to distinguish between friendly or hostile fire, it became all too much for him, and he howled plaintively before collapsing at his master's feet, shaking fearfully.

Soya was never quite the same again after that patrol. Whenever things kicked off, which was often, the sound of gunfire would reduce him to a quivering wreck. No longer able to perform his duties as a counter-IED dog, he would spend his days hanging around the command post. Even when rations were running low he was never short of scraps or love, willingly provided by the men who worked there manning the radios 24 hours a day.

The hapless dog was as much a part of our close-knit team as anyone else and it was agonising for all of   us to see his distress. None more so than his handler who was clearly heartbroken.

Just as our planners had hoped, our presence in the area was proving to be an irresistible draw. We had successfully, perhaps a little too successfully, distracted the Taliban from the main ANA operation. We were to learn later that this had gone off without a shot being fired, although it tragically cost the life of another Grenadier, Lance Corporal Duane Groom, killed by a roadside bomb while providing overwatch to the ANA as they withdrew.

Our plan had called for a 48 hour decoy. However, the insurgents had other ideas. As Haji Jalander had warned me, they seemed determined we should not leave alive, regardless of the cost to themselves.

In an almost exact facsimile of the moment captured by war artist Michael Alford two years earlier, No.2 Company now became trapped, or *fixed* as the military prefers to describe it, in Compound 24 X8C in the desert south of Zumbalay.

As compounds go it was pretty respectable. There was no hot and cold running water, nor any of the other basic amenities we have come to expect in the West, but it was clearly the comfortable home of a man of means. Intricately patterned, handwoven silk carpets covered the bare earth floors in many of the rooms, each of which was filled with sturdy hardwood furnishings. The master bedroom incorporated a generous walk-in wardrobe and elaborate tapestries adorned the walls.

The owner had not been expecting quite so many house guests. He was dismayed by our unexpected arrival. Dismay turned to disbelief when he was given just 30 minutes notice to pack up his possessions and his family and vacate his home. Even before he departed we had set about turning his once comfortable residence into a fortress.

This involved demolishing some of the outbuildings to accommodate our armoured vehicles as well as constructing fortified *sangar* or sentry positions from which to defend ourselves. Worst of all, the compound's fragrant courtyard garden was transformed into a foul smelling latrine.

A Company strength of fighting men generates a significant volume of shit each day. Each contribution is individually sealed by the producer in a WAG bag before being placed in a pit to which fuel oil is periodically added before burning. Separating soldiers from their faeces is an essential, if unpleasant, task if they are to remain fighting fit, but the damage to the poor man's garden must have been significant.

Nothing would grow there again for a very long time.

Whenever we requisitioned a compound we always generously compensated the owner for the inconvenience. I'd been told in training that the payments were so lucrative Afghans would queue up for the pleasure, but this was not borne out by my own experience. Not only did we evict the owner and his family, usually with little or no notice, but we also often modified the building to improve security. If we stayed any length of time the building would inevitably be further degraded by Taliban attacks. And finally there was all the smouldering feculence we'd leave behind.

Money might have repaired the damage, it might even have restored the shit-ravaged garden, but it seldom remained in the hands of the claimant long enough to do so. As soon as we departed Taliban enforcers would come knocking, roughly demanding the money be donated to the cause and not accepting *no* for an answer. I never met a compound owner who welcomed us into his home rubbing his hands with glee at the thought of the beating he would shortly receive before being relieved of the US dollars that had been so briefly in his possession.

Hollow assurances of a better life with GIRoA did little to sweeten the bitter pill.

Latitude:	31.79
Longitude:	64.67
Elevation:	852m
Met:	Sunny H:36°L:10°
DTG:	150644DSEP12

SARGE TAPPED TWO cigarettes, or *bangers* as he called them, from a battered pack and lit them both. Keeping one for himself he placed the other between my lips, tilted his head back and exhaled loudly, firing a plume of pale blue vapour skyward. I'm pretty sure he knew I didn't smoke but he was not a man who concerned himself with such trifling details.

At that moment, lung cancer was very low on the list of risk factors affecting my life expectancy. Fighting for our survival, trapped and cut off from our resupply chain, slowly but inexorably running out of supplies and ammunition, a choice blend of the world's finest tobaccos presented in a filter-tipped, king size cigarette was a precious commodity. It seemed churlish to decline his generosity.

Trying not to inhale, I let the smouldering cigarette dangle between my lips as I busied myself with the radio, attempting to re-establish comms with our ops room in Price, just a few klicks but a world away from our desperate and deteriorating situation.

A few hours earlier we'd learned that a Taliban suicide squad dressed in US Army uniforms had penetrated the Camp Bastion perimeter defences and destroyed a number of Harrier Jump Jets on the flight line.

A running battle had ensued and, even now, no one knew for sure if all the enemy fighters had been killed or captured. The Taliban had struck a devastating blow. Bastion was locked down and, from our lonely and isolated perspective, ISAF appeared to be in meltdown.

With our citadel breached we all knew, although it was not discussed, that our own position was now significantly more vulnerable. ISAF Main Effort[1] would be the restoration of security at Camp Bastion and

---

[1] **Main Effort (ME):** The Main Effort is a manoeuvre warfare concept that concentrates efforts on achieving objectives that lead to victory. It recognizes that, of all the activities going on within a command, one is the most critical to success at that moment in time. This becomes the focal point and receives priority for support of any kind.

until that was achieved we would be on our own. Resupply and extraction plans were on hold and all the surveillance and reconnaissance assets we might usually rely upon to support our lonely and exposed position were now reallocated to securing the Bastion perimeter.

To make matters worse, we simultaneously learned of the death of Lance Corporal Duane Groom. Duane was a Grenadier and was well known to many of the No. 2 Company men. His loss was keenly felt.

The deaths of Davo Davidson and now Duane, coupled with the hammer blow of the Bastion raid, preyed on all our minds but there was little time for reflection or mourning. Emboldened by their recent successes, the Taliban now pressed home their attacks on our own positions.

Over the course of the previous 48 hours a number of unsuccessful attempts had been made to extract our beleaguered force. An armoured relief column stalled when one of the *War Hammer* vehicles was knocked out by another massive IED, thankfully without any further casualties. Extraction by helicopter was now ruled out. Fighting had become so intense that the risk of losing one of the RAF's precious Chinook helicopters had been deemed too great.

Understanding the strategic impact the loss of a Chinook helicopter would have on the entire campaign, coming so soon after the raid on Camp Bastion, was one thing. Being on the tactical end of that decision was quite another. Knowing it was unquestionably the right decision did not bring any comfort to the defenders of Compound 24 X8C.

Given the gravity of our situation, Sarge was now considering a fighting withdrawal in contact, something we'd trained for in Canada the previous year but never seriously imagined we would be called upon to perform. Sarge's plan was to hike out under cover of darkness through the desert to a designated pick-up point on Highway One, the tarmac road to our south which linked Kandahar and Gereshk.

It was, without question, the option of last resort. The insurgents had now seeded the whole area with IEDs and I had no doubt they would harass the withdrawing force all the way to the highway. It was impossible to imagine we could make the distance without sustaining casualties.

I was reminded of another painting, this one by the Victorian artist Lady Elizabeth Butler, entitled 'Remnants of an Army'. It portrays William Brydon, the only British survivor of the 1842 retreat from Kabul, approaching the gates of Jalalabad fort on his dying horse. I was familiar with the painting because the artist had also painted a picture of my own unit, the London Irish Rifles at the battle of Loos. In her autobiography she wrote: *I never painted for the glory of war, but to portray its pathos and heroism.* Qualities which were not in short supply in Zumbalay that week as we contemplated the unthinkable.

By now, like pretty much everyone else in Task Force Helmand, I'd forgotten the reasons why we'd gone to war. It was certainly no longer *to help and protect the Afghan people to reconstruct their economy and democracy* as John Reid had directed back in 2006. I was simply fighting for the exceptional young men to the left and right of me, proud to be one amongst their number, determined not to let them or myself down. Undeniably old in comparison, creaking dangerously under the weight of all my equipment, but still able to do my bit when called upon.

It was all that now mattered. To me it mattered a very great deal.

Later that day Sarge called us together and briefed us that Mastiff Pete and his indomitable crews would make one last attempt to reach us by first light the following morning. If they were unsuccessful he warned us we should prepare to walk out.

The stakes could not have been higher.

After the briefing the No. 2 Company Sergeant Major, Warrant Officer Class Two Mark Cox organised a team photo. It would most likely be the last time we were all assembled in the same place and he wanted a record for the Company scrap book.

Just as he'd gathered everyone together in front of one of the sangars, yet another firefight kicked off. Incoming rounds peppered the walls of the compound only a few metres away and we all made to take evasive action. But Company Sergeant Major Cox was having none of it. In tones that brooked no disobedience he ordered us not to move. As I willed the hapless photographer to get on with it I evaluated the competing risks of sustaining a potentially lethal gunshot wound with that of incurring the displeasure of Sarge's iron enforcer.

I elected to comply with his direction.

With a few sideways glances, so too did everyone else.

Latitude:	31.80
Longitude:	64.51
Elevation:	834m
Met:	Sunny H:37°L:10°
DTG:	190730DSEP12

I HOIST MY bergan onto my shoulder as the RAF *Loadie* waves me forward from the Chinook's open ramp. I duck my head against the roar of the tail rotor and the downwash of exhaust fumes from the aircraft's twin Textron Lycoming turboshaft engines, and walk up the ramp and out of MOB Price for ever.

As my eyes adjust to the gloom of the interior I see that the aircraft is almost empty. Speech is impossible and the Loadie points me towards a small gaggle of soldiers sitting up front. I ignore his instructions, plonk myself on the seat closest to the tailgate and burst into tears. As the aircraft shudders into yet another cloudless Afghan sky the Loadie is kind enough to pretend he hasn't noticed and leaves me to it. I don't really know why I'm crying.

Tears of joy that I'm going home, soon to be reunited with my beloved sons, Harry and Alfie.

Tears of grief for those who have already returned in metal caskets and who will never again embrace the ones they love and died to protect.

Tears of frustration that we had achieved so little in Afghanistan, and at such a price.

Tears of sadness that my great mid-life adventure is all but over and I may never again thrill so keenly to the buzz of cheating death.

Tears of anguish that I must now face up to the realities of my failed marriage and my financial ruin.

48 hours earlier, Mastiff Pete had finally made it through the desert to relieve us. Not for the first time, he and his men had fearlessly risked their own lives to save those of others. They were an extraordinary, yet unassuming, band of brothers to whom I will forever be indebted. I am proud to say I have walked among them.

Inexplicably, after days of relentless combat, the Taliban

had let us go with barely a shot fired.

On our return to MOB Price we'd staged through Patrol Base Hazrat, another dusty and isolated ISAF base to the south of the Helmand River. Here we'd received a hot meal, and been stared at by men when they thought we were not looking. They had not shared our experience and wondered how it must have been. As we waited to depart, someone had taken a group photo of the half dozen London Regiment soldiers who'd been on the op.

When I look at it months later I see what caused those others to stare.

Six men sit in a tight huddle on the ground dressed in filthy, salt-rimed combat uniforms. Deep lines etched across dusty, unshaven faces. Discarded kit and equipment litters the scene, body armour, assault rifles, a Vallon mine detector. Each man appears lost in his own thoughts, gazing intently from the photo as if focussing on some unseen object very far away. It is the detached look of battle-weary men I'd seen in photographs from other wars made more shockingly personal because one of the faces is my own.

Although four of the six would drift away from the London Regiment in the months ahead, disillusioned by war, or perhaps by the absence of war, this same photo would later be used in an army recruiting poster.

Returning to MOB Price I found myself a stranger in my own home. While I'd been detained in Zumbalay the remainder of the headquarters staff had handed over to a new team. I imagined they must all now be sitting in the *Green Beans* café sipping iced cappuccinos waiting for the flight home. A flight I was in danger of missing if I didn't get a move on.

It was a curiously dislocating experience. After nine months I knew every grimy, dusty, sun-scorched corner of the base like I knew the back of my own hand. But where these spaces had once been filled with familiar faces, now there were only strangers. Everyone was very polite but it was clear they wanted me out of the way so they could get on with their own war.

I spent an hour with Colonel James' replacement briefing him on various aspects of the human terrain he was inheriting. Although he pretended to jot a few desultory notes in his pocketbook I could tell he wasn't listening. He already had his own plans and his own agenda.

I felt pushed aside, ruefully realising how it must have felt for Colonel Ken and his staff all those months ago when we'd arrived fresh-faced and eager to replace them.

It was impossible not to reflect on the shortcomings of six month operational rotations with the resultant institutional memory loss every time a headquarters changed hands. The majority of insurgents were engaged in the same struggle for power that had consumed their forebears for generations, in which progress was measured over decades and centuries, rather than over weeks and months.

With everyone eager to see the back of me, I packed my kit, booked a flight back to Bastion for the following morning and went in search of Sultaan to say my farewells. But the District Communications Advisor was nowhere to be found.

The following morning dawns just like any other in Afghanistan. The fumes from burning faeces catch at the back of my throat. A distant call to morning prayer competes with the incessant background hum of the camp's many generators. Orderly queues begin to form in all the usual places: at the egalitarian ablution blocks where there are no privileges of rank; outside the D-FAC where those standing in line must tussle with the daily conundrum of a full-fat, sodium enriched English breakfast or tinned grapefruit segments; in front of the ostentatiously titled Welfare Centre, lifeline to the world to which I will shortly return.

Despite the early hour the Kuffen is already doing a roaring trade as bleary-eyed citizens of MOB Price kick-start their day with a cup of coffee so strong it would carry a health warning back in Denmark. Siyal, the MOB Price laundryman is similarly busy, graciously accepting bags of dirty washing from all comers, the contents of which he will cheerfully transform to a homogeneous grey-green - the colour of true love.

In the nine months I've been here nothing much has changed in MOB Price. I've passed through its fortified walls almost unnoticed. My presence has done little, if anything, to alter the daily rhythms of the place as I'd hoped it might when I first embarked on my journey. With the benefit of hindsight I now know better. Nothing much has changed in Nahr-E-Saraj in half a millennium.

One more infidel, more or less, has made no difference.

I make my way down to the helipad weighed down by these thoughts. But there is one load that will shortly be lightened. I have one more appointment to keep before turning my back on Afghanistan. I'm party to one of the best kept secrets in Task Force Helmand and I'm about to exploit that knowledge.

Unbeknown to the vast majority of MOB Price's occupants, the three man Army Air Corps team who manage the busy HLS[1] have somehow sequestered a Tactical Base Ablution Unit fit for a President. While the rest of us have washed in communal stainless steel troughs and squatted over seatless latrines, they have relieved themselves behind hardwood partitions into luxury porcelain toilets with soft-close seats and lids. The walls are adorned with framed prints of exotic flowers and generous individual hand basins are accoutred with perfumed liquid soap dispensers. It is, without doubt, the finest toilet block in the whole of Afghanistan.

And so, my final act in MOB Price is to take a secret luxury shit.

---

[1] **HLS**: Helicopter Landing Site

APPENDICES

A MAN WHO HAS NOTHING WHICH HE

A man who has nothing which he
is willing to fight for, nothing
which he cares more about than he
does about his personal safety,
is a miserable creature.
MISERABLE CREATURE.

Red tape chokes Army's vital recruitment drive

One year on, an absent writer is still making her presence felt

Latitude:	51.75
Longitude:	-1.58
Elevation:	84m
Met:	Overcast H:18°L:8°
DTG:	241530ZSEP12

 Chris Green Thursday September 20, 2012 at 3:05pm

Leg 1 complete: PRICE to BASTION. Weapons, ammunition and body armour returned to the Quarter Master's stores. After 9 months I feel a bit naked without them. Next stop the Green Beans Cafe for iced frappucino. I now have a whole 24 hours with nothing to do before flying to Cyprus at stupid o'clock on Saturday morning. To those we've left behind, stay safe and we'll see you on the other side.

 Chris Green Sunday September 23, 2012 at 11:23am

Legs 2 and 3 complete: BASTION to MINHAD overnight and then MINHAD to CYPRUS this morning. Just enjoyed a morning swim in the Mediterranean and have mandatory briefings to look forward to this afternoon. Assuming the RAF can keep to the schedule we should be back in the UK tomorrow afternoon.

 Chris Green Monday September 24, 2012 at 3:30pm

Touchdown!

AS I HURRY from my train at London Bridge station I glance at my Citizen Divers watch, my constant companion of the last 20 years.

I don't want to be late for this appointment.

I notice that the black canvas military strap I fitted before departing for Afghan is caked in Helmand Province. Until this moment I've been oblivious to this but it's impossible to miss against the cuff of the white dress shirt I'm wearing under my velvet blazer.

Save for my watch, I'm in full   civilian mode, completely invisible amongst the multitude of commuters who criss-cross the station's concourse. Except, perhaps, that where they stride with confidence and purpose along unseen tramlines of relentless repetition my own trajectory is less certain. I'm an untethered element cast adrift in the throng.

I make my faltering way to the exit on London Bridge Street where The Shard towers above the railway lines that inspired it. The vast obelisk of glass and steel is a monument to a world of consumerism and excess that I turned my back on, but which I've been fighting to protect.

The irony is lost on me. At any moment two beautiful boys will appear at the station entrance and I'm straining to catch my first glimpse of them in the crowd.

Jane and I have been unable to agree on a reunion prior to this moment. Harry and Alfie are not waiting for the plane to touch down at RAF Brize Norton as I'd often daydreamed they might be. Nor are they present when our coach is mobbed by excited families as it swings onto the parade square at Lille Barracks in Aldershot – the start and end point of my Afghan Adventure.

I've been a forlorn bystander as colleagues push past me to embrace their partners or bundle their delighted children into their arms. Banners, balloons and even cakes are exchanged along with a multitude of kisses. Some affectionate, some passionate, some X-rated, but all of them heartfelt. Alone in this welter of excitement, I make my way through the happy throng and head disconsolately towards the camp exit. It dawns on me that I don't know where I'm going.

I keep walking.

As part of my mandatory 'decompression' programme I'm required to spend the next 48 hours on the base. But there's no accommodation for me. Eventually I'm quartered in a condemned block that is awaiting demolition in another part of the garrison. It is eerily silent, cold and gloomy and matches my mood perfectly.

General George Patton warned that *Glory is fleeting.* This doesn't feel like an especially warm welcome from a grateful nation.

In the end it is my sister, Edwina who comes to the rescue. As soon as I'm released from my military bonds of service she takes a day off work to travel to York and collect the boys. We're in constant contact throughout our respective journeys and so, by accident rather than design, our rendezvous is a railway station. I can't think of a better location for a reunion.

I catch a glimpse of Harry weaving through the crowd a split second before he's airborne and hurtling towards me at speed. I have just time to catch him in my arms but not quite enough time to stay on my feet. I go down hard, but the cold stone platform is a feather bed in the joy of that moment. Alfie is only a few paces behind his brother and with a glorious cry of *BUNDLE!* jumps knees first onto my chest.

We roll around on the floor for a while, just as we'd done on the lawns of Gooseberry Hall five months earlier, oblivious to the commuters who step around and over us. My wonderful sister, who has made it all possible, stands back and allows us to revel in the occasion.

The journey that started at the MOB Price helipad six days and 4,457 miles earlier is finally over.

I'm home at last.

In the years before I became disillusioned with my life of comfortable consumerism I would wake at 5.15am each workday morning in order to fund our pointlessly extravagant existence. In those days Harry and Alfie would often sleep in our bed and I would lie in the dark for a few minutes, enjoying the warmth of my family beside me. It increasingly became the highlight of my day and I wondered why I needed such a large house and quite so many belongings when everything in the world that actually mattered fitted comfortably within the precinct of our double bed.

As Harry and Alfie turn me black and blue with their love on the station concourse, I realise I've been right all along to exchange possessions for experiences. I haven't missed my designer clothes, my trophy house or my luxury goods even once.

Being reunited with my children, on the other hand, is an unforgettable moment that I will treasure for eternity.

Latitude:	51.49
Longitude:	-0.13
Elevation:	12m
Met:	Overcast, some showers H:10°L:3°
DTG:	102058ZOCT12

TWO WEEKS LATER I attended a dinner at which I was required to give a speech in front of Prince Edward, the Honorary Royal Colonel of the London Regiment. I still had Afghanistan in my head, under my fingernails and in my hair – what little I had left. Just a few weeks earlier I'd been sitting on the dusty floor of Compound 24, eating cold chicken pasta with a dirty spoon from a plastic bag in the company of unwashed men. Tonight I was sitting with Royalty enjoying a four course meal served from a silver salver.

I'd rehearsed my speech with Dad and my brother, Alex who both gave it the thumbs up. Of course, it didn't compare with the eve-of-battle speech made by Colonel Tim Collins to the 1st Battalion the Royal Irish Regiment in Iraq in 2003, but this was a different occasion and a different purpose. I hoped it would do the job:

Your Royal Highness, Honoured Guests, Sir, Ladies and Gentlemen.

It gives me great pleasure to report that VIMY Company, less seven men under the watchful eye of Company Sergeant Major Bland, are safely returned from combat operations in Afghanistan with Combined Force Nahr E Saraj North. Those remaining few are due to return home in the next five days when, Inshallah, we will be able to celebrate more fully.

Just a little over two years ago in September 2010, following the Regiment's annual training package at RAF St Mawgan, nearly 200 men and women from The London Regiment expressed interest in volunteering for operational service on Operation HERRICK 16 and 17.

This in itself was quite some achievement given that in the six years prior the Regiment had deployed over 350 infantrymen, the majority in the close combat role, to both Op TELIC and Op HERRICK and, at that time already had 60 soldiers in Afghanistan serving with 1st Battalion Scots Guards and the Duke of Lancaster's Regiment.

By 25 November 2011 the HERRICK 16 cohort had formed

and VIMY Company was raised comprising four Officers, three Warrant Officers and 51 other ranks who all successfully mobilised following a year long training package taking in the Canadian Prairie, Sunny Sennybridge, even sunnier Warcop and the habitual delights of every London based TA soldier, the Longmore Training area.

This, of course, was just the beginning. To borrow a phrase from Simon Cowell's X-Factor (which I know you all secretly watch) over the ensuing 11 months we have all embarked on our own incredible journey.

Each one of us has been tested and will forever be marked by the experience. For many it has been the self-acknowledged making of them – turning boys into men. For the majority it has fulfilled a desire to live a life less ordinary, to see something of the world and to give something back in the service of their country. A few, sadly, will bear the scars of their experience forever and must rebuild their lives completely. We must watch over all of them in the months and years ahead.

Whatever each of the men of VIMY Company takes from this experience it will be their story to tell their partners, friends, work colleagues, children and, one day perhaps, grandchildren. All of whom can re-tell these tales and be proud to have known a soldier from VIMY Company.

The statistics, however, give you some idea of their collective experience: During 239 days in Afghanistan the combined British, Danish and Afghan battlegroup with which VIMY Company served and fought was engaged in 402 small arms fire contacts, suffered 117 IED strikes and a further 241 IED finds. We also tragically lost 28 killed in action, including:

Guardsman Michael Rolland

Lance Corporal James Ashworth

Guardsman Jamie Shadrake

My voice cracked as I tried to read out the names of those soldiers from our battlegroup who would not be returning to their families, who would not be slapped on the back for a job well done at dinners such as this one. It was several long moments before I was able to regain my composure and continue:

Guardsman Karl Whittle

Guardsman Duane Groom

All from the 1st Battalion Grenadier Guards and

Sgt Lee Davidson from the Light Dragoons.

We also suffered a further 149 wounded in action, including our own Lance Corporal Wilson, Lance Corporal Costly and Private Lyon.

There have been individual acts of heroism and bravery which one hopes will be recognised in due course but what I am proud to be able to report to you this evening is that collectively the men and two women of VIMY Company have not been found wanting. They have lived and fought side-by-side and indistinguishable from their Regular counterparts without fear or favour.

I'm proud to count myself one amongst them.

History will ultimately judge whether this investment in blood and treasure was worthwhile but for the last six months at least a small town in Afghanistan, roughly the size of Aldershot, has been a significantly safer place to live. Violence in Gereshk is at a 5 year low and at a level where Afghan National Army and police forces have been able to take the lead in security provision. Governance is stable and taking its first tentative steps as a credible administration and most importantly of all, the economy is booming. These are significant advances, not yet irreversible, but we must hope we have created a sufficiently compelling glimpse of what life could be like that the majority of Afghans will support a GIRoA administration and resist sliding back into the bad old days of uncertainty and violence.

As proud as I am of VIMY Company we are, of course, already yesterday's men and our thoughts must now turn to the 22 men of GAZA Company, recently deployed on HERRICK 17. We wish them well as they take up the baton of the Regiment's ninth consecutive year of operational service and await their own safe return to the Regimental fold.

For now though, it's good to be   home.

By the time I finished my eyes were full of tears and I was shaking so much I could barely read my script.

It reminded me of the lunch many weeks before in the Bastion D-FAC when I lost the plot at some REMFs who were complaining that *Op Minimise* was interfering with their social lives. Like then, my colleagues sitting around the table look a little embarrassed for me, pretending not to notice that I've fluffed my speech in front of Royalty. Like then, I know they all think I've got PTSD but it's bollocks.

I'm fine.

I think.

After the dinner was over and the Royal Colonel had left I was approached by a soft-spoken officer who asked if he could have a copy of my speech. I was happy to oblige and gave him the tear-stained script that was still in my pocket. As we chatted I discovered that he was none other than Lieutenant Colonel Christopher MacGregor, author of *My Daddy's Going Away*. I was able to tell him how much I'd enjoyed reading his book with Harry and Alfie prior to deployment and how it had inspired me to seek out the Ursa Major constellation, known to the boys and me as the *Saucepan*, in the dazzling night skies over Afghanistan.

When writing my speech I was surprised by how easy it was to accede to the self-deception that enveloped the mission in Afghanistan. I brushed aside the flaws and failings that had been so painfully obvious to me, and to many others, at the time. As I wrote I was being at best naïvely optimistic, at worst deliberately duplicitous.

It rather depended on who you asked whether they thought *a small town in Afghanistan has been a significantly safer place to live.* There were many, like Haji Gul the hawaladar, who had felt compelled to flee the city.

I didn't really believe that the Afghan National Army and police forces had the credibility or the capacity *to take the lead in security provision.* Ghullie Khan, the District Chief of Police continued to prey on little boys whilst presiding over a corrupt and narco-compliant AUP. Captain Manan and many other ANA officers seemed set on local power sharing arrangements with their Taliban counterparts. They had little or no interest in securing the contested areas of the Kakoran Gap or

Zumbalay where we had endured the fiercest fighting and suffered the heaviest casualties.

Given what I knew about Salim Rodi, the dipsomaniac District Governor and the manner in which DfID had presided over the Community Council elections it was laughable for me to suggest that *Governance is stable and taking its first tentative steps as a credible administration.* Nor did I believe for one minute that the corrupt and broken Government of the Islamic Republic of Afghanistan had the support of the majority of ordinary Afghans, who would *resist sliding back into the bad old days of uncertainty and violence.*

About the only declaration I made that had even a shred of truth to it was the claim that *the economy is booming* but this was not something for which GIRoA, DfID or the British military could take any credit. Gereshk was booming because it had become the distribution centre for the billion dollar Helmand opium industry.

Making such outlandish and ridiculous claims, especially in the company of Royalty, was probably treasonable. So why did I say these things?

Latitude:	51.34
Longitude:	-0.74
Elevation:	86m
Met:	Sunny spells H: 12°L: 0°
DTG:	071242ZNOV12

AFTER A 28 year hiatus I'd returned to the Royal Military Academy Sandhurst to participate in the *Herrick 16* Mission Exploitation Symposium. Taking very great care not to park on The Colour Sergeant's parade square, I made my way across to the conference hall. According to the organisers the purpose of the seminar was *to lead and drive Army learning and rapid adaptation to deliver enhanced operational capability through improved doctrine, training, structures and equipment.*

This was to be delivered through *a responsive lessons-learned procedure, which aims to connect returning SMEs (Subject Matter Experts) with capability stakeholders, and provide a suitable forum to enable constructive discussion of current operational issues/challenges with rapid feedback to current training, driving short term adjustments to operational practice, set within a force development culture, that shapes medium term capability.*

I was, by now, familiar with the army's preference for convoluted syntax. But my own motivations for attending were not fully aligned with *force development culture*. I was much more interested in saying my goodbyes to the men and women of the British Army with whom I'd shared the last nine months of my life. After a period of well-deserved leave, the majority would be soldiering on, while my own life would be moving in a new, as yet uncharted, direction.

It was time to say goodbye to men like Lieutenant Colonel James Bowder, with whom I'd entered into a pact of fealty on a cold and frosty morning some 12 months earlier and who had presided over almost every aspect of my life since then. Men like Stumpy Keeley, who'd spared me from further travel on the Kandahar–Herat Highway in the *mobile fucking shower unit.* Young men like Ed Whitten, Owen Davis, Peter Eadon and others who had so warmly invited an ageing stranger to share their brews and their battlespace.

In the worlds we'd come from and were now returning to we had almost nothing in common and I knew it was unlikely we would meet again. For a few brief months our   lives had crossed and mine had been enriched by their generosity of spirit, their irrepressible good humour, their relentless banter and above all by their inspirational courage and devotion to duty.

There was, however, another reason why I was attending the symposium. Brigadier Douglas Chalmers, the Task Force Helmand Commander was to give a keynote address. I'd made some potentially treasonous claims in my after-dinner speech about the progress of the mission in Afghanistan. I was curious to hear what he had to say.

Naturally the senior British officer in Helmand Province could speak only of success. His military masters and his future career prospects depended upon this. But he chose some unusual metrics that suggested, perhaps, that he too had private reservations. He even touched upon the Helmand malaise of self-deception to which I had myself acceded.

His commanders and advisors, he told us, would often tell him what he wanted to hear. In order to get to the *crystal truth* about the state of Helmand he ended up talking to butchers and grocers instead.

I picked them because the Afghan capacity to eat meat is unrivalled on the planet, and the need for them to get a good supply is quite prevalent. On earlier tours I saw they were only really selling goat and chicken and on this tour I saw a lot more beef. Now, cattle are expensive and when you slaughter a cow, with a lack of refrigeration, you need to have the confidence to sell that cow. I saw a lot more cattle being slaughtered and a lot more cattle in people's compounds.

I became fixated by tomatoes... it is quite a soft fruit and easily damaged, and again there is a lack of refrigeration. The market stalls were never without tomatoes. And the ability for them to be moved from the villages to the market towns was a good indication of the freedom of movement that the stall holders have.

From those two elements I got a sense of the micro economics in the market towns and cities.

The Brigadier was right. Beef and tomatoes were both prevalent in the local markets and bazaars, and there seemed to be no shortage of customers with sufficient disposable income to purchase such luxury foodstuffs.

But I was less certain of the causality he presumed. The

explosion of poppy production over which the British had inadvertently presided was more likely to be at the heart of the economic growth he described. Nahr-E-Saraj remained the most violent district in the most violent province in the whole of Afghanistan, manifestly unable to sustain itself on beef and tomatoes rather than poppy.

I think the Brigadier knew this too. I think he also knew, but could not publicly state, that there could be no effective military solution when the political objective was so far from aligned with the country's underlying social framework.

DfID's state building hubris and incompetence, together with the tsunami of poorly regulated international aid and the vested interests of the narco-industry, had combined to create one of the most corrupt nations on earth, alongside Somalia and North Korea. These were metrics of which Brigadier Chalmers was surely aware but could not discuss. So instead he spoke of *cautious optimism* for the future.

I took this to be code for an excess of caution coupled with a lack of optimism.

If the Brigadier was visiting the bazaars and talking to the stall holders as he claimed, then he must have seen the same things I had seen. He too must have observed the dissonance between the official narrative of a better life with GIRoA and the evidence of his own eyes and ears. Or perhaps, despite his best efforts, the butchers and grocers he spoke to told him only what they thought he wanted to hear.

Brigadier Chalmers was clearly an intelligent and experienced officer and I did not believe he was blind to the realities of the failing Afghan mission. He did, however, have the unenviable task of motivating men for battle and of justifying whatever pain and suffering might then result. This may well have convinced him to keep his own counsel, for which I would not blame him.

In preparing for Afghanistan I'd been much motivated by the British 19th century philosopher, John Stuart Mill. Although Mill had no personal experience of combat he'd theorised that an *honest war* could be a means of personal regeneration.

At a time when I was trying to seek some purpose and guidance in my life beyond the accumulation of wealth and possessions I'd seized upon this notion to justify abandoning my wife and young children in the pursuit of some higher purpose.

With hindsight, despite our very best intentions, it seemed we all had fought under a misapprehension. Rather than *protect other human beings against tyrannical injustice* we had preserved tyrannical injustice in the form of a hopelessly corrupt and irredeemable government.

We had been *used as mere human instruments for firing cannon or thrusting bayonets, in the service and for the selfish purposes* of a governor in the pay of the illegal opium trade and of a police chief feathering his own nest and lining it with little boys for unspeakable purposes.

Rather than face up to the unpleasant reality of the things we knew to be happening around us, and which we appeared to be perpetuating, we blinded ourselves with self-deceit.

Perhaps it was fanciful thinking on my part to believe that Brigadier Chalmers might share my own deep misgivings. After all we had met only once before when he had misjudged my efforts to influence policy in Afghanistan as *deeply impressive.* But if I was right, we were not alone in self-deceit.

It enveloped us all:

In the pronouncements of the Provincial Reconstruction Team; in the declarations of successive Prime Ministers; in the statements of visiting government officials, movie stars, musicians and glamour models; in the *cautiously optimistic* reports of the international media; in the glittering array of honours and awards bestowed upon Afghan veterans, and in the millions donated to service charities.

Even though, in my heart of hearts, I knew these claims to be false I perpetuated them myself because I desperately wanted them to be true. Not because national pride or high profile political and military careers were at stake – although this was certainly the case. I wanted to record success because, in the previous nine months, I had seen men killed and others grievously wounded in the pursuit of these aims. Their sacrifice should mean something. The pain and suffering endured by their loved ones should not be in vain.

So, rather than admit the possibility of failure I embraced the deceit and, to my shame, I found myself   basking in its warming glow of self-satisfaction. I consoled any inner misgivings by telling myself I wasn't a government minister, or a glamour model, so what did I know?

Perhaps in years to come the fourth Anglo-Afghan War (2003–2014) would be seen as a blueprint for military intervention, counter-insurgency, international development and state building. Catriona Laing, the head of the Helmand PRT seemed to think so when she earnestly pronounced:

We have presented the people of Helmand with an opportunity. They have grabbed it enthusiastically, confidently… it's now in their hands for the future.

But I was having a hard time convincing my inner self that history would agree with her.

Latitude:	51.51
Longitude:	-0.09
Elevation:	29m
Met:	Overcast, some showers H:10°L:3°
DTG:	041333ZNOV12

THIS WAS MY big moment.

I raised myself up to my full height, pulled my shoulders back, puffed my chest out and sucked my belly in.

Vimy Company will move to the right in column of route, right turn!

I bellowed the words of command at the top of my voice, rolling my Rs for as long as I dared. As I did so 54 men pivoted in unison through 90 degrees on the heel of their right foot, raised their left knee until the thigh came parallel to the ground and then completed the movement by crashing their heel back into the tarmac. The resultant noise echoed down Aldermanbury Street.

Next, I moved off to take up my position at the head of the column. Setting aside the birth of my sons Harry and Alfie, this was quite possibly the proudest day of my life. I was about to lead 54 reservists, all of whom had risked life and limb in the service of their regiment, their capital and their country, into the ceremonial heart of the City of London.

In a few short moments, in front of hundreds of proud friends and family members, Alderman David Wootton the 684th Lord Mayor of London would welcome home the City's returning sons from the killing zone of Helmand's front line.

But not until I gave the order.

The world now stood still, waiting on my next word of command. I kept the world waiting, savouring the moment.

Somewhere behind me someone growled *Get a fucking move on, Sir* but I was not going to be rushed.

Over the course of the next few minutes I would take the Company through a series of predetermined drill movements that would culminate in the presentation of   operational service medals to each of the men. A lot was now riding on how well I'd memorised the words of command. If I gave the wrong orders, or gave them in the wrong sequence, chaos would ensue behind me.

I wasn't feeling the pressure though. To the bemusement of passing ramblers, I'd practised the routine on the lawns at Gooseberry Hall with ill-disciplined Labradors, impetuous teenagers and giggling children in the ranks. During one rehearsal, overcome by the solemnity of the occasion perhaps, one of the Labs had made off with the Lord Mayor's understudy, Kermit the Frog, clamped between his drooling jaws.

By comparison this was going to be easy.

Vimy Company…

…by the left…

quick march!

The combined pipes and drums of the London Regiment began to play and I led the Company, my heart bursting with pride, through the Aldermanbury Gate and onto the inner quadrangle of London's ancient Guildhall. The foundation stones across which we marched had been laid in 1411 in the reign of King Henry IV, the same year Ulugh Beg was coronated Sovereign Ruler of Afghanistan.

Our homecoming parade was to receive national press and television coverage and even feature on the army's own website and Facebook pages. But army bureaucrats at the Reserve Training and Mobilisation Centre had been shamefully determined to prevent it. They had insisted on demobilising the London Regiment reservists before the parade could take place. This had, no doubt, saved the taxpayer a few quid, but it was penny pinching I was certain the Chief of the General Staff – and the British public – would not have sanctioned.

After all that the men of the London Regiment had endured in the service of their Country they deserved much, much better, but the rear echelon mother fuckers at RTMC Chilwell had truly lived up to their name. In response to my complaint that my soldiers were being short-changed I was invited to an interview with a smug major. He appeared to have eaten a large quantity of doughnuts while we'd been away. Pale, soft and slowly running to fat behind his desk, it was pretty obvious he was not of the same warrior class as my own men. I deeply resented him sitting in judgement over them.

I resisted the very strong urge to beat some sense into him as he attempted to confuse me with obscure rules and regulations. A 2008 study commissioned by the Prime Minister's Office recommended *a systematic approach to Homecoming parades for units returning from combat.* This pathetic, lard-arsed excuse for a regular soldier informed me that this did not apply to reservists. A reserve soldier could attend a parade in his own time and at his own expense, but this would not be funded by the Ministry of Defence.

This prick was such a cunt he was giving other cunts a bad name.

Whatever the rights or wrongs of this ruling, what struck me was the obvious pleasure it gave this odious man. In the end the Commanding Officer of the London Regiment, Lieutenant Colonel Marc Overton intervened, rightly, to ensure that his soldiers were paid for attending their parade.

Today was not only a homecoming for the men of the London Regiment, but also a much anticipated personal reunion. As I marched past, swinging my arms a little higher than regulation demanded, I could just make out my father, standing in the crowd with his grandsons, a protective hand laid on their shoulders. Jane had been true to her word. She had refused to communicate with him during my absence, denying Harry and Alfie access to their grandfather as a consequence. Knowing she loved the boys as much as I did myself I was surprised at her cruelty. I also knew how much Harry and Alfie cherished their relationship with Jane's parents and vowed not to follow the same path myself.

I tried not to dwell on these thoughts. Today was a day for celebration, not bitterness, and the City of London was determined to show its appreciation.

Once the parade was over we all got stuck into some beers at a fabulous reception laid on by the Lord Mayor. Along with one or two others, I was asked to conduct some media interviews with the waiting press. I was a little surprised at all the attention our parade seemed to be attracting, but was more than happy to oblige. Leaving Harry with his grandfather and my other guests, I wandered outside with Alfie on my shoulders. We instantly became the centre of attention for a clutch of press photographers.

One of the journalists present was Deborah Haynes, The Times defence correspondent whom I'd met at Camp Bastion when Ben Birchall and I returned from the fighting patrol into Kakoran. A smart journalist, she first flattered me by recollecting that Ben and I had just returned from *somewhere terribly dangerous,* before quizzing me on some recruitment issues with which the army was struggling. Behind her the MoD's ever-present media handler caught my attention with a fixed stare and an almost imperceptible shake of the head. This was clearly a subject that was off-limits so I avoided the question, which was easy enough since I didn't know anything about army recruitment anyway.

When asked by the ITV News why the parade was so special I explained:

In terms of getting closure on our tour this is a really, really important moment. But, of course, it's also for the families as well. No doubt you heard the families cheer as we marched on and that sounded to me like a cheer of relief that their sons are home, they are safe and they can now relax. So for all of us, on many different levels, it's a really important day.

I managed to refrain from pointing out that the mother fuckers at RTMC Chilwell had done their best to prevent it. But I still hoped the smug major would choke on his doughnut when he saw me on the evening news.

Once the interviews were over, Alfie and I rejoined my guests in the Guildhall's splendid old library. The City of London had done us proud. It was a wonderful day and a night to remember.

Early the following morning I received a cryptic text message from my father informing me I should probably buy a newspaper. Sore headed and bleary-eyed I wandered down to the local news agent to find a picture of Alfie and me on the front cover of The Times under the headline:

Red Tape Chokes Army's Vital Recruitment Drive.

Latitude:	51.12
Longitude:	1.34
Elevation:	7m
Met:	Heavy rain H:6°L:2°
DTG:	091211ZJAN13

MEN WHO HAD never once criticised me when I lost my nerve in the Kakoran minefield ribbed me mercilessly for appearing on the front cover of The Times. Such is the logic of soldiers.

I knew, of course, that I was not the story and that Deborah had simply used me to illustrate her scoop on reserve recruitment. I also knew that it was Alfie's beatific face rather than my ugly mug that had helped to sell 397,549 copies of The Times that day.

Even so, as someone who had set out for Afghanistan with ambitions to make a difference and find some meaning to their life, it was still possible to believe that this was some form of vindication. According to a YouGov poll, readers of The Times are cat owning, analytical types who play rugby, wear Agent Provocateur and drive a Mercedes Benz. They rely on their newspaper to keep them abreast of important public affairs with an eye to the best interests of Britain.

Paradoxically, at the very point where The Times' editors had decided to use my image to illustrate important public affairs in Britain's best interests, I had personally concluded that my individual efforts to turn around foreign policy in Afghanistan had failed. Even worse, I'd concealed that failure by embracing the self-deceit that characterised official pronouncements on the mission but which did not bear out my own experiences.

I didn't regret going to Afghanistan, quite the opposite in fact. I was proud to have served my country, and would do so again if called upon. I was just more than a little sceptical about what we had achieved there and at what cost.

I reckoned John Stuart Mill had been right: *A man who has nothing which he is willing to fight for, nothing which he cares more about than he does about his personal safety, is a miserable creature.*

He had, however, been pretty much wrong about everything else. Men like me may well have been delivered to the battlefield on the rhetoric of *an honest purpose* and with   ideals to *protect other human beings against tyrannical injustice.* But, as in so many conflicts before this one, we had ended up fighting simply for each other.

In the weeks and months that followed my 15 minutes of fame I was kept busy. There seemed to be no end of parades, audiences with the Secretary of State, service chiefs and even Royalty to which I was invited and which happily distracted me from dealing with my doomed marriage.

On the day I visited wounded colleagues at Selly Oak hospital in Birmingham I was finally brought back to reality by a text message from Jane:

What the hell are you doing all day? You're not even working. BTW drop the 'just back from Afghan' bit as well – we're all sick of hearing it.

In the end, I let Jane have all our possessions, less a few personal items, and the lion's share of the proceeds of the sale of the Dulwich house. Not because of any magnanimity on my part, but because I made the mistake of hiring a thoroughly honourable and decent man to act as my lawyer. He was no match for Jane's pugnacious advocate.

The marriage was over and Jane quickly moved on to a better, wealthier and more dependable partner.

For my part, thanks to the generosity of friends, I was able to fulfil a long held ambition to spend a ski season in the Alps. It was the culmination of a dream hatched in 50 degree heat several thousand miles away in a dusty tent, shared with men I barely knew and would willingly have died for.

Latitude:	46.27
Longitude:	6.84
Elevation:	1,194m
Met:	Periods of snow H:6°L:-3°
DTG:	120505AFEB13

THE FIRST EXPLOSION woke me a little after 05.00. My mind raced as I tried to think who might be out on patrol at this early hour. The first blast was followed a short while later by a second, and then a third. Lying in the dark I surmised instantly what this meant. Someone had triggered an IED. As others had come to the aid of their beleaguered comrade they'd initiated secondary devices and were now victims themselves. I flinched involuntarily at the thought and as I did so my hand touched the naked body of another beside me.

Something was not quite right here.

A little careful exploration revealed, to my very great relief, that the body beside mine was unmistakeably female. Then it all made sense. I was not lying in my wretched cot in the honking transit accommodation at PB Clifton but in the sumptuous double bed of my chalet in the Porte du Soleil. The explosions that had set my spine tingling were not the work of Taliban bomb makers but that of the village pisteurs making the slopes safe after overnight snow.

This was very good news indeed, not only because there were no casualties spilling blood into Afghan soil, nor even because there was fresh snow on the ground - although both were cause for celebration. This was very good news because there was a beautiful, brown-eyed *Lyonnaise*[1] in my bed, and now it was not only my spine that was tingling. We'd been introduced just the evening before but in the small hours of the morning had stumbled home in each other's arms, our impetuosity hastened by the frosted velvet touch of languorous snowflakes as we hurried through the silent landscape.

Aroused by my gentle exploration of her sleeping form, it was clear that even with fresh snow on the ground I wouldn't be catching first chair today. But this was the second week in February and there would be many more overnight snowfalls in the coming months. Just as we'd

---

[1] **Lyonnaise**: An inhabitant of Lyon, France's third largest city situated in the Rhône-Alpes region between Paris and Marseille.

been told in our decompression briefing in Cyprus, sex now involved more than one person. It was infinitely more wonderful as a result.

Where are they now?
WHERE ARE THEY NOW?

GENERAL JOHN R ALLEN: As General Allen completed his tour in Afghanistan he became embroiled in a *sex and secrets* scandal that led to the downfall of his close friend and former boss, CIA Director David Petraeus. He had been due to take over as Supreme Allied Commander Europe – but instead was forced into early retirement.

AMEENA: Ameena and her father safely negotiated the *Highway to Hell* and she was admitted to the paediatric burns unit at the AISPO[1] hospital in Herat, where she responded well to treatment. Some weeks later, after she had been discharged and returned home to Gereshk, she visited MOB Price with her father. Through an interpreter she told Kara how she would never forget her and the kindness of the strangers who had saved her life.

SIYAL ATAR: I cannot say what happened to Mohammed after MOB Price closed in March 2014. I hope that for him the course of true love did run smooth. If, like many local contractors who risked their lives working for the British, he subsequently sought asylum in the UK for himself and his new bride then it is doubtful. In a move Lord Ashdown, the former Liberal Democrat leader, described as *inexplicable, inhumane and a matter of shame for all of us* the majority of asylum requests were denied.

CAPTAIN ALEX BAYLISS: Alex continues to serve in the British Army and is currently an instructor at the School of Infantry in Warminster. As he puts it, he plans to stay on in the services for as long as possible *in order to avoid getting a real job*.

BEN BIRCHALL: Ben still works for the Press Association and his photographs continue to adorn the front pages of the UK's national and regional newspapers. In October 2014, rather than covering the news he became the story as the last British civilian to leave Camp Bastion. He described the moment as *poignant and moving*.

TONY BLAIR: In an interview with the BBC in March 2015, Tony Blair stated: *It's important to understand that for all the challenges in Afghanistan there have been huge gains.* He illustrated his point with statistics highlighting improvements in healthcare, education and democracy, none of which apply to the areas in which British troops were fighting.

---

[1] **AISPO**: Italian Association for solidarity among people

LIEUTENANT COLONEL JAMES BOWDER: On return from Afghanistan, Colonel James was awarded the OBE to add to the list of operational honours and awards he has received, making him one of only a very small handful of men to be recognised on three consecutive tours of duty. He continues his meteoric path to the top of the army.

GORDON BROWN: In December 2014, Gordon Brown announced his decision to step down as MP for Kirkcaldy and Cowdenbeath, concluding a political career spanning three decades. In a speech to his constituents he claimed: *I still hold the belief in something bigger than ourselves. I still hold to the belief in the moral purpose of public service.*

DAVID CAMERON: In 2012, David Cameron announced MoD budget cuts that would reduce British Army numbers to their lowest level since the Crimean War of 1854, when British and French forces opposed the Russian annexation of the Crimean peninsula. In 2014, as past and present service chiefs expressed their concerns at the depth of these cuts, the Russian Federation again annexed the Crimea. Overlooking Britain's 2003 treaty obligation to defend Ukraine's borders from foreign aggression, David Cameron elected not to commit British troops to the Crimean peninsula for a second time.

BRIGADIER DOUGLAS CHALMERS: Brigadier Chalmers was awarded the Distinguished Service Order in the Operation *Herrick 16* honours and awards list. He is currently serving as the Assistant Chief of Staff for Operations at the Permanent Joint Headquarters in Northwood. His LinkedIn profile lists *Afghanistan*, *NATO* and *Counter-insurgency* as his top three skills.

GENERAL FRANCIS RICHARD DANNATT: General Dannatt retired from the British Army in 2009, taking up the largely honorary post of Constable of the Tower of London. In a 2010 autobiography, titled *Leading from the Front*, he was critical of Gordon Brown, as both Chancellor of the Exchequer and as Prime Minister, accusing him of *malign intervention.*

CAPTAIN OWEN DAVIS: Owen was awarded the Conspicuous Gallantry Cross *in recognition of acts of conspicuous gallantry during active operations against the enemy.* He left the Royal Marines a short while after and is currently studying medicine at a prestigious British University. The majority of his fellow students remain unaware of his former military service and fewer   still know he is the holder of a gallantry award second only to the Victoria Cross.

LIEUTENANT COLONEL RICHARD 'SKID' DORNEY: Skid's book *The Killing Zone* is a bestseller. He has donated all the profits from the sale of the book to service charities to support those *who will be affected by the consequences of war for years to come.*

CAPTAIN PETER EADON: Mastiff Pete received a commendation for *sustained exemplary leadership and numerous acts of personal bravery* while in Afghanistan. He hopes the next conflict in which Britain is engaged will be a conventional State-on-State war in order that he may deploy in his Challenger 2 Main Battle Tank, rather than the vehicle in which he earned his nickname.

CAPTAIN TOM GARDNER: Tom was awarded a Queen's Commendation for Valuable Service in the *Herrick 16* operational honours and awards list. He left the army shortly after returning from Afghanistan and married his long time girlfriend. He is now a father and works in the insurance industry.

THE GOOSEBERRY HALL GANG: The Gooseberry Hall Gang continues to be a constant source of laughter, love, lodging and skiing companionship. It's a debt that can never be repaid.

HAJI GUL: After being incarcerated in Torchlight for 25 days without charge and without access to legal representation, Haji Gul was released without explanation or apology. Shortly after his release he and his brother Ajip relocated to the city of Herat in the northern province of the same name. In December 2012 he was interviewed for a Reuters Special Report entitled *Stalking the Taliban* in which he claimed his business had collapsed: *People are afraid they will arrest me again.*

MAJOR GENERAL CHARLES M GURGANUS: General Gurganus was sacked by the United States Marine Corps in September 2013. An enquiry into the Taliban attack on Camp Bastion ruled that he had been negligent in assessing the Taliban's strength and intentions in the area and *did not take adequate force protection measures*. Like all true warriors, Gurganus fell on his sword saying: *I have complete trust and confidence in the leadership of our Corps and fully respect the decision of our Commandant.*

THOMAS HARDING: Thomas continues to write for The Telegraph and is their defence correspondent covering the

Army, Navy and RAF, defence politics and all operations involving the military.

REGIMENTAL SERGEANT MAJOR GLENN HAUGHTON: Glenn Haughton continues to strike fear into the hearts of the Queen's enemies, as well as a good number of Her subjects.

DEBORAH HAYNES: Deborah Haynes is the defence editor at The Times. She has championed the plight of Afghan interpreters who worked for the British forces and who have been denied asylum in the UK.

RANGER HEYWARD: Ninety was promoted to Lance Corporal on return from *Herrick 16*. The Grenadier Guards offered him a full-time post but he prefers life in the Reserves.

HAJI JALANDER: To the best of my knowledge Haji Jalander was never reunited with his son-in-law or with his opium resin. Both may have been figments of his imagination.

JANE: Jane drives a smart new SUV, updates her designer wardrobe each season and enjoys exotic holidays with her new partner.

CAPTAIN ANDREW 'STUMPY' KEELEY: As he has done all his adult life, Stumpy continues to *honestly and faithfully defend Her Majesty, Her Heirs and Successors, in Person, Crown and Dignity against all enemies.*

MAJOR DAVE KENNY: Dave avoided the SO1 Info Ops billet but returned to Afghanistan almost immediately to take up a staff job with Regional Command. He is currently the Commanding Officer of 2nd Battalion the Royal Irish Regiment.

BALOOL KHAN: On 14 January 2014 the Cabinet Office, the Foreign and Commonwealth Office, the Department for International Development, and the Ministry of Defence published a joint policy paper titled *The UK's Work in Afghanistan*. In it Balool Khan, the venerable Chairman of the Nahr-E-Saraj District Community Council states: *The District Councils are like a bridge over a river, they connect the people to the government and the government to the people.* Shortly afterwards, Balool Khan was replaced as Chairman of the Council by Mullah Daud, brother of Haji Qadus a former deputy, turned bitter rival, of Malim Mir Wali (see Ghullie Khan below). Mullah Daud and his brother are both alleged   to have made millions from lucrative construction and security contracts funded by international aid packages.

GHULLIE KHAN: Ghullie Khan was replaced as the Nahr-E-Saraj District Chief of Police in 2013 by Saymand Hekmatullah, son of Malim Mir Wali the Kabul parliamentarian rumoured to have duped TF196 into arresting Haji Gul. Hekmatullah was later killed in a Taliban suicide bomb attack and it is rumoured that Ghullie Khan may return to his old job.

SULTAAN KHAN: Sultaan continues to successfully navigate the murky waters of Helmandi politics and despite a change of Governor remains the District Communications Advisor. He is more optimistic about the future than many Western pundits and commentators, informing me in a recent email communication: *Here is everything good*.

LIAM AND RITCHIE: After our epic powder day in the Porte du Soleil, Liam, Ritchie and I never met again. I like to think they are out there somewhere, keeping the shred alive, getting stoked, carving freshies and celebrating their adventures with a giant reefer of Afghan skunk.

CAPTAIN ABDUL MANAN: In November 2012, BBC News journalist Caroline Wyatt travelled to Gereshk to produce a report on the progress of the British withdrawal from the kammarband. In her film she interviews Captain Manan who explains: *There are two wars going on in Afghanistan. One is for religion and one is for power. When NATO forces leave the people fighting here for religious reasons will stop but those battling for power will keep on fighting.*

LANCE CORPORAL RON McCABE: Ron crossed over from the porn industry and now works as an actor and model. He still turns out for the London Regiment and continues to enjoy the occasional bar fight. Following his career change he prefers to go by the name his mother gave him, Frankie.

GENERAL STANLEY McCHRYSTAL: Having been relieved of his command in June 2010, General McChrystal co-founded a consultancy business to *advance the best practices from Special Operations, business, and academia on organizational effectiveness in the 21st Century.*

A biography of McChrystal has been optioned by the actor Brad Pitt's production company, Plan B. It was written by the same Rolling

Stone magazine feature writer whose article cost McChrystal his job.

MIRAJDIN: There is only circumstantial evidence linking Mirajdin to the device that killed Sergeant Lee 'Davo' Davidson. He may, or may not, have been a bomb maker and I have no evidence that he ever visited a religious seminary in Baluchistan, although this is where many bombers learned their trade. I also cannot say for certain that Mirajdin met either Mohammed Momin or Haji Jalander, although in such a small community it is possible if not probable that he did.

A few days after Davo's death I visited a compound (21 X8L) a short distance from where the device detonated and found evidence of bomb-making, including piles of scrap metal (which may have been *shipyard confetti*) and discarded batteries from which the carbon rods had been removed (possibly for the purpose of making low metal content IEDs). The compound's elderly owner informed me he was an Ishaqzai who had been displaced by fighting before moving to Zumbalay to *live in peace*. He also informed me that his eldest son, Mirajdin was *visiting relatives*, although I suspected he was hiding in the women's quarters which I was unable to search following a directive from President Karzai. Either way, Mirajdin's father appeared to me to be a very frightened old man trying to protect his son. I concluded that bomb-making activity had been or was being conducted on the premises and that Mirajdin was the most likely fabricator.

My conclusions wouldn't have stood up to scrutiny in a British court of law, but this was Afghanistan. Many others had been branded *insurgent facilitators* and subjected to *priority effects* on weaker evidence. However, if Mirajdin was responsible for the bomb that killed Davo, he escaped both *kill* and *capture*. Our isolated location and the Bastion raid prevented me from calling in specialist search assets or detaining Mirajdin's father for further questioning, and when our patrol came under sustained attack we were forced to withdraw.

MOHAMMED MOMIN: What little was left of Objective Beninghaus following the Hellfire strike is buried in the Deh Adam Khan cemetery. Huge crowds attended his funeral. I watched the ceremony on CCTV cameras in Patrol Base Clifton. It is not known if his death encouraged his brothers to join the insurgency but the once peaceful suburb of Deh Adam Khan is now on the front line between pro-GIRoA and Taliban forces. According to some reports, hundreds of ANA soldiers have died in the fighting there.

MAJOR ANDREW 'MO' MORRISON: Mo left the army shortly after returning from Afghanistan to retrain as a paramedic. Caring for others, particularly the elderly and infirm must be a calling. It turned out Mo was the mystery benefactor who so thoughtfully provided the Zimmer frame I'd discovered by my desk in the J9 cell.

NICHOLAS: Nicholas and I continue to test Mother Nature's patience and enjoy epic ski adventures together. I still know very little else about him.

CHUCK NORRIS: In 2015, Chuck Norris celebrated his 75th birthday. If this book had been about him it would have been sub-titled *Man in Helmand.* Chuck doesn't get old because time can't keep up with him.

MULLAH MOHAMMED OMAR: The secretive Taliban supreme leader has not been seen publicly since late 2001, when he was ousted as Emir of the Islamic Emirate of Afghanistan. In 2011 he was alleged to have written to President Barack Obama expressing interest in peace talks. Although reports of his death have been greatly exaggerated in the past, he is believed to have succumbed to tuberculosis in 2013. It is unlikely that he ever borrowed books from the Camp Bastion library.

MAJOR UFFE GECKLER PEDERSON: Uffe and I forged a firm friendship over vigorous debate, filterless cigarettes and Danish coffee which survives to this day. He is currently the Danish Military Representative to the NATO Headquarters in Brussels and we ski together whenever his schedule allows. We still discuss the pros and cons of Danish and British interventionist foreign policy over Irish whiskey or Danish Gammel Dansk long after everyone else has taken to their beds.

PRIVATE PRICE-BROWN: On return from Afghanistan, PB resigned from the London Regiment and embarked on a new adventure with his girlfriend whose picture he had carried through thick and thin, tucked inside his helmet. They now live in Kenya where they work for an adventure tourism company.

JOHN REID: John Reid, who started his career in politics as a Young Communist, resigned as Home Secretary in 2007 following Gordon Brown's appointment as Prime Minister. In May 2010 the former communist accepted a life peerage and was ennobled as Baron Reid of Cardowan, of Stepps in Lanarkshire.

SALIM RODI: Salim Rodi was   replaced as District Governor of

Nahr-E-Saraj by Mohammed Fahim in early 2013. He no longer works for the GIRoA administration.

MAJOR CHRIS SARGENT: Sarge was awarded an MBE in the *Herrick 16* Operational Honours and Awards list for his *outstanding leadership*. He has since taken up the prestigious post of Academy Adjutant at the Royal Military Academy, Sandhurst, teaching the next generation of military commanders. It would be hard to find a better role model.

PADRE GARY SCOTT: Gary continues to serve as an army chaplain, neither judging, admonishing nor condemning the men and women to whom he ministers.

CAPTAIN THOR SOMMERSTRAND: Thor left the Danish Army soon after returning from Afghanistan. He prefers not to communicate with his former friends and colleagues from his time there.

SOYA: I don't know what happened to Soya, the beautiful fox red Labrador after that last, fateful patrol to Zumbalay. I like to think he is happily retired, spending his days lying idly in front of a warm hearth a long way away from anywhere hostile and dangerous, periodically making his presence felt with a malodorous fart.

CAPTAIN RUPERT STEVENS: Rupert left the Grenadier Guards shortly after returning from Afghanistan and a year later married his girlfriend, Victoria. He now works for Barclays Bank.

LIEUTENANT COLONEL MARK STOCKS: In order to spend more time with his wife and family, Mark relinquished the opportunity to command his regiment and instead took a well paid and comparatively undemanding staff job in Kuwait They are all enjoying their new life.

MAJOR JAMES SWANSTON: James continues to serve in the Army Reserve and is tipped one day to command the London Regiment. He has expanded his contact list of glamorous models to include, amongst others, Royalty, politicians and international sports personalities.

LIEUTENANT COLONEL ROLY WALKER: Having relinquished command of the Grenadier Guards, Roly Walker was promoted not once, but twice to become commander of 12th Armoured Infantry Brigade. The brigade is capable of a wide variety of missions anywhere in the world. Brigadier Walker still maintains an exacting standard of excellence and claims his brigade is *as ready as* *it can be should it be called upon.* I don't doubt him.

MAJOR KARA WATTERS: I briefly met Kara one last time at the Grenadier Guards medal parade in Aldershot in November 2012. Although I have no doubt there were many other instinctive acts of kindness and compassion that marked the British combat mission in Afghanistan, it was Kara's determined battle against cold-hearted bureaucracy and deadly infection to save a young life that I was privileged to witness first-hand. I failed to thank her for the hope and optimism she inspired. I hope this book corrects this omission.

LIEUTENANT ED WHITTEN: Ed stayed on in the army for a while, becoming a Middle East and North Africa specialist before taking a new job as a senior consultant with a private firm specialising in global strategic and operational risks. He remains close to Davo Davidson's family and visits them often.

1st BATTALION GRENADIER GUARDS: For their service in Afghanistan from 1 April – 30 September 2012, 11 members of the battalion received operational honours and awards as follows:

Victoria Cross:

Lance Corporal James Ashworth (killed in action)

Officer of the Order of the British Empire:

Lieutenant Colonel James Maurice Hannan Bowder MBE

Member of the Order of the British Empire:

Major Christopher 'Sarge' Sargent

Distinguished Service Order:

Major Piers Ashfield

Conspicous Gallantry Cross:

Captain Owen Davis RM

Military Cross:

Captain Michael Dobbin

Lance Sergeant Markus Strydom

Mention in Dispatches:

Guardsman Danny Bentley

Guardsman James Cornish

Lance Sergeant Ashley Hendy

Guardsman Micheal Ogden

Lance Sergeant Robert Pointon

Lance Corporal David Smith

Queen's Commendation for Bravery:

Lance Corporal Simon Dent

Queen's Commendation for Valuable Service:

Captain Tom Gardner

Operation Herrick 16 was to be the Grenadiers' last tour of Helmand Province and the battalion returned to State Ceremonial Public Duties before taking on a new role as the spearhead battlegroup for the Very High Readiness Joint Task Force (VJTF) for NATO with rifle companies from Albania, Holland and Latvia under command. The officer's mess lunchtime routine remains unchanged.

In the fight for peace
FOR PEACE

Latitude:	52.30
Longitude:	-1.57
Elevation:	62m
Met:	Thunderstorms H:18°L:12°
DTG:	311443AJUL14

FROM MY FIRST day in Afghanistan on 27th January to my last on 24th September 2012, 37 British servicemen were killed in action or died of wounds sustained in action.

Their deaths serve as a tragic chronology of my time in Helmand and I attended vigil services for them all. The most moving of these were often in austere patrol bases where, in the absence of army chaplains, the soldiers led and conducted the service themselves.

No matter what the circumstances, each vigil I attended concluded with the words of an epitaph first inscribed on a memorial in the Kohima cemetery in Nagaland, India and attributed to John Maxwell Edmonds:

When You Go Home, Tell Them Of Us And Say,
For Your Tomorrow, We Gave Our Today

For those of us who were there and have now come home these are not mere words, but a lifelong obligation.

Friday, 27 January 2012:
Lance Corporal Gajbahadur Gurung

Monday, 13 February 2012:
Senior Aircraftman Ryan Tomlin

Tuesday, 6 March 2012:
Sergeant Nigel Coupe
Corporal Jake Hartley
Private Anthony Frampton
Private Christopher Kershaw

Private Daniel Wade
Private Daniel Wilford

Wednesday, 21 March 2012:
Captain Rupert Bowers

Monday, 26 March 2012:
Sergeant Luke Taylor
Lance Corporal Michael Foley

Sunday, 8 April 2012:
Corporal Jack Leslie Stanley

Wednesday, 18 April 2012:
Sapper Connor Ray

Friday, 27 April 2012:
Guardsman Michael Roland

Friday, 4 May 2012:
Corporal Andrew Steven Roberts
Private Ratu Manasa Silibaravi

Saturday, 12 May 2012:
Corporal Brent John McCarthy RAFP
Lance Corporal Lee Thomas Davies

Saturday, 26 May 2012:
Captain Stephen James Healey

Friday, 1 June 2012:
Corporal Michael John Thacker

Sunday, 3 June 2012:
Private Gregg Thomas Stone

Wednesday, 13 June 2012:
Lance Corporal James Ashworth

Friday, 15 June 2012:
Corporal Alex Guy

Sunday, 1 July 2012:
Warrant Officer Class 2 Leonard Thomas
Guardsman Craig Roderick
Guardsman Apete Tuisovurua

Thursday, 9 August 2012:
Lieutenant Andrew Chesterman

Friday, 10 August 2012:
Lance Corporal Matthew David Smith

Friday, 17 August 2012:
Guardsman Jamie Shadrake

Friday, 7 September 2012:
Guardsman Karl Whittle

Sunday, 9 September 2012:

Sergeant Lee Paul Davidson

Friday, 14 September 2012:

Lance Corporal Duane Groom

Saturday, 15 September 2012:

Sergeant Gareth Thursby
Private Thomas Wroe

Friday, 21 September 2012:

Sergeant Jonathan Eric Kups
Captain James Anthony Townley

Monday, 24 September 2012:

Captain Carl Manley

4B:1T (*Four bit*): Four Ball: One Tracer. The standard configuration of tracer to ball rounds in UK 7.62mm belted ammunition for use with the GPMG machine gun.

ACOG: Advanced Combat Optical Gunsight (fitted to the SA80 assault rifle in Afghanistan)

AGC: Adjutant General's Corp

AH: Attack Helicopter

AISPO: Italian Association for solidarity among people

AK47: selective-fire, gas-operated 7.62×39mm assault rifle, first developed in the Soviet Union by Mikhail Kalashnikov

AK74: an assault rifle developed in the early 1970s in the Soviet Union as the replacement for the AKM (itself a refined version of the AK47)

ALP: Afghan Local Police

ANA: Afghan National Army

ANAL: Ammonium Nitrate and Aluminium (HME components)

ANCOP: Afghan National Civil Order Police

ANFO: Ammonium Nitrate and Fuel Oil (HME components)

Angrezi: English/British

ANP: Afghan National Police

ANS: Ammonium Nitrate and Sugar (HME components)

ANSF: Afghan National Security Forces

AOB: Any other business

APC: Armoured   Personnel   Carrier

ARM: Afghanistan Rights Monitor

ATP: Annual Training Package

Aunt Mary: A slang term for marijuana derived from the Mexican Spanish meaning of the word: *Maria* (Mary) and *Juana* (Joan or Jane). Hence, *Aunt Mary*.

AUP: Afghan Uniformed Police

AO: Area of Operations

Battle: At various times also known as **Battle Action Force**, **Battle Picture Weekly** and **Battle with Storm Force**, was a British war comic published by IPC Magazines from 8 March 1975 to 23 January 1988. Most stories were set in World War II.

BDL: Bed Down Location

Bergan: A large rucksack, supported by a frame.

Berm: A low earth wall, usually adjacent to a ditch. The digging of the ditch often providing the soil from which the berm is constructed.

BFBS: British Forces Broadcasting Station

BGHQ: Battlegroup Headquarters

Blue on Blue: An attack by a military force on friendly forces while attempting to attack the enemy, either misidentifying the target as hostile, or due to errors or inaccuracy.

Bluey: Free and postage free British Forces Post Office airmail letter forms supplied to troops on active service and their families.

Bravo: Male. For brevity of reporting different targets are assigned different letters of the phonetic alphabet. Alpha: Building. Bravo: Male. Charlie: Vehicle. Echo: Female.

Bullpup: A firearm with its action behind its trigger group. This configuration permits a shorter overall weapon for a given barrel length. This maintains the advantages of a longer barrel in muzzle velocity and accuracy, while improving manoeuvrability and reducing weight.

Bund line: Built-up natural defence line, such as a low hedgerow or berm.

C2: Command and Control

Camber: Camber refers to the curvature along the length of a ski. Camber affects the way the skis react on different types of terrain. The most common types of camber include traditional camber, rocker (or reverse camber), flat camber (or zero camber), and cambered medley (or camber combination). A ski with traditional camber curves such that if it's sitting flat on a hard surface, the middle of the ski will be raised off the ground.

Casevac: Casualty Evacuation

Casrep: Casualty Report

CF NES(N): Combined Force Nahr-E-Saraj (North)

Chaff: A radar countermeasure in which aircraft spread a cloud of aluminium, metallised glass fibre or plastic, to distract radar-guided missiles.

Chuck Norris facts: Deliberately absurd facts focussing on Chuck Norris's virility, manliness and all round heroism. Major Uffe Pederson, the battlegroup's Danish Deputy Commander regularly travelled around in an unarmoured 4x4 vehicle which he would drive himself. This contravened regulations and exposed him to considerable risk from IEDs but it also drew grudging admiration and respect. The vehicle quickly came to be known as the *Chucknorrismobile*, imbuing it with Chuck Norris' invincibility.

Chuff Chart: A chart or calendar used by servicemen and women to count down the days until the end of a tour of duty.

CIED: Counter Improvised Explosive Device

CNO: Casualty Notification Officer

CoD: Call of Duty, a first- and third-person shooter video game franchise.

COEFOR: Contemporary Operating Environment Force

COIN: Counter-insurgency

Contact: An engagement with the enemy in which rounds are exchanged

COS: Chief of Staff

CP: Checkpoint

CPIED: Command Pull Improvised Explosive Device

CQB: Close Quarter Battle

CWIED: Command Wire Improvised Explosive Device

Crab Air: Royal Air Force

CUB: Commander's Update Briefing

CULAD: Cultural Adviser

D&V: Diarrhoea and vomiting

Danger Close: The term *danger close* is included in the request for supporting fires such as artillery or mortars when there are friendly troops or positions in close range of the intended target and inside the blast radius of the munition.

Dashte: Desert

DCA: District Communications Advisor

D-CoP: District Chief of Police

DCSU: Defence Cultural Specialist Unit

D-FAC: Dining Facility

DfID: Department for International Development

DG: District Governor

Dicker: A term originally coined   in Northern Ireland to describe low level, usually unarmed informants, often children, who follow patrols and hang around outside military bases providing basic intelligence on troop movements and dispositions to the enemy.

Dishdash: Long one-piece tunic worn by men

DMOC: Defence Media Operations Centre

DNBI: Disease and non-battle injury

Doobie: Marijuana cigarette

DOW: A battle casualty who dies of wounds or other injuries received in action after having reached a medical treatment facility.

DPHQ: District Police Headquarters

DROPS: Demountable Rack Offload and Pickup System

DSO: Distinguished Service Order

DST: District Stabilisation Team (See also HPRT)

DShKM/Dushka: Russian designed 50-calibre heavy machine gun, sometimes nicknamed Dushka (literally, *Sweetie, Dear*), from the abbreviation.

DTG: Date Time Group

Using the DTG, 10.30 GMT on 11th April 2012 is written as 1110.30ZAPR12.

The Armed Forces use the 24 hour clock. This means that 20.15 hours, pronounced twenty-fifteen hours, is 8.15pm.

Soldiers usually avoid midnight and refer to 23.59 or 00.01 hours.

Time zones: The suffix Z (Zulu) denotes Greenwich meantime (GMT). A (Alpha) denotes GMT + 1 hour. B (Bravo) denotes GMT + 2 hours and so on. Afghanistan is 4½ hours ahead of GMT but uses the suffix D (Delta).

ECBA: Enhanced Combat Body Armour

EOD: Explosive Ordnance Disposal

Fast Mover: Military slang for fighter jet.

FCO: Foreign and Commonwealth Office

FEO: Female Engagement Officer

FFUI: **Find, Feel, Understand, Inform**: In January 2010, Major General Michael T. Flynn USA wrote an influential paper titled *Fixing Intel: A blueprint for making intelligence relevant in Afghanistan.* His paper recommended sweeping changes to the way the intelligence community thinks about itself – from a focus on the enemy to a focus on the people of Afghanistan. This involved modifying the five components of the kinetic targeting approach: find, fix, finish, exploit and analyze into a non-kinetic social engineering construct: find, feel, understand, inform.

Fifty, Fifty Cal or **Point Five-O (.50)**: Any machine gun that fires 50 BMG (Browning Machine Gun) 12.7×99mm standard NATO ammunition.

FLET: Forward Line of Enemy Troops

FOB: Forward Operating Base

Freshies: Fresh snow on which there are no ski or snow board tracks.

FTTT (F triple T): First to the truth

Ganja: Marijuana

GHG: Gooseberry Hall Gang

GIRoA: Government of the Islamic Republic of Afghanistan

GPMG: General Purpose Machine Gun

Green on Blue: Attacks on ISAF soldiers by members of the Afghan Security forces

Green Zone (GZ): Fertile, cultivated land irrigated by the Helmand River.

H16: HERRICK 16. *Herrick* is the randomly assigned codename under which all British military operations in Afghanistan have been conducted since 2002. *Herrick 16* covered the period March – September 2012.

H4H: Help for Heroes

HAF: Helicopter Assault Force

Helipad: helicopter landing pad

Hesco Bastion: a modern gabion used for flood control and military fortification and the name of the British company that developed it in the late 1980s. It comprises a collapsible wire mesh container and heavy-duty fabric liner which is filled with sand, soil or gravel and used as a temporary to semi-permanent dike or barrier against explosions or small arms. It has been widely used in Afghanistan and is routinely adapted by soldiers to fashion rudimentary furniture to make living accommodation a little more comfortable and homely.

Hexie TV/watching Hexie TV: Squaddie slang referring to the preparation of hot rations or boiling water using army issue hexamine cookers.

HIND (Mil Mi24): Russian designed and built armed assault and attack helicopter operated by the Soviet Air Force and its successors since 1972. Known to pilots as the *flying tank* it is a combination of armoured gunship and troop transport and was greatly exploited by airborne units of the Soviet Army during the 1979–89 Soviet war in Afghanistan.

HIP (Mil Mi8): A Soviet designed medium twin-turbine helicopter. Among the world's most produced helicopters, numerous versions were built including an armed gunship variant (Mi8TVK) used by Russian forces in Afghanistan from 1979–89.

HLS: Helicopter Landing Site

HME: Home-made Explosive

HMMWV (Humvee): High Mobility Multipurpose Wheeled Vehicle

HPRT: Helmand Provincial Reconstruction Team. The HPRT was a multi-national, multi-department team funded by DfID dedicated to

Helmand Province. It was established in Sep 2004, and ceased operations in Dec 2013.

HQ: Headquarters

HVO: Hydrogenated vegetable oil

IBP: Intelligence Preparation of the Battlefield

IDC: International Development Committee

IDF: Indirect Fire

IED: Improvised Explosive Device

Iron Triangle: A defensive position in which three armoured vehicles park nose to tail in a triangular formation.

Iron Sight: A system of shaped alignment markers (usually metal) used as a sighting device to assist in the aiming of a firearm. Iron sights are composed of two component parts; a rear sight, usually an aperture mounted perpendicular to the line of sight, and a front sight post.

ISAF: International Security Assistance Force

ISTAR: Intelligence, surveillance, target acquisition, and reconnaissance. ISTAR is a practice that links several battlefield functions together to assist a combat force in employing its sensors and managing the information they gather.

JFEOD: Joint Force Explosive Ordnance Disposal

JIOTAT: Joint Information Operations Training and Advisory Team

JPEL: Joint Priority Effects List. Also known as the *kill/capture* list, the JPEL is a list of individuals whom coalition forces in Afghanistan wish to capture or kill.

Kandak: Afghan National Army formation equivalent to a British battalion.

Keep the shred alive: the pure pleasure, freedom and exhilaration that comes from skiing, snowboarding or skateboarding to a high standard of proficiency.

Khareji: foreigner

KIA: Killed in Action. KIA is a battle casualty who is killed outright or dies as a result of other wounds before reaching a medical treatment facility.

Kinetic/Kinetic military action: Military action involving the use of lethal force.

KLE: Key Leadership Engagement

Klick: Kilometre

Km: Kilometre

Leaguer (from South African Dutch **Laager)**: A temporary defensive encampment surrounded by armoured vehicles – a military term originating from the Boer War.

LEGAD: Legal Advisor

LFTT: Live Firing Tactical Training

LN: Local National

LNE: Local National Engagement

Loadie: [Loadmaster] An aircraft crew member in charge of loading and unloading cargo.

Lyonnaise: An inhabitant of Lyon, France's third largest city situated in the Rhône-Alpes region between Paris and Marseille.

M4: M4 carbine, a shorter and lighter version of the M16-A2 assault rifle

Mag: slang for magazine. A container or detachable receptacle for holding a supply of ammunition cartridges to be fed automatically into the breech of a weapon.

Man Away: A term used by British Forces to indicate that a man is missing or unaccounted for.

Mastiff: A heavily armoured 6 x six-wheel-drive patrol vehicle which carries eight troops, plus two crew.

MBE: Member of the Most Excellent Order of the British Empire

MCCP: Movement Control Check Point

MDCoA: Most dangerous course of action.

ME: Main Effort. The Main Effort is a manoeuvre warfare concept that concentrates efforts on achieving objectives that lead to victory. It recognises that, of all the activities going on within a command, one is the most critical to success at that moment in time. This becomes the focal point and receives priority for support of any kind.

MERT: Medical Emergency Response Team

MIB: Men in Black. A fictional secret organisation that supervises extraterrestrial life forms living on Earth and hides their existence from ordinary humans.

Mirab: (Pashtu) Water Master. Afghanistan is an agricultural society and water for irrigation is a precious resource. Historically – and in the present – villagers have not trusted each other to take only their share. The job of the Mirab is to equitably distribute irrigation water to each household, usually based on the size of their landholdings. The Mirab is paid collectively by the community and because of the importance of the job is a very influential figure.

MLCoA: Most likely course of action.

MOB: Main Operating Base

MoD: Ministry of Defence

MoIA: Ministry of Interior Affairs

MPOPC: Military Psychological Operations Planners Course

MRAP: Mine-resistant ambush-protected vehicle

MSSG: Military Stabilisation Support Group

MT: Mechanical Transport

MTP: Multi-terrain pattern

Muj: Mujahideen

Nanawatai: (Pashtu: *sanctuary*) is a tenet of the Pashtunwali code of the Pashtun people. It allows a beleaguered person to enter the house of any other person and request sanctuary or protection. This cannot be refused, even at the cost of the host's own life or fortune.

NCO: Non-commissioned officer

NGO: Non-governmental organisation

Nine Liner: Medical evacuation request, so called because of the nine point reporting format

NIOC: National Information Operations Course

No Fall line: An imaginary line drawn on any descent above which a fall may lead to serious injury, but more probably will result in death.

NOTICAS: The formalised system of reporting casualties within the UK Armed Forces. The NOTICAS report contains information on the severity of the casualty's injuries to inform what next of kin are told. Only the most serious casualties are subject to a NOTICAS notification.

OBE: Officer of the Most Excellent Order of the British Empire

Ops Room: Operations Room

OPTAG: Operational Training and Advisory Group

ORBAT: Order of Battle

OSW: Operational Staff Work

PAT: Police Advisory Team

PB: Patrol Base

P-CoP: Provincial Chief of Police

PCS: Personal Clothing System

Phyllotaxy: The arrangement of leaves on a plant stem (from Ancient Greek phýllon "leaf" and táxis "arrangement").

PID: Positively Identify

Pink List: An internal Army document listing those eligible for promotion to Lieutenant Colonel.

Pikatinny Rail: (also known as a MIL-STD-1913 rail or tactical rail) is a bracket on some firearms that provides a standard mounting platform for accessories and attachments such as vertical pistol grips, bipods, electro-optical sights, image intensifiers; flashlights and laser sights.

PJHQ: Permanent Joint Headquarters. Situated in Northwood, London PJHQ is the UK's tri-service headquarters from where all overseas military operations are planned and controlled.

PKM: Gas-operated, belt fed, air-cooled, automatic only, machine gun. Originally designed and manufactured in Russia in the late 1960s, copies are still in production in Bulgaria, China, Iran, Poland and Serbia.

Platoon: In the British Army, a rifle platoon from an infantry company consists of three sections of eight men, plus a signaller (radio operator), a platoon sergeant and the platoon commander (either a second lieutenant or lieutenant).

PMAG: Police Mentoring and Advisory Group

POG: PsyOps Group

Point Five-O (.50), Fifty or **Fifty-Cal**: Any machine gun that fires 50 BMG (Browning Machine Gun) 12.7×99mm standard NATO ammunition.

Point of Fire: A location from which an enemy can be engaged with suppressive fire threatening casualties to those who expose themselves to it and which, when coordinated with the manoeuvre of forces achieves the destruction, neutralisation or suppression of the enemy.

POLAD: Political Advisor

Pow or **Pow-pow**: Powder snow

PM: Protected Mobility

PPE: Personal protection equipment

PPIED: Pressure Plate Improvised Explosive Device

PRR: Personal Role Radio

PRT: Provincial Reconstruction Team (see HPRT)

PsyOps: Psychological Operations

PsyOper: A PsyOps practitioner

PT: Pysical Training

PTSD: Post Traumatic Stress Disorder

QM: Quartermaster

Qur'an (also **Quran, Koran, Kuran)**: The central religious text of Islam, which Muslims believe to be a revelation from Allah. Respect for the written text of the Qur'an is an important element of religious faith for most Muslims, and the Qur'an is treated with reverence. Based on tradition and a literal interpretation of Qur'an 56:79 *(none shall touch but those who are clean)*, many Muslims believe that they must perform a ritual cleansing with water before touching a copy of the Qur'an, although this view is not universal. Worn-out copies of the Qur'an are wrapped in a cloth and stored indefinitely in a safe place, buried in a mosque or a Muslim cemetery, or burned and the ashes buried or scattered over water.

Quetta Shura: A militant organization composed of the leaders of the Afghan Taliban, believed to be based within the city of Quetta in the Balochistan province of Pakistan.

RAP: Regimental Aid Post

RCO: Range Conducting Officer

RCSW: Regional Command South West

Reefer: Marijuana cigarette

Rebar: Reinforcing bar, a steel bar or mesh of steel wires commonly used as a tension device in reinforced concrete and reinforced masonry structures, to strengthen and hold the concrete in compression.

Re-bomb *(re-bomb my mags)*: to refill magazines with ammunition

REMF: Rear Echelon Mother Fucker

RIAB: Radio-in-a-box. A portable broadcasting system containing a laptop, mixer, CD/Cassette player, digital audio recorder, microphones and equipment needed to establish a radio station in remote locations

Ribs/fighting Ribs: Inkerman Company, First Battalion The Grenadier Guards are known as the Ribs or fighting Ribs after their predecessors took part in the Anglo-Dutch Wars (1652–74) as marines, accommodated in the ship's hold amongst the ribs.

RMO: Regimental Medical Officer

RMP: Royal Military Police

RPG: Ruchnaya Protivotankovaya Granata. A World War Two era high explosive anti-tank (HEAT) hand grenade first developed by the Soviet Union.

Rocker: Rocker (also known as reverse camber) refers to the curvature along the length of a ski. Rocker is a curve opposite to that of traditional camber (see Camber). A rockered ski placed on a flat surface will make contact with the surface in the middle of the ski while the tips of the ski will be raised. Rocker helps to float in powder but reduces the amount of edge contact during turns, so it's not well suited for riding high-speeds or hard carving.

RoE: Rules of Engagement

ROG: Rear Operations Group

RSOI: Reception, Staging and Onward Integration

RTMC: Reserves Training and Mobilisation Centre

SA80 A2 L85: The SA80 A2 L85 is a 5.56mm gas-operated assault rifle manufactured by Heckler & Koch. It is a member of the SA80 family of assault weapons and serves the British Armed Forces as Individual Weapon (IW) and Light Support Weapon (LSW).

The SA80 series of rifles entered service with the British Army in 1985 and underwent a major mid-life update in 2002, during which the SA80 A1 rifles were upgraded to the SA80 A2 standard.

SAF: Small Arms Fire

Sangar: A small protected structure used for observing or firing from.

SAS: Special Air Service

Seasonaire: A Seasonaire is a person who lives in multiple locations during the different seasons of the year.

SF: Special Forces

Shade Shift: An analysis of human terrain that acknowledges the complexity of different allegiances and interests between and amongst target audiences.

Shalwar Kameez: A long tunic (kameez) worn over a pair of baggy trousers (shalwar).

Shemagh: traditional Middle Eastern headdress designed to protect the wearer from sand and heat, typically worn by men.

Shred: to perform an athletic sport such as surfing, skiing, or skateboarding to a high standard of proficiency.

Shura: an Arabic word meaning "consultation", often used by ISAF troops to describe a meeting between ISAF and Afghan security forces or local nationals.

Skin up: to roll a marijuana cigarette

SNAFU: Situation Normal, All Fucked Up

SNCO: Senior Non-Commissioned Officer

SO1: Staff Officer grade 1, Lieutenant Colonel

SOF: Special Operations Forces

SOP: Standard Operating Procedure

SOTF (West): Special Operations Task Force (West)

SPG-9: The SPG-9 Kopye (Spear) is a Russian, tripod-mounted, man-portable recoilless rifle. It fires fin-stabilised, rocket-assisted high explosive and anti-tank projectiles.

Spin Zhira (Pashtu): literal meaning White Beard, denoting Old/Wise Man or Village Elder.

STABAD: Stabilisation Advisor

Stoked: To be exhilarated or excited

SU: Stabilisation Unit

SUSAT: Sight Unit Small Arms Trilux. A x4 optical gunsight with tritium-powered illumination for use in low light conditions fitted to the SA80 but now largely replaced by the ACOG (Advanced Combat Optical Gunsight) or the ELCAN Specter OS x4 Lightweight Day Sight (LDS).

SUV: Suburban Utility Vehicle

TA: Territorial Army now renamed the *Army Reserve*

TBAU: Tactical Base Ablution Unit

TCP: Temporary Checkpoint

TF196: Task Force 196

TFH: Task Force Helmand

THC: Tetrahydrocannabinol. The principal psychoactive constituent (or cannabinoid) of cannabis.

TONTINE BOX: Tontine boxes were popular amongst the officer class in the 18th and 19th centuries. Prior to departing on a military campaign or expedition, each participating officer paid an agreed sum into a fund which was used to purchase a piece of silverware, usually a box, on which their names were engraved. On return from duty the box would then be sold and the proceeds divided amongst the surviving members. In some cases no officers survived and the boxes have remained the property of the officers' mess to which they belonged, a poignant reminder to their successors of their sacrifice.

Toke: inhale from a cigarette, typically one containing cannabis.

TRANAD: Transition Advisor

Twin-tips: A modified version of their alpine counterparts, twin-tip skis are designed to enable a skier to take off and land backward while jumping and to ski backwards (switch) down a slope. The name "twin-tip" comes from the shape of the ski. While most alpine skis have a defined, curved-up front end (or "tip") as well as a flat rear end (or "tail"), twin-tip skis have a curved-up tip and tail.

UAV: Unmanned Aerial Vehicle

UBACS: Under Body Armour Combat Shirt

UGV: Upper Gereshk Valley

UN: United Nations

UNAMA: United Nations Assistance Mission to Afghanistan

US AID: United States Agency for International Development

USMC: United States Marine Corps

UXO: Unexploded Ordnance

Vallon: German made hand-held mine and IED detector used extensively by US and coalition troops in Afghanistan.

VCP: Vehicle Checkpoint

VOIED: Victim Operated Improvised Explosive Device

VP: Vulnerable Point

VSO: Village Stability Operations. A US SOF initiative the aim was to provide *enhanced security, governance, and development in strategically important rural areas critical to the Afghanistan campaign but beyond the effective reach of the Afghan government and U.S. conventional forces.* It perhaps provides insight that the Parschow VSO was just 3km due south of Gereshk, the seat of GIRoA District Governance and home to the District Police Headquarters, the main Afghan National Army base and ISAF's Main Operating Base Price, yet it was still beyond the reach of the Afghan government and US conventional forces.

WAG Bag: Waste Activated Gel bag. Single use, zip-close human waste bags. Literally a toilet in a bag, complete with toilet paper and hand sanitiser.

Warthog: an armoured twin chassis articulated tracked troop carrier

WIA: Wounded in Action

WMD: Weapons of Mass Destruction

WO2: Warrant Officer Class Two

Printed in Great Britain
by Amazon

26248418R00275